Autodesk®
Authorized Publisher

AutoCAD® 2011
ESSENTIALS

COMPREHENSIVE EDITION

Munir M. Hamad
Autodesk® Approved Instructor

JONES & BARTLETT
LEARNING

World Headquarters

Jones & Bartlett Learning
40 Tall Pine Drive
Sudbury, MA 01776
978-443-5000
info@jblearning.com
www.jblearning.com

Jones & Bartlett Learning
Canada
6339 Ormindale Way
Mississauga, Ontario L5V 1J2
Canada

Jones & Bartlett Learning
International
Barb House, Barb Mews
London W6 7PA
United Kingdom

Jones & Bartlett Learning books and products are available through most bookstores and online booksellers. To contact Jones & Bartlett Learning directly, call 800-832-0034, fax 978-443-8000, or visit our website, www.jblearning.com.

Substantial discounts on bulk quantities of Jones & Bartlett Learning publications are available to corporations, professional associations, and other qualified organizations. For details and specific discount information, contact the special sales department at Jones & Bartlett Learning via the above contact information or send an email to specialsales@jblearning.com.

Production Credits

Publisher: David Pallai
Editorial Assistant: Molly Whitman
Production Director: Amy Rose
Associate Production Editor: Tiffany Sliter
Associate Marketing Manager: Lindsay Ruggiero
V.P., Manufacturing and Inventory Control:
   Therese Connell

Cover and Title Page Design: Kristin E. Parker
Composition: Glyph International
Cover Image: © Happy Alex/ShutterStock, Inc.
Printing and Binding: Malloy, Inc.
Cover Printing: Malloy, Inc.

Library of Congress Cataloging-in-Publication Data

Hamad, Munir M.
   AutoCAD 2011 essentials / Munir Hamad. -- Comprehensive ed.
      p. cm.
   Includes index.
   ISBN-13: 978-0-7637-9800-0 (pbk.)
   ISBN-10: 0-7637-9800-2 (ibid)
   1. Computer graphics. 2. Computer-aided design. 3. AutoCAD. I. Title.
   T385.H329335 2010b
   620'.00420285536—dc22
                                                                    2010018695

6048
Printed in the United States of America
14 13 12 11 10   10 9 8 7 6 5 4 3 2 1

License, Disclaimer of Liability, and Limited Warranty

TABLE OF CONTENTS

*P*REFACE

INTRODUCTION

◇ AutoCAD® has been the de facto drafting tool for PC users since 1982.

◇ As you read this, millions of engineers, draftsmen, project managers, engineering students, and anyone else working with drawings are using AutoCAD.

◇ Whether you are with a university, company, or factory, if you have decided to use AutoCAD instead of other CAD software, you have made the right choice. Autodesk (the creator of AutoCAD) is an established company that will be around for a long time to come.

◇ This book is perfect for both novice and experienced users of AutoCAD 2011 alike. It is a very handy tool for college and university drafting instructors who are using the software.

◇ If you do not have much experience using AutoCAD 2011, you will want to review the first 10 chapters, which cover the basics, before moving on to the final 7 chapters, which are intended for advanced users.

◇ Almost 75% of current AutoCAD users rely solely on the core commands covered in the first 10 chapters of this book. By mastering the commands and techniques discussed in the advanced chapters, you will place yourself among the top 25% of AutoCAD users in the world. In other words, you can expect a better position, better income, and fewer work hours.

◇ This book will not explain what engineering drafting is or how it is produced. Knowing the fundamentals of drafting by having at least read a book or taken a course on the subject is a prerequisite to understanding this text.

◊ This text can be instructor-led or self-taught:

- If an instructor presents the text, the estimated time requirement is six days at eight hours a day.
- If the text is self-taught, the reader can approach it at his or her convenience.

◊ At the end of each chapter, you will find a Chapter Review that will help you test your understanding of the material.

◊ There are 112 exercises throughout the book to help you implement what you have learned. Some of these exercises are presented using both metric and imperial units. We encourage you to solve all exercises, regardless of your preference.

◊ There are eight workshops (projects), in which you will complete a full (small) project. These workshops:

- Simulate a real-life project from beginning to end, thereby allowing you to implement what you have learned.
- Help you organize the information in a logical order.
- Teach and reinforce all of the basic and necessary commands and functions in AutoCAD 2011.

PURPOSE AND OBJECTIVES

◊ This text is for all levels of AutoCAD 2011 users. The first 10 chapters cover the basic and intermediate levels of AutoCAD. The final 7 chapters consider the advanced features of AutoCAD, often by delving deeper into subjects introduced in the earlier chapters. The courseware demonstrates in a very simple step-by-step procedure how to create an engineering drawing, modify it, annotate it, dimension it, and, finally, print it.

◊ Upon the completion of this text, the reader will be able to do the following:

- Understand AutoCAD 2011 and its basic operations, including the filing system
- Set up drawings
- Draw various objects with speed and precision
- Construct drawings using simple steps
- Modify any object in a drawing

- Create, insert, and edit blocks
- Create dynamic blocks
- Create, edit, and extract block attributes
- Hatch using different hatch patterns and methods
- Create text and tables
- Insert and edit dimensions
- Prepare and plot a drawing
- Use the advanced two-dimensional drafting commands
- Understand the most important advanced techniques
- Understand parametric constraints
- Use the **External Reference** feature for team collaboration
- Understand sheet sets
- Understand the process of checking CAD standards
- Use the more advanced layer functions
- Use Autodesk Design Review for markups
- Use the **Markup Set Manager**

PREREQUISITES

◊ This text is written with the assumption that readers have experience using computers and the Microsoft® Windows® operating system.

◊ Readers should know how to start new files, open existing files, save files, use the "save as" option, close files with or without saving, and exit software.

◊ Because these commands are similar in all software packages, they are not explained in this text unless doing so helps demonstrate a command specific to AutoCAD.

◊ AutoCAD 2011 comes with a dark gray background. However, the backgrounds of the illustrations in this text have been changed to white for greater clarity.

◊ If you need to download sample files that come with AutoCAD, you can do so by following this link: http://www.autodesk.com/autocad-samples.

ABOUT THE DVD

◇ A DVD is included with this book. It contains the following:

- The AutoCAD 2011 trial version: This software will last for 30 days starting from the day of installation. You will need it to solve the exercises and workshops.

- Exercise and workshop files: These files will be your starting point to solve all exercises and workshops in the book. Copy the folder named "Exercises & Workshops" into a hard drive on your computer.

- Two folders for the workshops: The first folder, named "Metric," is for the metric units workshops; the second one, named "Imperial," is for the imperial units workshops.

- Solutions to the even-numbered exercises so that you may check your work.

For Instructors

Solutions to all exercises and workshops, files for the completed projects, Microsoft® PowerPoint® slides for lectures, and more are available for qualified instructors at http://www.jblearning.com/catalog/9780763798000/. Designated instructors' materials are for qualified instructors only. Jones & Bartlett Learning reserves the right to evaluate all requests.

1

INTRODUCTION TO
AUTOCAD 2011

In This Chapter

◊ What is AutoCAD?
◊ Starting AutoCAD
◊ Understanding the AutoCAD interface
◊ Understanding the AutoCAD defaults
◊ Viewing commands
◊ Creating a new file and opening an existing file

1.1 WHAT IS AUTOCAD?

- AutoCAD was one of the first computer-aided design/drafting (CAD) software applications in the world.
- The first version of AutoCAD was released at the end of 1982, and it was designed to be used on personal computers (PCs) only.
- Since then, AutoCAD has enjoyed an ever-expanding user base all over the world.
- The user can draw both two-dimensional (2D) drawings and three-dimensional (3D) designs.
- There is another version of AutoCAD called AutoCAD LT, which is dedicated to 2D drafting only.
- In this book, we will cover AutoCAD 2011.

1.2 STARTING AUTOCAD 2011

- Start AutoCAD 2011 by double-clicking on the shortcut that appears on your computer's desktop. This shortcut was created during AutoCAD's installation.
- AutoCAD will show the **Initial Setup** dialog box:

- This step will be discussed in Appendix A. For now, we will skip it by clicking **Skip** in the lower right corner. In the following dialog box, click **Start AutoCAD 2011**.

- Once AutoCAD loads and opens, a **Welcome Screen** will pop up:

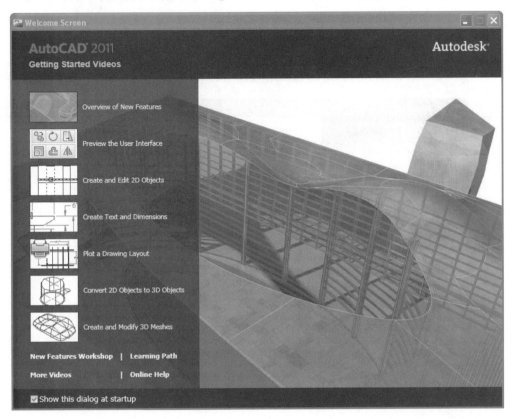

- For now, we will close this window.

1.3 AUTOCAD 2011 SCREEN

■   AutoCAD 2011 will start with a drawing file. Some key features of this screen are labeled in the following image:

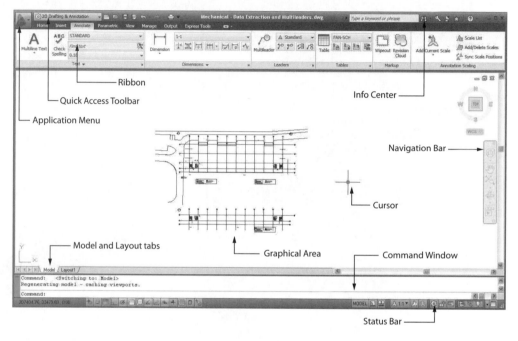

1.4 UNDERSTANDING THE AUTOCAD 2011 INTERFACE

■   The **Ribbons** and **Application Menu** will be your primary methods of reaching commands in AutoCAD 2011.

■   You will use **Ribbons** instead of the normal toolbars.

■   This interface will give you more space for the **Graphical Area**, which is your drawing area.

Application Menu

- Click on the **Application Menu**, and you will see the following:

- Using this menu, you can:
  - Create a new file
  - Open an existing file
  - Save the current file
  - Save the current file under a new name (Save As) and/or in a different folder
  - Export the current file to a different file format
  - Print the current file
  - Publish the current file
  - Send the current file to eTransmit or email
  - Use all the functions related to your drawing
  - Close the current file
  - Exit AutoCAD

Quick Access Toolbar

▪   The **Quick Access Toolbar** is the small toolbar located at the top left of the screen:

▪   Using this toolbar, you can:
   •   Change the workspace
   •   Start a new file
   •   Open an existing file
   •   Save the current file
   •   Save the current file under a new name (Save As) or in a different folder
   •   Undo and redo changes to the file
   •   Print the current file
▪   If you click the arrow at the end of the toolbar, the following list is displayed:

▪   Using this list, you can add or remove commands.
▪   Also, you can choose **Show Menu Bar**, which is sometimes needed if the command you need is not found in the **Application Menu** or **Ribbons**.

Ribbons

- **Ribbons** consist of two parts:
  - Tabs
  - Panels

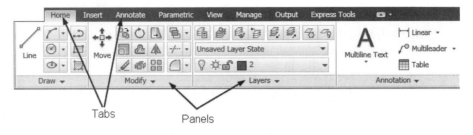

Tabs

Panels

- For example, the tab called **Home** consists of eight panels: **Draw**, **Modify**, **Layers**, **Annotation**, **Block**, **Properties**, **Utilities**, and **Clipboard.**
- For each tab, you will see different panels.
- The following is the **Draw** panel:

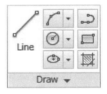

- Some panels (such as the **Draw** panel) have a small triangle near the title, which indicates that there are more buttons. If you click this triangle, you will see the following:

■ At the lower left-hand corner of the panel, you will see a small pushpin. If you click on it, this will become the default view. To return to the previous view, simply click the pushpin again:

■ Some panel buttons have a small triangle to the right, which indicates more options:

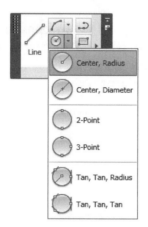

■ If you hold the cursor over any button for 1 second, a small help screen will appear:

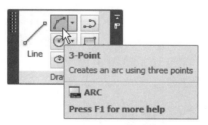

- However, if you hold the cursor over the button for 3 seconds, an extended help screen will appear:

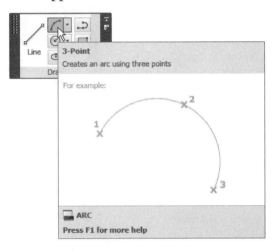

- Panels can be *docked* or *floating*. By default, all panels are docked. To change a panel to floating, simply click the name of the panel, hold it, and drag it to the desired location.
- If all panels remain docked, you will *not* see any panel outside the tab to which it belongs. However, if you make any panel floating, then you will be able to see it in all other tabs.
- Two small buttons will appear at the right-hand side of floating panels. The following images show the function of each button:

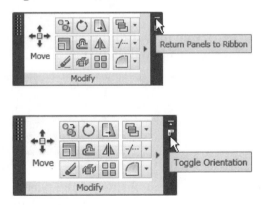

- All panels have two orientations, as displayed here:

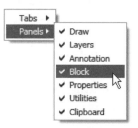

- The number of tabs and panels are predefined by default.
- However, you can turn off/on any tab/panel by right-clicking on any tab/panel and selecting the desired tab/panel to be turned off or on:

- **Ribbons** can be viewed in four different formats:
  - You can view the panels and their contents:

  - You can view the names and icons of the panels. If you hold your cursor over the name/icon, the panel's contents will appear:

- You can view only the names of the panels. If you hold your cursor over a name, the panel's contents will appear:

- You can view only the names of the tabs. Once you click on a tab, the related panels will appear:

- If you click the small arrow to the right of the tabs, a list of these formats will appear:

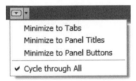

- From this list, you can pick any **Ribbon** format you wish right away, or you can cycle through the options.

InfoCenter

- At the top right of the screen, you will see the **InfoCenter**:

- If you type keywords into the **InfoCenter**, AutoCAD will search all of its online and offline resources to find you related help topics. See the following example:

■ However, if you prefer using the conventional help topics, you can access them by clicking the arrow at the right side of the **InfoCenter**:

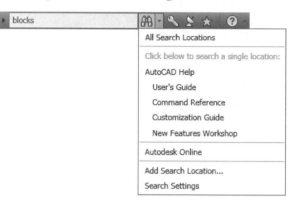

Command Window

■ Those who used AutoCAD 25 years ago may recall that the only way to input commands was with the **Command Window**. Users had to memorize all the AutoCAD commands and type them in. There were no menus, toolbars, panels, or ribbons. Although users can still type in commands, we don't recommend this approach.

Graphical Area

■ The **Graphical Area** is where you do your drafting. You will use the crosshairs to specify points in the X,Y plane.
■ You can monitor the coordinates of the crosshairs using the left part of the **Status Bar**.

Status Bar

■ The **Status Bar** in AutoCAD contains many functions to help you draft with precision. We will discuss most of the buttons on the **Status Bar** throughout this book.
■ There are two views for the **Status Bar**:
  • Icons (by default):

- Buttons:

| INFER | SNAP | GRID | ORTHO | POLAR | OSNAP | 3DOSNAP | OTRACK | DUCS | DYN | LWT | TPY | QP | SC |

  - To switch between the two views, right-click on the **Status Bar**. The following menu will appear:

Enabled	
Use Icons	
Settings…	
Display	▶

  - Select **Use Icons**, and the view will change accordingly.

1.5 POINTS IN AUTOCAD

  - Points are defined (and saved) in AutoCAD using the Cartesian coordinate system.
  - The coordinates will look something like **3.25,5.45**, which is in the format of **X,Y**.
  - The first and most traditional way of specifying points in AutoCAD is to type the coordinates whenever you are asked to do so by typing X,Y (pronounced "X comma Y"). See the following illustration:

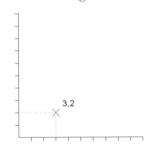

1.6 AUTOCAD DEFAULT SETTINGS

- Sign convention: positive is up and right.
- Angle convention: positive is counterclockwise (CCW) starting from the *east* (i.e., 0 angle). See the following illustration:

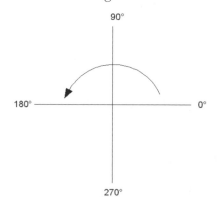

1.7 THINGS YOU SHOULD KNOW ABOUT AUTOCAD

- The mouse is the primary input device:
  - The left button is always used to select, or click.
  - The right button offers a drop-down menu when pushed.
- The wheel in the mouse has zooming functions:
  - Zoom in on your drawing by moving the wheel forward.
  - Zoom out on the drawing by moving the wheel backward.
  - Pan (i.e., move through the drawing) by pressing the wheel and holding it, then moving the mouse.
  - Zoom to the edges of your drawing by double-clicking the wheel.
- If you typed an AutoCAD command or any input in the **Command Window**, you must press [Enter] to execute it.
- [Enter] = [Spacebar] in AutoCAD.
- To repeat the most recent AutoCAD command, press [Enter] or [Spacebar].
- To cancel an AutoCAD command, press [Esc].
- Press [F1] to see the **Help Window**.
- Press [F2] to see the **Text Window**.

1.8 DRAWING LIMITS

- AutoCAD offers the user an infinite drawing sheet on all sides.
- When you start a new AutoCAD drawing, your viewpoint will be at 0,0,1.
- You are looking at the X,Y plane using a camera's lens; hence, you will see part of your infinite drawing sheet. This part is called the **limits**. See the following illustration:

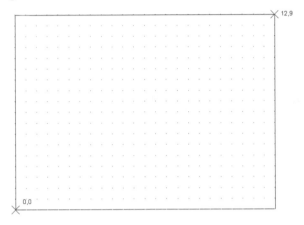

- In this example, you can see that the **limits** of the drawing are from 0,0 (lower left-hand corner) to 12,9 (upper right-hand corner). This is your working area.
- We will learn to change **limits** in the following chapters.

1.9 AUTOCAD UNITS AND SPACES

- One of the lesser-known facts about AutoCAD is that it does not deal with a certain length unit while drafting. Note the following points:
  - AutoCAD uses AutoCAD units.
  - An AutoCAD unit can be anything you want. For example, it can be a meter, centimeter, millimeter, inch, or foot.
  - All of these units are correct as long as you later remember the unit you have chosen and are consistent in both X and Y.
- There are two spaces in AutoCAD, **Model Space** and **Layout** (or **Paper Space**). You can switch between the two spaces from the **Status Bar**.

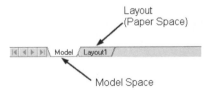

- By default, when you start a new drawing file, you are in **Model Space**.
- In **Model Space** you can create and modify your drawing.
- When you are ready to make a hard copy of your drawing file, switch to the **Layout** (**Paper Space**) so you can prepare your page setup.
- This is the moment you need to ask yourself, "What is my unit assumption?" so you can properly scale your drawing.
- We will discuss printing in a later chapter.

1.10 VIEWING COMMANDS

- Earlier in this chapter we discussed the benefits of the mouse wheel for zooming in, zooming out, and panning. You can also zoom in, zoom out, and pan using the zooming and panning commands.
- Make sure you are at the **View** tab on the **Ribbon**. From the **Navigate** panel, click the third option down, **Extents**. A list of zooming commands will appear:

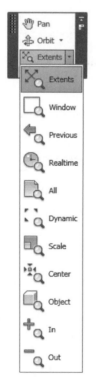

- **Zoom Extents** is used to zoom to limits or all objects, whichever is bigger.
- **Zoom Window** is used to specify a rectangle. By specifying two opposite corners, whatever is inside the rectangle will look larger.
- **Zoom Previous** is used to restore the previous view, up to the last 10 views.
- **Zoom Realtime** is used by clicking the left button of the mouse and holding it. If you move forward, you are zooming in; if you move backward you are zooming out.
- **Zoom All** is used to zoom to all objects.
- **Zoom Dynamic** is used with the **Zoom Window** first. You will see the whole drawing and your current place (it will be shown by a green dotted line). Go to the new location and press [Enter].
- **Zoom Scale** is used by inputting a scale factor (i.e., typing in a number). If the scale factor typed is less than 1, the drawing will decrease in size. If the scale factor is greater than 1, the drawing will increase in size. If you insert the letter *x* after the number (e.g., 2x), the scale will adjust relative to the current view.
- **Zoom Center** is used to specify a new center point for the zooming, along with a new height.
- **Zoom Object** is used to zoom to selected objects. AutoCAD will ask you to select objects. The selected objects will fill the screen.
- **Zoom In** is not really a zoom option; rather, it is a programmed option that equals the **Zoom Scale** with a scale factor of 2x.
- **Zoom Out** is just like **Zoom In** but with a zoom factor of 0.5x.

1.11 CREATING A NEW FILE

■ To create a new file based on a premade template, click **New** from the **Quick Access Toolbar**:

- The following dialog box will appear:

- This dialog box will allow you to select the desired template.
- AutoCAD template files have the extension *.dwt*.
- AutoCAD 2011 has many premade templates you can use. If you do not want to use these templates, you can create your own template (see Appendix A).
- For now, we will use *acad.dwt* to help us do some of our exercises and workshops.
- Click **Open** to start a new file.

1.12 OPENING AN EXISTING FILE

- To open an existing file for further editing, click **Open** from the **Quick Access Toolbar**.

- The following dialog box will appear:

Select File	

Look in: Mechanical Sample

Views ▾ Tools ▾

Name ▲	Size
Mechanical - Data Extraction ...	268 KB
Mechanical - Data Links.dwg	164 KB
Mechanical - Multileaders.dwg	135 KB
Mechanical - Text and Tables....	133 KB
Mechanical - Xref.dwg	318 KB

Preview

☐ Select Initial View

File name: Mechanical - Data Links.dwg   Open

Files of type: Drawing (*.dwg)   Cancel

History · My Documents · Favorites · FTP · Desktop · Buzzsaw

- Specify the hard drive, and select the folder your file resides in.
- AutoCAD drawing files have the extension *.*dwg*.
- If you want to open a single file, select the file and click open (or double-click on the file's name).
- If you want to open more than one file, select the first file name, then hold the [Ctrl] key on the keyboard and click the other file names. You can open as many files as you wish. When you are done selecting files, click **Open**.

Quick View

- If you open more than one file, you can use two functions in the **Status Bar**: **Quick View Drawings** and **Quick View Layouts**.

Quick View Layouts
Quick View Drawings

MODEL

- If these two buttons are switched on, you will see the following:

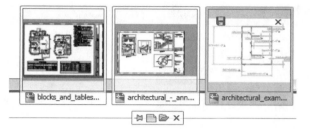

- You will see all the opened files.
- To jump from one file to another, click the window of the desired file.
- When you hover over any of the files, you will see the layouts of the file, and the picture will change to the following:

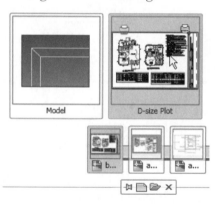

- Also, you will see a small toolbar at the bottom, which will enable you to:
  - Close the **Quick View**
  - Open a file
  - Start a new file
  - Pin **Quick View Drawings**
- If you right-click the **Quick View** button of any file, the following menu will appear:

- Using **Windows**, you can **Arrange Icons**, **Tile Vertically**, **Tile Horizontally**, or **Cascade**.
- You can copy your current file as a hyperlink and paste it in another document.
- You can close all files.
- You can close files other than the current file.
- You can save all files.
- You can close the current file.

Organizing Files

▪ Make sure you are at the **View** tab on the **Ribbon**. There are several ways to organize files Using the **Window** panel:

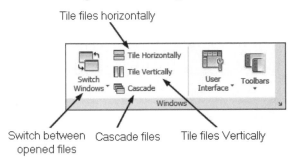

Tile files horizontally

Switch between opened files   Cascade files   Tile files Vertically

▪ The **Switch Windows** button will show you a list of opened files. The current file will be listed with a checkmark (✓); if you want another file, select the name of the desired file.

NOTE ▪ Using [Ctrl] + [Tab] you can browse between opened files.

▪ The rest of the file commands are identical to other Windows® applications, including **Save**, **Save As**, and **Exit**.

1.13 CLOSING FILES

■   To close a file using the **Application** menu, select **Close**, then select either
Current Drawing or **All Drawings**:

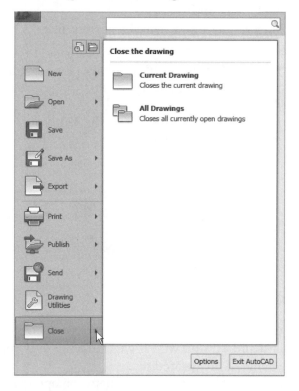

INTRODUCING AUTOCAD 2011

Exercise 1-1

1. Start AutoCAD 2011.
2. From the **Quick Access Toolbar**, click **Open**.
3. Go to the **Samples** folder under the AutoCAD 2011 folder. Open the
    following three files:
    a. Blocks and Tables—*Metric.dwg*
    b. Blocks and Tables—*Imperial.dwg*
    c. Architectural and Annotation Scaling—*Multileader.dwg*
4. Using **Quick View Drawings**, jump from one file to another. Using **Quick
    View Layouts**, look at the layouts in each file.

5. Using [Ctrl] + [Tab], browse the three opened files, stop at Blocks and Tables (*Metric.dwg*), and click the **Model** tab at the lower end. Using the wheel on your mouse or any of the zoom commands, zoom in on the drawing, zoom out (using different methods), and pan.

6. Press [F2] to see the **Text Window**, which includes all the history of the current session.

7. Go to the **Home** tab and drag the **Layers** panel to make it floating. Then go to the **Insert** tab and see if the **Layers** panel is still visible.

8. Return the **Layers** panel to its original location.

9. Change the format of the **Ribbon** and test all four options.

10. Using the right-click menu on **Quick View Drawings**, select **Close All** without saving.

CHAPTER REVIEW

1. All opened files can be closed using a single command.
   a. True
   b. False

2. CAD stands for _____.

3. In AutoCAD, there are two available spaces: **Model Space** and **Paper Space**. Which of the following statements is true?
   a. You draw on **Model Space** and print from **Paper Space**.
   b. You draw on **Paper Space** and print from **Model Space**.
   c. There is only one space in AutoCAD.
   d. **Model Space** is only for 3D design.

4. Positive angles start from the *north*.
   a. True
   b. False

5. AutoCAD is one of few software applications that allows users to:
   a. Connect through the Internet.
   b. Type commands using the keyboard.
   c. Accept Cartesian coordinates.
   d. Create positive angles that are CCW.

6. _____ is a tool in AutoCAD that allows users to see all opened files in small windows.

7. Press _____ to see the **Text Window**.

CHAPTER REVIEW ANSWERS

1. a
2. computer-aided design/drafting
3. a
4. b
5. b
6. **Quick View Drawings**
7. [F2]

Chapter 2

DRAFTING USING AUTOCAD 2011

In This Chapter

◇ The **Line** command and precision drawing methods
◇ The **Arc** and **Circle** commands
◇ The **Object Snap (OSNAP)** tool
◇ The **Object Snap Tracking (OTRACK)** tool
◇ The **Polyline** command
◇ The **Polar Tracking (POLAR)** tool
◇ **Erase** and basic selecting methods

2.1 INTRODUCTION

- The two most important considerations in drafting are:
  - Precision
  - Speed
- You always want to finish your drawing as fast as possible, yet, you do not want to undermine your drawing's precision.
- Always put precision before speed; it is easier to learn to speed up the creation process than it is to improve accuracy.
- In this chapter we will tackle many commands, but our primary goal is drafting with precision.

2.2 THE LINE COMMAND

- The **Line** command is used to draw segments of straight lines.
- Many methods will allow us to draw precise shapes using the **Line** command, as will be discussed later. For now, we will use the only method we know—typing the coordinates in the **Command Window**.

- On the **Ribbon**, use the **Home** tab. From the **Draw** panel, click the **Line** button:

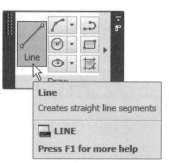

- The following prompts will appear:

```
Specify first point: (type in the coordinate of
the first point)
Specify next point or [Undo]: (type in the
coordinate of the second point)
Specify next point or [Undo]: (type in the
coordinate of the third point)
Specify next point or [Close/Undo]: (type in the
coordinate of the fourth point)
```

- At any time, you can use the **Undo** option to undo the last specified point, and hence the last specified segment.
- After you draw two segments, the **Close** option will be available to connect the last point to the first point and to end the command.
- You can also end the command by pressing [Enter] or the spacebar.
- Pressing [Esc] also ends the **Line** command.
- If you are using the **Line** command and you right-click, the following menu will appear, which is identical to the command prompts:

2.3 DRAFTING USING DYNAMIC INPUT

- By default, the **Dynamic Input** is turned on, so anything you type in the **Command Window** will appear on the screen beside the AutoCAD cursor.

- Make sure the **Dynamic Input** button is turned on:

- For example, if you type the word "line," it will appear on the screen as follows:

- When you press [Enter], the following will appear:

- Type the X coordinates, then press [Tab]:

- Type the Y coordinate, then press [Enter]. **Dynamic Input** will show the length and the angle of the line to be drawn (the angle is measured from the east and incremented by 1 degree):

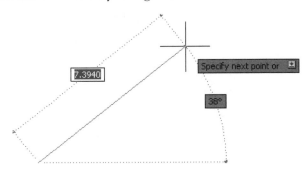

■ Specify the length and press [Tab]; then type the angle and press [Enter]:

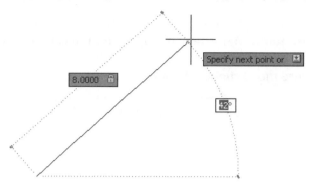

DRAWING LINES: FIRST METHOD

Exercise 2-1

1. Start AutoCAD 2011.
2. Open the file *Exercise 2-1.dwg*.
3. Make sure that:
   a. **Polar Tracking** is off.
   b. **Object Snap** is off.
   c. **Object Snap Tracking** is off.
   d. **Dynamic Input** is on.
4. Draw the following lines using the **Line** command and **Dynamic Input** (without dimensions):

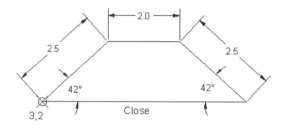

5. Save and close the file.

■ Start the **Line** command and type the coordinates of the first point. With **Dynamic Input** on, specify the length, press [Tab], and specify the angle. Do the same for the other line segments.

2.4 PRECISION METHOD 1: SNAP AND GRID

- As you can see, the only method we have used to precisely specify points in the X,Y plane was to type the coordinates using **Dynamic Input**.
- We do this because we cannot depend on the mouse to specify precise points.
- For the mouse to work precisely, we need to control its movement.
- **Snap** is the only tool in AutoCAD that can help us control the movement of the mouse.
- Using the **Status Bar**, click the **Snap Mode** button:

- Now move in the **Graphical Area** and watch the mouse jump to exact points. (If you did not see any change, you may need to change the X and Y spacing, which will be discussed in a moment.)
- The **Grid** will show a grid of lines on the screen to simulate grid paper, which is used in drawing diagrams.
- By default, the **Grid** is turned on.
- On its own, the **Grid** is not accurate, but it is a helpful tool when used with **Snap**.
- Using the status bar, click the **Grid Display** button to turn it on:

- You can now see lines displayed on the screen.
- If the default values for either **Snap Mode** or **Grid Display** do not satisfy your needs, simply right-click on either button and the following shortcut menu will appear:

■   Select **Settings**. The following dialog box will appear:

■   By default, **Snap X spacing** and **Snap Y spacing** are equal. **Grid X spacing** and **Grid Y spacing** are also equal. To keep this setup, make sure that the **Equal X and Y spacing** box is checked.

■   Select **Grid On** if you would like to use the old method of **Grid Display**, which uses dots instead of lines, and where you want to display it. You have three choices: **2D model space**, **Block editor**, and **Sheet/layout**.

■   Set the **Major line** spacing for the **Grid Display**.

■   By default, **Grid** lines will extend beyond limits (we will discuss limits in Chapter 3); hence, no matter how much you zoom in or out, you will still see grid lines. You can make the grid adhere to the limits by unchecking the **Display grid beyond Limits** box.

■   Leave the other options in their default settings. Some of them will be discussed shortly, and some of them are discussed in *AutoCAD® 2010 3D Modeling Essentials* by Munir Hamad.

■   If you want **Grid** to follow **Snap**, set the two grid values to zero.

NOTE ■   You can use function keys to turn on both **Snap** and **Grid**:
   •   [F9] = **Snap** on/off
   •   [F7] = **Grid** on/off

SNAP AND GRID

Exercise 2-2

1. Start AutoCAD 2011.
2. Open the file Exercise 2-2.dwg.
3. Using **Snap** and **Grid**, draw the following lines *without typing* any coordinates. Start from the lower left-hand corner with 2.75,2.25 (do not draw the dimensions).

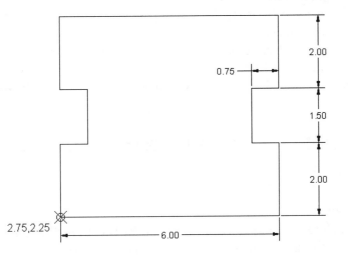

4. Save and close the file.

- Change the **Snap X spacing** to 0.25 first, and set the grid values to 0. Switch both **Snap** and **Grid** on, and draw the lines as required.

2.5 PRECISION METHOD 2: DIRECT DISTANCE ENTRY AND ORTHO

- Because lines in AutoCAD are *vectors*, we must specify a length and an angle to successfully draw them.
- **Ortho** is a tool that forces the cursor to always give us orthogonal angles (i.e., 0, 90, 180, and 270).
- **Direct Distance Entry** is a very handy tool in drafting; if the mouse is already directed toward an angle, just type in the distance and press [Enter].
- Combining these two tools will allow us to draw lines with precise lengths and angles.

- Follow these steps:
  - From the **Status Bar**, click the **Ortho Mode** button:

  - Start the **Line** command.
  - Specify the first point.
  - Move the mouse to the right, up, left, or down, noting that it gives you only orthogonal angles.
  - Use the desired angle, type in the distance, and press [Enter].
  - Continue with other segments using the same method.
- NOTE ➤ You can use **Direct Distance Entry** with **Dynamic Input** as well.

DIRECT DISTANCE ENTRY AND ORTHO

Exercise 2-3

1. Start AutoCAD 2011.
2. Open file *Exercise 2-3.dwg*.
3. Using **Ortho** and **Direct Distance Entry**, draw the following shape. Start from the lower left-hand corner with 3,2 (without dimensions).

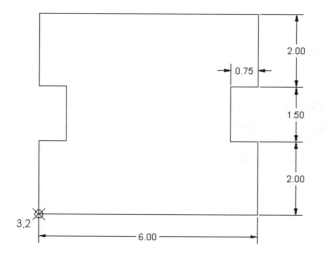

4. Save and close the file.

2.6 THE ARC COMMAND

- The **Arc** command is used to draw circular arcs (the arc part of a circle).
- Look at the following illustration:

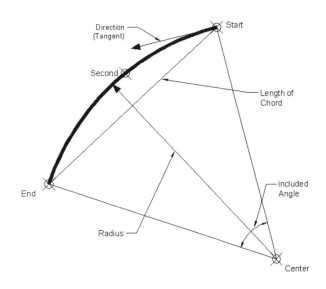

- The information that AutoCAD recognizes about an arc includes:
  - Start point
  - Second point (not necessarily the midpoint)
  - Endpoint
  - Center point
  - Radius
  - Length of chord
  - Included angle (angle created by **Start**, **Center**, and **End**)
  - Direction (the tangent passes through the start point)
- AutoCAD needs only three pieces of information to draw an arc, but not just any three.
- AutoCAD will start by asking you to make your first input, choosing between the start point and the center point. Based on your choice, it will ask you to specify the second piece of information, and so on.
- On the **Ribbon**, go to the **Home** tab. From the **Draw** panel, click the **Arc** button (the small arrow at the right). You will see the following:

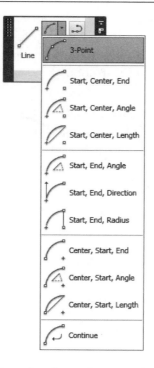

- Before you start, select the desired method from the menu. AutoCAD will take it from there.

 ■ Always think counterclockwise when specifying points.

DRAWING ARCS

Exercise 2-4

1. Start AutoCAD 2011.
2. Open the file *Exercise 2-4.dwg*. You will see the following shape:

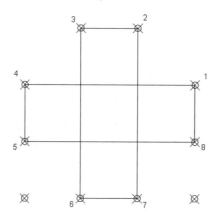

3. Turn on **Snap** and **Grid**.
4. Draw the first arc between point 1 and point 2 using **Start**, **End**, **Angle**, where point 1 is the start point, and the angle = –90.
5. Draw the second arc between point 3 and point 4 using **Start**, **End**, **Direction**, where point 3 is the start point and the direction = 270.
6. Draw the third arc between point 5 and point 6 using **Start**, **Center**, **End**, where point 6 is the start point and the point at the lower left is the center point (you can specify it easily using **Snap** and **Grid**).
7. Draw the fourth arc between point 7 and point 8 using **Start**, **Center**, **Length**, where point 8 is the start point, the point at the lower right is the center point, and the length of the chord is the distance between point 8 and point 7.
8. The shape should appear as follows:

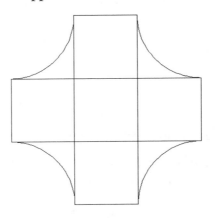

9. Save and close the file.

2.7 THE CIRCLE COMMAND

- The **Circle** command is used to draw a circle in AutoCAD.
- There are six different methods to draw a circle.
- To use the first two methods, you must know the center of the circle. This will give you the radius and the diameter:

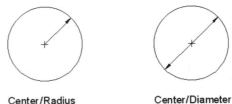

Center/Radius   Center/Diameter

- To use the third method, you must know any three points on the parameter of the circle.
- To use the fourth method, you must know two points on the parameter of the circle such that the distance between them is equal to the diameter:

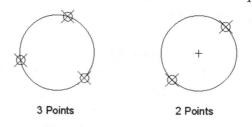

3 Points   2 Points

- To use the fifth method, you should have two objects already drawn. We can consider them as tangents, then specify a radius.
- To use the sixth method, you should specify three tangents by selecting three objects:

Tangent/Tangent/Tangent   Tangent/Tangent/Radius

- On the **Ribbon**, go to the **Home** tab. From the **Draw** panel, click the **Circle** button (the small arrow at the right). You will see the following:

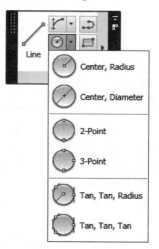

- Before you start, select the desired method from the menu. AutoCAD will take it from there.

DRAWING CIRCLES

Exercise 2-5

1. Start AutoCAD 2011.
2. Open the file *Exercise 2-5.dwg*.
3. Make sure that **Snap** and **Grid** are on.
4. Draw five circles to make your file look like the following:

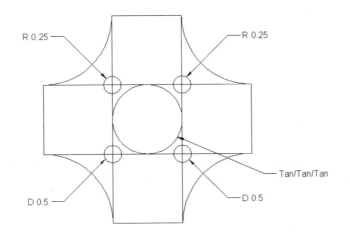

5. Save and close the file.

2.8 PRECISION METHOD 3: OBJECT SNAP (OSNAP)

- AutoCAD keeps a full record of each object in each drawing.
- **Object Snap (OSNAP)** is a tool that helps you use these records when you need to specify points on objects already precisely drawn without knowing the points.
- Example:
  - Assume we have the following shape:

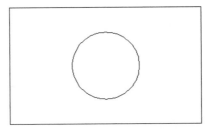

- We have no information about any object in this shape.
- We have been asked to draw a precise line from the midpoint of the right vertical line to the top of the circle as a tangent.
- The command to draw is **Line**. AutoCAD asked us to specify the first point, and we typed **mid** and pressed [Enter] (or the spacebar), then went directly to the right line where a yellow triangle appeared. We clicked:

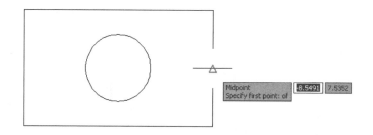

- AutoCAD then asked us to specify the next point, and we typed **tan** and pressed [Enter] (or the spacebar), then went directly to the top of the circle, where a yellow circle appeared. We clicked:

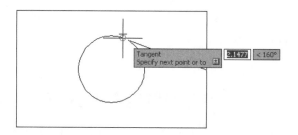

- We then pressed [Enter] to end the command.

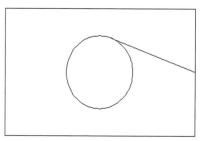

- Mission accomplished.

■ Some of the **OSNAPs** are:

End

● To catch the endpoint of an object

Mid

● To catch the midpoint of an object

Intersection

● To catch the intersection of two objects

Center

● To catch the center of an arc or a circle

Quadrant

● To catch the quadrant of an arc or a circle

Tangent

● To catch the tangent of an arc or a circle

Perpendicular

● To catch the perpendicular point on an object

Nearest

● To catch a point on an object nearest to your click point

NOTE ■ We will discuss more **OSNAPs** when we learn more commands.

■ There are three ways to use the **OSNAPs** when you are asked to specify a point:

Typing

■ Type the first three letters of the desired **OSNAP**—for example, **end**, **mid**, **cen**, **qua**, **int**, **per**, **tan**, **nea**. This is an old method, but still widely used among the veterans of AutoCAD.

[Shift] + Right-Click

■ Hold [Shift] and right-click. The following menu will appear. Select the desired **OSNAP**:

Running OSNAP

- This method is the most practical of those discussed.
- You will select an **OSNAP** and it will run all the time. The next time you are asked to specify an endpoint, for example, simply go to the desired point and it will be acquired immediately.
- There are two ways to activate running **OSNAP**:
  - In the first option, starting from the **Status Bar**, right-click the **OSNAP** button. The following menu will appear:

- In this example, **Endpoint**, **Center**, **Intersection**, and **Extension** are all running (as indicated by the frame around each icon).
- In the second option, select **Settings** and the following dialog box will appear:

Drafting Settings

Snap and Grid | Polar Tracking | Object Snap | 3D Object Snap | Dynamic Input | Quic ◄ ►

☑ Object Snap On (F3)   ☑ Object Snap Tracking On (F11)

Object Snap modes

☐ ☑ Endpoint   ☐ ☐ Insertion   [Select All]
△ ☐ Midpoint   ┴ ☐ Perpendicular   [Clear All]
○ ☑ Center   ○ ☐ Tangent
⊠ ☐ Node   ✕ ☐ Nearest
◇ ☐ Quadrant   ⊠ ☐ Apparent intersection
✕ ☑ Intersection   // ☐ Parallel
--- ☑ Extension

💡 To track from an Osnap point, pause over the point while in a command. A tracking vector appears when you move the cursor. To stop tracking, pause over the point again.

[Options...]   [OK] [Cancel] [Help]

- Switch on the desired **OSNAP** and click **OK**.

2.9 OBJECT SNAP TRACKING (OTRACK)

- If you have a rectangle and you want to draw a circle, the center of which coincides exactly with the center of the rectangle, **Object Snap Tracking (OTRACK)** will help you do this without drawing any new objects to facilitate specifying the exact points.
- **OTRACK** uses **OSNAPs** of existing objects to "steal" the coordinates of the new point.
- From the **Status Bar**, click the **Object Snap Tracking** button:

- Make sure that **OSNAP** is also on, as **OTRACK** alone would not do anything.

Example of Two-points OTRACK

- Let's consider an example in which we use two points to specify one point:
  - Assume we have the following rectangle:

  - Make sure that **OSNAP** and **OTRACK** are both turned on. Also make sure that **Midpoint** in **OSNAP** is turned on.
  - Start the **Circle** command, which will ask you to specify the center point.
  - Go to the upper (or lower) horizontal line and move to the midpoint. Hover there for a couple of seconds, then move up or down. You will see an infinite line extending in both directions (do not click):

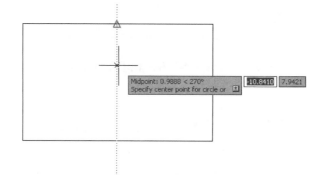

  - Go to the right (or left) vertical line and move to the midpoint. Hover there for a couple of seconds, then move right or left. You will see an infinite line extending in both directions:

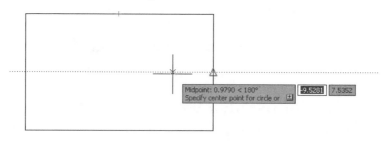

- Now move your cursor to where you think the two infinite lines should intersect:

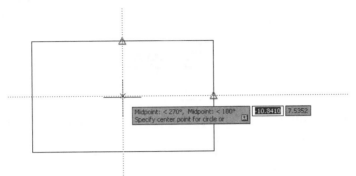

- Once you see the two infinite lines, click. You have thus specified the center point of the circle. You can now type in the radius (or diameter) of the circle:

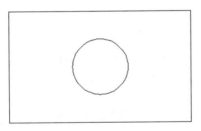

Example of One-point OTRACK

- Let's consider another example. This time we will use one point to specify one point:
  - Continue with the shape we used in the last example.
  - Start the **Circle** command, which will ask you to specify the center point.
  - Make sure both **OSNAP** and **OTRACK** are turned on, and also turn on **Center** in **OSNAP**.
  - Move your cursor to the center point of the existing circle and hover for a couple of seconds, then move to the right. An infinite line will appear:

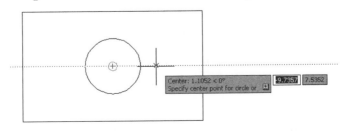

- Type "2" (or any distance) and press [Enter]:

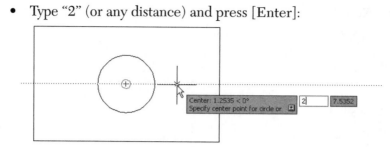

- The center of the new circle will be specified, then type in the radius. You will see the following:

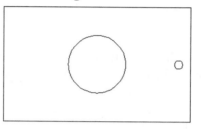

 ■ If you hover over a point for a couple of seconds to produce the infinite line and discover that this is not the desired point, simply hover over the same point again and it will be disabled.

DRAWING USING OSNAP AND OTRACK

Exercise 2-6
1. Start AutoCAD 2011.
2. Open the file *Exercise 2-6.dwg*.

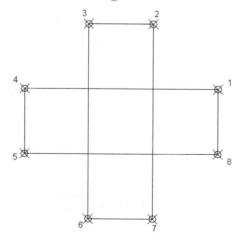

3. Make sure that **Snap** and **Grid** are both turned off.

4. Using running **OSNAP**, switch on **Endpoint**.

5. Draw the first arc between point 1 and point 2 using **Start**, **End**, **Angle**, where point 1 is the start point and the angle = –90.

6. Draw the second arc between point 3 and point 4 using **Start**, **End**, **Direction**, where point 3 is the start point and the direction = 270.

7. Draw the third arc between point 5 and point 6 using **Start**, **Center**, **End**, where point 6 is the start point. To specify the center point, use **OTRACK** between point 5 and point 6.

8. Draw the fourth arc between point 7 and point 8 using **Start**, **Center**, **Length**, where point 8 is the start point. To specify the center point, use **OTRACK** between point 7 and point 8, and the length of the chord is the distance between point 8 and point 7.

9. The shape should appear as follows:

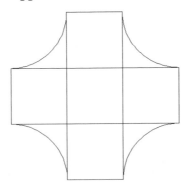

10. Using the following picture, and using running **OSNAP**, turn **Intersection** on. Then specify five circles using **Intersection** to specify the center points for the small circles. (By default, AutoCAD will activate **Tangent** when you use the **Tan**, **Tan**, **Tan** method.)

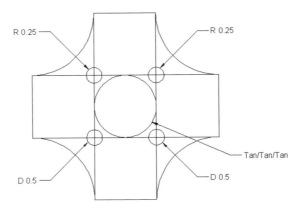

11. Save and close the file.

DRAWING USING OSNAP AND OTRACK

Exercise 2-7
1.   Start AutoCAD 2011.
2.   Open the file *Exercise 2-7.dwg*.
3.   Turn **OSNAP** on, and set the following **OSNAPs** on: **Endpoint**, **Midpoint**, and **Center**.
4.   Turn on **OTRACK**.
5.   Draw the four circles while specifying the center using **OSNAP** and **OTRACK**.

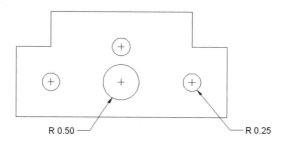

6.   Save and close the file.

2.10 THE POLYLINE COMMAND

- Poly means many. If you exchange the word *poly* with *many* in the term *Polyline*, you would in essence have *many lines*.
- To start, let's compare the **Line** command to the **Polyline** command:

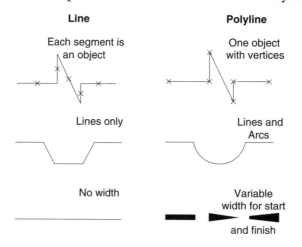

- As you can see from the comparison, there are mainly three differences between the two commands.
- On the **Ribbon**, use the **Home** tab. From the **Draw** panel, click the **Polyline** button:

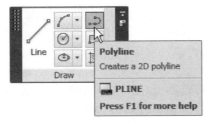

- The following prompt will appear:

```
Specify start point:
Current line-width is 0.9000
Specify next point or [Arc/Halfwidth/Length/Undo/Width]:
```

- After you specify the first point, the **Polyline** command will report to you the current polyline width (in our example it is 0.90), then it will ask you to specify the next point. You can use all the methods we learned with the **Line** command.
- If you do not want to specify the second point, you can choose from **Arc**, **Halfwidth**, **Length**, and **Width**.

Arc

- By default, the **Polyline** command will draw lines.
- You can change the mode to draw arcs by selecting the **Arc** option. The following prompt will appear:

```
Specify endpoint of arc or
[Angle/CEnter/CLose/Direction/Halfwidth/Line/Radius/
Second pt/Undo/Width]:
```

- We learned in the **Arc** command that AutoCAD needs three pieces of information to draw an arc.
- AutoCAD already knows the start point of the arc, which is the start point of the polyline or the endpoint of the last line segment.
- AutoCAD will assume that the direction of the arc will be the same angle as the last line segment. Users can accept or reject this assumption.
- If you accept this assumption, then AutoCAD will ask you to specify the endpoint of the arc.

- If you reject this assumption, then specify the second piece of information from the following:
    - Angle of arc, then center or radius
    - Center, then angle or length
    - Direction, then end
    - Radius, then end or angle
    - Second, then end

Halfwidth

- The first method is to specify the width of the polyline.
- Specify the halfwidth of the polyline from the center to one of its edges, which should resemble the following:

- When you select this option, AutoCAD will show the following prompt:

```
Specify starting half-width <1.0000>:
Specify ending half-width <1.0000>:
```

- In our example, the halfwidth is 1.0 for both the start point and the endpoint.

Length

- In the **Polyline** command, if you draw an arc then switch to the **Line** command, and you want the line to be tangent to the arc, then select this option.
- This option will assume the angle to be the same as that of the last segment, hence you will be asked only for the length. The following prompt will appear:

```
Specify length of line:
```

Width

- **Width** is the same as **Halfwidth**, with the exception that you must input the full width:

NOTE

- The **Undo** and **Close** options are the same options in the **Line** command.
- If you choose to close in the **Arc** option, it will close the shape by an arc.

2.11 CONVERTING OBJECTS

- Now we have two sets of commands, the **Polyline** command, which can draw lines and arcs as well as make them one unit, and the **Line** and **Arc** commands, which will draw segments of both lines and arcs.
- To convert a polyline to a line and arc, we will use the **Explode** command.
- On the **Ribbon**, go to the **Home** tab. From the **Modify** panel, click the **Explode** button:

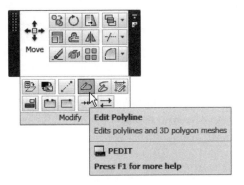

- You will see the following prompts:

```
Select objects:
```

- Select the desired polyline and press [Enter] or right-click. The polyline will be turned into lines and arcs; hence, it will loose some of its characteristics, such as width.
- In order to convert lines and arcs to polylines, we will use the **Edit Polyline** (or **PEDIT**) command.
- On the **Ribbon**, go to the **Home** tab. From the **Modify** panel, click to show more buttons, then click the **Edit Polyline** button:

```
Select polyline or [Multiple]: (Select one object)
Object selected is not a polyline
Do you want to turn it into one? <Y>
Enter an option [Close/Join/Width/Edit vertex/Fit/Spline/
Decurve/Ltype gen/Reverse/Undo]: J
```

- Select one of the objects to be converted.
- AutoCAD will discover that the selected object is not a polyline and will tell you, "Object selected is not a polyline." It will then give you the option to "Turn it into polyline." If you answer yes, then a small menu will appear. Select the **Join** option.
- Next, AutoCAD will ask you to select the other objects you want to join to the first selected object.
- Once done, press [Enter] twice.

DRAWING POLYLINES

Exercise 2-8
1. Start AutoCAD 2011.
2. Open the file *Exercise 2-8.dwg*.
3. Using **Ortho** and **Direct Distance Entry**, draw the following shape (without dimensions) using the **Polyline** command with width = 0.1.

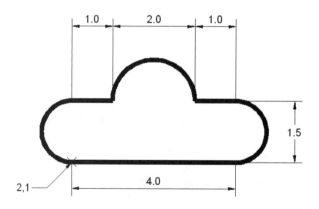

4. Using the **Explode** command, explode the polyline, noting how the width is lost. Using the **Undo** command, change it back to a polyline.
5. Save and close the file.

- Consider the following tips:
  - To draw the large arc, use angle = 180.
  - Before you draw the last arc, change the mode to **Arc** and select **Close**.

2.12 POLAR TRACKING

- We learned that we can force the cursor to give us four orthogonal angles (0, 90, 180, 270) using **Ortho**.
- If we want other angles, such as 30 and its multiples, **Ortho** will not help us. Thus, AutoCAD provides another powerful tool, called **Polar Tracking**.
- **Polar Tracking** allows you to extend rays from your current point toward angles such as 30, 60, 90, 120, and so on. You can use **Direct Distance Entry**, just like we did with **Ortho**.
- From the **Status Bar**, click the **Polar Tracking** button:

- To select the desired angle, right-click on the button and you will see the following menu:

```
✔ 90
  45
  30
  22.5
  18
  15
  10
  5
✔ Enabled
✔ Use Icons
  Settings...
  Display      ▶
```

- Select the desired angle, and you will get it along with its multiples.
- If you want more control, right-click on the button and select **Settings**. The following dialog box will appear:

Increment Angle

- Under **Polar Tracking**, select the **Increment angle** drop-down menu for a list of predefined angles. Select the desired angle.
- If the angle you want is not among the list, simply type your own angle.
- Based on this example, the user will have rays in angles of 0, 30, 60, 90, 120, etc.

Additional Angles

- There may be times in the design process when you will need odd angles that the **Increment angle** cannot provide, such as 56 or 112.
- The **Additional angles** option will help you set these odd angles.
- Using the same dialog box, check the **Additional angles** box.
- Click the **New** button and type in the angle.
- To delete an existing additional angle, select it and click the **Delete** button.
- NOTE ▸ AutoCAD will not give the multiples of the additional angles.

PolarSnap

- We previously discussed the **Snap** command, which helped us use the mouse to specify exact points on the X,Y plane.
- The **Snap** command can help us only along the *x*-axis (+ and −) and along *y*-axis (+ and −).

- If you want to snap to a point along the ray produced by **PolarSnap**, you have to change the type of the **Snap** from **Grid snap** to **PolarSnap**.
- From the **Status Bar**, turn on **Snap**. Right-click on the **Snap** button and select **Settings**. Under **Snap type**, select **PolarSnap** instead of **Grid snap**, as shown:

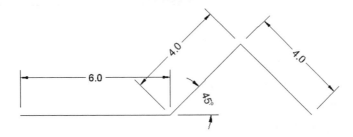

- Now set the **Polar spacing** value:

Polar spacing	
Polar distance:	1.00

Example

- We want to draw the following shape:

- Let's assume we set the **Increment angle** to 45 and we changed the type of **Snap** to **PolarSnap** with a distance = 1.0. To draft using **Polar Tracking**, follow these steps:
  - Start the **Line** command, then specify a starting point.
  - Move to the right until you see a ray. Read the distance and the angle. When you reach your distance, click to specify a point, as shown:

6.0000   0°

Polar: 6.0000 < 0°

  - Move the cursor toward the angle 45 until you see the ray, then move the mouse to the desired distance and click:

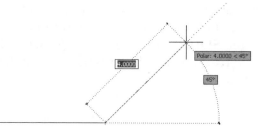

- Move the cursor toward the angle 315 until you see the ray, then move the mouse to the desired distance and click:

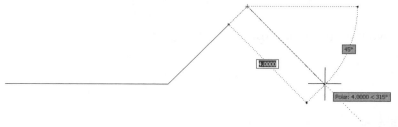

DRAWING USING POLAR TRACKING

Exercise 2-9

1. Start AutoCAD 2011.
2. Open the file *Exercise 2-9.dwg*.
3. Switch both **Polar Tracking** and **PolarSnap** on, and select the following settings:
   a. Increment angle = 30
   b. Additional angles = 135
   c. Polar distance = 0.5
4. Draw the following shape (without dimensions) starting from 3,2:

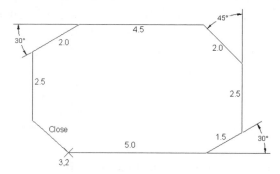

5. Save and close the file.

2.13 THE ERASE COMMAND

- **Erase** is the first modifying command discussed.
- The only purpose of this command is to delete any object you select.
- On the **Ribbon**, go to the **Home** tab. From the **Modify** panel, click the **Erase** button:

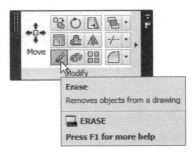

- The following prompt will appear:

```
Select objects:
```

- Once this prompt appears, the cursor will change to a pick box:

- Basically, you can do three things with the pick box:
  - Touch an object and click to select it.
  - Go to an empty place, click, and go to the right; this will get you a **Window**.
  - Go to an empty place, click, and go to the left; this will get you a **Crossing**.

Window

- A window is a rectangle specified by two opposite corners. The first corner is created when you click on the empty place. Release your mouse's button, move the cursor to a suitable place, and click to create the second corner.

First Point

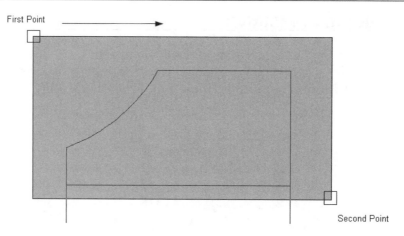

Second Point

- Whatever is *fully* inside the rectangle will be selected. If any part (even a tiny part) is outside the rectangle, it will not be selected. See the following illustration:

Crossing

- A crossing is just like a window, except that in addition to anything inside it being selected, anything touching it will be selected:

First Point

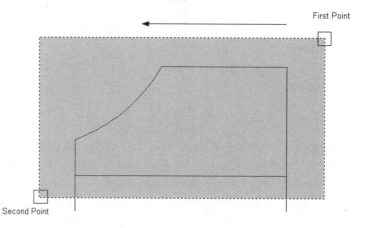

Second Point

- The result will be:

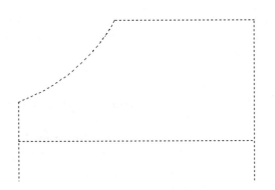

NOTE

- These three methods can be used with almost all the modifying commands, not just the **Erase** command.
- The **Select Objects** prompt is repetitive. You must always finish by pressing [Enter] or by right-clicking and using the menu.
- Other ways to erase objects are:
  - Without issuing any command, click on the desired object(s) and press [Delete].
  - Without issuing any command, click on the object(s) desired and right-click. The following shortcut menu will appear. Select **Erase**:

<u>R</u>epeat LINE
Recent Input ▸
Clipboard ▸
<u>I</u>solate ▸
Erase
<u>M</u>ove
Cop<u>y</u> Selection
Sc<u>a</u>le
R<u>o</u>tate
Dra<u>w</u> Order ▸
A<u>d</u>d Selected
Selec<u>t</u> Similar
Deselect <u>A</u>ll
Subobject Selection Filter ▸
<u>Q</u>uick Select...
Propertie<u>s</u>
Quick Properties

2.14 THE OOPS, UNDO, AND REDO COMMANDS

- This group of commands can help you correct your mistakes.
- They can be used in the current session only (i.e., once you close the file, they are useless).

Oops

- **Oops** is used to retain the last group of erased objects.
- It works only with the **Erase** command.
- This command is only available in the **Command Window**.
- You have to type the full command, **Oops**, in the **Command Window**.
- No prompt will be displayed, but you will see the last group of erased objects come back to the drawing.

Undo

- **Undo** is used to undo the last command.
- You can reach this command using one of the following methods:
  - From the **Quick Access** toolbar, click the **Undo** button:

  - Type **u** at the **Command Window** (do not type **undo**, because it has a different meaning).
  - Press [Ctrl] + Z.
- The last command will be undone.
- You can undo as many commands as you want in the current session.

Redo

- The **Redo** command allows you to undo the undo.
- You can apply this command using one of the following methods:
  - From the **Quick Access** toolbar, click the **Redo** button:

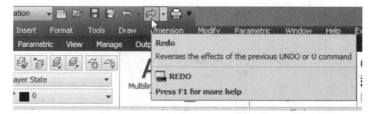

- Type **redo** in the **Command Window**.
- Press [Ctrl] + Y.

■ The last undone command will be redone.

■ You can redo as many commands as you want in the current session.

2.15 THE REDRAW AND REGEN COMMANDS

■ You will often need to refresh the screen for one reason or another.

■ Or you will need AutoCAD to regenerate the whole drawing to show the arcs and circles as smooth curves.

■ Neither command has a toolbar button, which is why we need to show the **Menu Browser** by using the **Quick Access** toolbar.

Redraw

■ From the **Menu Browser**, select **View/Redraw**, or type **r** in the **Command Window**.

■ The screen will be refreshed.

Regen

■ From the **Menu Browser**, select **View/Regen**, or type **re** at the command prompt.

■ See the following example:
  - This is how the drawing looks before the **Regen** command:

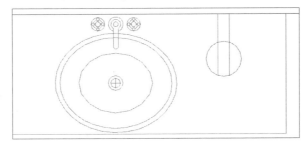

  - This is how it looks after the **Regen** command:

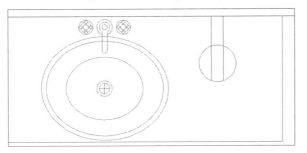

ERASE, OOPS, UNDO, AND REDO

Exercise 2-10
1. Start AutoCAD 2011.
2. Open the file *Exercise 2-10.dwg*.
3. Using the **Erase** command and either **Window** or **Crossing**, perform the following steps:
   a. Using **Window**, try to erase all the rectangles in the middle. Press [Enter], then use the **Oops** command to retain the objects.
   b. Using **Crossing**, try to erase the circles to the right of the shape. Press [Enter] and then **Undo**. Also try to **Redo** to see the effect.
   c. Using a pick box, try to erase the lines of the frame, press [Enter], and then use **Undo** to undo the erasing.
4. Close the file *without* saving.

CHAPTER REVIEW

1. Which of the following statements is true:
   a. **Snap** helps control the mouse, whereas **Grid** is complementary to **Snap**.
   b. **Ortho** and **Direct Distance Entry** help us draw exact orthogonal lines.
   c. You can use **Direct Distance Entry** with **Dynamic Input**, **Ortho**, and **Polar Tracking**.
   d. All of the above.
2. The **Arc** command in AutoCAD will draw a _____ arc.
3. Using **OTRACK**, you can:
   a. Specify a point using two existing points.
   b. Specify the radius of an arc.
   c. Specify the endpoint of an existing line.
   d. None of the above.
4. **OTRACK** does not need **OSNAP** to work:
   a. True
   b. False

5. In **Polar Tracking**, if the **Increment angle** does not fulfill all your needs, you need to:
   a. Use **Ortho**.
   b. Set additional angles.
   c. Use the command **Polar New Angles**.
   d. None of the above.
6. There are _____ ways to draw a circle in AutoCAD.
7. Use the _____ command to convert polylines to lines and arcs.

CHAPTER REVIEW ANSWERS

1. d
2. circular
3. a
4. b
5. b
6. 6 (six)
7. **Explode**

Chapter 3
SETTING UP YOUR DRAWING

In This Chapter
◊ Things to consider before setting up your drawing
◊ Drawing units
◊ Drawing limits
◊ Layer functions
◊ **Quick Properties, Properties,** and **Match Properties**

3.1 THINGS TO CONSIDER BEFORE SETTING UP YOUR DRAWING

- There are many considerations when setting up a drawing file. We cannot cover them all in this chapter, but we will address the most important things.

Drawing Units

- First, define the drawing distance and angle units, along with their precision.

Drawing Limits

- Try to figure out the workspace size (area) that will be sufficient to accommodate your drawing.

Layers

- Layers are the most effective way to organize a drawing. We will learn what they are, how to create them, and how to control them.

NOTE ▶ ■ In Appendix A we will discuss how to create templates in AutoCAD, which is more applicable for businesses than individuals.

3.2 STEP 1: DRAWING UNITS

■ This will be your first step.
■ This command will allow you to select the proper length and angle units.
■ From the **Application Menu**, select **Drawing Utilities/Units**.

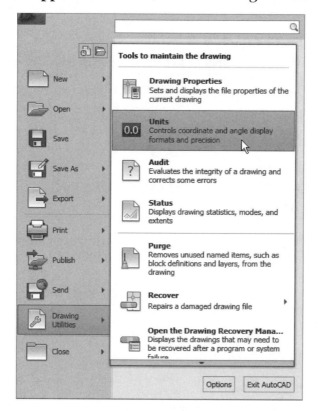

- The following dialog box will appear:

- Under **Length**, set the desired **Type**. You will have five choices:
  - **Architectural** (example: 1'-5 3/16")
  - **Decimal** (example: 20.4708)
  - **Engineering** (example: 1'-4.9877")
  - **Fractional** (example: 17 1/16)
  - **Scientific** (example: 1.6531E+01)
- Under **Angle**, set the desired **Type**. You will have five choices:
  - **Decimal Degrees** (example: 45.5)
  - **Deg/Min/Sec** (example: 45d30'30")
  - **Grads** (example: 50.6g)
  - **Radians** (example: 0.8r)
  - **Surveyor's Units** (example: N 45d30'30" E)
- For the desired **Length** and **Angle**, select the **Precision**. For example:
  - Architectural precision can be 0'-0 1/16", or 0'-0 1/32", etc.
  - Decimal precision can be 0.00, or 0.000, etc.
  - Deg/Min/Sec precision can be 0d00'00", or 0d00'00.0", etc.
- By default, AutoCAD deals with the positive angles as counterclockwise. If you want it the other way around, check the **Clockwise** box.
- Under **Insertion scale**, specify **Units to scale inserted content**, which is your drawing's scale against the scale of any object (e.g., a block) new to your drawing. This function will help AutoCAD make the suitable conversion.

- Click the **Direction** button to see the following dialog box:

- As we discussed in Chapter 1, AutoCAD always starts the zero angle measuring from the east. If you want to change it, select the desired angle to be considered as the new zero.

3.3 STEP 2: DRAWING LIMITS

- In Chapter 1, we said that AutoCAD offers an unlimited drawing sheet, which extends in all directions. However, we will not use it all; instead, we will specify an area that will set our limits.
- **Drawing Limits** is the area you select to work in. It should be specified using two points, the lower left-hand corner and the upper right-hand corner.
- Because we will draw in **Model Space** and print from **Paper Space**, we do not need to think about the drawing scale at this point.
- To know exactly what limits are needed, make sure you have the following information:
  - The longest dimension in your sketch in both X and Y.
  - The AutoCAD unit you have selected (e.g., m, cm, mm, inch, or foot).

Example

- Assume we have the following case:
  - We want to draw an architectural plan, which extends in X for 50 m, and in Y for 30 m.
  - Also, assume that an AutoCAD unit = 1 m.
- Because an AutoCAD unit = 1 m, 50 m is equal to 50 AutoCAD units. The same reasoning applies for the 30 m.
- Note that 0,0 is always the favored lower left-hand corner, so no need to change it. The upper right-hand corner will be 50,30.

- Using the **Quick Access Toolbar**, show the **Menu Bar** and select **Format/Drawing Limits**. The following prompt will appear in the **Command Window**:

```
Specify lower left corner or [ON/OFF] <0,0>: (Press [Enter]
to accept the default value.)
Specify upper right corner <12,9>: (Type in the coordinate
of the upper right-hand corner.)
```

ON/OFF

- To forbid yourself from using any area outside this limit, turn the limits on.

DRAWING UNITS AND LIMITS

Exercise 3-1

1. Start AutoCAD 2011.
2. Open the file *Exercise 3-1.dwg*.
3. Note the current units, which are displayed in the lower left-hand corner of the screen.
4. From the **Application Menu**, select **Drawing Utilities/Units**. Change the units as follows:
   a. Length type = Architectural
   b. Length precision = 0'-0 1/32"
   c. Angle type = Deg/Min/Sec
   d. Angle precision = 0d00'00"
5. Now check the coordinates again, noting how the numbers changed to the new units.
6. Using the **Limits** command, do the following:
   a. Accept the default point for the lower left-hand corner.
   b. For the upper right-hand corner, type **30',20'**.
7. Using the **Snap** or **Grid** button at the **Status Bar**, right-click and select **Settings**. Then uncheck the **Display grid beyond Limits** box and click **OK**.
8. Double-click the mouse wheel to get **Zoom Extents**. Now you can see the new limits.
9. Turn on **Limits** and try to draw any line outside the limits. What is AutoCAD's response?
10. Save and close the file.

3.4 STEP 3: LAYERS

What Are Layers?

- Let's assume that we have a huge number of transparent papers, along with 256 color pens.
- Being careful not to draw anywhere except the top of the paper, we use the red pen to draw the border of the drawing.
- Then we move the second paper to the top and draw an architectural wall plan using the yellow pen.
- Next, we move the third paper to the top and draw the doors using the green pen. Repeating the procedure, we draw windows, furniture, electrical outlets, hatching, text, dimensioning, etc.
- If you view all the papers at the same time, what will you see? A full architectural plan!
- In AutoCAD, we call each paper a layer.
- Each layer should have a name, color, linetype, lineweight, and lots of other information.
- One layer will be in all of AutoCAD's drawings. This layer is 0 (zero). You cannot delete or rename it.
- To draw on a layer, first make it **current**. Only one layer will be current at a time.
- The objects drawn on a layer will automatically inherit the properties (color, linetype, and lineweight, etc.) of the current layer. Hence, a line in a red layer, with dashdot linetype and 0.3 lineweight, will have the exact same properties.
- By default, the setting of the object's color is BYLAYER.
- By default, the setting of the object's linetype is BYLAYER.
- By default, the setting of the object's lineweight is BYLAYER.
- NOTE ▶ It is highly recommended to keep these settings intact, as changing them may lead to creating objects with non-standard properties.
- On the **Ribbon**, go to the **Home** tab. Using the **Layers** panel, click the **Layer Properties** button.

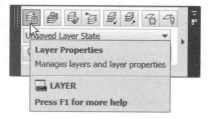

- The following dialog box will appear:

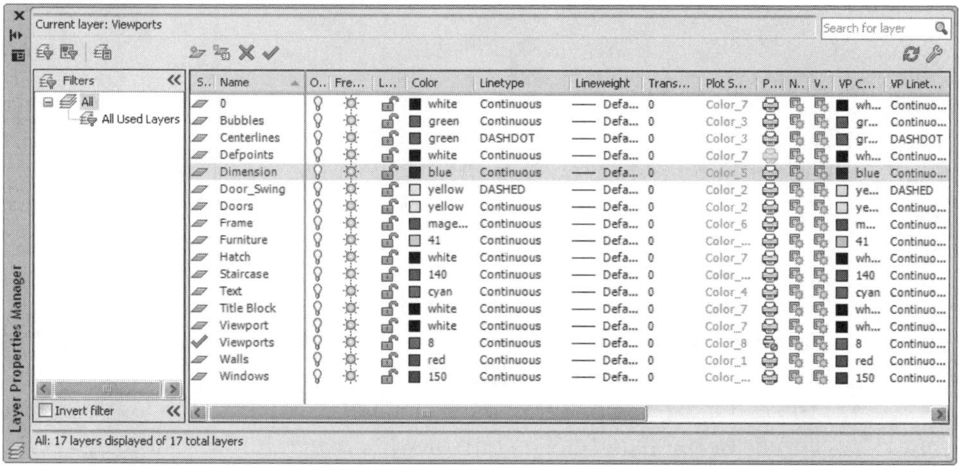

- The **Layer Properties Manager** is not a normal dialog box. It is a palette, which can be docked, resized, and hidden.
  - Drag the title of the palette to the right, left, top, or bottom of the screen, and you will see the **Layer Properties Manager** palette change its size and dock at the place you select.
  - You can hide the entire palette and show only the title bar by clicking the **Auto-hide** button, as shown in the following image. Whenever you want to see the palette again, simply go back to the title and the palette will appear.

  - You can show the **Properties** menu to control the palette. Click the **Properties** button as shown:

- The following menu will appear:

- The most important options using this menu are **Anchor Left** and **Anchor Right**, which automatically dock the palette at the right or the left and switch on **Auto-hide**.
- You can make the palette larger or smaller. Move to the lower right-hand corner of the palette. The cursor will change to the following:

- Click and drag to the right to make the palette larger. Click and drag to the left to make it smaller.

Creating a New Layer

- To create a new layer in the drawing, you must prepare all the necessary information of the new layer.
- Click the **New Layer** button:

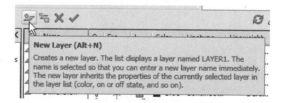

- AutoCAD will add a new layer with the temporary name *Layer1*. The **Name** field will be highlighted. Type the desired name of the layer (you can use up to 255 characters with spaces allowed). Use *only* the following characters:
  - Letters (a, b, c, . . . z)—lowercase or capital does not matter
  - Numbers (0, 1, 2, . . . 9)
  - (-) hyphen, (_) underscore, and ($) dollar sign

- Good layer naming is a common practice to use. This means using names that give an idea about the contents of the layer. For example, a layer that contains the walls of a building would be named "walls."

Setting a Color for a Layer

- After creating a layer, you will set its color.
- AutoCAD uses 256 colors for the layers (although technically, they are only 255 if we exclude the color of the **Graphical Area**).
- The first seven colors can be called by their names or numbers:
  - Red (1)
  - Yellow (2)
  - Green (3)
  - Cyan (4)
  - Blue (5)
  - Magenta (6)
  - Black/White (7)
- The rest of the colors can be called only by their numbers.
- You can use the same color for more than one layer.
- Select the desired layer under the **Color** field, and click either the name of the color or the icon. The following dialog box will appear:

- Move to the desired color (or type in the name/number) of the color, and then click **OK**.

NOTE ➤
- You can also set the layer's color through the pop-up list in the **Layers** panel by selecting the color icon in the list:

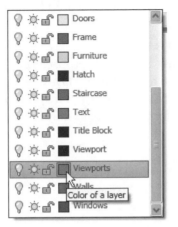

Setting a Linetype for a Layer

- AutoCAD comes with several generic predefined linetypes saved in the files *acad.lin* and *acadiso.lin*.
- You can buy other linetypes from third parties located on the Internet. Just go to any search engine and type "autocad linetype." You will find lots of linetype files, some free of charge and some available for a fee (usually a few dollars).
- Not all of the linetypes are loaded into the drawing files; hence, you may need to load the desired linetype before you use it.
- First, select the desired layer. Under the **Linetype** field, click the name of the linetype. The following dialog box will appear:

- If your desired linetype is there, select it; otherwise, you need to load another linetype. Click the **Load** button, and the following dialog box will appear:

- Select the desired linetype to be loaded and click **OK**. Now that the linetype is loaded, it will appear in the **Select Linetype** dialog box. Select it and click **OK**.

Setting a Lineweight for a Layer

- Select the desired layer under the **Lineweight** field. Click either the number or the shape of the lineweight, and the following dialog box will appear:

- Select the desired lineweight and click **OK.**

- If you want to view the lineweight of any layer on the screen, click the **Show/ Hide Lineweight** button on the **Status Bar**:

NOTE ▶ ■ We prefer to see the lineweight using **Plot Style** (discussed later), which will affect the hard copy.

Making a Layer the Current Layer

- There are three ways to make a certain layer the current layer:
  - In the **Layer Properties Manager** palette, double-click on the name or the status of the desired layer.
  - In the **Layer Properties Manager** palette, select the desired layer and click the **Set Current** button.

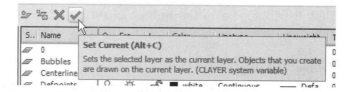

  - On the **Ribbon**, go to the **Home** tab. On the **Layers** panel, there is a pop-up list for the layers. Select the desired layer name, and it will become the current layer:

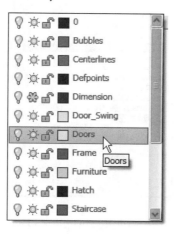

LAYER NAMES, COLORS, LINETYPES, AND LINEWEIGHTS

Exercise 3-2

1. Start AutoCAD 2011.
2. Open the file *Exercise 3-2.dwg*.
3. Create the following layers:

Layer Name	Color	Linetype	Lineweight
Shaft	Magenta	Continuous	0.3
Body	Cyan	Continuous	0.3
Base	Green	Continuous	0.3
Centerlines	9	Dashdot2	0.5

4. Make **Centerlines** the current layer. (Make sure that **Dynamic Input** is off.)
5. Draw a line from 6,7.5 to 6,4.5, and draw another line from 8,6 to 4,6.
6. Save and close the file.

3.5 LAYER FUNCTIONS

Adding More Layers

- The easiest way to add more layers is to click on the name of any layer while you are in the **Layer Properties Manager**, and then press [Enter].
- Or you can use the **New Layer** button.
- NOTE ▶ By default, AutoCAD will always sort the layers according to their names.

Selecting Layers

- All of the methods discussed will be performed using the **Layer Properties Manager** dialog box.
- There are many ways to select layers:
  - To select a single layer, simply click on it.
  - To select multiple nonconsecutive layers, select the first layer, then hold [Ctrl] and click on the other layers.

- To select multiple consecutive layers, select the first layer, then hold [Shift] and click on the last layer you wish to select.
- To select multiple layers all at once, click on an empty area and hold the mouse. Move to the right or to the left, and a rectangle will appear. Cover the layer you want to select and release the mouse.
- To select all layers, press [Ctrl] + A.
- To unselect a selected layer, hold [Ctrl] and click the layer.

NOTE ▶ ■ One of the most important advantages of selecting multiple layers is setting the color, linetype, or lineweight for a group of layers all in one step.

Deleting a Layer

- You cannot delete a layer that contains objects, so the first step is to empty the layer of any objects in it.
- Using the **Layer Properties Manager** palette, select the desired layer (or layers) to be deleted, and do one of the following:
  - Press [Delete].
  - Click on the **Delete Layer** button.

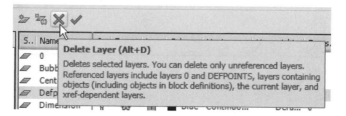

Renaming a Layer

- To rename a layer using the **Layer Properties Manager** palette, click the name of the desired layer once.
- The name will be available for editing.
- Input the new name and press [Enter].

Right-Clicking Functions

- Right-clicking here is done in the **Layer Properties Manager** palette.
- If you select any layer and right-click, the following shortcut menu will appear:

```
✓ Show Filter Tree
  Show Filters in Layer List

  Set current
  New Layer
  Rename Layer                          F2
  Delete Layer
  Change Description
  Remove From Group Filter

  New Layer VP Frozen in All Viewports
  VP Freeze Layer in All Viewports
  VP Thaw Layer in All Viewports

  Isolate selected layers

  Select All
  Clear All
  Select All but Current
  Invert Selection

  Invert Layer Filter
  Layer Filters                          ▶

  Save Layer States...
  Restore Layer State...
```

- Through this shortcut menu, you can perform many of the functions we have discussed, such as:
  - Set the current layer
  - Create a new layer
  - Delete a layer
  - Select all layers
  - Clear the selected layer(s)
  - Select all but the current layer
  - Invert the selected layer(s) (make the selected unselected, and vice versa)
- The first two choices in this shortcut menu are:
  - **Show Filter Tree** (which by default is turned on)
  - **Show Filters in Layer List** (which by default is turned off)

- By turning off **Show Filter Tree**, the dialog box will have more space, as shown:

- Or you can you use the two arrows at the left panel, as in the following:

Changing an Object's Layer

- Each object should exist in a layer.
- The fastest method to change the object's layer is the following:
  - Without issuing any command, select the object by clicking it.
  - In the **Layers** toolbar, the object's layer will be displayed. Click the layer's pop-up list and select the new layer name.
  - Press [Esc] one time.
- Other methods to change an object's layer will be discussed later.

Making an Object's Layer Current

- This function is very handy if there are too many layers in your drawing to manage easily.
- It is also useful if you see an object in your drawing but do not know in which layer the object resides.
- In these cases, you want to make this object's layer the current layer. To do so, follow these steps:
  - On the **Ribbon**, go to the **Home** tab. Using the **Layers** panel, click the **Make Object's Layer Current** button:

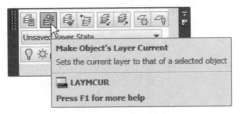

  - The following prompt will be shown:

```
Select object whose layer will become current: (Click on the
desired object.)
Walls is now the current layer.
```

  - Now the current layer is the object's layer.

The Four Switches of a Layer

- Each layer has four switches, which will determine its state.
- You can see these switches in both the **Layer Properties Manager** palette and the layer pop-up list from the **Layer** panel.
- These switches are:
  - On/Off
  - Thaw/Freeze
  - Unlock/Lock
  - Plot/No Plot

- See the following example:

- In this example, you can see that:
  - The switches for the **Bubbles** layer are On, Thaw, Unlocked, and Plot.
  - The switches for the **Dimension** layer are Off, Frozen, Locked, and No Plot.
- These four switches are independent from each other.
- By default, the layers are On, Thaw, Unlocked, and Plot.
- When you turn a layer off, the objects in it will not be shown on the screen, and if you plot the drawing, they will not be plotted. But the objects in this layer will be included in the total count of the drawing; hence, the drawing size will not change.
- When you freeze a layer, the objects in it will not be shown on the screen, and if you plot the drawing, they will not be plotted. Also, the objects in this layer will *not* be included in the total count of the drawing; hence, the drawing size will be less.
- When you lock a layer, none of the objects in it are modifiable.
- When you make a layer No Plot, you can see the objects on the screen, but when you issue **Plot** commands, these objects will not be plotted.
- Three of these switches can be changed using either the **Layer Properties Manager** palette or the layer pop-up list from the **Layer** panel; the fourth (Plot/No Plot) can be changed only from the **Layer Properties Manager** palette.

- To change the switch, simply click it.
NOTE
- You cannot freeze the current layer, but you can turn it off. See the following dialog box:

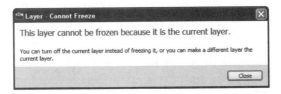

- You should be careful when you turn the current layer off because every time you draw a new object, it will disappear right away. Therefore, when you try to turn a layer off, AutoCAD will issue the following warning:

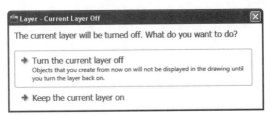

Layer Previous

- While you are working in AutoCAD, you will change the state of layers many times. Thus, you need a tool to help you quickly return to the previous state.
- **Layer Previous** provides this ability.
- On the **Ribbon**, go to the **Home** tab. Using the **Layers** panel, click the **Previous** button:

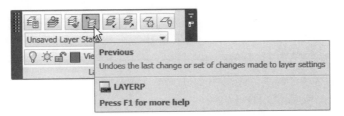

- AutoCAD will report the following:

```
Restored previous layer status
```

- **NOTE** ■ While you are using the **Layer Properties Manager** palette, or the layer pop-up list from the **Layer** toolbar, if you make several changes on several switches for several layers, AutoCAD will consider them all as one action. Thus, they will be restored in one **Previous** command.

Layer Match

- To convert objects from one layer to another, you can use the **Layer Match** tool. It will help you unify several objects belonging to different layers.
- On the **Ribbon**, go to the **Home** tab. Using the **Layers** panel, click the **Match** button:

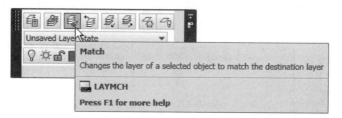

- The following prompt will appear:

```
Select objects to be changed: (Select the desired objects.
Once you are done, press [Enter].)

Select object on destination layer or [Name]:
```

- Once the command is done, a message resembling the following will appear:

```
8 objects changed to layer "Dimensions"
```

LAYER FUNCTIONS

Exercise 3-3
1. Start AutoCAD 2011.
2. Open the file *Exercise 3-3.dwg*.
3. Change the object's layer as follows:
   a. Change the layer of the two circles from 0 to Shaft.
   b. Change the layer of the two arcs from 0 to Body.
   c. Change the layer of the lines from 0 to Base.

4. Using the **Status Bar**, switch on **Show/Hide Lineweight** to see the objects displaying the assigned lineweight.
5. Lock the layer Shaft. Then try to erase the objects in it. What is AutoCAD's response?
6. Unlock the layer Shaft.
7. Using the **Make Layer Objects Current** button, select one of the centerlines. Which layer becomes current?
8. Click the **Layer Previous** button twice. What happens?
9. Try to freeze the current layer. What is AutoCAD's response?
10. Try to rename layer 0? What is AutoCAD's response?
11. Rename the layer Centerlines as Center_lines.
12. Try to delete the layer Shaft. What is AutoCAD's response, and why?
13. Save and close the file.

3.6 QUICK PROPERTIES, PROPERTIES, AND MATCH PROPERTIES

- Earlier in this chapter, we learned that each object inherits the properties of the layer in which it resides. By default, the setting of the current color, linetype, and lineweight is BYLAYER, which means that the object follows the layer in which it resides.
- This makes it easier to control the drawing, because it is easier to control a handful of layers than to control hundreds of thousands of objects. Thus, we recommend not changing these settings in normal use.
- However, sometimes we may need to change some properties. To do so, we can use three commands:
  - **Quick Properties**
  - **Properties**
  - **Match Properties**

Quick Properties

- **Quick Properties** is a function that will pop up automatically when you select any object.
- By default, this command is always on, but if it is off, you can turn it on from the **Status Bar**:

- To start the **Quick Properties** command, simply click any object and a small panel resembling the following will appear:

Line		
Color	■ ByLayer	
Layer	Walls	
Linetype	—————— ByLayer	

- In this panel, you can change the color, layer, and linetype.
- If you move the mouse over either of the two sides, the panel will expand as shown:

Line		
Color	■ ByLayer	
Layer	Walls	
Linetype	—————— ByLayer	
Length	6000	

Properties

- The easiest way to initiate the **Properties** command is to right-click the desired object(s). When the shortcut menu appears, select **Properties**. Proceed as follows:
  - The selection set you made consists of different object types (lines, arcs, circles, etc.). In the case of the illustration below, you can change only the general properties of these objects:

All (35)	
General	
Color	ByLayer
Layer	*VARIES*
Linetype	—————— ByLayer
Linetype scale	1
Plot style	ByColor
Lineweight	—————— ByLayer
Transparency	ByLayer
Hyperlink	

- However, if you select the upper pop-up list, you will see the following:

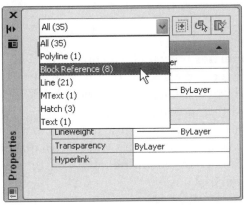

- You can filter the objects by selecting the desired type of object. You can then change all or any of the properties.
- The selection set you made consists of a single object type. In the case of the illustration below, you can change the general properties and the object-specific properties:

NOTE ➤ ■ **Properties** is a palette, hence all the things we learned about the **Layer** palette are applicable.

Match Properties

■ **Match Properties** is useful if you open a drawing and find that the creator of the drawing did not stick with the concept of BYLAYER. For example, you may find that a green line resides in a red layer and that a dashdot circle is in a layer with continuous linetype.

■ The best way to correct such misconduct is to find one object in each layer that holds the correct properties and to then match the other objects to it.

■ On the **Ribbon**, go to the **Home** tab. Using the **Clipboard** panel, click the **Match Properties** button:

```
Paste
▼
Clipboard
```

Match Properties
Applies the properties of a selected object to other objects

⊟ MATCHPROP

Press F1 for more help

■ AutoCAD will show the following prompt:

`Select source object:`

■ Click on the object that holds the right properties.
■ The cursor will change to a paintbrush:

■ AutoCAD will show another prompt:

`Select destination object(s):`

■ Click on the objects you want to correct. Once you are done, press [Enter].

QUICK PROPERTIES, PROPERTIES, AND MATCH PROPERTIES

Exercise 3-4
1. Start AutoCAD 2011.
2. Open the file *Exercise 3-4.dwg*.
3. We "mistakenly" draw all objects in layer 0. Using all the commands you have learned, put each object in its right layer.
4. Save and close the file.

CREATING OUR PROJECT (METRIC)

Workshop 1-M
1. Start AutoCAD 2011.
2. Close any opened file.
3. Create a new file based on the *acad.dwt* template.
4. Double-click on the mouse wheel to **Zoom Extents**.
5. From the **Application Menu**, select **Drawing/Units** and make the following changes:
   a. Length Type = Decimal, Precision = 0
   b. Angle Type = Decimal Degrees, Precision = 0
   c. Unit to scale inserted content = Millimeters
6. Assume that an AutoCAD unit = 1 mm and that you have a 30-m × 20-m plan you want to draw. Your limits will be:
   a. Lower left-hand corner = 0,0
   b. Upper right-hand corner = 30000,200000
7. Type **Limits** in the **Command Window**, and set the limits accordingly.
8. Double-click on the mouse wheel to **Zoom Extents** to the new limits.
9. Create the following layers:

Layer Name	Color	Linetype	Special Remarks
Frame	Magenta	Continuous	
Walls	Red	Continuous	
Doors	Yellow	Continuous	
Door_Swing	Yellow	Dashed	

Layer Name	Color	Linetype	Special Remarks
Windows	150	Continuous	
Centerlines	Green	Dashdot	
Bubbles	Green	Continuous	
Furniture	41	Continuous	
Staircase	140	Continuous	
Text	Cyan	Continuous	
Hatch	White	Continuous	
Dimension	Blue	Continuous	
Viewports	8	Continuous	No Plot

10. Save the file in the **Metric** folder (in the copied folder from the DVD) as *Workshop_01.dwg*.

CREATING OUR PROJECT (IMPERIAL)

Workshop 1-I
1. Start AutoCAD 2011.
2. Close any opened file.
3. Create a new file based on the *acad.dwt* template.
4. Double-click on the mouse wheel to **Zoom Extents**.
5. From the **Application Menu**, select **Drawing/Units** and make the following changes:
   a. Length Type = Architectural, Precision = 0'-0"
   b. Angle Type = Decimal Degrees, Precision = 0
   c. Unit to scale inserted content = Inches
6. Assume that an AutoCAD unit = 1 inch and that you have a 70' × 60' plan you want draw. Your limits will be:
   a. Lower left-hand corner = 0,0
   b. Upper right-hand corner = 70',60'
7. Type **Limits** in the **Command Window**, and set the limits accordingly.
8. Double-click on the mouse wheel to **Zoom Extents** to the new limits.
9. Create the following layers:

Layer Name	Color	Linetype	Special Remarks
Frame	Magenta	Continuous	
Walls	Red	Continuous	
Doors	Yellow	Continuous	
Door_Swing	Yellow	Dashed	
Windows	150	Continuous	
Centerlines	Green	Dashdot	
Bubbles	Green	Continuous	
Furniture	41	Continuous	
Staircase	140	Continuous	
Text	Cyan	Continuous	
Hatch	White	Continuous	
Dimension	Blue	Continuous	
Viewports	8	Continuous	No Plot

10. Save the file in the **Imperial** folder (in the copied folder from the DVD) as *Workshop_01.dwg*.

CHAPTER REVIEW

1. Which of the following statements about layer names is correct?
   a. They can be up to 255 characters long.
   b. They can contain spaces.
   c. They can contain letters, numbers, hyphens, underscores, and dollar signs.
   d. All of the above.
2. There are _____ different length units in AutoCAD.
3. What do you need to know to set limits in a file?
   a. The paper size you will print on.
   b. The longest dimension of your sketch in both X and Y.
   c. The measure of an AutoCAD unit.
   d. B and C.

4. Only the first seven colors can be called by their names and numbers:
   a. True
   b. False

5. Which of the following statements about linetypes in AutoCAD is true?
   a. They are stored in *acad.lin* and *acadiso.lin*.
   b. They are loaded in all AutoCAD drawings.
   c. To use a linetype, you must first load it.
   d. A and C.

6. If you assign a lineweight to a layer and draw lines on this layer, you must switch on the _____ button from the **Status Bar** to see this lineweight on the screen.

7. I can change only the _____ properties of non-similar objects using the **Properties** command.

CHAPTER REVIEW ANSWERS

1. d
2. 5 (five)
3. d
4. a
5. d
6. **Show/Hide Lineweight**
7. General

A FEW GOOD CONSTRUCTION COMMANDS

Chapter **4**

In This Chapter

◇ Creating a parallel duplicate using the **Offset** command
◇ Creating neat intersections using the **Fillet** and **Chamfer** commands
◇ Trimming and extending objects
◇ Lengthening and joining objects

4.1 INTRODUCTION

- So far, we have learned only four drawing commands: **Line, Arc, Circle**, and **Polyline**.
- These alone can help you accomplish only 20% of your drawing.
- If you think that each and every line (or arc or circle) should be drawn by you, you are wrong!
- In this chapter, we will discuss seven commands, which, as if by magic, will help us construct the most difficult drawings in no time.
- These commands are:
  - The **Offset** command, which creates parallel copies of your original objects.
  - The **Fillet** command, which allows you to close unclosed shapes either by extending the two ends to an intersecting point or by using an arc.
  - The **Chamfer** command, which is the same as the **Fillet** command, except that it will create a slanting edge.
  - The **Trim** command, which allows some objects to act as cutting edges for other objects to be trimmed.
  - The **Extend** command, which allows you to extend objects to a boundary.
  - The **Lengthen** command, which allows you to extend or trim length from an existing line.
  - The **Join** command, which allows you to join similar objects (e.g., lines to lines, and polylines to polylines).

4.2   THE OFFSET COMMAND

- **Offset** will create a new object parallel to a selected object.
- The new object (by default) will have the same properties as the original object and will reside in the same layer.
- There are two methods for using **Offset**:
  - Offset distance
  - Through point
- On the **Ribbon**, go to the **Home** tab. Using the **Modify** panel, click the **Offset** button:

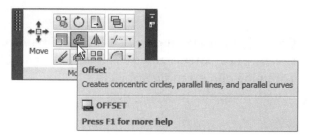

- The following prompt will appear:

```
Current settings: Erase source=No  Layer=Source
OFFSETGAPTYPE=0
Specify offset distance or [Through/Erase/Layer] <Through>:
```

Offset Distance

- To use this method, you must know the distance between the original object and the parallel duplicate (i.e., the offset distance).
- Select the object that will be offset.
- Then specify the side of the offset by clicking to the right or left, up or down, etc.
- The prompts will be as follows:

```
Specify offset distance or [Through/Erase/Layer] <Through>:
(Type in the desired distance.)
Select object to offset or [Exit/Undo] <Exit>: (Select a
single object.)
Specify point on side to offset or [Exit/Multiple/Undo]
<Exit>: (Click on the desired side.)
```

- The command will repeat the last two prompts for further offsetting.
- To end the command, press [Enter], or right-click.

Through Point

- With this method, instead of needing to know the distance between the objects, you must know a point that the new parallel object will pass through.
- The prompt will be as follows:

```
Specify offset distance or [Through/Erase/Layer] <Through>:
(Type t and press [Enter].)
Select object to offset or [Exit/Undo] <Exit>: (Select a
single object.)
Specify through point or [Exit/Multiple/Undo] <Exit>:
(Specify the point that the new image will pass through.)
```

- The command will repeat the last two prompts for further offsetting.
- To end the command, press [Enter], or right-click.
- Here is an example:

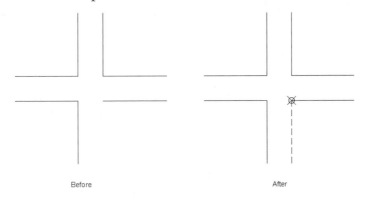

Before   After

Multiple

- With either of the preceding methods, you can use the **Multiple** option.
- Instead of repeatedly selecting the object and specifying the side, **Multiple** will allow you to specify only the side of the offset.
- The prompt will be as follows:

```
Specify offset distance or [Through/Erase/Layer] <Through>:
(Select a method.)
Select object to offset or [Exit/Undo] <Exit>: (Select a
single object.)
Specify through point or [Exit/Multiple/Undo] <Exit>:
(Type m and press [Enter].)
Specify point on side to offset or [Exit/Undo]
<next object>: (Simply click on the desired side, repeating
as needed. Once you are done, press [Enter].)
```

Undo

- At any time while you are offsetting, you can use the **Undo** option to undo the last offsetting action.
- AutoCAD will recall the last offset distance, so there is no need to reenter it, unless you want to use another value.
- **Offset** will produce a bigger or smaller arc, circle, or polyline.
- You can right-click to see shortcut menus that show the different options of the **Command Window**.
- In the **Offset** command, you can use only one offset distance. If you want another offset distance, end the current command and issue a new **Offset** command. (Hopefully, in the next versions of AutoCAD, the **Offset** command will allow more than one offset distance per command.)

OFFSETTING OBJECTS

Exercise 4-1
1. Start AutoCAD 2011.
2. Open the file *Exercise 4-1.dwg*.
3. Offset the walls (magenta) to the inside using the distance = 1'.
4. Offset the stair using the distance = 1'-6" and using the **Multiple** option to create eight lines representing eight steps.
5. Explode the inner polyline.
6. Offset the right vertical line to the left using the through point option and the left endpoint of the upper-right horizontal line.
7. Offset the new line to the right using distance = 6".
8. The new shape of the plan should look like the following:

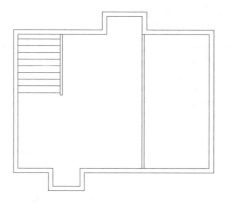

9. Save and close the file.

4.3 THE FILLET COMMAND

- ▪ If you have lines that appear as follows:

- ▪ And you want them to look like this:

- ▪ Or you want them to look like this:

- ▪ Then you need to use the **Fillet** command.
- ▪ To issue the **Fillet** command, select the first object and then the second object. It is a very simple AutoCAD command.
- ▪ The **Fillet** command works with two different settings:
  - • Radius = 0, which will create a neat intersection.
  - • Radius > 0, which will create an arced corner.
- ▪ When closing the shape with an arc, the **Fillet** command offers two methods of handling the original shapes:
  - • **Trim:** The arc will be produced, and the original objects will be trimmed accordingly.
  - • **No trim:** The arc will be produced, but the original objects will stay intact.

- Here is an example:

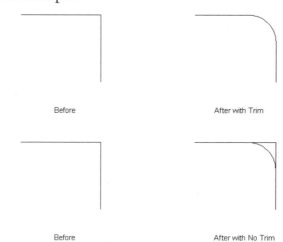

Before   After with Trim

Before   After with No Trim

- On the **Ribbon**, go to the **Home** tab. Using the **Modify** panel, click the **Fillet** button:

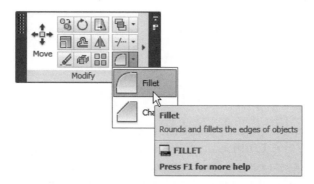

- The following prompt will appear:

```
Current settings: Mode = TRIM, Radius = 0.0000
Select first object or [Undo/Polyline/Radius/Trim/Multiple]:
```

- The first line reports the current value of the mode and the radius.
- Choose between the different options: **Radius, Trim, Multiple**, and **Undo**.

Radius

- To set a new value for the radius, the following prompt will appear:

`Specify fillet radius <0.0000>:` *(Type in the new radius.)*

Trim

- To change the mode from **Trim** to **No trim**, and vice versa, the following prompt will appear:

`Enter Trim mode option [Trim/No trim] <Trim>:` *(Type t or n.)*

Multiple

- By default, you can perform a single fillet per command by selecting the first object and the second object.
- If you want to perform multiple fillets in a single command, you have to select the **Multiple** mode first.

Undo

- At any time while you are filleting, you can use the **Undo** option to undo the last filleting action.
- When you fillet with a radius, the radius will be created in the current layer. So make sure you are in the right layer.
- To end the command when you use the **Multiple** option, press [Enter] or right-click.
- Even if R > 0, you can still fillet with R = 0. To do so, simply hold [Shift] and click on the desired objects. Regardless of the current value of R, you will fillet with R = 0.
- You can use the **Fillet** command to fillet two parallel lines with an arc. AutoCAD will calculate the distance between the two lines and take the radius to be one-half of this length.

FILLETING OBJECTS

Exercise 4-2

1. Start AutoCAD 2011.
2. Open the file *Exercise 4-2.dwg*.

3. Using the **Fillet** command, make the shape look like the following:

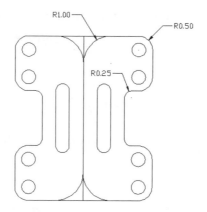

4. Save and close the file.

4.4 THE CHAMFER COMMAND

- The **Chamfer** command is identical in many ways to the **Fillet** command. **Chamfer**, however, creates a slanting edge rather than an arc.
- To create the slanted edge, we will use one of two methods:
  - Two distances
  - Length and angle

Two Distances

- There are three different approaches to this method:
  - (Dist1 = Dist2) = 0.0, as in the following example:

- (Dist1 = Dist2) > 0.0, as in the following example:

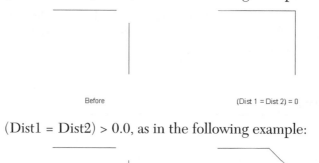

- (Dist1 ≠ Dist2) > 0.0, as in the following example (no matter which is selected first, Dist1 will be used):

Before   (Dist 1 ≠ Dist 2) > 0

Length and Angle

- To use this method, specify a length (which will be removed from the first object) and an angle, as in the following example:

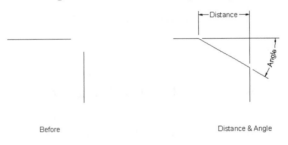

Before   Distance & Angle

- On the **Ribbon**, go to the **Home** tab. Using the **Modify** panel, click the **Chamfer** button:

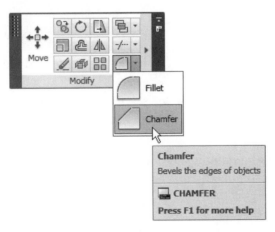

- The following prompt will appear:

```
(TRIM mode) Current chamfer Dist1 = 0.0000, Dist2 = 0.0000
Select first line or [Undo/Polyline/Distance/Angle /Trim/
Method/Multiple]:
```

- The first line reports the current mode and the distances (or length and angle).
- Choose between the different options: **Distances, Angle, Trim, Method**, and **Multiple**.

Distances

- To set a new value for the distances, the following prompt will appear:

```
Specify first chamfer distance <0.0000>: (Input the first
distance.)
Specify second chamfer distance <0.0000>: (Input the second
distance.)
```

Angle

- To set the new values for both length and angle, the following prompt will appear:

```
Specify chamfer length on the first line <0.0000>: (Input the
length on first line.)
Specify chamfer angle from the first line <0>: (Input the
angle.)
```

Trim

- To change the mode from **Trim** to **No trim**, and vice versa, the following prompt will appear:

```
Enter Trim mode option [Trim/No trim] <Trim>: (Type t or n.)
```

Method

- To specify the default method to be used in the **Chamfer** command, the following prompt will appear:

```
Enter trim method [Distance/Angle] <Distance>: (Type d or a.)
```

Multiple

- By default, you can perform a single chamfer per command by selecting the first object and the second object. If you want to perform multiple chamfers in a single command, you have to select the **Multiple** mode first.

- When you chamfer, the slanted line will be created in the current layer. So make sure you are in the right layer.
- To end the command when using the **Multiple** option, press [Enter] or right-click.
- The mode of **Trim** or **No Trim** in the **Fillet** command will affect the **Chamfer** command, and vice versa. Thus, if you change the mode in one of these two commands, the other command will reflect this change.

CHAMFERING OBJECTS

Exercise 4-3
1. Start AutoCAD 2011.
2. Open the file *Exercise 4-3.dwg*.
3. Using the **Chamfer** command, do the following:
   a. For the inside lines, set distances = 1.0 and 0.5.
   b. For the outside lines, set the distance = 2 and the angle = 20.
4. The illustration should appear as follows:

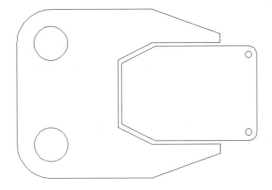

5. Save and close the file.

4.5 THE TRIM COMMAND

- Trimming is used when we want to remove part of an object by cutting the edge(s).
- The **Trim** command is a two-step command:
  - The first step is to select the cutting edge(s). You can select one object or as many as you wish.
  - The second step is to select the objects to be trimmed.

- The following example will illustrate the process of trimming:

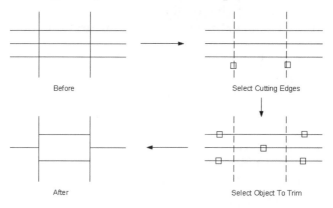

- On the **Ribbon**, go to the **Home** tab. Using the **Modify** panel, click the **Trim** button:

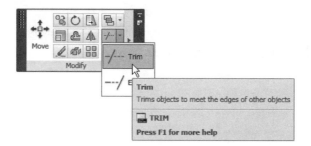

- The following prompt will appear:

```
Current settings: Projection=UCS, Edge=Extend
Select cutting edges ...
Select objects or <select all>:
```

- The first line displays the current settings.
- The second line tells you to select the cutting edges.
- Use any of the methods we discussed in the **Erase** command. Once you are done, press [Enter] or right-click.
- You can also use the fastest way—the **Select All** option—which will select all the objects to act as cutting edges.
- The following prompt will appear:

```
Select object to trim or shift-select to extend or
[Fence/Crossing/Project/Edge/eRase/Undo]:
```

- Now click on the parts you want to trim, one by one.
- If you make a mistake, either right-click to access the shortcut menu and select **Undo**, or type **u** in the **Command Window.**

Fence

- You can use the **Fence** option to speed up the process of selecting the objects to be trimmed. This can be done by specifying two points or more. A dotted line will be created, and objects that touch it will be selected.

Crossing

- The same function is offered by the **Crossing** option. When you specify two opposite corners, a crossing window will appear, and any object touched by the crossing will be trimmed.

Erase

- Sometimes, as a result of trimming, unwanted objects will be created. Instead of finishing the command and issuing an **Erase** command, AutoCAD offers this command so you can erase objects while you are still in the **Trim** command.
- Type **r** in the **Command Window**. AutoCAD will ask you to select the objects you want to erase. Once you are done, press [Enter], and you will be prompted again to select another option.

TRIMMING OBJECTS

Exercise 4-4

1. Start AutoCAD 2011.
2. Open the file *Exercise 4-4.dwg*.
3. Using the **Trim** command, try to create the following shape.

   If you get a residual object, you can use the **Erase** option in the **Trim** command to get rid of it.

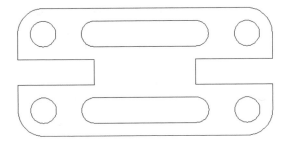

4. Save and close the file.

4.6 THE EXTEND COMMAND

- The **Extend** command is the opposite of the **Trim** command.
- It allows you to extend selected objects to the boundary edge(s).
- The **Extend** command is a two-step command:
    - The first step is to select the boundary edge(s). You can select one object or as many as you wish.
    - The second step is to select objects to be extended.
- The following example illustrates the process of extending:

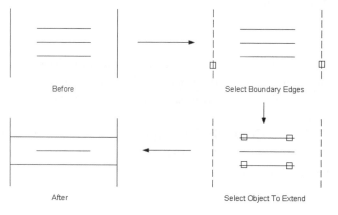

- On the **Ribbon**, go to the **Home** tab. Using the **Modify** panel, click the **Extend** button:

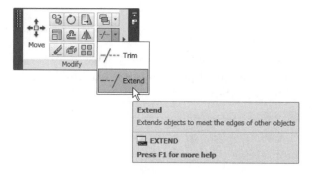

- The following prompt will appear:

```
Current settings: Projection=UCS, Edge=Extend
Select boundary edges ...
```

```
Select objects or <select all>:
```

- The first line displays the current settings.
- The second line tells you to select the boundary edges.

- Use any of the methods you know. Once you are done, press [Enter] or right-click (you can use the **Select All** option as well).
- The following prompt will appear:

```
Select object to extend or shift-select to trim or
[Fence/Crossing/Project/Edge/Undo]:
```

- Now click on the parts you want to extend, one by one.
- If you make a mistake, either right-click to access the shortcut menu and select **Undo**, or type **u** in the **Command Window**.
- The rest of the options are the same as the **Trim** command.

- While you are in the **Trim** command, and while you are clicking on the objects to be trimmed, if you hold [Shift] and click, you will extend the objects rather than trim them. Also note that by following these same steps while in the **Extend** command, you will trim the objects rather than extend them.
- See the following example:

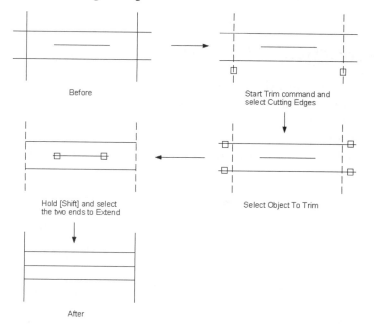

Before

Start Trim command and select Cutting Edges

Select Object To Trim

Hold [Shift] and select the two ends to Extend

After

EXTENDING OBJECTS

Exercise 4-5

1. Start AutoCAD 2011.
2. Open the file *Exercise 4-5.dwg*.

3. The creator of this file was really confused about the final result. Using the **Extend** and **Trim** commands, try to clarify the final product so it appears as follows:

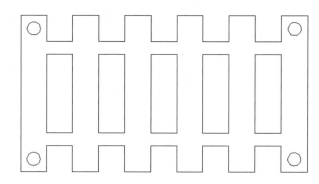

4. Save and close the file.

4.7 THE LENGTHEN COMMAND

■ Using the **Extend** command, we needed an object to serve as a boundary in order to extend the rest of the objects to it.

■ The **Lengthen** (or shorten, as it serves both purposes) command will do this without the need for any boundary.

■ On the **Ribbon**, go to the **Home** tab. Extend the **Modify** panel and select the **Lengthen** button:

■ The following prompt will appear:

```
Select an object or [DElta/Percent/Total/DYnamic]:
```

■ Click any object to receive the current length.

■ The command will perform the lengthening (or shortening) using the **Delta**, **Percent**, **Total**, and **Dynamic** commands.

Delta

- The **Delta** command allows you to add (or remove) length to (or from) the current length.
- If you input a negative value, **Lengthen** shortens the line.
- The following prompt will appear:

```
Enter delta length or [Angle] <0.0000>: (Input the extra
length to be added.)
```

Percent

- The **Percent** command allows you to add (or remove) length to (or from) the length by specifying a percentage of the current length.
- The number should be positive and non-zero. If it is >100, it will lengthen. If it is <100, it will shorten.
- The following prompt will appear:

```
Enter percentage length <100.0000>: (Input the new
percentage.)
```

Total

- The **Total** command allows you to make the new total length of the line equal to the number you will input.
- If the new number is greater than the current length, the line will lengthen. If the new number is less than the current length, the line will shorten.
- The following prompt will appear:

```
Specify total length or [Angle] <1.0000)>: (Input the new
total length.)
```

Dynamic

- The **Dynamic** command allows you to specify a new length for the object based on the dynamic movement of the mouse.
- The following prompt will appear:

```
Select an object to change or [Undo]: (Select the desired
object.)
Specify new endpoint: (Move the mouse up until you reach the
desired length.)
```

NOTE
- You can use only one method per command.

LENGTHENING OBJECTS

Exercise 4-6

1. Start AutoCAD 2011.
2. Open the file *Exercise 4-6.dwg*.
3. Using the **Lengthen** command and the **Delta** option, shorten the two vertical lines by 1 unit.
4. Using the **Lengthen** command and the **Total** option, make the total length of the two horizontal lines = 5.
5. As you can see, the lower line does not end like the upper line.
6. Using the **Lengthen** command and the **Percent** option, set the percent at **104**, and select the end of the line.
7. The output should look like the following:

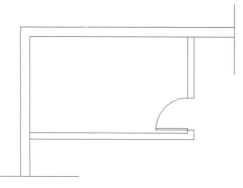

8. Save and close the file.

4.8 THE JOIN COMMAND

- While modifying your drawing, you may end up with a line broken into segments that you need to join into a single line. The same may happen with arcs.
- If you have a polyline, you can join other objects, such as lines and arcs, to it.
- On the **Ribbon**, go to the **Home** tab. Extend the **Modify** panel and select the **Lengthen** button:

- AutoCAD will show the following prompts:

```
Select source object:
Select lines to join to source: (Select the source object.)
Select lines to join to source: (Depending on the source
object, the following prompt will ask you to select the
objects to join. Once you are done, press [Enter].)
1 line joined to source
```

- If you select a line object, the other lines should be collinear. Gaps are allowed.
- If you select an arc object, the other arcs should be part of the same imaginary circle. Gaps are allowed.
- There is a special prompt in the **Arc** option to close the arc and formulate a circle.
- You can join any other objects (e.g., lines, arcs) to a polyline, but no gaps are allowed.

JOINING OBJECTS

Exercise 4-7
1. Start AutoCAD 2011.
2. Open the file *Exercise 4-7.dwg*.
3. This file resembles what you may find after recovering a corrupt file. You will find broken lines, and a broken arc and polyline.
4. Using the **Join** command, make the arc a full circle.
5. Using the **Join** command, connect the two broken lines.
6. Join all the lines to the polyline.
7. Save and close the file.

DRAWING THE PLAN (METRIC)

Workshop 1-M
1. Start AutoCAD 2011.
2. Open the file *Workshop_02.dwg*.
3. Make the layer **Walls** current.
4. Using the **Polyline** command, first draw the outer lines (without the dimension) starting from point 8000,3000. Use all the methods you learned in Chapter 2.

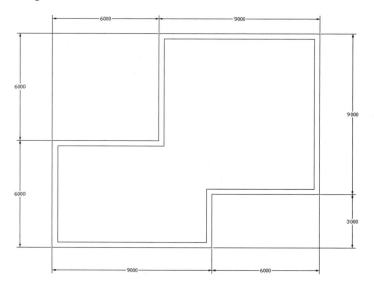

5. Using the **Offset** command, offset the polyline to the *inside* with the offset distance = 300.
6. Explode the inner polyline.

7. Using the **Offset**, **Fillet**, **Chamfer**, **Trim**, **Extend**, **Lengthen**, and **Zoom** commands, create the interior walls using the following dimensions:

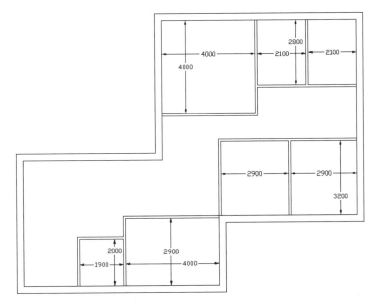

NOTE ▸ ▪ The thickness of all inner walls = 100.

8. Make the door openings, taking the following into consideration:

   a. All door openings = 900.

   b. Always set the distances from the walls to the door openings at 100, except for the outside door, which should be 500.

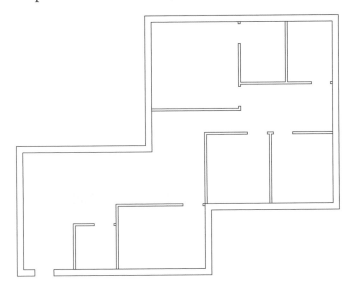

NOTE ■ To make the door openings, use the following technique:

- Offset an existing wall (say, 100 for internal doors).
- Offset the new line (say, 900 for room doors).
- You will have the following shape:

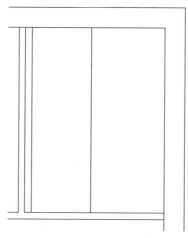

- Extend the two vertical lines to the lower horizontal line, as shown:

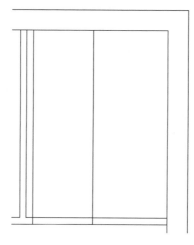

- Using the **Trim** command, select all the horizontal and vertical lines as cutting edges, then press [Enter]. As for the objects to trim, click on the unneeded parts (you can use **Crossing**, which is quicker).

- You will get the following:

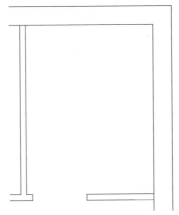

9. Save and close the file.

DRAWING THE PLAN (IMPERIAL)

Workshop 2-I
1. Start AutoCAD 2011.
2. Open the file *Workshop_02.dwg*.
3. Make the layer **Walls** current.
4. Using the **Polyline** command, draw the outer lines (without the dimension) starting from point 16',10'. Use all the methods you learned in Chapter 2.

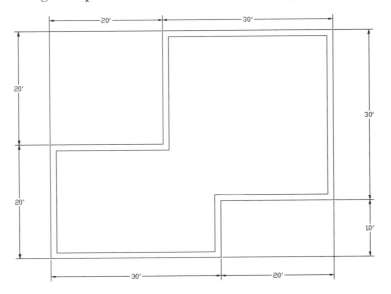

5. Using the **Offset** command, offset the polyline to the *inside* with the offset distance = 1'.

6. Explode the inner polyline.

7. Using the **Offset, Fillet, Chamfer, Trim, Extend, Lengthen,** and **Zoom** commands, create the interior walls using the following dimensions:

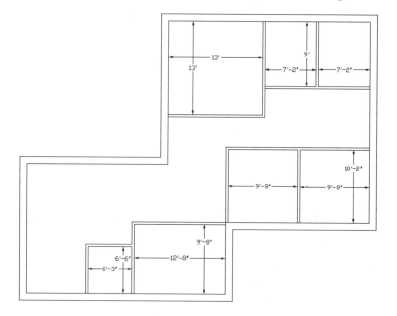

NOTE ▶ ■ The thickness of all inner walls = 4".

8. Make the door openings, taking into consideration the following:

   a. All door openings are 3'.

   b. Always set the distance from the walls to the door openings at 4", except for the outside door, which should be 1'6".

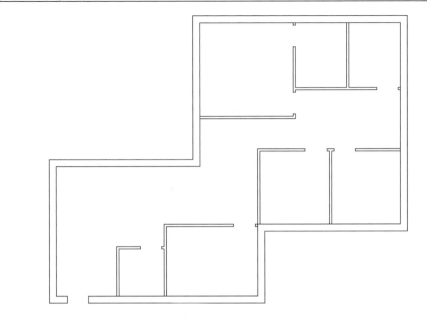

NOTE ■ To make the door openings, use the following technique:
- Offset an existing wall (say, 4" for internal doors).
- Offset the new line (say, 3' for room doors).
- You will have the following shape:

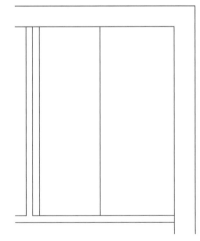

- Extend the two vertical lines to the lower horizontal line, as shown:

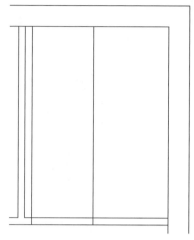

- Using the **Trim** command, select all the horizontal and vertical lines as cutting edges, then press [Enter]. As for the objects to trim, click on the unneeded parts (you can use **Crossing**, which is quicker).
- You will get the following:

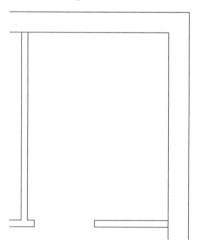

9. Save and close the file.

CHAPTER REVIEW

1. Using the same **Offset** command, you can offset more than one distance.
   a. True, but only two offset distances are allowed.
   b. True, I can offset as many as I wish.
   c. False, only one offset distance is allowed per command.
   d. The only method available in the **Offset** command is the through point method.
2. In the **Lengthen** command, using the **Percent** option, 150% should be input as _____.
3. While you are trimming, you can extend, and vice versa.
   a. True
   b. False
4. You can fillet using an arc, but you must specify:
   a. Distances
   b. Radius
   c. Radius and distances
   d. Length and angle
5. There are two methods for using the **Chamfer** command: distances and length/angle.
   a. True
   b. False
6. The first step in the **Extend** command is to select the _____, and the second step is to select the _____.
7. If I want to join lines, they should be _____, and _____ are allowed.

CHAPTER REVIEW ANSWERS

1. c
2. 150
3. a
4. b
5. a
6. boundary edge(s), objects to extend
7. collinear, gaps

5 MODIFYING COMMANDS

In This Chapter
◊ Selecting objects using advanced techniques
◊ Moving and copying objects
◊ Rotating and scaling objects
◊ Creating duplicates using the **Array** command
◊ Mirroring objects
◊ Stretching objects
◊ Breaking objects
◊ Using **Grips** to modify objects

5.1 INTRODUCTION

- In this chapter, we will learn the core of the modifying commands in AutoCAD.
- We will cover nine commands that will enable you to make any type of change in the drawing.
- First, we will discuss the selection process (using more advanced methods than we discussed in Chapter 2).
- Then we will discuss the following commands:
  - The **Move** command, which allows you to move objects from one place to another.
  - The **Copy** command, which allows you to copy objects.
  - The **Rotate** command, which allows you to rotate objects using rotation angles.
  - The **Scale** command, which allows you to create larger or smaller objects using a scale factor.

- The **Array** command, which allows you to create copies of objects either in a matrix fashion or in a circular or semicircular fashion.
- The **Mirror** command, which allows you to create mirror images of selected objects.
- The **Stretch** command, which allows you to increase or decrease the length of objects.
- The **Break** command, which allows you to break an object into two pieces.
- We will conclude this chapter by discussing **Grips** in AutoCAD.

5.2 ADVANCED METHODS OF SELECTING OBJECTS

- All of the modifying commands (with some exceptions) will ask you the same question:

```
Select objects:
```

- In Chapter 2, we looked at some of the methods used to select objects. We will now expand our knowledge in this area.
- All the methods we discuss will involve typing at least one letter into the **Command Window** at the **Select objects** prompt.

W (Window)

- If you type **W**, the **Window** mode will be available whether you go to the right or to the left.

C (Crossing)

- If you type **C**, the **Crossing** mode will be available whether you go to the right or to the left.

WP (Window Polygon)

- If you want to select multiple objects without the constraint of the rectangle window, you can use the **Window Polygon** mode.
- When you type **WP** and press [Enter], the following prompt will appear:

```
First polygon point: (Specify the first point of the
polygon.)
Specify endpoint of line or [Undo]: (Specify the second
point.)
Specify endpoint of line or [Undo]: (Specify the third
point, etc.)
```

- When you are done, press [Enter] to end the **WP** mode.
- Any objects that are *fully* inside the **Window Polygon** will be selected. If any part (even a tiny part) is outside the shape, the object will not be selected. See the example:

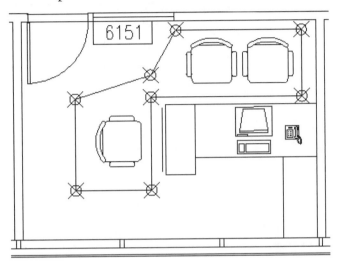

CP (Crossing Polygon)

- The **Crossing Polygon** mode is the same as the **Window Polygon** mode, except it has the features of the **Crossing** mode. Thus, whatever objects it fully contains—as well as any objects touching them—will be selected:

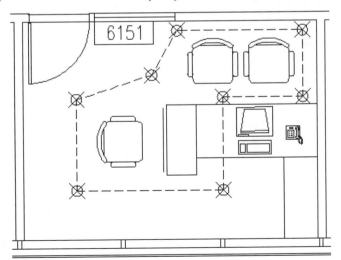

F (Fence)

- The main function of the **Fence** mode is to touch objects.
- It was discussed when we introduced the **Trim** and **Extend** modes.

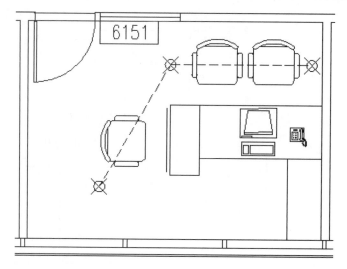

L (Last)

- The **Last** mode allows you to select the last object drawn.

P (Previous)

- The **Previous** mode allows you to select the last selection set used.

All

- The **All** mode allows you to select all objects in the current file.

Deselect

- If, while selecting a group of objects, you inadvertently select one or two items, how do you deselect them?
- Simply hold [Shift] and click the objects. They will be deselected.

Other Methods for Selecting Objects

- There are other methods used to select objects that will make your life easier.
- One helpful technique, called **Noun/Verb selection**, will allow you to select an object first and then issue a command.

- The cursor appears as follows:

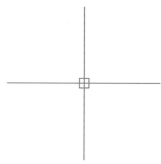

- As you can see, there is a pick box inside the cursor.
- Without issuing any command, you can do any of the following:
  - Click on any object to select it.
  - Find an empty space, click, then go to the right to get the **Window** mode.
  - Find an empty space, click, then go to the left to get the **Crossing** mode.
- Once you select the desired objects, right-click to get the following shortcut menu:

Repeat HELP
Clipboard ▶
Isolate ▶
Erase
Move
Copy Selection
Scale
Rotate
Draw Order ▶
Add Selected
Select Similar
Deselect All
Subobject Selection Filter ▶
Quick Select…
Properties
✔ Quick Properties

- From this shortcut menu, you can access five modifying commands without typing a single letter on the keyboard or issuing any commands from menus or the toolbars. These commands are **Erase, Move, Copy Selection, Scale**, and **Rotate**.

- Make sure that the **Noun/verb selection** technique is checked in the **Selection modes** dialog box. You can reach this option by right-clicking without selecting an object, then selecting **Options** followed by the **Selection** tab:

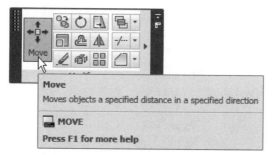

 - This technique will not work with the **Offset, Fillet, Chamfer, Trim, Extend**, or **Lengthen** commands. It does, however, work with the **Join** command.

5.3 THE MOVE COMMAND

- The **Move** command allows you to move objects from one place to another.
- On the **Ribbon**, go to the **Home** tab. Using the **Modify** panel, select the **Move** button:

- The **Move** command is a three-step process.
- The first step is to:

```
Select objects:
```

- Once you are done, press [Enter] or right-click.

- The next prompt will ask you to:

```
Specify base point or [Displacement] <Displacement>:
```
(Specify the base point.)

- The *base point* will be used in four other commands. What is a base point?
  - The simplest way to define a base point is to call it a *handle* point.
  - There is no golden rule that defines the correct point to be a base point.
  - Rather, you must take it case by case. It could be the center of a group of objects in one situation and the upper left-hand corner in another.
  - This is true for commands such as **Move, Copy**, and **Stretch**. But for a command such as **Rotate**, the base point refers to the point around which the whole shape rotates. In the **Scale** command, it is the point relative to which the whole shape will shrink or enlarge.
- The third prompt will be:

```
Specify second point or <use first point as displacement>:
```
(Specify the second point.)

- The command will end automatically.
- See the following example:

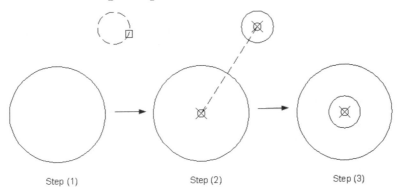

| Step (1) | Step (2) | Step (3) |

MOVING OBJECTS

Exercise 5-1
1. Start AutoCAD 2011.
2. Open the file *Exercise 5-1.dwg*.

3. Move the four objects (bathtub, toilet, sink, and door) to their respective places to make the bathroom look like the following:

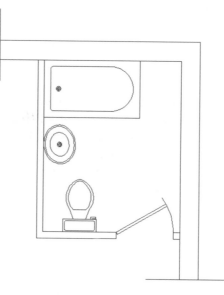

4. Save and close the file.

- For the toilet, use the midpoint of the inside wall as the second point.
- For the sink, use the left quadrant and the midpoint of the inside wall.

5.4 THE COPY COMMAND

- The **Copy** command allows you to copy objects.
- On the **Ribbon**, go to the **Home** tab. Using the **Modify** panel, select the **Copy** button:

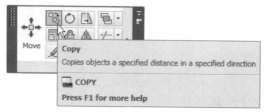

- This command is a three-step process.
- The first step is to:

`Select objects:`

- Once you are done, press [Enter] or right-click.

- The next prompt will ask you to:

```
Specify base point or [Displacement] <Displacement>:
(Specify the base point.)
```

- The third prompt will be:

```
Specify second point or [Exit/Undo] <Exit>:
(Specify the second point.)
Specify second point or [Exit/Undo] <Exit>:
(Specify another second point.)
```

- Once you are done, press [Enter] or right-click.
- If you made a mistake, simply type **u** into the **Command Window** to undo the last action.
- See the following example:

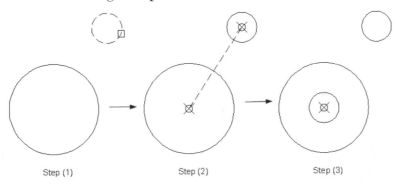

Step (1)   Step (2)   Step (3)

COPYING OBJECTS

Exercise 5-2

1. Start AutoCAD 2011.
2. Open the file *Exercise 5-2.dwg*.
3. Copy the guest chair twice, setting the copies to the right of the original and leaving proper distance between them.
4. Copy the rounded sofa once, setting the copy to the right of the original.
5. Copy the whole office twice, using the upper left-hand corner of the office.
6. Save and close the file.

- Use **Polar Tracking, OSNAP**, and **OTRACK** to make sure the objects are aligned.

5.5 THE ROTATE COMMAND

- The **Rotate** command allows you to rotate objects around a point using a rotation angle.
- On the **Ribbon**, go to the **Home** tab. Using the **Modify** panel, select the **Rotate** button:

- This command is a three-step process.
- The first step is to:

```
Select objects:
```

- Once you are done, press [Enter] or right-click.
- The next prompt will ask you to:

```
Specify base point: (Specify the base point.)
```

- The third prompt will be:

```
Specify rotation angle or [Copy/Reference] <0>:
(Specify the rotation angle, -=CW, +=CCW.)
```

- You can use the **Copy** option if you want to rotate a copy of the objects selected and keep the original intact.
- The command will end automatically.
- See the following example:

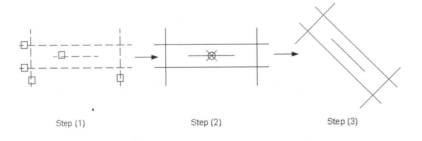

Step (1)   Step (2)   Step (3)

ROTATING OBJECTS

Exercise 5-3

1. Start AutoCAD 2011.
2. Open the file *Exercise 5-3.dwg*.
3. Rotate the door, two windows, the chair, and the desk to look like the following, bearing in mind that counterclockwise is positive and clockwise is negative (angles used are either 45 or –45):

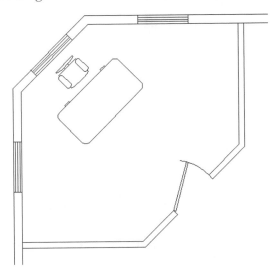

4. Save and close the file.

  •   The best way to do this exercise is by either using **Polar Tracking** or typing the angles. You may need to move some objects to make the room look perfect.

5.6 THE SCALE COMMAND

- The **Scale** command allows you to enlarge or shrink objects using a scale factor.
- On the **Ribbon**, go to the **Home** tab. Using the **Modify** panel, select the **Scale** button:

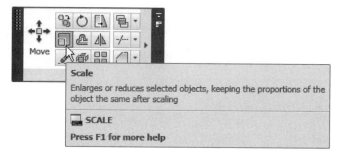

- This command is a three-step process.
- The first step is to:

```
Select objects:
```

- Once you are done, press [Enter] or right-click.
- The next prompt will ask you to:

  ```
  Specify base point: (Specify the base point.)
  ```

- The third prompt will be:

```
Specify scale factor or [Copy/Reference] <1.0000>:
(Specify the scale factor. The number should be a non-zero
positive number.)
```

- You can use the **Copy** option if you want to scale a copy of the objects selected and keep the original intact.
- The command will end automatically.
- See the following example:

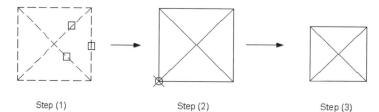

Step (1)   Step (2)   Step (3)

SCALING OBJECTS

 Exercise 5-4
1. Start AutoCAD 2011.
2. Open the file *Exercise 5-4.dwg*.
3. Set the scale factor = 0.8 to scale the bathtub, using the upper left-hand corner as the base point.
4. Set the scale factor = 1.2 to scale the sink, using the quadrant on the left side as the base point.
5. Set the scale factor = 0.75 to scale the door, using the endpoint at the left-hand side of the door as the base point.
6. Save and close the file.

5.7 THE ARRAY COMMAND

- The **Array** command allows you to create duplicates of objects using two methods:
  - Rectangular array (matrix shape)
  - Polar array (circular or semicircular shape)
- On the **Ribbon**, go to the **Home** tab. Using the **Modify** panel, select the **Array** button:

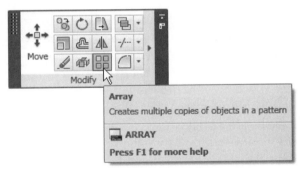

Rectangular

- To create a duplicate of objects simulating the matrix shape, select the **Rectangular Array**.

- The following dialog box will appear:

- First, click the **Select objects** button to select the desired objects. Once you are done, press [Enter] or right-click.
- Then, specify the number of **Rows** and the number of **Columns** (the original object is inclusive).
- Specify the **Row offset** (the distance between rows) and the **Column offset** (the distance between columns). While you are doing this, keep two things in mind:
  - You must be consistent. Measure the distance from the same reference (e.g., from top to top, from bottom to bottom, from center to center).
  - You must note the direction in which you are copying. If you input a positive number, it will be either to the right or up. If you input a negative number, it will be either to the left or down.
- Specify the **Angle of array**. By default, it will be set to repeat the objects using the orthogonal angles.
- Click the **Preview** button to see the result of your inputs.
- AutoCAD will display the result, and the following prompt will appear:

```
Pick or press Esc to return to dialog or
<Right-click to accept array>:
```

- If you like the results, press [Enter] or right-click.
- If not, press [Esc].

- See the following example:

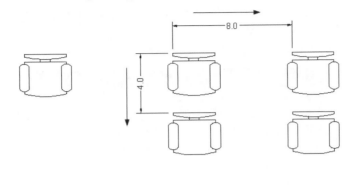

Step (1)   Step (2)

RECTANGULAR ARRAY

 Exercise 5-5
1. Start AutoCAD 2011.
2. Open the file *Exercise 5-5.dwg*.
3. Using the **Rectangular array**, array the chairs to look like the following:

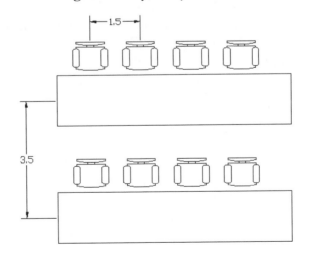

4. Save and close the file.

Polar Array

- To create a duplicate of objects simulating a circular or semicircular shape, use the **Polar Array**.
- The following dialog box will appear:

- First, click the **Select objects** button to select the desired objects. Once you are done, press [Enter] or right-click.
- Then, specify the **Center point** of the array, either by inputting the coordinates in **X** and **Y** or by clicking the **Pick center point** button and specifying the point by using the mouse.
- You have three pieces of data to input, and AutoCAD will only take two of them:
  - Total number of items
  - Angle to fill
  - Angle between items

■ The following diagram illustrates the relationship between the three parameters:

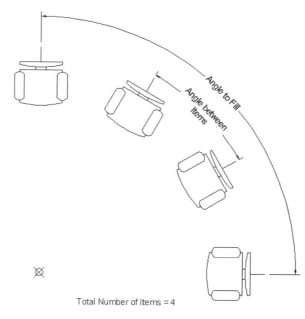

Total Number of Items = 4

■ You can specify two of the three parameters, which gives you three methods:
  • Method 1: Specify the total number of items and the angle to fill. AutoCAD will figure out the angle between items.
  • Method 2: Specify the total number of items and the angle between items. AutoCAD will know the angle to fill.
  • Method 3: Specify the angle to fill and the angle between items. AutoCAD will calculate the total number of items.
■ Under **Methods and values**, select the proper method and input the corresponding values.

- Specify if you want to **Rotate items as copied**. See the following example:

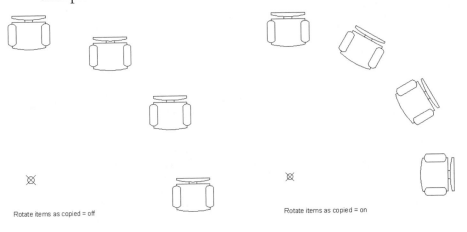

Rotate items as copied = off   Rotate items as copied = on

POLAR ARRAY

Exercise 5-6

1. Start AutoCAD 2011.
2. Open the file *Exercise 5-6.dwg*.
3. Using the **Polar Array** command array the square to look like the following:

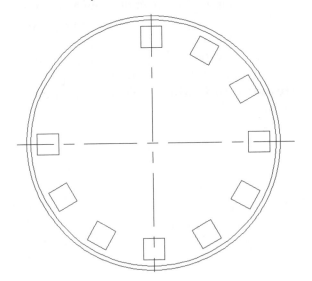

4. Save and close the file.

5.8 THE MIRROR COMMAND

- The **Mirror** command allows you to create a mirror image of selected objects.
- On the **Ribbon**, go to the **Home** tab. Using the **Modify** panel, select the **Mirror** button:

- The first step is to:

```
Select objects:
```

- Once you are done, press [Enter] or right-click.
- Now you need to specify the mirror line by specifying two points:

```
Specify first point of mirror line: (Specify the first point
of the mirror line.)
Specify second point of mirror line: (Specify the
second point of the mirror line.)
```

- The following applies to the mirror line:
  - There is no need to draw a line to act as a mirror line; two points will do the job.
  - The length of the mirror is not important, but the location and angle of the mirror line will affect the final result.
- The last prompt will be:

```
Erase source objects? [Yes/No] <N>: (Type n or y.)
```

- The **Mirror** command will produce an image in all cases. You can decide whether you want AutoCAD to keep the source objects or erase them.
- The **Mirror** command ends automatically.
- NOTE ▶ If part of the objects to be mirrored is text, you must indicate whether you want to treat it as other objects and mirror it, or simply copy it.
- To do so, prior to issuing the **Mirror** command, type **mirrtext** in the **Command Window**. The following prompt will appear:

```
Enter new value for MIRRTEXT <0>:
```

- If you input 0 (zero), then the text will be copied.

- If you input 1, then the text will be mirrored.
- See the following example:

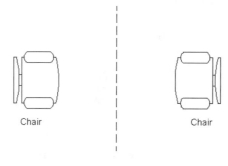

Chair   Chair

Mirrtext = 0 & Erase Source Objects = No

MIRRORING OBJECTS

Exercise 5-7

1. Start AutoCAD 2011.
2. Open the file *Exercise 5-7.dwg*.
3. Using the **Mirror** command, mirror the door labeled D15 (main entrance) to show it opening to the inside.
4. Using the **Mirror** command, mirror the door at the right of the main entrance, which opens to the left, to open to the right. To specify the mirror line, press [Shift] and right-click. Select the **Mid Between 2 Points** option, then select the edges of the door. One point will be specified. Using **Polar Tracking**, specify the second point.
5. Using the **Mirror** command, mirror the two windows on the right wall to the left wall.
6. Using the **Mirror** command, mirror the two windows on the top wall (the one at the right and the one in the middle) to the bottom wall.
7. Save and close the file.
   - The doors and windows are all objects and not blocks; hence you may find it difficult to select them. To solve this problem, use the advanced techniques you have learned in this chapter to quickly select the desired objects.

5.9 THE STRETCH COMMAND

- The **Stretch** command allows you to either increase or decrease the length of selected objects.
- On the **Ribbon**, go to the **Home** tab. Using the **Modify** panel, select the **Stretch** button:

- The first step is to:

```
Select objects to stretch by crossing-window or
crossing-polygon...
```

- The **Stretch** command is one of the few commands that insists on a certain method of selecting.
- The **Stretch** command asks the user to select using either **C** or **CP**.
- As we discussed earlier, **C** and **CP** will select any object contained inside and any object touched (crossed) by **C** or **CP** lines.
- The **Stretch** command will use both facilities by setting the following rules:
  - Any object *fully* contained inside **C** or **CP** will be moved.
  - Any object crossed by **C** or **CP** will be stretched.
- Once you are done, press [Enter] or right-click.
- The second prompt will be:

```
Specify base point or [Displacement] <Displacement>:
```
(Specify the base point.)

- The third prompt will be:

```
Specify second point or <use first point as displacement>:
```
(Specify the destination point.)

- The **Stretch** command ends automatically.

- See the following example:

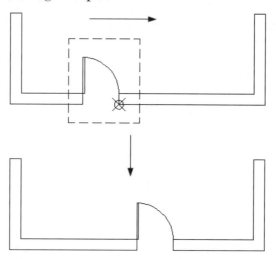

STRETCHING OBJECTS

Exercise 5-8

1. Start AutoCAD 2011.
2. Open the file *Exercise 5-8.dwg*.
3. Using the **Stretch** command and **CP**, stretch the shape to look like the following image (you may need to switch **OSNAP** off while specifying **CP**). Keep in mind that the distance of the stretching on both sides is 1.5.

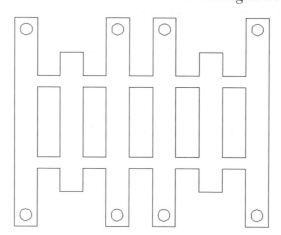

4. Save and close the file.

5.10 THE BREAK COMMAND

- The **Break** command allows you to break an object into two pieces.
- On the **Ribbon**, go to the **Home** tab. Expand the **Modify** panel and select the **Break** button:

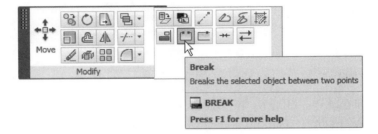

- The first step is to:

```
Select object:
```

- You can break one object at a time. When you select this object, AutoCAD will prompt you with the following:

```
Specify second break point or [First point]:
```

- To understand this prompt, note the following:
  - To break an object, you must specify two points on it.
  - Your selection can be considered either a selection and also a first point or a selection only. If you consider the selection to be a selection and a first point, respond to this prompt by specifying the second point.
  - However, if you want the selection to be only a selection, type **F** in the **Command Window**, and AutoCAD will respond with the following prompt:

```
Specify first break point: (Specify the first breaking point.)
Specify second break point: (Specify the second breaking
point.)
```

- If you want to break a circle, take care to specify the two points counter-clockwise.
- See the following example:

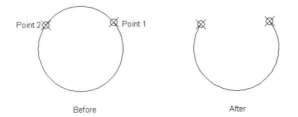

Before   After

- Within the **Modify** panel (located on the **Home** tab of the **Ribbon**), there is a tool called **Break at Point**:

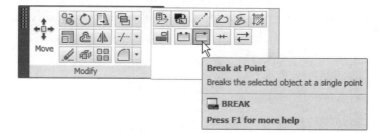

- This tool is similar to the **Break** command, except:
  - You will be asked to select only one point.
  - AutoCAD will assume that the first point and the second point are in the same place.
  - The object will be broken into two objects, but they will be connected.

BREAKING OBJECTS

Exercise 5-9
1. Start AutoCAD 2011.
2. Open the file *Exercise 5-9.dwg*.
3. Using the **Break** command, break the two circles to resemble the following:

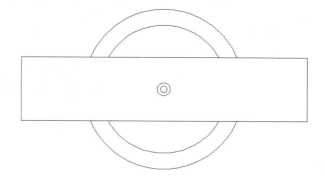

4. Save and close the file.

5.11 GRIPS

Introduction

- **Grips** is a quick and easy method for modifying your objects.
- **Grips** simply requires clicking on the object(s); commands are not needed.
- **Grips** will do two things for you:
  - It will select the objects, which will act as a selection set. Thus, they will be ready for any modifying command to be issued.
  - Blue (default color) squares will appear at certain places depending on the object's type. Here are some examples:

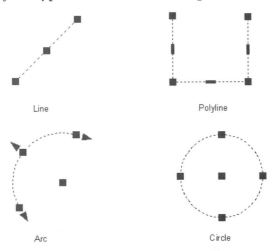

- These squares are the grips.
- There is a magnet relationship between these squares and the pick box of the crosshairs.
- Also, if you hover over grips, the blue will turn to green to indicate that this is the current grip.
- If you click on one of these blue squares, you will:
  - Make it hot, turning it to red
  - Make this grip a base point
  - Start a group of five **Modify** commands (using the right-click)
- On polylines, small rectangles at the midpoint of each segment help users perform one of three additional functions:
  - Stretch
  - Add a vertex
  - Convert to an arc

The Five Commands

- Once you make one of the blue squares hot (by clicking on it), this grip will become the base point for five commands:
  - **Move**
  - **Mirror**
  - **Rotate**
  - **Scale**
  - **Stretch**
- To see these commands, right-click and the following shortcut menu will appear:

```
Enter
Recent Input          ▶
Dynamic Input         ▶

Stretch
Move
Rotate
Scale
Mirror

Base Point
Copy
Reference
Undo           Ctrl+Z

Exit
```

- The other options available in the shortcut menu are:
  - **Base Point**, which is used to define a base point other than the one you started with.
  - **Copy**, which is more a mode than a command. The **Copy** mode works with all the other commands and, therefore, will give you the ability to **Rotate with Copy, Scale with Copy**, etc.

Steps

- The steps to use **Grips** are as follows:
  - Select the object(s) desired (direct clicking, **Window** mode, or **Crossing** mode).
  - Select one of the grips to be your base point, and click it. It will become hot (red by default).
  - Right-click and select the desired command from the shortcut menu. You can now specify another base point and/or select the **Copy** mode.

- Perform the steps of the desired command.
- Once you are done, press [Esc] once or twice, depending on the command.

- You can use **OSNAP** with **Grips** with no limitations. Also you can use **Polar Tracking** and **OTRACK** to assure the modification's accuracy.
- **Mirror** is the only command that does not ask explicitly for the base point. The reason it is listed with the other four commands is that AutoCAD considers the first point of the mirror line to be the base point.
- To keep both the original and the mirrored image using **Grips**, you must select the **Copy** mode after you select the **Mirror** command.
- You can *deselect* objects from the grips by holding [Shift] and clicking on the object, thus avoiding the grips.
- You can select more than one grip as the base point if you hold [Shift] while picking the base point.
- After finishing, select one of them as your base point by clicking it.

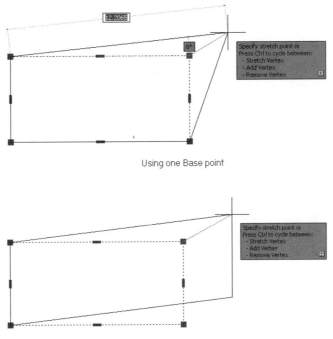

Using one Base point

Multiple Base points using [Shift]

- So AutoCAD will remember the last input you made (e.g., distance, angle), hold [Ctrl] while moving, rotating, stretching, or scaling.

Dynamic Input

- **Dynamic Input** can give you information about objects by using their grips.
- If you hover over an end grip of a line, **Dynamic Input** tells you the length and the angle of that line:

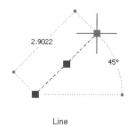

Line

- If you hover over an end grip shared between two lines, **Dynamic Input** tells you the length and angle of both lines:

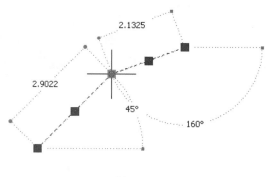

Line

- If you hover over the middle grip of an arc, **Dynamic Input** tells you the radius and the included angle of the arc:

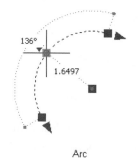

Arc

- If you hover over the endpoint of an arc, **Dynamic Input** tells you the circle's radius and the angle formed from the center point to the arc endpoints, starting from the east:

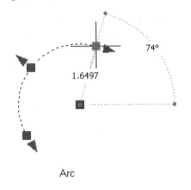

Arc

- If you hover over the quadrant grip of a circle, **Dynamic Input** tells you the radius of the circle:

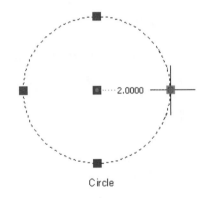

Circle

- If you hover over the intermediate grip of a polyline, **Dynamic Input** tells you the lengths of the line segments (without the angles):

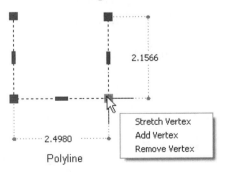

Polyline

Special Polyline Functions

- When working with polylines, grips offer additional functions.
- The grips are the rectangles at the midpoint of each segment.
- They will enable you to do the following:
  - Stretch a polyline using the grip as the base point.
  - Add a new vertex to a polyline.
  - Convert a line segment to an arc segment, and an arc segment to a line segment.
- In the following example, a user hovers over a line segment:

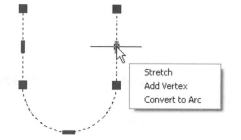

- In the following example, a user hovers over an arc segment:

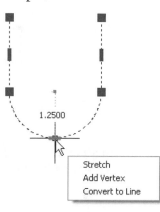

- The following is an example of stretching:

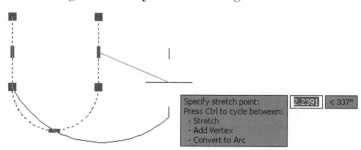

■ The following is an example of adding a vertex:

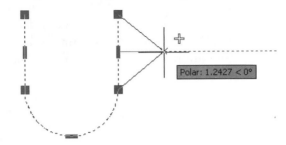

■ The following is an example of converting a line to an arc:

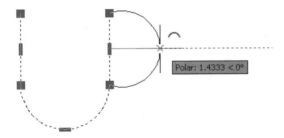

 ■ While you are in any one of these three commands, you can press [Ctrl] to cycle between the current command and the other two commands.

USING GRIPS

Exercise 5-10

1. Start AutoCAD 2011.

2. Open the file *Exercise 5-10.dwg*.

3. Without issuing any commands, select the upper circle. Make the center hot, then right-click and select **Scale**. Right-click again and select **Copy**. For the **Scale factor** prompt, type **0.5**. Press [Esc] twice.

4. In the right part of the base, without issuing any command, select the rectangle. Make one of the blue grips hot, right-click, select **Rotate**, then right-click again and select **Base Point**. You can now specify a new base point, which is the center of the rectangle (using **OSNAP** and **OTRACK**). Set the rotation angle = 90. Press [Esc] twice.

5. Select the rotated rectangle at the right part of the base, select any grip to make it hot, then right-click and select **Mirror**. Right-click again and select **Copy**, and right-click for a third time and select **Base Point**. Specify one of the two endpoints of the vertical lines separating the two parts of the base, then specify the other endpoint. Press [Esc] twice. The shape should appear as follows:

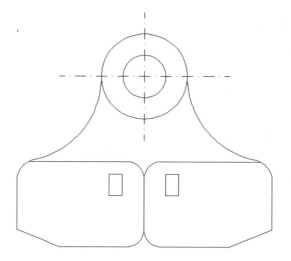

6. Save and close the file.

CHAPTER REVIEW

1. What do the commands **Move, Copy, Rotate, Scale**, and **Stretch** have in common?
    a. They are all modifying commands.
    b. They all use the base point concept.
    c. They all change the length of an object.
    d. A and B.
2. In the **Stretch** command, you have to use _____ or _____ while selecting the objects.
3. **Mirrtext** is used to control whether to copy or to mirror the text in the **Mirror** command.
    a. True
    b. False

4. If you break a circle, you have to specify the two points in which direction?

    a. Counterclockwise.

    b. Clockwise.

    c. It doesn't matter.

    d. You cannot break a circle.

5. You can scale using a scale factor = –1.

    a. True

    b. False

6. In the **Array** command, using the **Rectangular** option, the **Row offset** must be _____ if you want to repeat the objects downward.

CHAPTER REVIEW ANSWERS

1. d

2. **C, CP**

3. a

4. a

5. b

6. negative

Chapter 6

WORKING WITH BLOCKS

In This Chapter
◊ Creating and inserting blocks
◊ Exploding blocks
◊ Using the **Design Center** and automatic scaling
◊ Using Tool Palettes and their effect on blocks
◊ Editing blocks

6.1 WHAT ARE BLOCKS?

- A block in AutoCAD is any shape used in one or more drawings more than once.
- Instead of drawing the shape every time you need it, follow these steps:
  - Draw it once.
  - Store it as a block.
  - Insert it as many times as you wish.
- Blocks in AutoCAD have changed a lot over the years, making some procedures obsolete.
- In this chapter, we will mention the old methods, but we will concentrate more on the new methods of using blocks.

6.2 CREATING BLOCKS

- The first step in creating blocks in AutoCAD is to draw the desired shape.
- While drawing the shape, consider the following three guidelines:
  - Draw the shape in layer 0 (zero).
  - Draw the shape in certain units.
  - Draw the shape in the correct dimensions.

Why Layer 0?

- Layer 0 is different from any other layer in AutoCAD, because it will allow the block to be transparent both in color and in linetype.
- If you draw the shape that will be a block while layer 0 is current and you then insert it into another layer with red color and a dashdot linetype, the block will be red and dashdot.

Why Certain Units?

- If you want AutoCAD to automatically rescale your block to fit into the current drawing units, you must specify the units of the block.

What Are the Correct Dimensions?

- The correct dimensions are either:
  - The real dimension of the shape.
  - Values with simple distances such as 1, 10, 100, and 1000 that will make it easy for you to scale the block once you insert it.
- Let's assume we draw the following shape:

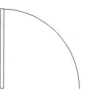

- The next step would be to decide the base point (the "handle" for this block).
- Also, think of a good name for this block.
- Now you can now issue the command.
- On the **Ribbon**, go to the **Home** tab. Using the **Block** panel, select the **Create** button:

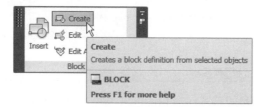

- The following dialog box will appear:

- Type the name of the block. The name should not exceed 255 characters as with (layer naming).
- Under **Base point**, click the **Pick point** button to input the base point of the block. Once you are done, press [Enter] or right-click. Or you can click on the **Specify On-screen** checkbox to specify the base point after the dialog box closes.
- Under **Objects**, click the **Select objects** button to select the objects. Once you are done, press [Enter] or right-click. Or you can click on the **Specify On-screen** checkbox to specify the objects after the dialog box closes.
- Now determine what you want AutoCAD to do with the objects you draw while creating the block. You have three choices:
  - Retain them as objects
  - Convert them to blocks
  - Delete them

- Under **Behavior**, set the following:

- Leave **Annotative** unchecked (this is an advanced feature).
- Click on the **Scale uniformly** checkbox if you want the block to always be scaled uniformly (i.e., X-scale = Y-scale).
- Click on the **Allow exploding** checkbox if you want to be able to explode the block.
- Under **Settings**, select the **Block unit** you want to use for your drawing. This will help AutoCAD in the **Automatic scaling** feature.

- Click the **Hyperlink** button. The following dialog box will appear:

- This dialog box allows you to insert a hyperlink inside the block to lead to a website, a drawing file with more details, an MS Word document, an Excel document for calculation, etc.
- After you finish, when you approach the block, you will see something like the following:

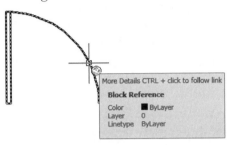

- As you can see, the shape of the hyperlink will be displayed, and a help message will appear telling you to hold [Ctrl] + click the block to open the desired link.
- Write any description for your block.
- Select whether to allow this block to be opened in the block editor (the block editor is an advanced feature used to create dynamic blocks). Keep it turned off for the time being.
- When you are done, click **OK**.
- Now, let's imagine that our drawing has a cabinet. The door of the cabinet will be opened, and the defined block will be placed inside it. This block will be intact. Even when you insert it, you will insert only a copy of it.
- You can define as many blocks as you wish.

CREATING BLOCKS

 Exercise 6-1

1. Start AutoCAD 2011.
2. Open the file *Exercise 6-1.dwg*.
3. All the shapes were made in layer 0 (zero).
4. Create three blocks—door, window, and double door—using the following settings in **Block Definition**:
   a. For all blocks, the base point is the lower left-hand point.
   b. Delete the objects after defining the block.
   c. Allow exploding.
   d. Set block units as meters.
5. Save and close the file.

6.3 INSERTING BLOCKS

- Once you create a block, you can use it in your drawing as many times as you wish.
- Consider the following guidelines when inserting a block in your drawing:
  - Set the desired layer to be current.
  - Prepare the drawing to accommodate the block (e.g., finish the door openings before inserting the door block).
- After considering these guidelines, issue the command.
- On the **Ribbon**, go to the **Home** tab. Using the **Block** panel, select the **Insert** button.

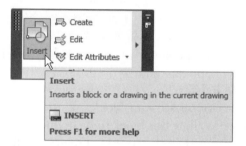

- The following dialog box will appear:

- Select the name of the desired block from the list.
- Specify the **Insertion point** using one of two methods:
  - Click on the **Specify On-screen** checkbox, which means you will specify the insertion point using the mouse. (This is usually the easier method.)
  - Type the coordinates of the insertion point.

- Specify the **Scale** of the block by using one of the following methods:
  - Click on the **Specify On-screen** checkbox, which means you will specify the scale using the mouse.
  - Type the scale factor in all three directions, which means you can set the X-scale factor unequal to the Y-scale factor.
  - Click on the **Uniform Scale** checkbox, which will allow you to input only one scale. The others will follow.
- Specify the **Rotation** of the block by using one of the following methods:
  - Click on the **Specify On-screen** checkbox, which means you will specify the rotation angle using the mouse.
  - Type the rotation angle.
- The **Block unit** part will be read-only, thereby showing you the unit you specified when you created this block. Also, it will show the **Factor**, which is based on the **Block unit** and the **drawing unit** (which is defined in the **Application Menu**). According to this factor, AutoCAD will automatically scale the block to suit the current drawing.
- Click **OK** to end the command.
- Using the **Scale** of the block, you can use negative values to insert mirror images of your block. See the following example:

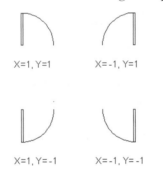

INSERTING BLOCKS

Exercise 6-2
1. Start AutoCAD 2011.
2. Open the file *Exercise 6-2.dwg*.

3. Insert the blocks for the doors, windows, and double door in the proper layer. For the windows, insert the top and right-hand windows, then use the **Mirror** command to mirror the rest of the windows. The plan should look like the following:

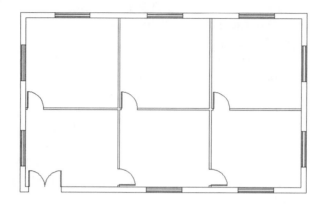

4. Save and close the file.

6.4 EXPLODING BLOCKS

- When you insert incidences of blocks, keep them as blocks, and do not try to change their nature.
- However, in some (rare) cases, you may want to explode the block (which is one object) to the objects forming it.
- To do so, you must use the **Explode** command.
- On the **Ribbon**, go to the **Home** tab. Using the **Modify** panel, select the **Explode** button:

- AutoCAD will prompt you to:

```
Select objects:
```

- Once you are done, press [Enter] or right-click.
- Once you explode a block, it will go back to its original layer (the layer in which the block was created).
- Do not use this command unless you really need it.
- In older versions of AutoCAD, a block could not be defined as a cutting edge or a boundary edge in the **Trim** and **Extend** commands. Starting with AutoCAD 2005, you can select blocks as cutting edges and boundary edges. Thus, there is no need to explode the block for this purpose.
- You can use this command to explode polylines to lines and arcs.

6.5 USING THE DESIGN CENTER

- AutoCAD has a very helpful tool called the **Design Center**, which allows you to share blocks, layers, and other data among different files.
- In this chapter, we will concentrate on blocks.
- The file you want to take the blocks from could be anywhere:
  - It could be in your computer.
  - It could be in your colleague's computer, which is connected to your computer through your company's local area network.
  - It could be on a website.
- On the **Ribbon**, go to the **Insert** tab. Using the **Content** panel, select the **Design Center** button:

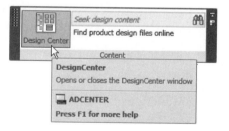

- The following will appear:

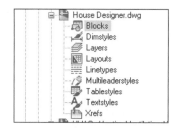

- As you can see, the **Design Center** palette is split into two parts:
  - On the left, you will see the hierarchy of your computer, including all your hard disks and network places (just like My Computer in Windows).
  - Select (by double-clicking) the desired hard disk, folder, and drawing. You will see something like the following:

- You can select these functions:
  - Blocks
  - Dimstyles
  - Layers
  - Layouts
  - Linetypes
  - Multileaderstyles
  - Tablestyles
  - Textstyles
  - Xrefs

- Once you click (you do not need to double-click) the word **Blocks**, look at the right part of the **Design Center**. You will see the blocks available in this drawing.
- There are several ways to move the blocks from this drawing to your drawing:
  - Drag and drop (using the left button)
  - Drag and drop (using the right button)
  - Double-click
  - Right-click

Drag and Drop Using the Left Button

- Perform the following steps:
  - In your drawing, make sure you are in the correct layer.
  - Make sure you switched on the correct **OSNAP** settings.
  - Click and hold the desired block from the **Design Center**.
  - Drag the block into your drawing; you will be holding it from the base point.
  - Once you catch the correct **OSNAP**, release the mouse button.

Drag and Drop Using the Right Button

- Perform the following steps:
  - In your drawing, make sure you are in the correct layer.
  - Make sure you switch on the correct **OSNAP** settings.
  - Right-click and hold the desired block from the **Design Center**.
  - Drag the block into your drawing.
  - Release the mouse button. The following shortcut menu will appear:

Insert Block...
Cancel

  - It is the same as the **Insert** command discussed earlier.
  - Follow the same steps as the **Insert** command.

Double-Click

- If you double-click any block in the **Design Center**, the **Insert** dialog box will appear, and you can follow the same steps.

Right-Click

■ Right-click the desired block. The following shortcut menu will appear:

> **Insert Block...**
> Insert and Redefine
> Redefine only
>
> Block Editor
>
> Copy
>
> Create Tool Palette

- If you select **Insert Block**, the **Insert** dialog box will appear as discussed previously.
- You will notice two options, **Insert and Redefine** and **Redefine only**. We will be discussing these shortly.
- Select the **Block Editor** option if you want to open this block in the block editor to add dynamic features to it.
- If you select **Copy**, then you will copy the block to the Windows clipboard; hence, you can use it in AutoCAD or other software. To use it, select **Edit/Paste** or press [Ctrl] + V.
- We will discuss the last option in this shortcut menu, the **Tool Palette**, shortly.

6.6 AUTOMATIC SCALING

■ If you are using the **Design Center** to move blocks from other drawings and find that the block is either too big or too small, you will know there is a problem with the **Automatic Scaling** feature.

■ To control **Automatic Scaling**, do the following:
- While you are creating the block, make sure you are setting the right **Block unit**.
- Before you bring the block from the **Design Center**, set the **Units to scale inserted contents** in the **Drawing Utilities/Units** from the **Application Menu**.

Block Unit

- When you are creating a block, the following dialog box will appear:

- Under the part labeled **Block unit**, select the desired unit.

Units to Scale Inserted Content

- Before using any block, select **Drawing Utilities/Units** from the **Application Menu**. The following dialog box will appear:

- Under the area labeled **Units to scale inserted content**, set the desired scale used in your drawing.
- Using the two scales, AutoCAD will calculate the proper scale of the block.

USING THE DESIGN CENTER

Exercise 6-3

1. Start AutoCAD 2011.
2. Open the file *Exercise 6-3.dwg*.
3. Make the **Furniture** layer current.
4. Using the **Application Menu**, select **Drawing Utilities/Units**. What is the setting of **Units to scale inserted content**?
5. In the **Design Center**, go to **Sample/Design Center**, then check the blocks in the *Home Space Planner.dwg* file.
6. Double-click on the **Chair – Desk** block. The Insert dialog box will appear. What is the block unit, and what is the conversion factor?
7. Using the **Design Center**, insert the blocks as shown in the following illustration in the upper right room:

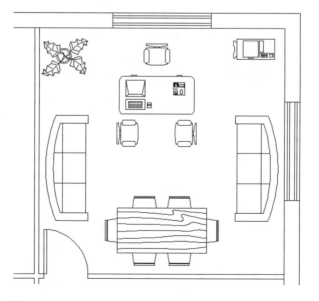

8. Save and close the file.

6.7 TOOL PALETTES: INTRODUCTION

- The **Design Center** gives us the ability to share data from other files. However, you must make sure you are at the right layer and specify the correct rotation angle, scale factor, etc. Also, you need to search for the desired content each time.
- **Tool Palette** solves all of these problems.
- **Tool Palette** will keep blocks, hatches (discussed in the next chapter), and other items available for you regardless of which drawing you are working on. You can keep virtually anything inside a Tool Palette.
- **Tool Palette** works with the same drag-and-drop method we used with the **Design Center**, but in **Tool Palette** the method will occur in two ways: *from* **Tool Palette** and *to* **Tool Palette**.
- **Tool Palette** is unique to each computer. If you create (or customize) a Tool Palette, it will be available for all your drawings.
- On the **Ribbon**, go to the **View** tab. Using the **Palettes** panel, select the **Tool Palettes** button:

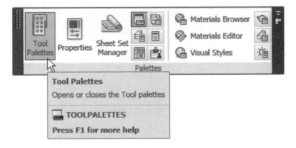

■   The following will appear on the screen:

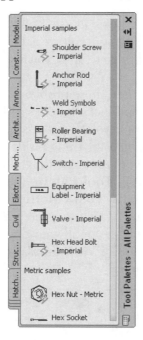

■   You will see several premade Tool Palettes created by Autodesk® for your immediate use.
■   You can create your own Tool Palette using different methods, depending on the source.
■   You can copy, cut, or paste tools inside each Tool Palette.
■   You can customize the tools inside each Tool Palette.

6.8 CREATING A TOOL PALETTE

■   Right-click over the name of any existing Tool Palette. The following shortcut menu will appear:

- Select the **New Palette** option, and a new Tool Palette will be added. Type in the name of the new Tool Palette:

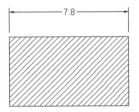

- A new empty Tool Palette will be added.
- To fill this Tool Palette, use the drag-and-drop method, either from the graphical screen or from the **Design Center**.

NOTE
- By default, the local blocks of the current drawing are *not* automatically available in your Tool Palettes.

Example

- Assume we are working with the following drawing. This drawing contains polylines, a hatch, and a linear dimension:

- Without issuing any command, click on the polyline, hold it (avoid the grips), and drag it into the empty Tool Palette. Do the same thing for the hatch and the linear dimension (avoiding grips). Your Tool Palette will look like the following:

Creating a Tool Palette Using the Design Center

- You can copy all the blocks in one drawing using the **Design Center** and then create a Tool Palette from them, retaining the name of the drawing.
- To do so, follow these steps:
  - Open the **Design Center**.
  - Go to the desired folder, then to the desired file.

• Right-click on the **Blocks** icon. The following shortcut menu will appear:

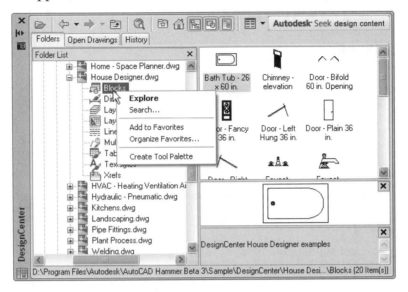

■ Select the **Create Tool Palette** option. A new Tool Palette will be added, retaining the name of the file you chose and containing all the blocks.

NOTE ▶ ■ You can also drag and drop any block from the **Design Center** to any desired Tool Palette.

6.9 CUSTOMIZING TOOL PALETTES

■ Blocks and hatches in a Tool Palette can be copied then pasted in the same Tool Palette or any other Tool Palette. This allows you to assign different properties to each tool.

■ For example, there is a block called **chair**. If you want to make three copies of it, each would hold a different rotation angle. The same thing applies to hatch patterns, as each copy can have a different scale factor.

■ Also, you can specify that a certain block (or hatch) go to a certain layer regardless of what the current layer is.

How to Copy and Paste a Tool

- Follow these steps:
  - Right-click on the desired tool, and a shortcut menu will appear. Shortcuts vary depending on the tool chosen. The shortcut shown here is for **Blocks**:

Redefine
Block Editor
Cut
Copy
Delete
Rename
Update tool image
Specify image...
Properties...

  - Select the **Copy** option.
  - In any Tool Palette, right-click to see the following shortcut:

✔ Allow Docking
🔍 Seek Design Content
Auto-hide
Transparency...
View Options...
Sort By   ▶
Paste
Add Text
Add Separator
New Palette
Delete Palette
Rename Palette
Customize Palettes...
Customize Commands...

  - Select the **Paste** option. The copied tool will reside at the bottom of the Tool Palette and will have the same name.

How to Customize a Tool

- To customize a tool, follow these steps:
  - Right-click on the copied tool. The following shortcut menu will appear:

  - Select the **Properties** option. The following dialog box will appear:

- You can change the **Name** and **Description** of the tool.
- There are two types of properties:
  - **Insert** properties, in which a block's properties are different from a hatch's properties.
  - **General** properties, such as color, layer, linetype, plot style, and lineweight.

- By default, the **General** properties are all **use current**, which means the current settings are applied.
- All **Insert** properties and **General** properties are customizable.

USING TOOL PALETTES

Exercise 6-4

1. Start AutoCAD 2011.
2. Open the file *Exercise 6-4.dwg*.
3. Make layer 0 current.
4. Open the **Design Center** and select **Sample/Design Center**. Open the file *Home Space Planner.dwg*.
5. Right-click the **Blocks** icon and select **Create Tool Palette**. A new Tool Palette named **Home Space Planner** will be added.
6. Select the file *House Designer.dwg*.
7. Show the blocks of this file.
8. Locate the **Bath Tub – 26 × 60 in** block, and drag and drop it into your newly made Tool Palette.
9. Repeat these steps with the **Sink – Oval Top** block.
10. Right-click on the name of the Tool Palette and select **Rename**. Change the name to **My Tools**.
11. In the **My Tools** Tool Palette, right-click on the tool named **Chair – Rocking** and select **Properties**. In the dialog box, change the **Layer** from **use current** to **Furniture**.
12. Right-click on the same tool again, and select **Copy**. Select an empty space and **Paste** it three times.
13. Using the same method as in step 11, change the rotation angle of these blocks to be 90, –90, and 180.
14. Now you have a Tool Palette that you can use in all of your drawings on this computer.
15. Save and close the file.

6.10 EDITING BLOCKS

- Assume that after you have created a block and inserted it several times in your drawing, you discover something wrong with it.
- To solve your problem, you need to redefine the original block using **Block Editor**.

- In the **Block Editor**, you can create a **Dynamic Block**. This is an advanced feature in AutoCAD, and we will use it (for now) only to edit blocks.
- On the **Ribbon**, go to the **Home** tab. Using the **Block** panel, select the **Edit** button:

- AutoCAD will show the following dialog box:

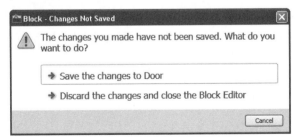

- Select the name of the block to be edited and click **OK**.
- The **Block Editor** will open with a different background color. A new tab will be added, titled **Block Editor**, and will have many new panels.
- You should not be intimidated by these changes. Simply ignore them and proceed with the changes to your block (adding, modifying, and erasing).
- Once you are done, click the **Close Block Editor** button at the right. The following message will appear:

- You have two choices: either save the changes to the block or simply discard these changes.

 - If you double-click on a block, it will start the same command.

CREATING A BLOCK (METRIC)

Workshop 3-M

1. Start AutoCAD 2011, and open the file *Workshop_03.dwg*.
2. Make the layer 0 current.
3. Choose an empty space and draw the following shape (without dimensions):

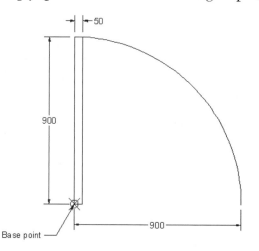

4. Using the **Block** panel, select the **Create** button. Create a block by entering the following information in the **Block Definition**:
   a. Block name = Door
   b. Specify the designated base point
   c. Delete the shape after creating the block
   d. Block unit = Millimeters
   e. Scale uniformly = off
   f. Allow exploding = on
   g. Description = Door to be used inside the building. Refer to the door table
   h. Open in block editor = off
5. Make the **Doors** layer current.

6. Using the **Insert** command, insert the **Door** block in the proper places as shown:

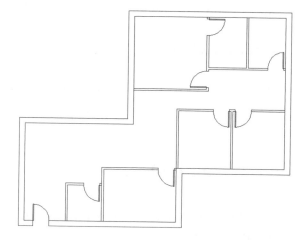

7. Make the **Furniture** layer current.

8. Select **Drawing Utilities/Units**, and make sure that **Units to scale inserted content** is **Millimeters**.

9. Open the **Design Center**, and select **Sample/Design Center**.

10. Using *Home Space Planner.dwg*, *House Designer.dwg*, and *Kitchens.dwg*, and with **OSNAP** off, drag and drop the following blocks as shown:

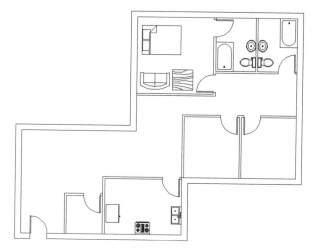

11. Start the **Edit** command in the **Block** panel.

12. Select one of the doors you inserted. Once the dialog box appears, click **OK**.

13. Select the arc representing the swing of the door. Right-click and select **Properties**.
14. Change its layer to be **Door_Swing**.
15. Change the Linetype scale = 200.
16. Close the **Properties** palette.
17. Save your changes.
18. You will see that the swing of all the doors is now a dashed linetype.
19. Save and close the file.

CREATING A BLOCK (IMPERIAL)

 Workshop 3-I

1. Start AutoCAD 2011, and open the file *Workshop_03.dwg*.
2. Make the layer 0 current.
3. Choose an empty space and draw the following shape (without dimensions):

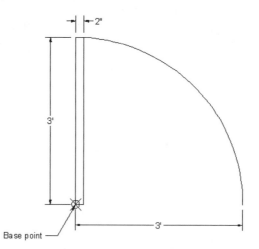

4. Using the **Block** panel, select the **Create** button. Create a block by entering the following information in the **Block Definition**:
   a. Block name = Door
   b. Specify the designated base point
   c. Delete the shape after the creation of the block
   d. Block unit = Inches
   e. Scale uniformly = off

  f. Allow exploding = on

  g. Description = Door to be used inside the building. Refer to the door table

  h. Open in block editor = off

5. Make the **Doors** layer current.

6. Using the **Insert** command, insert the **Door** block in the proper places as shown:

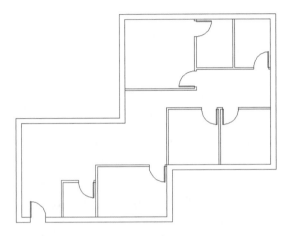

7. Make the **Furniture** layer current.

8. Select **Drawing Utilities/Units**, and make sure that **Units to scale inserted content** is **Inches**.

9. Open the **Design Center** and select **Sample/Design Center**.

10. Using *Home Space Planner.dwg*, *House Designer.dwg*, and *Kitchens.dwg*, and with **OSNAP** off, drag and drop the following blocks as shown:

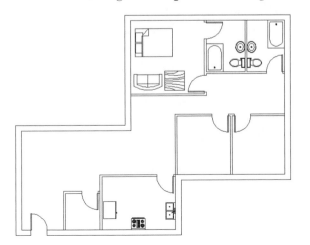

11. Start the **Edit** command in the **Block** panel.
12. Select one of the doors you inserted. Once the dialog box appears, click **OK**.
13. Select the arc representing the swing of the door. Right-click and select **Properties**.
14. Change its layer to be **Door_Swing**.
15. Change the Linetype scale = 10.
16. Close the **Properties** palette.
17. Save your changes.
18. You will see that the swing of all the doors is now a dashed linetype.
19. Save and close the file.

CHAPTER REVIEW

1. You should draw your original shape, which will be a block, in layer 0.
    a. True
    b. False
2. Which of the following statements is true regarding the **Automatic Scaling** feature in AutoCAD?
    a. It will change the scale of the block to fit in the current drawing.
    b. AutoCAD will ask for two scales to convert the block.
    c. Automatic scaling works for both blocks and hatches.
    d. None of the above.
3. Which of the following statements is true regarding Tool Palettes?
    a. They can be created from blocks coming from the **Design Center**.
    b. You can drag and drop objects both from and to a Tool Palette.
    c. You can customize the block inside a Tool Palette.
    d. All of the above.
4. Which of the following commands cannot be used for blocks?
    a. **Explode**
    b. **Insert**
    c. **Makelocalblock**
    d. **Block Editor**
5. To make the **Design Center** and **Tool Palettes** occupy less space in the **Graphical Area**, use _____.

CHAPTER REVIEW ANSWERS

1. a
2. a
3. d
4. c
5. Auto-hide

Chapter **7** **HATCHING**

In This Chapter
◇ Hatching in AutoCAD
◇ Using the **Hatch** command
◇ Hatching using Tool Palettes
◇ Using the **Gradient** command
◇ Editing hatching in AutoCAD

7.1 HATCHING IN AUTOCAD

- To hatch in AutoCAD, you must draw objects forming a closed area. Beginning with AutoCAD 2005, it became acceptable to hatch an area with a small opening.
- AutoCAD comes with several generic predefined hatch patterns saved in the files *acad.pat* and *acadiso.pat*. You can buy other hatch patterns from third parties, which can be found on the Internet.
- A hatch, like any other object, should be placed in a separate layer.
- There are two methods to hatch in AutoCAD: using the **Hatch** command and using **Tool Palette**.

7.2 SELECTING THE HATCH PATTERN

- Using the **Hatch** command is the old method of hatching in AutoCAD.

- On the **Ribbon**, go to the **Home** tab. Using the **Draw** panel, select the **Hatch** button:

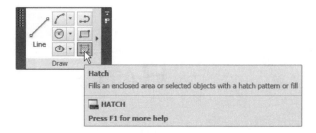

- Once the command starts, a new tab will be added called **Hatch Creation**.
- It has six panels:
  - Boundaries
  - Pattern
  - Properties
  - Origin
  - Options
  - Close
- By default, the hatch pattern in new drawings is **ANSI31**.
- Without clicking, hover over the desired areas. You will see a preview of the hatch. If you are satisfied, simply click inside the area. Once you are done, press [Enter].
- If you want another hatch pattern, go to the **Pattern** panel and select the desired pattern either by using the scroll arrows or by clicking the small button at the bottom of the scroll bar to show all available hatch patterns:

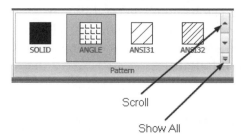

Scroll

Show All

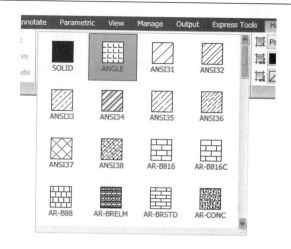

7.3 HATCH TYPES

- ■ There are four types of hatches in AutoCAD:
  - Solid
  - Gradient
  - Pattern
  - User defined

Solid

- ■ A solid hatch will fill a selected area with a single color. If you are in a layer, it will take the color of the layer, or you can set a desired color.
- ■ After you start the **Hatch** command, using the **Properties** panel, select **Solid**, as shown:

Gradient

- ■ A gradient hatch will fill an area with two colors of your choice, using a method which involves mixing these two colors (we will discuss this method later in more detail).

- After you start the **Hatch** command, using the **Properties** panel, select **Gradient**, as shown:

Pattern

- All the predefined patterns, which serve all types of engineering drawings, are found in the **Pattern** hatch.
- After you start the **Hatch** command, using the **Properties** panel, select **Pattern**, as shown:

User Defined

- The simplest hatch pattern has parallel lines.
- After you start the **Hatch** command, using the **Properties** panel, select **User defined**, as shown:

7.4 SELECTING THE AREA TO BE HATCHED

- By default, the **Pick Points** mode is selected. When you hover over the desired area, you will see a hatch preview.
- You can select more than one area with the same command, and you can control whether AutoCAD will consider the areas a single object or multiple objects.

- There are two ways to select the objects forming the area:
  - **Pick Points**
  - **Select**

Add Pick Points

- This method is very simple. Click inside the desired area, and AutoCAD will recognize the area automatically.
- This method will also detect any objects (called islands) within the outer area and automatically deselect them so they are not hatched.
- Islands can be any object type: circle, closed polyline, text, etc.
- Once you start the **Hatch** command, the following prompt will appear:

```
Pick internal point or [Select objects/seTtings]:
```

- Click inside the area(s) desired. Once you are done, press [Enter].

Add Select Objects

- This is the same method used to select any object, as previously discussed.
- After you start the **Hatch** command, using the **Boundaries** panel, click the **Select** button, as shown:

- The following prompt will appear:

```
Select objects or [picK internal point/seTtings]:
```

- Select the desired objects, which form a closed area. Once you are done, press [Enter].

- After you select using either method, and while you are still in the command, you will be able to **Remove Boundary Objects**:

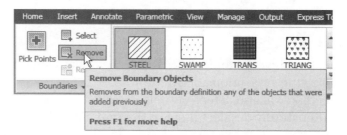

- You will see the following prompt:

```
Select boundary to remove:
```

- Click on any selected boundary. You will see that the hatch was removed from this boundary.

7.5 HATCHING: PROPERTIES

- While using the **Hatch** command, you can change the following properties:
  - Hatch Color
  - Background Color
  - Hatch Angle
  - Hatch Pattern Scale

Hatch Color

- **Hatch Color** allows you to specify a color for the hatch pattern (in particular, the fill color) other than the BYLAYER settings.
- Using the **Properties** panel, click **Hatch Color** and set the color:

Background Color

- **Background Color** allows you to specify a color for the background of the hatch.
- Using the **Properties** panel, click **Background Color** and set the color:

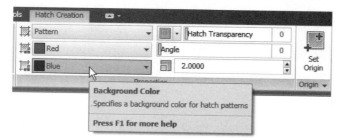

Hatch Angle

- **Hatch Angle** allows you to change the angle of the hatch lines from the default value.
- Using the **Properties** panel, click **Hatch Angle** and move the slider to change the angle, or type in the new value:

Hatch Pattern Scale

- **Hatch Pattern Scale** allows you to specify the scale for the selected pattern.

- Using the **Properties** panel, click **Hatch Pattern Scale** and type in the new value:

Special Properties for a User-Defined Hatch

- If you select your pattern to be **User Defined**, you will have the following variation:
  - **Hatch Pattern Scale** will become **Hatch Pattern Spacing**, which means you will specify the distance between two lines instead of an overall scale:

  - You can specify if the user-defined hatch uses parallel lines or crosshatch by expanding the **Properties** panel and selecting **Double**:

HATCHING USING THE HATCH COMMAND

Exercise 7-1

1.   Start AutoCAD 2011.
2.   Open the file *Exercise 7-1.dwg*.
3.   Make the **Hatch** layer current.
4.   Start the **Hatch** command.
5.   Select hatch pattern **ANSI32**.
6.   Click inside the desired area to see the hatch preview.
7.   Click all the areas except the two bolt holes.
8.   Change the hatch scale = 1.5.
9.   Change the angle = 90.
10. Change the background color to yellow.
11. Click **Close Hatch Creation** to end the command.
12. Start the **Hatch** command again, and select the solid pattern.
13. Change the hatch color to black.
14. Click inside the bolt holes.
15. Click **Close Hatch Creation** to end the command.
16. Save and close the file.

7.6 HATCHING: OPTIONS

- While you are hatching, there are some options in the **Hatch** command you should know in order to have full control over the hatching process.
- At the right side of the dialog box, check the **Options** panel:

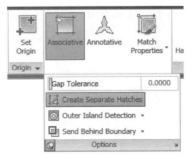

Associative

- Associative means there is a relationship between the hatch and the boundary. Whenever the boundary changes, the hatch automatically changes. It is recommended to keep this option on.
- To help illustrate the associative function, assume you have hatched the following shape. What happens when you move the circle?

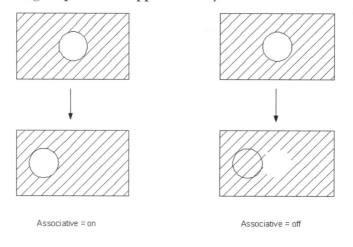

Associative = on   Associative = off

Annotative

- This is an advanced feature related to printing.

Match Properties

- This feature helps quickly hatch a new area using the exact features of an existing hatch.
- After clicking the **Match Properties** button, you will be presented with two choices: **Use current origin** and **Use source hatch origin**. (We will discuss origin shortly.)

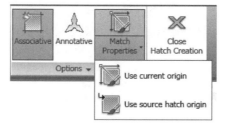

- Click the **Match Properties** button. The following prompt will appear:

```
Select hatch object:
```

- The mouse will change to a paintbrush:

- Click the source hatch pattern. The following prompt will happen:

```
Pick internal point or [Select objects/seTtings]:
```

- Click inside the desired area(s). Once you are done, press [Enter].

Gap Tolerance

- AutoCAD will hatch areas with small gaps. How small is up to the user.
- Using the **Gap Tolerance** adjuster, you can set the maximum gap that AutoCAD will ignore:

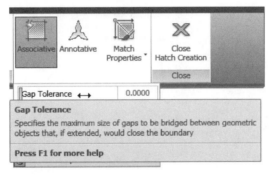

Create Separate Hatches

- By default, when you hatch several areas using the same command, all of the hatches will be considered one object. Hence, they will move together and will be erased together.
- By clicking on the **Create Separate Hatches** option, you can hatch several areas using the same command. Each hatch will still be considered a separate object.

Outer Islands Detection

- Islands in AutoCAD are the inner objects inside the outer boundary of an area to be hatched.
- Click **Outer Island Detection** to see a drop-down list with four choices:
  - **Normal Island Detection**: When there are three objects or more nested inside each other, AutoCAD will hatch the outer object, leave the second, hatch the third, etc.

- **Outer Island Detection**: When there are three or more objects nested inside each other, AutoCAD will hatch the outer only and leave the inner objects intact.
- **Ignore Island Detection**: When there are three or more objects nested inside each other, AutoCAD will ignore all the inner objects, thus hatching the outer area fully.
- **No Islands Detection**: AutoCAD will not recognize the inner objects.

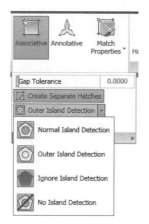

Draw Order

- If hatched areas intersect with other hatched areas (specifically those hatched with **Solid** hatching), you must set the **Draw** order while you are inserting the hatch to ensure the right appearance of each area.
- The five cases are:
  - **Don't assign** (which applies the default)
  - **Send to back**
  - **Bring to front** (see the following):

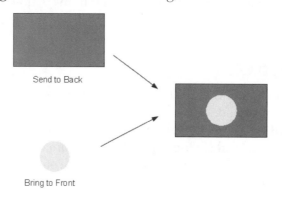

- **Send behind boundary**
- **Bring in front of boundary** (see the following):

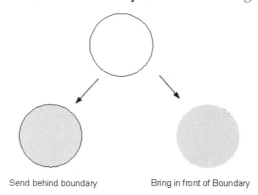

Send behind boundary   Bring in front of Boundary

7.7 HATCH ORIGIN

- By default, AutoCAD uses 0,0 as the starting point for any hatch. Therefore, if you want to hatch using a brick-like hatch and you need it to start from a point in the area you want to hatch, you must use the settings in this part of the dialog box.
- Using the **Origin** panel, specify your desired action:

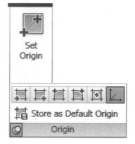

- You can click the **Set origin** button and set the desired point on the boundary, or you can use the predefined points available: bottom left point, bottom right point, top left point, top right point, or center of the area.

- See the following example:

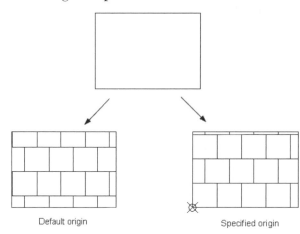

Default origin   Specified origin

HATCH OPTIONS AND ORIGIN

Exercise 7-2
1. Start AutoCAD 2011.
2. Open the file *Exercise 7-2.dwg*.
3. Make the **Hatch** layer current.
4. Start the **Hatch** command.
5. Pick the steel hatch pattern.
6. Click inside all the areas except the two holes.
7. Go to the **Options** panel and turn off **Create Separate Hatches**.
8. Select **Normal Island Detection**. What areas are recognized?
9. Select **Outer**, then **Ignore**, noting the difference between the three cases.
10. Finally, select **Outer**.
11. Press [Enter] to end the command.
12. Thaw the **Objects** layer.
13. Start the **Hatch** command. Using the angle hatch pattern, click inside the shape.
14. Using the **Origin** panel, select the five different origins, noting the differences between them.

15. Make sure **Associative** is on.
16. Press [Enter] to end the command.
17. Move the big circle to the right by 0.5. What happened? Why?
18. Hover over the first hatch. Is it one object or multiple objects? Why?
19. Save and close the file.

7.8 ADVANCED FEATURES

- There are some useful advanced features in the **Hatch** command, including **Boundary retention** and **Boundary set**.

Boundary Retention

- By default, AutoCAD creates a polyline around the detected area. Once the **Hatch** command is finished, AutoCAD will delete this polyline.
- Using the **Boundaries** panel, you can indicate whether to keep this temporary object. You have three choices:
  - **Don't Retain Boundaries**
  - **Retain Boundaries—Polyline**
  - **Retain Boundaries—Region**

Boundary Set

- When you use the **Pick Points** option to define the boundary to be hatched, AutoCAD will by default analyze all the objects in the **Current Viewport**.
- This may take a long time depending on the complexity of the drawing. To minimize the time, you can provide a selection set for AutoCAD to use when analyzing the boundary.

■ Using the **Boundary** panel, click **Boundary Set**:

● By default, the selected option is **Current Viewport**.
● Click the small button at the left. The following prompt will appear:

```
Select objects:
```

● Select the desired objects and press [Enter], or right-click. This time the selected option will be **Use Boundary Set**, as follows:

● Now when you ask AutoCAD to select a boundary by clicking inside it, AutoCAD will not analyze all objects in the current viewport; rather, it will analyze only the objects you selected.

7.9 HATCHING USING TOOL PALETTES

■ In Chapter 6, we discussed Tool Palettes, which include both blocks and hatches.
■ The main feature of Tool Palettes is the drag-and-drop feature. We will use this feature to speed up the process of hatching.
■ Perform the following steps:
  ● Create a new Tool Palette and name it (for example, "My Hatches").
  ● Use the **Hatch** command to add hatches to your different drawings.

- While hatching, you are changing the hatch settings.
- If you think you may reuse a hatch (with all of its settings) in other drawings, simply drag and drop it into your newly created Tool Palette.
- You can make several copies of your hatch and customize the different settings of each hatch. Right-click on any hatch in your Tool Palette and select **Properties**. The following dialog box will appear:

- After several drawings, you will have a big library of hatches that you can use in your drawings.
- Now, use the drag-and-drop feature to move hatches from your Tool Palettes to your drawing.

NOTE ■ By default, there will be a Tool Palette (called **Hatches and Fills**) that you can use if you do not want to create your own.

7.10 THE GRADIENT COMMAND

- Use the **Gradient** command if you want to shade a 2D area with two colors.
- This command uses the same method as the **Hatch** command, so the steps will not be reiterated here.

- On the **Ribbon**, go to the **Home** tab. Expand the **Draw** panel and select the **Gradient** button:

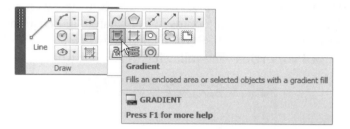

- A new tab will be added showing nine different patterns:

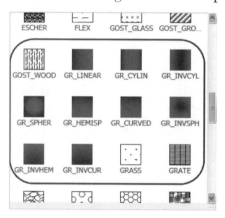

- Select the desired pattern, then select the two colors desired using the **Properties** panel:

- You can also control the angle of the color gradation. See the following illustration:

Angle = 0   Angle = 90

USING THE GRADIENT COMMAND

Exercise 7-3
1. Start AutoCAD 2011.
2. Open the file *Exercise 7-3.dwg*.
3. Start the **Gradient** command.
4. Select the first color to be 142 and the second to be 61.
5. Choose the GR_CYLIN pattern.
6. Click inside the area to preview the gradient hatch.
7. Save and close the file.

7.11 EDITING AN EXISTING HATCH OR GRADIENT

- Ways to edit a hatch or gradient include:
  - Single-clicking (**Grips**)
  - **Quick Properties**
  - **Properties**
  - Double-clicking

Single-Clicking (Grips)

- When you single-click any hatch, the following will happen:
  - A single grip appears (a filled circle at the center of the area).
  - A new tab appears named **Hatch Editor**. It is identical to the **Hatch Creation** tab and allows you to change settings.
  - The **Quick Properties** window appears.
- To modify an object, simply use the new tab and its panels.
- The grip at the center of the area will enable you to make extra modifications. Hover over the grip to see the options, as shown:

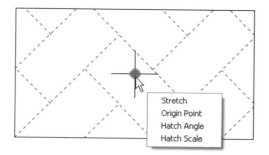

■ You can do any or all of the following:
  • Stretch the hatch pattern (it is actually moving, not stretching)
  • Change the origin point dynamically
  • Change the hatch angle dynamically
  • Change the hatch scale dynamically

Quick Properties

■ Whenever you click a hatch, the **Quick Properties** window will appear. It allows you to edit only the most important properties:

Hatch	
Color	■ ByLayer
Layer	0
Type	Predefined
Pattern name	AR-HBONE
Annotative	No
Angle	0
Scale	0.5000
Associative	Yes
Background color	☑ None

■ As you can see, you can modify the following:
  • Color
  • Layer
  • Type
  • Pattern name
  • Annotative (or not)
  • Angle
  • Scale
  • Associative (or not)
  • Background color

Properties

■ If you double-click the desired hatch (or select the hatch), right-click, then select **Properties** from the shortcut menu, the following **Properties** palette will appear:

Hatch			
General			▲
Color	■ ByLayer		
Layer	0		
Linetype	—————— ByLayer		
Linetype scale	1.0000		
Plot style	ByColor		
Lineweight	—————— ByLayer		
Transparency	ByLayer		
Hyperlink			
Pattern			▲
Type	Predefined		
Pattern name	AR-HBONE		
Annotative	No		
Angle	0		
Scale	0.5000		
Origin X	-19.4687		
Origin Y	6.2184		
Spacing	0.5000		
ISO pen width	0.50 mm		
Double	No		
Associative	Yes		
Island detection style	Outer		
Background color	☑ None		
Geometry			▲
Elevation	0.0000		
Area	52.1837		
Cumulative Area	52.1837		

- In the **Properties** palette, you can edit all the data related to the selected hatch. Some of the settings will be applicable to user-defined hatch patterns, such as **Spacing** and **Double**.
- Note that at the bottom of the **Properties** palette you will find two fields, **Area** and **Cumulative Area**.
- **Area** is the area of a single hatch area selected.
- **Cumulative Area** is for all the areas selected.

Recreate Boundary

- If you hatch an area and for some reason the boundary is lost and the hatch is kept, this option allows you to recreate the boundary of an existing hatch.

- Click the hatch without the boundary. The **Hatch Editor** tab will appear. From the **Boundaries** panel, click the **Recreate** button:

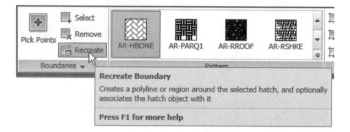

- The following prompt will appear:

```
Enter type of boundary object [Region/Polyline] <Polyline>:
```

- Type **P** for polyline or **R** for region. The following prompt will appear:

```
Associate hatch with new boundary? [Yes/No] <Y>:
```

- Type **Y** for yes or **N** for no.
- The command will end automatically by creating a new boundary.

HATCHING USING THE HATCH COMMAND (METRIC)

Workshop 4-M

1. Start AutoCAD 2011, and open the file *Workshop_04.dwg*.
2. Make the **Hatch** layer current.
3. Start the **Hatch** command and select the type to be **Pattern**.
4. Select the **AR-CONC** pattern.
5. Set the scale = 100.
6. Click inside the area representing the outer wall. Press [Enter] to end the command.
7. Start the **Hatch** command and select the type to be **Pattern**.
8. Select the **ANSI32** pattern.
9. Set the scale = 500.
10. Click inside the area representing the inner walls. When done, press [Enter].
11. Zoom to the kitchen at the lower right of the plan.
12. Start the **Hatch** command and select the type to be **Pattern**.
13. Select the **ANGLE** pattern.

14. Set the scale = 1000. Make sure **Associative** is on.

15. Zoom to the kitchen and click inside the area.

16. Using the **Origin** panel, click the four buttons representing the bottom left and right and the top left and right. We will choose the lower left button. When done, press [Enter].

17. Move the oven to the right. What happens to the hatch? Does it react correctly?

18. Start **Tool Palettes**. Create a new Tool Palette, and name it "My Hatches."

19. Drag and drop the three hatches we used in our file, which are **AR-CONC**, **ANSI32**, and **ANGLE**.

20. In the new Tool Palette, select any of the three hatches and right-click. Select **Properties**, making sure that the layer is always **Hatch**, not **Use current**.

21. Click the **AR-CONC** hatch. Using the **Hatch Editor** tab, change the scale of the hatch to be 75. Press [Enter] to end the command.

22. Click the **ANGLE** hatch and hover over the only grip. Using **Hatch Angle**, change the angle to be 45 (type the command or use **Polar Tracking**).

23. What is the area of the outer wall?

24. Save and close the file.

HATCHING USING THE HATCH COMMAND (IMPERIAL)

Workshop 4-I

1. Start AutoCAD 2011, and open the file *Workshop_04.dwg*.

2. Make the **Hatch** layer current.

3. Start the **Hatch** command and select the type to be **Pattern**.

4. Select the **AR-CONC** pattern.

5. Set the scale = 5.

6. Click inside the area representing the outer wall. Press [Enter] to end the command.

7. Start the **Hatch** command and select the type to be **Pattern**.

8. Select the **ANSI32** pattern.

9. Set the scale = 20.

10. Click inside the area representing the inner walls. When done, press [Enter].

11. Zoom to the kitchen at the lower right of the plan.

12. Start the **Hatch** command and select the type to be **Pattern**.

13. Select the **ANGLE** pattern.

14. Set the scale = 50. Make sure that **Associative** is on.

15. Zoom to the kitchen and click inside the area.

16. Using the **Origin** panel, click the four buttons representing the bottom left and right and the top left and right. We will choose the lower left button. When done, press [Enter].

17. Move the oven to the right. What happens to the hatch? Does it react correctly?

18. Start **Tool Palettes**. Create a new Tool Palette, and name it "My Hatches."

19. Drag and drop the three hatches we used in our file, which are **AR-CONC**, **ANSI32**, and **ANGLE**.

20. In the new Tool Palette, select any of the three hatches and right-click. Select **Properties**, making sure that the layer is always **Hatch**, not **Use current**.

21. Click the **AR-CONC** hatch. Using the **Hatch Editor** tab, change the scale of the hatch to be **2.5**. Press [Enter] to end the command.

22. Click the **ANGLE** hatch and hover over the only grip. Using **Hatch Angle**, change the angle to be 45 (type the command or use **Polar Tracking**).

23. What is the area of the outer wall?

24. Save and close the file.

CHAPTER REVIEW

1. The origin of a hatch area is defined by AutoCAD, and you cannot change it.
    a. True
    b. False

2. You can create a boundary for an existing hatch using the _____ button.

3. When you click a hatch, the multigrip will appear.
    a. True
    b. False

4. Which of these statements is *not* true about hatching in AutoCAD?
    a. You can set the **Draw** order of the hatch.
    b. You can use the **Hatch** command and the drag-and-drop method.
    c. You can only hatch closed areas.
    d. You can use hatch or gradient colors.

5. Which of the following tasks cannot be done using the **Hatch** command?
   a. Separate hatches using the same command.
   b. Hatch areas with gaps.
   c. Set the scale of the hatch pattern.
   d. Hatch with a three-color gradient.

6. If you want the hatch to react to any change in the boundary, click the _____ button in the **Options** panel.

CHAPTER REVIEW ANSWERS

1. b
2. **Recreate Boundary**
3. b
4. c
5. d
6. **Associative**

Chapter **8** **TEXT AND TABLES**

In This Chapter
◇ Creating a text style
◇ **Single Line Text** Command
◇ **Multiline Text** Command
◇ Editing text (using **Quick Properties** and **Properties, Spell Check, Find** and **Replace,** and **Grips**)
◇ Creating a table style
◇ The **Table** Command

8.1 INTRODUCTION

- To write text in AutoCAD, you must first create your own text style.
- In **Text Style**, you will specify the characteristics of your text, which will apply to all the text you input in your drawing file.
- You should have several text styles in your drawing to cover all the requirements (big fonts for titles, small fonts for remarks, a special text style for dimensions, etc.).
- Text styles can be shared between files using the **Design Center**.
- After you create your text style, you can use two commands to write text in your drawing:
  - **Single Line Text** (old method)
  - **Multiline Text** (new method)
- When you are finished writing, you can edit and spell check the text.
- To create tables with text, you must create a **Table Style**.
- Then you can insert tables and write text inside them.
- Table styles can be shared between files using the **Design Center**.

8.2 TEXT STYLE

- The first step in writing text in AutoCAD is to create a text style.
- **Text Style** is where you define the characteristics of your text.
- On the **Ribbon**, go to the **Annotate** tab. Using the **Text** panel, click the small arrow in the lower right-hand corner, then click the **Text Style** button:

- The following dialog box will appear:

- As you can see, AutoCAD comes with a default text style called **Standard**.
- This style contains the default settings of the text style.
- This style is very simple, so you should consider creating your own.
- To create a new text style, click the **New** button. The following dialog box will appear:

- Type in the name of the new text style using the naming convention you used with the layers.
- When done, click **OK**.

Font Name

- First, select the desired font.
- There are two types of fonts you can use in AutoCAD:
  - Shape files (*.*shx*), which are the old type of fonts.
  - True type fonts (*.*ttf*), which are the new type of fonts.
- The following illustration shows the difference between the two types:

True Type Font   Shape File

Font Style

- If you select a true type font, you will be able to select the font style from the following choices:
  - Regular
  - Bold
  - Bold and italic
  - Italic
- See the following illustration:

Regular   Bold   Bold/Italic   Italic

Annotative

- This is an advanced feature. We will leave it off for now.

Height

- The next step is to specify the height of the text. See the following illustration:

- As you can see, the height mentioned in the dialog box is for capital letters.
- There are two methods for specifying the height of text:
  - Leave the value equal to 0 (zero), which means you must specify the height each time you use this style.
  - Specify a height value that will always be used after you have created this style.

Effects

- There are five effects you can add to your text:
  - **Upside down**:

Regular   Upside down

  - **Backwards**:

Regular   Backwards

  - **Width Factor**:

Regular   Width Factor = 1.50   Width Factor = 0.75

- **Oblique Angle**:

Bag — Regular
Bag — Oblique Angle = +15
Bag — Oblique Angle = -15

- **Vertical**, which is only applicable for **.shx* fonts. It will write the text from top to bottom (good for any **.shx* Chinese fonts).
- When you are done, click the **Apply** button, then the **Close** button.

- At the left part of dialog box, there is a popup list showing **All styles**. Using this list you can show all defined text styles (whether used or not), or only the text styles that are used in this drawing.

CREATING A TEXT STYLE

Exercise 8-1
1. Start AutoCAD 2011.
2. Open the file *Exercise 8-1.dwg*.
3. Create the following text style:
   a. Name = Drawing Info
   b. Font = Arial
   c. Font Style = Italic
   d. Height = 0
4. Create the following text style:
   a. Name = Notes
   b. Font = Garamond
   c. Font Style = Regular
   d. Height = 5
5. Save and close the file.

8.3 SINGLE LINE TEXT COMMAND

- **Single Line Text** is the first of two commands you can use to write text in AutoCAD.
- Although you write several lines of text in each command, each line is considered a separate object.

- On the **Ribbon**, go to the **Annotate** tab. Using the **Text** panel, select the **Single Line Text** button:

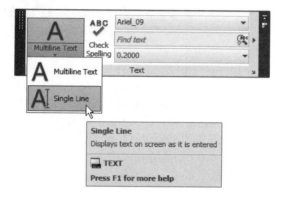

- The following prompt will appear:

```
Current text style:   "arial_09"   Text height:   0.9000
Annotative No
Specify start point of text or [Justify/Style]: (Specify the
start point of the baseline.)
Specify rotation angle of text <0>: (Specify the rotation
angle of the baseline, then press [Enter] and start writing.)
```

- You will see the text on the screen. Press [Enter] once each time you want to start a new line, and press [Enter] twice to end the command.
- As noted earlier, AutoCAD will use the current text style to write the desired text. In the **Text** panel, you will see something like the following:

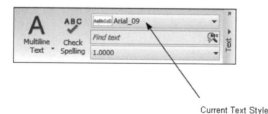

Current Text Style

8.4 MULTILINE TEXT COMMAND

- The **Multiline Text** command simulates Microsoft Word® simplicity in creating text, so it is easier for users who have experience using Word.
- All the text you write in a single command is considered a single object.

- On the **Ribbon**, go to the **Annotate** tab. Using the **Text** panel, select the **Multiline Text** button:

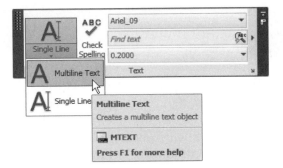

- The following prompt will appear:

```
Current text style:  "arial_09"  Text height:  0.9000
Annotative  No
Specify first corner: (Specify the first corner.)
Specify opposite corner or [Height/Justify/Line spacing/
Rotation/Style/Width]: (Specify the opposite corner.)
```

- At the first prompt, the cursor will change to a crosshair:

- After you specify the first point, you will get something like the following:

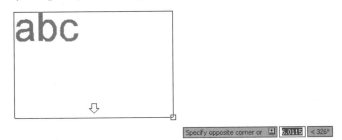

- Select two opposite corners to specify the area in which you will write.
- After you specify the two corners, a text editor with a ruler will appear:

■ AutoCAD will automatically show a new tab called **Text Editor** (which will disappear when you are done with this command):

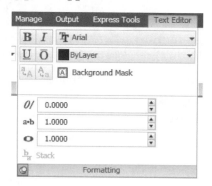

■ A blinking cursor will appear in the text editor so you can type your text. Using the **Text Editor** tab, you can format the text as you wish.

■ If you created a text style (highly recommended), then at the left part of the tab you will see the name and height of the current text style.

■ To format any text, you should select it first just like you do in MS Word.

Formatting Panel

■ The **Formatting** panel appears as follows:

■ Use the **Formatting** panel to change all or any of the following:
   • Change the text to **Bold**.
   • Change the text to **Italic**.
   • Change the text to **Underlined**.
   • Change the text to **Overlined**.
   • Change the font (it is recommended to keep the font specified by the current text style).
   • Change the color of the text (it is recommended to keep the color of the current layer).
   • Convert an uppercase letter to a lowercase letter, and vice versa.

- Specify the **Background Mask** (the background color). You will see the following dialog box:

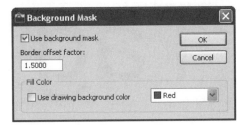

- Specify the **Oblique Angle**.
- Specify the **Tracking** to increase or decrease the spaces between letters. Values greater than 1 mean more space between letters, and values less than 1 mean less space.
- Specify the **Width Factor**.

Paragraph Panel

- The **Paragraph** panel is as follows:

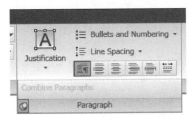

- Use the **Paragraph** panel to change any or all of the following: **Justification**, **Bullets and Numbering**, and **Line Spacing**.
  - Change the **Justification** to one of the nine options listed in the following illustration:

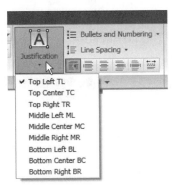

- To understand **Justification**, see the following illustration:

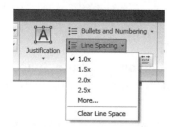

- You can use **Bullets and Numbering** and choose between letters (lowercase or uppercase), numbers, and bullets:

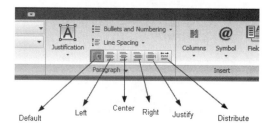

- You can set the **Line Spacing** of the paragraph. You have the choice of 1.0×, 1.5×, 2.0×, 2.5×, or you can set your own:

- You can change the justification of the paragraph by using the six buttons illustrated here:

Insert Panel

■ The **Insert** panel is as follows:

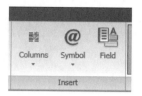

• You can use **Columns** to create two columns or more of your text. If you click the **Columns** button, the following menu will appear:

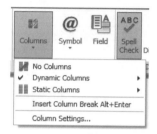

• You can select **Dynamic Columns** to specify **Auto height** or **Manual height**:

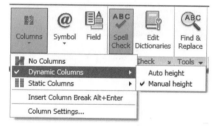

• You can select **Static Columns** to specify the desired number of columns:

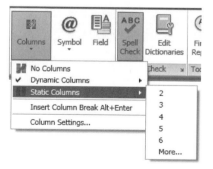

- Click **Insert Column Break [Alt] + [Enter]** to insert a column break at a certain line.
- Click **Column Settings** and you will see the following dialog box:

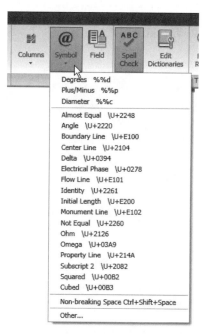

- You can add symbols to your text. If you click the **Symbol** button, the following menu will appear, allowing you to add one of 20 available symbols:

Spell Check Panel

- The **Spell Check** panel is as follows:

- By default, the **Spell Check** button is on. While you are typing, a dotted red line will appear under misspelled words, as shown:

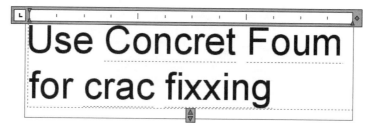

- Go to the misspelled word and right-click. Suggestions for the correct spelling will appear at the top of the shortcut menu. If you need more suggestions, you can view them as follows:

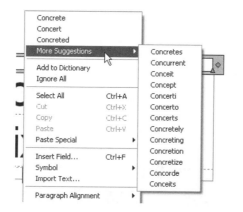

- To use other dictionaries, click the **Edit Dictionaries** button. You will see the following dialog box:

Tools Panel

- The **Tools** panel is as follows:

- In the Tools panel, you can **Find and Replace** text, **Import Text**, and apply **AutoCAPS**:
  - Click the **Find and Replace** button to see the following dialog box:

- You can replace one or all occurrences of a specified term.
- The **Import Text** function allows you to import text already stored as a text file. Click on the **Import Text** button to see the following dialog box:

- Select the desired drive and folder, then select the desired *.txt* file. Once you click **Open**, you will see the text in the editor available for formatting.
- Use the **AutoCAPS** function to write in uppercase letters (just like using **Caps Lock** on the keyboard).

Options Panel

- The **Options** panel is as follows:

- Using the **Options** panel, you can do all or any of the following:
  - Undo any mistake you make while typing or redo any command.
  - Show or hide the ruler.

- Or show more options, as shown:

Character Set

- To choose a different character set, select from the sub-menu:

Remove Formatting

- To make **Remove Formatting** active, first select the text. AutoCAD enables you to remove the formatting on the selected text:

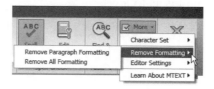

Editor Settings

- To control the **Editor Settings**, choose it from the sub-menu:

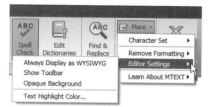

Close Panel

- The **Close** panel allows you to close the **Text Editor** tab:

Set Indents

- Setting indents in the **Text Editor** is identical to the process in MS Word. See the following illustration:

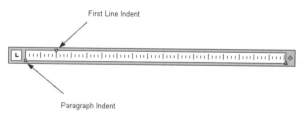

- Move the **First Line Indent** to specify where the first line will start.
- Move the **Paragraph Indent** to specify where the next line will start.
- You can also set **Tabs** in your text by clicking anywhere on the ruler.

Right-Click While You Are in the Text Editor

- While you are in the **Text Editor**, you will see the following menu when you right-click:

```
Select All            Ctrl+A
Cut                   Ctrl+X
Copy                  Ctrl+C
Paste                 Ctrl+V
Paste Special              ▶

Insert Field...       Ctrl+F
Symbol                     ▶
Import Text...

Paragraph Alignment        ▶
Paragraph...
Bullets and Lists          ▶

Columns                    ▶

Find and Replace...   Ctrl+R
Change Case                ▶
AutoCAPS
Character Set              ▶

Combine Paragraphs
Remove Formatting          ▶
Background Mask...

Editor Settings            ▶
Help                  F1

Cancel
```

- This menu includes all the functions in the **Text Editor** tab, so you can use whichever method you find more suitable.

Increasing the Height and Width of the Writing Area

- When you started the **Multiline** command, you specified two opposite corners to indicate the area in which you wanted to write.
- You can change the width and height of the writing area using the controls shown in the following illustrations:

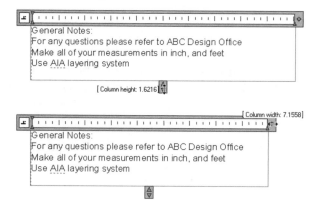

WRITING USING SINGLE LINE TEXT AND MULTILINE TEXT

Exercise 8-2

1. Start AutoCAD 2011.
2. Open the file *Exercise 8-2.dwg*.
3. Make the **Drawing Info** text style current.
4. Make the **Text** layer current.
5. Switch off **OSNAP**.
6. Type the following using **Single Line Text**. Input the following using Height = 2.5 and Height = 5:

Itemref	Quantity	Title/Name, designation, material, dimension etc		Article No./Reference	
Designed by George	Checked by Jimmy	Approved by – date	Filename	Date	Scale
ABC Investment		Architectural Plan			
		No. ABC-01-0099		Edition	Sheet
14		15		16	

7. Make the **Notes** text style current.
8. Zoom out until you see the whole frame.
9. Zoom to the rectangle at the top right.
10. Start the **Multiline Text** command, and specify the two edges of the rectangle as your text area.
11. Import the *General Notes.txt* file.
12. Select the text starting with "If you have any architectural" and ending with "detailing."
13. Using **Bullets and Numbering**, select **Numbered** and move the **First line indent** one step to the left.
14. Select the text starting with "All architectural drawing" and ending with "ABC-03-NNN."
15. Using **Bullets and Numbering**, select **Bulleted** and move the **First line indent** one step to the left.
16. Select the text "General Notes:" and make it bold and underlined.
17. Correct the spelling of the word "guidelines."
18. Erase the rectangle.
19. Zoom to the rectangle at the lower left of the sheet.
20. Start the **Multiline Text** command, and specify the two edges of the rectangle as your text area.
21. Import the *General Notes.txt* file again.

22. If the ruler expands to the right, use the shape at the right of the ruler to shrink it to fit the area you want.

23. Do the same for the numbered and bulleted areas.

24. Using **Columns**, select **Static Columns** and specify three columns.

25. Go to the **Column Settings** dialog box and specify Column Width = 100 and specify Gutter Width = 10.

26. Change the column height so point 2 will end in column 1 and point 3 will start at column 2.

27. At the end of point 6, insert a column break.

28. In column 3, you will see point 7 was added. Delete it, and delete any empty lines.

29. Close the **Text Editor**.

30. Save and close the file.

8.5 EDITING TEXT USING QUICK PROPERTIES AND PROPERTIES

- To edit the *contents* of text, simply double-click the text.
- If you double-click multiline text, the editor will reappear with the **Multiline Text** tab, which can be used for adding or deleting text, or simply for reformatting.
- If you double-click single line text, the text will be available for adding and deleting.
- You can also select **Multiline Text**, right-click, and select **Mtext Edit**.

Single Line Text

- To edit the properties of single line text, simply click it. The **Quick Properties** window will appear:

Text	
Layer	0
Contents	AutoCAD 2011 Essentials
Style	Standard
Annotative	No
Justify	Left
Height	0.2000
Rotation	0

- You can change the **Layer, Contents, Style, Annotative** status, **justification, Height**, and **Rotation** angle.
- If you want to do more editing than this, select **Properties**, and you will see the following:

- You can change the **General** properties of the single line text (**Color, Layer, Linetype**, etc.).
- You can change the properties of the text (**Contents, Style, Justify, Height, Rotation**, etc.).
- You can change the **Geometry** of the text (**Position X, Y**, and **Z**).
- Finally, you can change the miscellaneous properties (**Misc**) of the single line text (**Upside down** and **Backward**).

Multiline Text

- To edit the properties of multiline text, simply click the text. The **Quick Properties** window will appear:

MText	
Layer	0
Contents	AutoCAD 2011 Essentials
Style	Standard
Annotative	No
Justify	Top left
Text height	0.2000
Rotation	0

- Your options are the same as for editing single line text.
- To have full editing power, you must start the **Properties** command. You will see the following:

MText	
General	
Color	ByLayer
Layer	0
Linetype	ByLayer
Linetype scale	1.0000
Plot style	ByColor
Lineweight	ByLayer
Transparency	ByLayer
Hyperlink	
3D Visualization	
Material	ByLayer
Text	
Contents	AutoCAD 2011 Essentials
Style	Standard
Annotative	No
Justify	Top left
Direction	By style
Text height	0.2000
Rotation	0
Line space factor	1.0000
Line space distance	0.3333
Line space style	At least
Background mask	No
Defined width	7.2362
Defined height	0.0000
Columns	Dynamic
Geometry	
Position X	15.1319
Position Y	7.7653
Position Z	0.0000

- You can change the **General** properties of the multiline text (**Color**, **Layer**, **Linetype**, etc.).

- You can change the properties of the text (**Contents, Style, Justify, Height, Rotation**, etc.).
- You can change the specific features of multiline text, such as **Line space factor, Line space distance, Line space style, Background mask, Defined width, Defined height**, and **Columns**.

NOTE ▶ - If you select both single line text and multiline text, you can change only the **General** properties.

- You can select either multiple single line text or multiple multiline text and change their properties in one step.

Text and Grips

- If you click on single line text, you will see the following:

Elevation

- The grip appears at the start point of the baseline.
- On the other hand, if you click on multiline text, you will see the following:

Elevations and Cross Sections will be modified together

- You will see a grip at the top left, which will allow you to move the multiline text.
- The arrow at the top right allows you to extend the horizontal dimension of the multiline text. If you stretch it to the right, it will increase; if you stretch it to the left, it will decrease:

Elevations and Cross Sections will be modified together

- The arrow at the bottom will place the text in multiple columns:

Elevations ▸   will be   ▸
and Cross   modified
Sections   together
▾

Check Spelling

- In this chapter, we have discussed how to **Spell Check** and **Find and Replace** inside the multiline text editor. But, what if we want to check existing single line or multiline text? We can use two tools: **Check Spelling** and **Find and Replace**.
- AutoCAD will spell check the entire drawing, the current space/layout, or selected text.
- On the **Ribbon**, go to the **Annotate** tab. Using the **Text** panel, click the **Check Spelling** button:

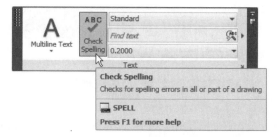

- The following dialog box will appear:

Check Spelling	
Where to check:	
Entire drawing	Start
Not in dictionary:	Add to Dictionary
	Ignore
Suggestions:	Ignore All
	Change
	Change All
Main dictionary:	
American English	Dictionaries...
Settings... Undo	Close Help

- This is identical to the MS Word spelling checker. If AutoCAD finds any misspellings, it will offer suggestions. You can select, alter, or ignore the suggestions.

Find and Replace

- AutoCAD can find any text and replace it in the entire drawing file.
- On the **Ribbon**, go to the **Annotate** tab. Using the **Text** panel, type the desired text in the ***Find text*** field:

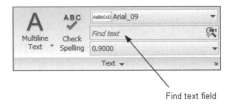

Find text field

- Type the word or phrase you are looking for in the edit box and click the key at the right. AutoCAD will locate the text and show the following dialog box:

- Under **Replace with**, type the new word(s) you want to appear in place of the word(s) given in **Find what**.
- You can search the entire drawing or a selection of text.
- You have three choices to select from: **Find, Replace**, and **Replace All**.
- When you are finished, click **Done**.

EDITING TEXT

Exercise 8-3

1. Start AutoCAD 2011.
2. Open the file *Exercise 8-3.dwg*.
3. Zoom to the text at the right side.

4. Select the text. Using **Quick Properties**, set Justify = Top Left, and change Height = 4. Press [Esc].

5. Select the text again. Using the arrow at the bottom, move it up to make the text two columns. Make sure all six points are in the first column.

6. Using the grip at the left, move the whole text inside the sheet.

7. Move the second column closer to the first column by dragging the arrow at the right to the left.

8. Double-click on the text and erase "Head of Design Department," then insert your initials.

9. Click outside the **Text Editor** to close it.

10. Using the **Annotate** tab on the **Ribbon**, go to the **Text** panel and click ***Find text***. Type **ABC**, then press [Enter].

11. In **Replace with**, type **Halabi**, then click **Replace All**.

12. Zoom to the lower right part and click **Halabi Investment**. Using **Quick Properties**, change Height = 4 and set Justify = Middle Center. Now the sentence has two grips.

13. Using the middle center grip, **OSNAP**, and **OTRACK**, move the sentence to the center of the rectangle.

14. Zoom to see the whole page.

15. Save and close the file.

8.6 TABLE STYLE

- As with text, to create a table in AutoCAD, you must perform the following two steps:
  - Create a table style.
  - **Insert** and **Fill** the table.
- In **Table Style**, you will define the main features of your table.
- On the **Ribbon**, go to the **Annotate** tab. Using the **Tables** panel, click the **Table Style** button:

- You will see the following dialog box:

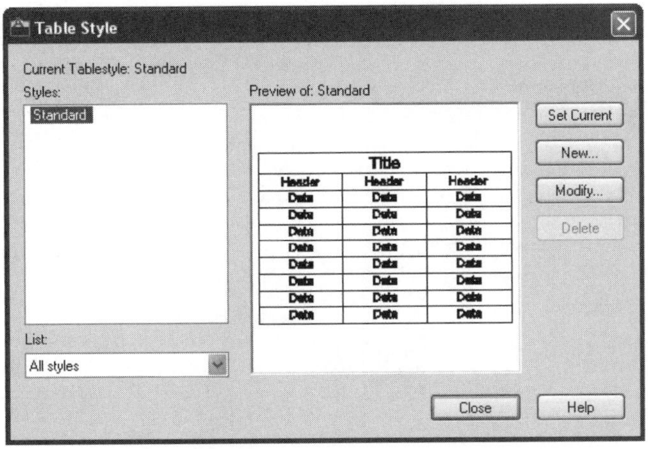

NOTE
- As you can see, there is a predefined style called **Standard**.
- There will always be a preview that shows you the changes you are making, so it is easy to see if you have made the right choice.
- To create a new table style, click the **New** button. You will see the following dialog box:

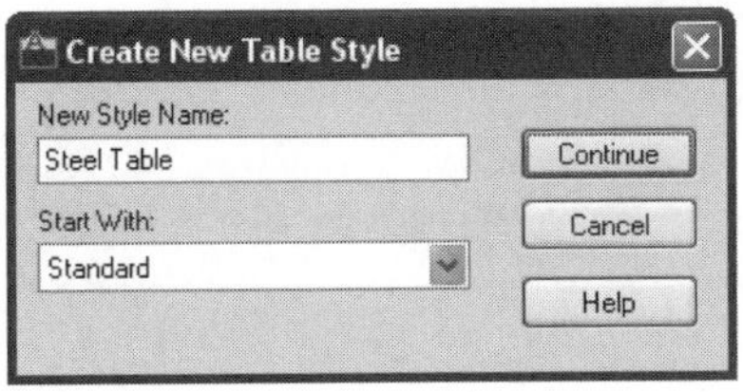

- Type in the name of your new style.
- Select the **Start With** style (you will start with a copy from this style).

■   Click the **Continue** button. The following dialog box will appear:

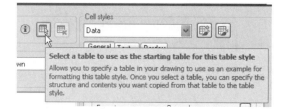

■   Under **Starting table**, you can select an existing table and copy its style instead of starting from scratch:

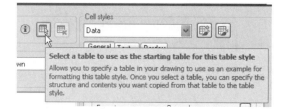

■   Under **General**, specify the **Table direction**:
   •   **Down** means the title and column headers are at the top of the table, and the cells will go below them.
   •   **Up** means the title and column headers are at the bottom of the table, and the cells will go above them.

■ Under **Cell styles**, you have three choices: **Data, Header**, and **Title**. This feature controls the table's three parts:

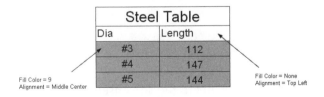

■ You can control the **General** properties, **Text** properties, and **Border** properties of these three parts.

General Tab

■ The **General** properties tab appears as follows:

■ You can control the following settings:
  • **Fill Color**: Specify whether the cells will have a colored background.
  • **Alignment**: Specify the justification of the text compared to the cell (you have nine choices). See the following example:

- **Format**: Specify the format of the numbers. Click on the small button with the three dots and you will see the following dialog box:

- Set the **Type** to be **Data** or **Label**.
- **Margins**: Specify the **Horizontal** and **Vertical** distances to be taken around the **Data** relative to the borders.

Text Tab

- The **Text** properties tab appears as follows:

- You can control the following settings:
    - **Text style**: This refers to the style used in the cells.
    - **Text height**: This is only applicable if the text style selected has a height = 0.
    - **Text color**: You should most likely leave it as **ByLayer** or **ByBlock**.
    - **Text angle**: This sets the oblique angle of the text.

Borders Tab

- The **Borders** properties tab appears as follows:

- You can control the following settings:
  - Specify the **Lineweight, Linetype**, and **Color** of the borders (either choose **ByBlock** or specify the desired value from the list).
  - Specify whether you want the border to be single line (the default setting) or double line. If you specify double line, you must also specify the spacing.
  - Set the type of border (inside, outside, etc.).
- Once you set all the variables, click **OK** to go back to the first dialog box and do any or all of the following:
  - Select the current style from many available styles. This style becomes the default, which you will see the next time you use the **Table** command.
  - Select one of the existing styles and make any type of modification. You will see the same dialog box that you see when you create a new style.

CREATING A TABLE STYLE

Exercise 8-4

1. Start AutoCAD 2011.
2. Open the file *Exercise 8-4.dwg*.
3. Start the **Table Style** command.
4. Create a new style and call it **Sheet Table**.
5. Under **Cell styles**, select **Title** and make the following changes:
   a. Text style = Table Title
   b. Remove all border lines

6. Select **Header** and make the following changes:
    a. Fill color = 9
    b. Alignment = Middle Center
    c. Text style = Table Header
7. Select **Data** and make the following changes:
    a. Alignment = Middle Center
    b. Text style = Table Data
8. Save and close the file.

8.7 THE TABLE COMMAND

- The **Table** command allows you to insert a table in an AutoCAD drawing using a predefined style.
- You will specify the number of columns and rows and fill the cells with the desired data.
- On the **Ribbon**, go to the **Annotate** tab. Using the **Tables** panel, click the **Table** button:

- The following dialog box will appear:

- Select the predefined **Table style** name.
- If you did not create a table style before this step, simply click the small button beside the list and create the desired table style:

- Specify the **Insert options**. You have three choices:
  - **Start from empty table**: Normally this option should be used.
  - **From a data link**: This option allows you to bring in data from spreadsheets such as those created in MS Excel®.
  - **From object data in the drawing (data extraction)**: Use this option only if you have block attributes.

- There are two insertion methods:
  - **Specify insertion point**
  - **Specify window**

Specify Insertion Point

- To use this method, the upper left-hand corner of the table, and set up the following:
  - Number of columns
  - Column width
  - Number of rows (not counting the title and column heads)
  - Row height (in lines)
- Click **OK** and AutoCAD will present the following prompt:

```
Specify insertion point:
```

- Specify the upper left-hand corner of the table, and the table will be ready for data to be filled in each row.
- You will first fill the title, then the column headers, and then the data. You can move between rows using [Tab] to go to the next cell and [Shift] + [Tab] to go back to the previous cell.

Specify Window

- If you use this method, you will be asked later to specify a window. You must specify a total height and a total width.
  - If you specify the number of columns, the column width will be calculated automatically (total width divided by the number of columns). If you instead specify the column width, the number of columns will be calculated automatically (total width divided by a single column width).
  - The same applies to rows. Either specify the number of rows, and the row height will be calculated automatically (total height divided by the number of rows), or specify the row height, and the number of rows will be calculated automatically (total height divided by a single row height).
- Click **OK** and AutoCAD will present the following prompt:

```
Specify first corner:
Specify second corner:
```

- Specify two opposite corners, and the table will be available for input, just like in the previous method.
- To edit a cell's content, simply double-click the cell.

THE TABLE COMMAND

Exercise 8-5
1. Start AutoCAD 2011.
2. Open the file *Exercise 8-5.dwg*.
3. Make the table style **Sheet Table** current.
4. Make the **Text** layer current.
5. Start the **Table** command. Using the following information, insert the table using the drawn rectangle at the center of the sheet:
   a. Specify window
   b. Columns = 3
   c. Row height = 3
6. Input the data as follows:

Sheet Table		
Sheet No.	Sheet Description	Remarks
ABC-01-NNNN	Architectural	Eng. George
ABC-02-NNNN	Structural	Eng. Gupta
ABC-03-NNNN	Mechanical/Electrical	Eng. Halabi

7. Save and close the file.

CREATING A TEXT STYLE (METRIC)

Workshop 5-M
1. Start AutoCAD 2011, and open the file *Workshop_05.dwg*.
2. Create a text style named **Title** with the following settings:
   a. Font = Arial
   b. Font Style = Bold
   c. Height = 900
   d. Width Factor = 2

3. Create a text style named **Inside_Annot** with the following settings:
   a. Font = Times New Roman
   b. Font Style = Regular
   c. Height = 300
   d. Width Factor = 1
4. Create a text style named **Dimension** with the following settings:
   a. Font = Arial
   b. Font Style = Regular
   c. Height = 400
   d. Width Factor = 1
5. Refer to the following plan when completing the next steps:

6. Make the **Text** layer current.
7. Using the **Single Line Text (DTEXT)** command and using the **Inside_ Annot** text style, type the words **Master Bedroom, Toilet, Living Room**.
8. Using the **Single Line Text (DTEXT)** command and using the **Title** text style, type the words **Ground Floor Plan**.
9. Switch off the **OSNAP** button.
10. Using the **Multiline Text** command, specify the area in the lower right part of the plan (as shown) and using the **Inside_Annot** text style, import the file named *Notes.txt*. Do not close the editor.
11. Select the word "three" and make it red, bold, and underlined. Close the editor.
12. Select the multiline text. The four grips will appear. Select one of the right grips to make it hot, and stretch it to the right so you will make the text one line shorter.

13. Double-click the multiline text, and make the following changes:

    a. Select the word "solely" and make it italic.

    b. Add a comma before the word "which."

    c. Press [Enter] after the last word to add a new line, and type your initials.

14. While you are in the editor, you can see three words with a dashed red line beneath them. Spell check these three words, and select the correct spelling.

15. Create a new table style based on **Standard** and call it **Door Schedule**.

    a. For **Title**, Text Style = Inside_Annot and Alignment = Middle Center.

    b. For **Data**, Text Style = Inside_Annot and Alignment = Middle Center.

    c. For **Header**, Text Style = Inside_Annot and Alignment = Middle Center.

    d. For **Cell** margins, Horizontal = 100 and Vertical = 100.

16. Make this table style current.

17. Make the **Text** layer current.

18. Looking at the following plan, and using the **Door Schedule** table style, add a table just like the one shown. Use the following:

    a. Specify the insertion point

    b. Columns = 5

    c. Column Width = 2000

    d. Data Rows = 4

    e. Row Height = 1 Line(s)

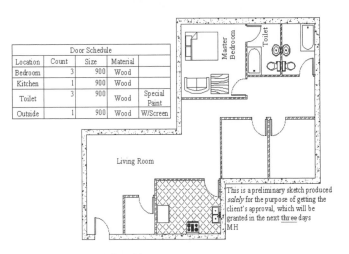

19. Save and close the file.

CREATING A TEXT STYLE (IMPERIAL)

Workshop 5-I

1. Start AutoCAD 2011, and open the file *Workshop_05.dwg*.
2. Create a text style named **Title** with the following settings:
   a. Font = Arial
   b. Font Style = Bold
   c. Height = 3'-0"
   d. Width Factor = 2
3. Create a text style named **Inside_Annot** with the following settings:
   a. Font = Times New Roman
   b. Font Style = Regular
   c. Height = 1'-0"
   d. Width Factor = 1
4. Create a text style named **Dimension** with the following settings:
   a. Font = Arial
   b. Font Style = Regular
   c. Height = 1'-4"
   d. Width Factor = 1
5. Refer to the following plan while completing the next steps:

6. Make the **Text** layer current.
7. Using the **Single Line Text (DTEXT)** command and using the **Inside_Annot** text style, type the words **Master Bedroom, Toilet, Living Room**.

8. Using the **Single Line Text** (**DTEXT**) command and using the **Title** text style, type the words **Ground Floor Plan**.

9. Switch off the **OSNAP** button.

10. Using the **Multiline Text** command, specify the area in the lower right part of the plan (as shown), and using the **Inside_Annot** text style, import the file named *Notes.txt*. Do not close the editor.

11. Select the word "three" and make it red, bold, and underlined. Close the editor.

12. Select the multiline text. The four grips will appear. Select one of the right grips to make it hot, and stretch it to the right so you will make the text one line shorter.

13. Double-click the multiline text, and make the following changes:

    a. Select the word "solely" and make it italic.

    b. Add a comma before the word "which."

    c. Press [Enter] after the last word to add a new line, and type your initials.

14. While you are in the editor, you can see three words with a dashed red line beneath them. Spell check these three words, and select the correct spelling.

15. Create a new table style based on **Standard** and call it **Door Schedule**.

    a. For **Title**, Text Style = Inside_Annot and Alignment = Middle Center.

    b. For **Data**, Text Style = Inside_Annot and Alignment = Middle Center.

    c. For **Header**, Text Style = Inside_Annot and Alignment = Middle Center.

    d. For **Cell margins**, Horizontal = 100 and Vertical = 100.

16. Make this table style current.

17. Make the **Text** layer current.

18. Looking at the following plan, and using the **Door Schedule** table style, add a table just like the one shown. Use the following:

    a. Specify the insertion point

    b. Columns = 5

    c. Column Width = 6'-8"

    d. Data Rows = 4

    e. Row Height = 1 Line(s)

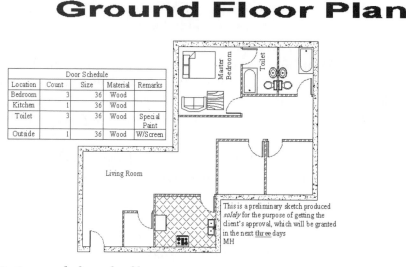

19. Save and close the file.

CHAPTER REVIEW

1. The height given in **Text Style** is for lowercase letters.
   a. True
   b. False

2. There are two types of fonts in AutoCAD: _____ and
   _____ .

3. There is no relation between **Text style** and **Table style**.
   a. True
   b. False

4. While using the **Multiline Text** command, you cannot:
   a. Import any *.txt* file.
   b. Format text.
   c. Change the indents.
   d. Bring in an MS Word document as OLE.

5. Which of the following is *not* true about tables?
   a. There are two methods to insert a table.
   b. You can control the cell style for **Title, Header**, and **Data**.
   c. You can convert multiline text to a table.
   d. You can define whether the table direction is **Down** or **Up**.

6. In **Table style**, Top Left and Middle are considered to be _____
   options.

CHAPTER REVIEW ANSWERS

1. b
2. **.shx* , **.ttf*
3. b
4. d
5. c
6. **Justification**

Chapter **9** **DIMENSIONING YOUR DRAWING**

In This Chapter

◊ Dimension types
◊ Creating dimension styles
◊ An introduction to dimensioning commands
◊ Dimension blocks and grips
◊ Multileader styles and commands

9.1 INTRODUCTION

- Dimensioning in AutoCAD is a semi-automatic process; users contribute part of the job and AutoCAD does the rest.
- Users in linear dimensioning, for example, specify three points. The first and the second are the length to be dimensioned; the third is the position of the dimension line.
- Accordingly, AutoCAD will automatically generate the **Dimension block**, as shown:

- A **Dimension block** consists of four parts:
  - Dimension line
  - Extension lines
  - Arrowheads
  - Dimension text

- See the following illustration:

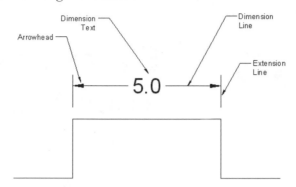

- The dimensioning process has two parts:
  - Creating dimension style(s)
  - Dimensioning your drawing
- The dimension style will control the appearance of the **Dimension block**. Each user will set up the style according to their needs.
- Creating a dimension style can be a lengthy and tedious job, but it will be done only once, and users can then focus on the other job—is dimensioning the drawing.

9.2 DIMENSION TYPES

- AutoCAD supports the following dimension types:
  - Linear and Aligned
  - Arc Length, Radius, and Diameter
  - Angular
  - Continuous
  - Baseline
  - Ordinate

Linear and Aligned

■   See the following illustration:

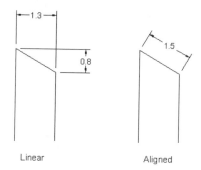

Linear   Aligned

Arc Length, Radius, and Diameter

■   See the following illustration:

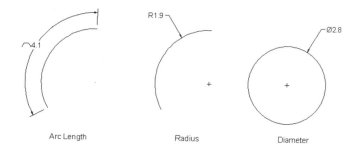

Arc Length   Radius   Diameter

Angular

■   See the following illustration:

Angular

Continuous

- See the following illustration:

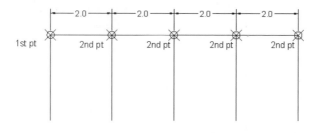

Baseline

- See the following illustration:

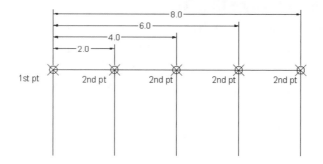

Ordinate

- See the following illustration:

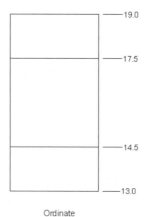

Ordinate

9.3 CREATING DIMENSION STYLES

- On the **Ribbon**, go to the **Annotate** tab. Using the **Dimensions** panel, click the **Dimension Style** button:

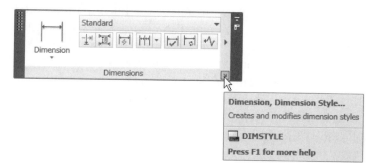

- The following dialog box will appear:

- By default, there will be a premade dimension style called **Standard**.
- You can modify this style or create your own (which is recommended).
- To create a new style, click the **New** button. The following dialog box will appear:

- Type in the new style name using the same naming convention you used when creating the layers.
- Select the **Start With** style (you will start with a copy of this style).
- Keep **Annotative** off for now.
- By default, the changes you make will be implemented for all types of dimensions. However, you can also create a new dimension style that will affect only a certain type of dimension.
- Click the **Continue** button and begin modifying the settings. We will cover each tab of the **Dimension Style** dialog box in the following pages.
- NOTE ► In this dialog box, whenever you find a **Color** setting leave it as is. It is better to control colors through layers and not through individual objects. This also applies for **Linetype** and **Lineweight**.

9.4 THE LINES TAB

- The first tab in the **Dimension Style** dialog box is **Lines**. This is where we control **Dimension lines** and **Extension lines**. When you click this tab, you will see the following:

- Under **Dimension lines**, you can control the following settings:
  - **Color**, **Linetype**, and **Lineweight** of the dimension line.

- **Extended beyond ticks**: To edit this value, go to the **Symbols and Arrows** tab and set the **Arrowhead** to be either **Architectural tick** or **Oblique**. See the following illustration:

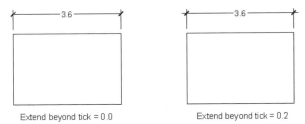

- **Baseline spacing**: See the following illustration:

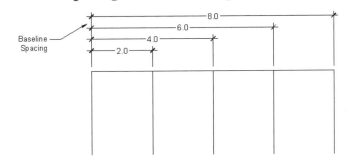

- Select to **Suppress Dim line 1** for one of them or **Dim line 2** for both:

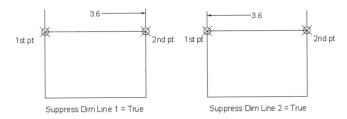

- Under **Extension lines**, control the following settings:
  - **Color**, **Linetype**, and **Lineweight** of the extension lines.
  - Select to **Suppress Ext line 1** for one of them or **Ext line 2** for both:

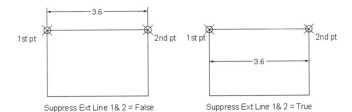

- Specify **Extend beyond dim lines** and **Offset from origin**:

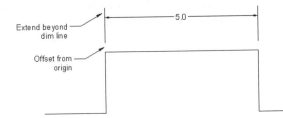

- To set **Fixed length extension lines**, you must specify the **Length**. See the following example:

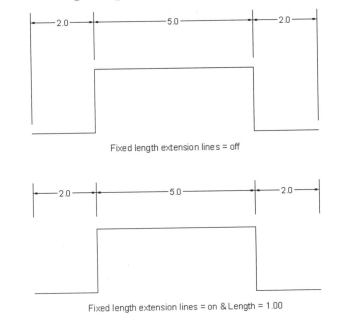

Fixed length extension lines = off

Fixed length extension lines = on & Length = 1.00

- NOTE ▪ The **Length** you specify will be calculated from the dimension origin up to the dimension line.

9.5 THE SYMBOLS AND ARROWS TAB

- When you click the **Symbols and Arrows** tab, you will see the following:

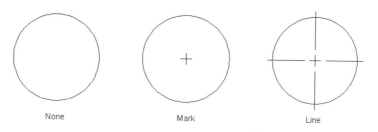

- Under **Arrowheads**, you can control the following settings:
  - The shape of the **First** arrowhead.
  - The shape of the **Second** arrowhead.
  - The shape of the arrowhead to be used in the **Leader**.
  - The **Size** of the arrowhead.

NOTE
- If you change the first arrowhead, the second will change automatically, but if you change the second, the first will not change.
- Under **Center marks**, you can:
  - Select whether to show the center mark or the centerlines.
  - Set the **Size** of the center mark.

None   Mark   Line

- Under **Dimension Break**, set the **Break size**, which is the width of the break of the dimension lines in a dimension break:

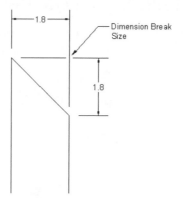

- Under **Arc length symbol**, control whether to show the symbol **Preceding** the dimension text, **Above** the dimension text, or not at all (**None**):

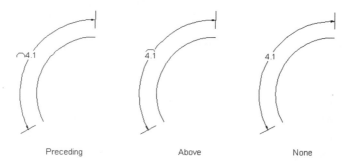

- Under **Radius jog dimension**, set the value of the **Jog angle**:

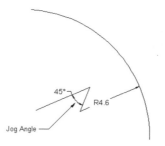

- Under **Linear Jog dimension**, set the **Jog height factor** as a percentage of the text height:

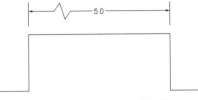

Jog height factor = 3 times the height of text

9.6 THE TEXT TAB

- When you click the **Text** tab, you will see the following:

- Under **Text appearance**, you can control the settings as follows:
  - Select the desired premade **Text style** to be used to write the dimension text. If you did not create a text style prior to this step, you can click the three dots button and create one now.
  - Specify the **Text color**.

- Specify the **Fill color**, which is the background color:

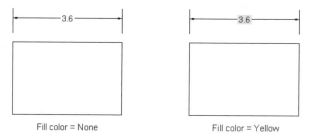

Fill color = None   Fill color = Yellow

- Input the **Text height** (only applicable if the assigned text style has a text height = 0.0).
- Go to the **Primary Units** tab and assign the **Unit format** to be **Architectural** or **Fractional**. The dimension text will appear, for example, as 1¼. Set **Fraction height scale** according to whether you want the fraction to appear smaller than the ordinary number.
- Select whether to **Draw frame around** the dimension text:

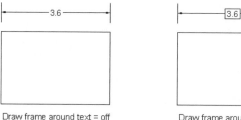

Draw frame around text = off   Draw frame around text = on

- As an introduction to **Text placement**, see the following illustration:

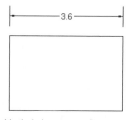

Vertical placement = Centered
Horizontal placement = Centered

■ Under **Text placement**, you can control the settings as follows:

   • Select the **Vertical** placement. You have five choices: **Centered**, **Above**, **Outside**, **JIS** (Japanese Industrial Standard), and **Below**. See the following illustration:

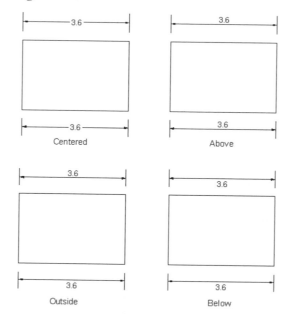

   • Select the **Horizontal** placement. You have five choices: **Centered**, **At Ext Line 1**, **At Ext Line 2**, **Over Ext Line 1**, and **Over Ext Line 2**. See the following illustration:

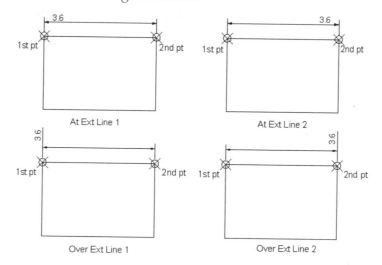

- Set the **View Direction** of the dimension text to be either **Left-to-Right** or **Right-to-Left**.
- Set the **Offset from dim line**, which is the distance between the dimension line and the baseline of the dimension text. See the following illustration:

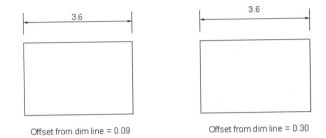

Offset from dim line = 0.09   Offset from dim line = 0.30

- Under **Text alignment**, control whether the text will always be **Horizontal**, **Aligned with dimension line**, or according to **ISO standard**. See the following illustration:

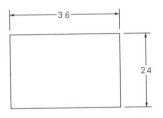 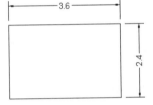

Text alignment = Horizontal   Text alignment = Aligned with dimension line

NOTE
- The only difference between **Aligned with dimension line** and **ISO standard** is the **Radius** and **Diameter** types. **Aligned with dimension line** is considered, like the other types, to be aligned with the dimension line, and **ISO standard** is considered a special case of horizontal.

9.7 THE FIT TAB

- When you click the **Fit** tab, you will see the following:

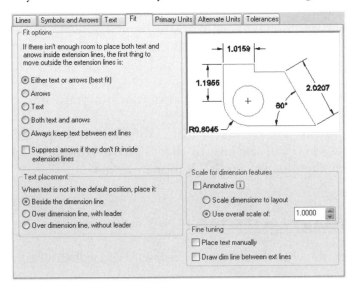

- As an introduction to the **Fit** tab, notice that there are three things within the two extension lines: **Dimension line**, **Arrowheads**, and **Dimension text**. AutoCAD will put them all inside the two extension lines when the distance can accommodate all three. Next, we will discuss what happens if there is not enough room.
- Under **Fit options**, you can control the settings as follows:
  - Select one of the five options to decide how AutoCAD will treat **Arrowheads** and **Dimension text**.
  - Specify whether to **Suppress arrows if they don't fit inside extension lines**.
- Under **Text placement**, control the placement of the text. If it does not fit inside the extension lines, you have three options: **Beside the dimension line**, **Over dimension line with leader**, and **Over dimension line without leader**. See the following illustration:

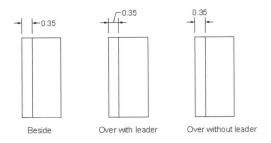

Beside   Over with leader   Over without leader

- Under **Scale for dimension features**, set the following:
  - Keep **Annotative** off for now.
  - Set the **Scale dimension to layout** (we will discuss layouts in the next chapter).
  - For any distance, length, or size, input a value. **Use overall scale of** is a setting that will magnify or shrink the whole values in one step. This will not affect the distance measured.
- Under **Fine tuning**:
  - If you want to place your text yourself, you can choose **Place text manually**.
  - You can also choose to force AutoCAD to draw the dimension line between extension lines by choosing **Draw dim line between ext lines**, whether the distance is appropriate or not.

9.8 THE PRIMARY UNITS TAB

- When you click the **Primary Units** tab, you will see the following:

- As an introduction to the **Primary Units**, let's assume your client wants the dimension in Decimal format and a subcontractor wants it in Architectural format. The solution is to show two numbers for each dimension. The first will be the **Primary Units**, and the second will be the **Alternate Units**. In this tab, we will cover the **Primary Units**.

- Under **Linear dimensions**, you can control the settings as follows:
  - Choose a **Unit format** from the six presented.
  - Select the **Precision** of the unit format selected.
  - If you select the Architectural or Fractional format, then specify the **Fraction format**, which includes **Horizontal**, **Diagonal**, and **Not Stacked**.
  - If you select **Decimal**, then specify the **Decimal Separator**; the options are **Period**, **Comma**, and **Space**.
  - Specify the **Round off** number. If you select 0.5, for example, then AutoCAD will round off any dimension to the nearest 0.5.
  - Input the **Prefix** and/or the **Suffix**. To illustrate this setting, see the following:

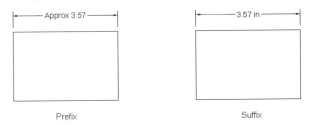

- Under **Measurement scale**:
  - Input the **Scale factor**. To explain the importance of this setting, let's assume we have a drawing that uses the millimeter as the unit—hence, a length of 10 m will be 10,000—but we want the value 10 to appear and not 10,000. To do so, we must set the **Scale factor** to be 0.001.
  - Select **Apply to layout dimensions only** (we will discuss layouts in the next chapter).
- Under **Zero suppression**, select to suppress the **Leading** and/or the **Trailing** zeros. See the following illustration:

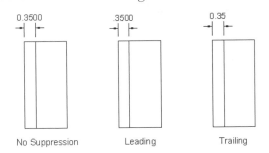

- If you have meters as your unit, and the measured value is less than 1 cm, we call this a sub-unit. Set the **Sub-unit factor** (in our example 1 m = 100 cm, so the factor = 100) and the suffix for it.

- Under **Angular dimensions**, select the **Unit format** and the **Precision**.
- Under **Zero suppression**, select to suppress the **Leading** and/or the **Trailing** zeros for the angular measurements.

9.9 THE ALTERNATE UNITS TAB

- When you click the **Alternate Units** tab, you will see the following:

- If you want two numbers to appear for each dimension, click on **Display alternate units**.
- Specify the **Unit format**, its **Precision**, the **Multiplier for all units** value, the **Round distance to** value, the **Prefix**, the **Suffix**, and the **Zero suppression** criteria.
- Specify whether to show the alternate units **After primary value** or **Below primary value**. See the following illustration:

After primary value   Below primary value

9.10 THE TOLERANCES TAB

- When you click the **Tolerances** tab, you will see the following:

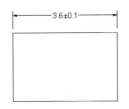

(Dialog box screenshot: Tolerances tab)

- There are several ways to show the tolerances:
  - **Symmetrical**
  - **Deviation**
  - **Limits**
  - **Basic**
- See the following illustration:

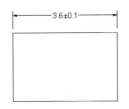

Symmetrical

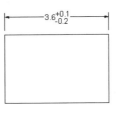

Deviation

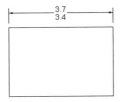

Limits

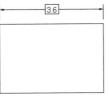

Basic

- Under **Tolerance format**, control the settings as follows:
  - Specify the desired **Method** from the preceding list.
  - Specify the **Precision** of the numbers to be shown.
  - If you select **Symmetrical**, specify the **Upper value**.
  - For **Deviation** and **Limits**, specify the **Upper value** and **Lower value**.
  - If you want the tolerance values to appear smaller than the dimension text, specify **Scaling for height**.
  - Specify the **Vertical position** of the dimension text with regard to the tolerance values (**Bottom**, **Middle**, or **Top**).
- If **Deviation** or **Limits** is selected, choose whether to **Align decimal separators** or **Align operational symbols**. See the following illustration:

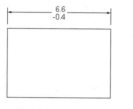

Align decimal seperators

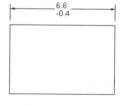

Align operational symbols

- If you are showing **Alternate units**, specify the **Precision** of the numbers under the **Alternate units tolerance**.
- Accordingly, specify the **Zero suppression** for both the **Primary units** tolerance and the **Alternate units** tolerance.

9.11 CREATING A SUB-STYLE

- Sometimes you will need a dimension style identical to almost all types of dimensions except, perhaps, for **Diameter** or some other setting(s).
- In this case, we create a dimension style for all types, and then we create a sub-dimension style from it.
- Perform the following steps:
  - Create your dimension style.
  - Select it from the list in the **Dimension Style** dialog box.
  - Click the **New** button to create a new style.

- The following dialog box will appear:

- For **Use for**, select **Diameter** (for example). The dialog box will change to:

- Now click **Continue** and make the desired changes. These changes will affect only the diameter dimensions.
- In the **Dimension Style** dialog box, you will see something like the following:

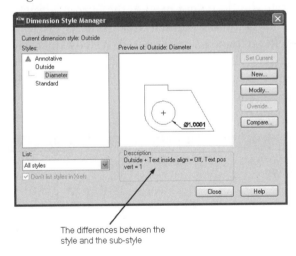

The differences between the style and the sub-style

- You can see how AutoCAD relates the new sub-style to the existing style. Also, you can see in the **Description** area how AutoCAD lists the differences between the style and its sub-style.

9.12 CONTROLLING DIMENSION STYLES

- Once you create more than one dimension style, you can control them using the **Current, Modify,** and **Delete** buttons.

Set Dimension Style Current

- While you are in the **Dimension Style** dialog box, select the desired dimension style and click the **Current** button.
- On the **Ribbon**, go to the **Annotate** tab. From the **Dimensions** panel, use the pop-up list to set the current dimension style:

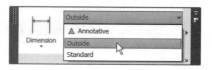

Modify Dimension Style

- While you are in the **Dimension Style** dialog box, select the desired dimension style and click the **Modify** button. The same dialog box will appear for more editing.

Delete Dimension Style

- There are three conditions for deleting a dimension style:
  - The style should be not used in the current drawing.
  - It should not be the current dimension style.
  - It should not have any sub-style. If it does, delete the sub-style first, then delete the style.
- If these three conditions are fulfilled, then select the desired dimension style to be deleted and press [Del] (or you can right-click it and select **Delete**). The following dialog box will appear:

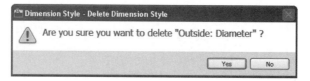

- If you click **Yes**, the style will be deleted. If you click **No**, the whole process will be canceled.

CREATING DIMENSION STYLES

Exercise 9-1

1. Start AutoCAD 2011.
2. Open the file *Exercise 9-1.dwg*.
3. Create a dimension style with the following specifications:
   a. Name = Mechanical, Start with = Standard, Use for = All dimensions
   b. Baseline spacing = 0.5
   c. Extend beyond dim lines = 0.2
   d. Offset from origin = 0.2
   e. Center marks = None
   f. Text alignment = Align with dimension line
   g. When text is not in the default position, place it = Over dimension line with leader
   h. Primary unit format = Decimal
   i. Precision = 0.00
4. Create two sub-styles, one for **Radius** and the other for **Diameter**, with Text alignment = Horizontal.
5. Save and close the file.

9.13 AN INTRODUCTION TO DIMENSIONING COMMANDS

- Dimensioning commands insert dimensions using the points specified by the user.
- You will find all commands under the **Annotate** tab in the **Dimensions** panel.

- See the following illustration:

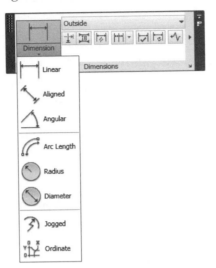

- More commands can be found in the hidden part of the **Dimensions** panel:

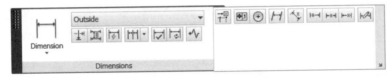

- All dimensioning commands used in this book are found in the **Dimensions** panel.

9.14 THE LINEAR COMMAND

- Use the **Linear** command to create a horizontal or vertical dimension.
- On the **Ribbon**, go to the **Annotate** tab. Using the **Dimensions** panel, click the **Linear** button.
- The following prompts will appear:

```
Specify first extension line origin or <select object>:
(Specify the first point.)
Specify second extension line origin: (Specify the second
point.)
Specify dimension line location or
[Mtext/Text/Angle/Horizontal/Vertical/Rotated]: (Specify the
location of the dimension line.)
```

- There are three steps to follow:
  - Specify the first point of the dimension distance to be measured.
  - Specify the second point of the dimension distance to be measured.
  - Specify the location of the dimension block by specifying the location of the dimension line.
- The following is the result:

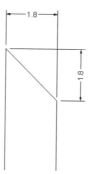

- You can also use the other available options:
  - **Mtext**
  - **Text**
  - **Angle**
  - **Horizontal**
  - **Vertical**
  - **Rotated**

Mtext

- This option allows you to edit the measured distance in the **MTEXT** command.

Text

- This option allows you to edit the measured distance in the **DTEXT** command.

Angle

- This option allows you to change the angle of the text.

Horizontal

- This option allows you to create a horizontal dimension.

- The following is the result:

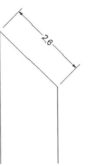

- The rest of the options are the same as the **Linear** command.

9.16 THE ANGULAR COMMAND

- The **Angular** command allows you to create an angular dimension.
- On the **Ribbon**, go to the **Annotate** tab. Using the **Dimensions** panel, click the **Angular** button.
- There are four ways to place an angular dimension in AutoCAD:
  - Select an arc. AutoCAD will measure the included angle.
  - Select a circle. The position that you select the circle from will be the first point and the center of the circle will the second point. AutoCAD will ask you to specify any point on the diameter of the circle and will place the angle accordingly.
  - Select two lines. AutoCAD will measure the inside angle or the outside angle.
  - Select a vertex, which will be considered the center point. AutoCAD will ask you to specify two points and will measure either the inside angle or the outside angle:

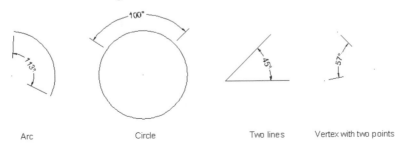

Arc   Circle   Two lines   Vertex with two points

- The following prompts will appear:

```
Select arc, circle, line, or <specify vertex>: (Select the
desired method as discussed, assuming we select arc.)
Specify dimension arc line location or [Mtext/Text/Angle]:
(Specify the dimension block location.)
```

9.17 THE ARC LENGTH COMMAND

- Use the **Arc Length** command to create a dimension showing the length of a selected arc.
- On the **Ribbon**, go to the **Annotate** tab. Using the **Dimensions** panel, click the **Arc Length** button.
- The following prompts will appear:

```
Select arc or polyline arc segment: (Select the desired arc.)
Specify arc length dimension location, or [Mtext/Text/Angle/
Partial/Leader]: (Specify the location of the dimension
block.)
```

- There are two steps to follow:
  - Select the desired arc.
  - Specify the location of the dimension block.
- The following is the result:

- The options **Mtext**, **Text**, and **Angle**—which are available in the **Arc Length** command—were discussed in the **Linear** command section.

Partial

- If you want **Arc Length** to measure part of the arc and not the entire arc, specify two points on the arc. The result will resemble the following:

Leader

- To add a leader, see the following example:

9.18 THE RADIUS COMMAND

- Use the **Radius** command to insert the radius dimension on an arc and/or a circle.
- On the **Ribbon**, go to the **Annotate** tab. Using the **Dimensions** panel, click the **Radius** button.
- The following prompts will appear:

```
Select arc or circle: (Select the desired arc or circle.)
Specify dimension line location or [Mtext/Text/Angle]:
(Specify the location of the dimension block.)
```

- There are two steps to follow:
  - Select the desired arc or circle.
  - Specify the location of the dimension block.
- The result will appear as follows:

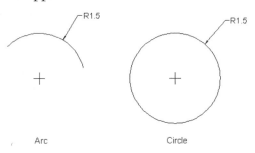

9.19 THE DIAMETER COMMAND

- Use the **Diameter** command to insert diameter dimensions on an arc and/or a circle.
- On the **Ribbon**, go to the **Annotate** tab. Using the **Dimensions** panel, click the **Diameter** button.

- The following prompts will appear:

```
Select arc or circle: (Select the desired arc or circle.)
Specify dimension line location or [Mtext/Text/Angle]:
(Specify the dimension block location.)
```

- The result will appear as follows:

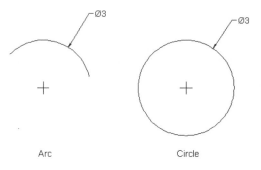

Arc   Circle

9.20 THE JOGGED COMMAND

- If you have a large arc with a center very far from the arc itself, it will be difficult to apply a normal radius dimension.
- The solution is to add a jogged radius dimension.
- Use the **Jogged** command to add a jogged radius to an arc or a circle.
- On the **Ribbon**, go to the **Annotate** tab. Using the **Dimensions** panel, click the **Jogged** button.
- The following prompts will appear:

```
Select arc or circle: (Select the desired arc or circle.)
Specify center location override: (Specify a point that will
act as a new center point.)
Dimension text = 1.5
Specify dimension line location or [Mtext/Text/Angle]:
(Specify the dimension line location.)
Specify jog location: (Specify the location of the jog.)
```

- There are four steps to follow:
  - Select the desired arc or circle.
  - Specify the point that will act as the new center point.
  - Specify the dimension line location.
  - Specify the location of the jog.

- The result will appear as follows:

R10.01

9.21 THE ORDINATE COMMAND

- Use the **Ordinate** command to add several measurements to objects relative to a certain point.
- On the **Ribbon**, go to the **Annotate** tab. Using the **Dimensions** panel, click the **Ordinate** button.
- The **Ordinate** command allows you to set dimensions relative to a datum, either in X or in Y. See the following illustration:

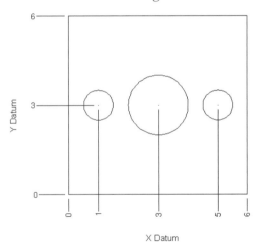

- NOTE You must change the UCS (User Coordinate System) origin location to the desired location so the readings will be right; otherwise, the values will be relative to the current location of 0,0.
- The following prompts will appear:

```
Specify feature location: (Click on the desired point.)
Specify leader endpoint or [Xdatum/Ydatum/Mtext/Text/Angle]:
(Specify the dimension location.)
```

- By default, when you select a point, you may go in the direction of either X or Y. If you want the **Ordinate** command to go exclusively in the X direction, then select the **Xdatum** option. Select **Ydatum** if you want to go exclusively in the Y direction.
- The rest of the options are the same as those in the **Linear** command.

DIMENSION COMMANDS: PART 1

Exercise 9-2
1. Start AutoCAD 2011.
2. Open the file *Exercise 9-2.dwg*.
3. Make the **Dimension** layer current.
4. Make the dimension style **Mechanical** current.
5. Dimension the drawing to look like the following:

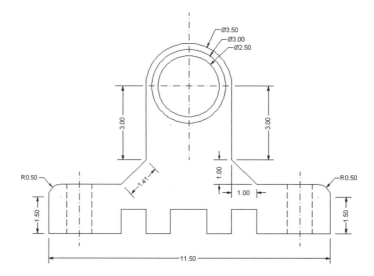

6. Save and close the file.

DIMENSION COMMANDS: PART 2

Exercise 9-3
1. Start AutoCAD 2011.
2. Open the file *Exercise 9-3.dwg*.
3. Make the **Dimension** layer current.

4. Dimension the drawing to look like the following:

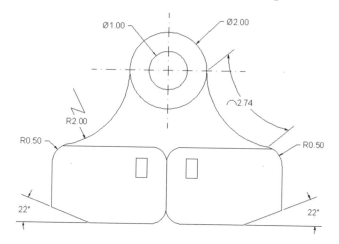

5. Save and close the file.

DIMENSION COMMANDS: PART 3

Exercise 9-4

1. Start AutoCAD 2011.
2. Open the file *Exercise 9-4.dwg*.
3. Make the **Dimension** layer current.
4. Apply the ordinate dimensions as shown:

5. Save and close the file.

9.22 THE CONTINUE COMMAND

- After you put a dimension in your drawing (i.e., linear, aligned, angular, or ordinate), you can ask AutoCAD to continue using the same type and to allocate it along the first one.
- Use the **Continue** command to input many dimensions swiftly.
- On the **Ribbon**, go to the **Annotate** tab. Using the **Dimensions** panel, click the **Continue** button.

If No Dimension Was Created in This Session

- The following prompt will appear:

Select continued dimension: *(Select either Linear, Aligned, Ordinate, or Angular.)*

- AutoCAD will consider the selected dimension as the base dimension and will continue accordingly.

If a Dimension Was Created in This Session

- The following prompt will appear:

Specify a second extension line origin or [Undo/Select] <Select>: *(Specify the second point of the last Linear, Aligned, Ordinate, or Angular dimension, or select an existing dimension.)*

- AutoCAD will allow you to do one of three things:
  - If you already input a linear dimension (for example), then you can continue by specifying the second point. Keep in mind that the second point of the first dimension is the first point of the continuing dimension.
  - Select an existing dimension and continue from there.
  - Undo the last continue dimension.
- See the following illustration:

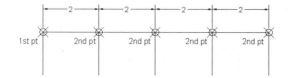

9.23 THE BASELINE COMMAND

- The **Baseline** command works just like the **Continue** command except the dimensions will always be related to the first point the user selected.
- On the **Ribbon**, go to the **Annotate** tab. Using the **Dimensions** panel, click the **Baseline** button.
- All the prompts and procedures are identical to the **Continue** command.
- See the following illustration:

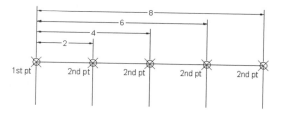

CONTINUOUS AND BASELINE DIMENSIONS

Exercise 9-5

1. Start AutoCAD 2011.
2. Open the file *Exercise 9-5.dwg*.
3. Make the **Dimension** layer current, and make **Mechanical** your current dimension style.
4. Zoom to the shape to the right.
5. Set the **Continuous** dimension as shown:

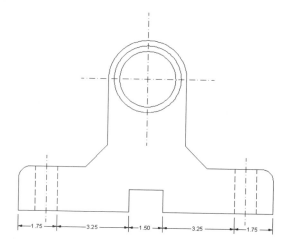

6. Zoom to the shape at the left, and set the **Baseline** dimension as shown:

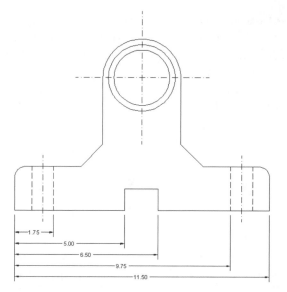

7. Save and close the file.

9.24 THE QUICK DIMENSION COMMAND

-   Use the **Quick Dimension** command to place a group of dimensions in a single step.
-   On the **Ribbon**, go to the **Annotate** tab. Using the **Dimensions** panel, click the **Quick Dimension** button.
-   The following prompt will appear:

```
Select geometry to dimension: (Select either by clicking,
using Window, or using Crossing. After you are done, press
[Enter].)
Specify dimension line position, or [Continuous/Staggered/
Baseline/Ordinate/Radius/Diameter/datumPoint/Edit/SeTtings]
<Continuous>:
```

- At this prompt, you can right-click. The following shortcut menu will appear:

- From this shortcut menu, you can select the proper dimension type. The choices are **Continuous, Staggered, Baseline, Ordinate, Radius**, or **Diameter**.
- Select the type and then specify the dimension line location; a group of dimensions will be placed in a single step.
- See the following **Staggered** example:

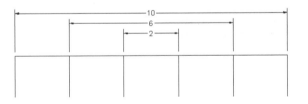

9.25 DIMENSION BLOCKS AND GRIPS

- You can edit dimension blocks using **Grips**.
- If you click a dimension block, five grips will appear:

- As you can see, the grips appear in the following places:
  - The two ends of the dimension line.
  - The two origins of the dimension line.
  - The dimension text.
- You can change the position of the text by clicking its grip and moving it parallel to the dimension line.
- You can change the position of the dimension line by clicking one of the two grips and moving it closer to, or farther from, the origin.
- You can change the measured distance by moving one of the two grips of the origin and the distance will change accordingly.
- See the following example:

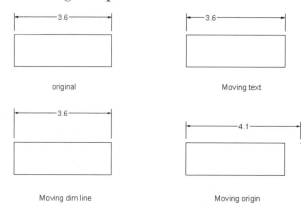

- Also, if you select a dimension block and right-click, the following shortcut menu will appear (only the part concerning the dimension is shown):

- You can change four things in the selected dimension block: **Dim Text position, Precision, Dim Style**, and **Flip Arrow**.

Dim Text Position

■ You can change the position of the dimension text using the options shown here:

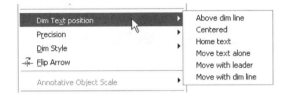

- **Above dim line**: The dimension text will change from any other position to **Above**.
- **Centered**: The dimension text will change from any other position to **Centered**.
- **Home text**: The dimension text will return to its original position according to its dimension style.
- **Move text alone**: Allows you to position the text freely.
- **Move with leader**: Allows you to position the text freely, but with a leader.
- **Move with dim line**: Allows you to move both the dimension text and the dimension line in one step.

Precision

■ Select **Precision** to set the number of decimal places for the number shown.
■ You can select from zero to eight decimal places:

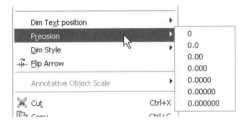

Dim Style

■ The changes made using this method can be saved in a new dimension style. Select the option **Save as New Style**, and type in a new name.

- You can change the dimension style of any dimension block in the drawing. The existing dimension styles will appear. Select the new desired dimension style:

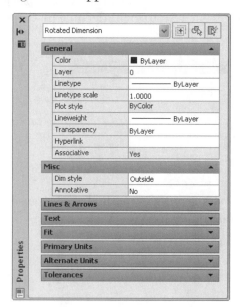

Flip Arrow

- Select **Flip Arrow** to flip the arrows from inside to outside, and vice versa.
- The process can be done on only one arrow at a time.

9.26 DIMENSION BLOCK PROPERTIES

- Select a dimension block and right-click, then select **Properties**. The following dialog box will appear:

- Under **General**, you will see the general properties of the selected dimension block.
- You will also see **Misc, Lines & Arrows, Text, Fit, Primary Units, Alternate Units**, and **Tolerances**. These options are identical to those of the **Dimension Style** command. Thus, using **Properties**, you can change any of the characteristics of the dimension block after you place it.

QUICK DIMENSION AND EDITING

Exercise 9-6

1. Start AutoCAD 2011.
2. Open the file *Exercise 9-6.dwg*.
3. Using the **Quick Dimension** command, select the bottom horizontal and vertical line using **Crossing**.
4. Hold [Shift] and deselect the two outer dashed lines, along with the centerlines. Press [Enter], right-click, and select **Continuous**.
5. Start **Quick Dimension** again, and select the three small circles. Press [Enter], right-click, and select **Radius**, then move the mouse to the right and create an angle that does not measure 0° or 90°. Click to end the command.
6. Use the grips to move the circle at the right away from the dashed lines.
7. Start **Quick Dimension** again, and select the outer arc and two big circles. Press [Enter], right-click, and select **Diameter**, then move the mouse to the right and create an angle that does not measure 0° or 90°. Click to end the command.
8. Using the grips, rearrange the three dimension blocks so they look better.
9. Double-click the mouse wheel to discover another shape. Zoom to it.
10. Using **Quick Dimension**, dimension the lines the way we did in steps 3 and 4, but this time using **Baseline**.
11. Select the horizontal dimension and right-click. Select **Precision** and set it to 0.00. Select the same dimension and right-click. Select **Dim text position**, then **Above dim line**.
12. Zoom to the **Radius** dimension and select it. Right-click and select **Dim style**, then **Mechanical**.
13. Zoom out, click the vertical dimension, and move it closer to the object.
14. Move the grip touching the quadrant of the upper arc to be the top point of the small vertical line at the left, then press [Esc].
15. Save and close the file.

9.27 AN INTRODUCTION TO MULTILEADERS

- A leader in AutoCAD is an arrow pointing to a part of the drawing, with two lines and some text to explain certain facts about that part.
- A multileader can be one arrow with a single set of lines or multiple arrows with multiple sets of lines. The following illustration shows a single leader:

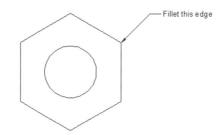

- The following illustration shows a multileader:

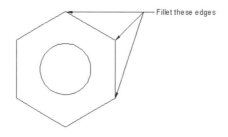

NOTE
- Normally you will create a single leader; then, using other commands, you can create a multileader from it.
- You will specify (by default) two points. The first point indicates where the arrow will point; the second specifies the length and angle of the leader. Another small horizontal landing will be added automatically. See the following illustration:

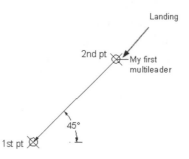

- Multileader has its own style and set of commands, which we will discuss in the following pages.

9.28 MULTILEADER STYLES

- As we discussed in **Dimension Style**, you will use the **Multileader Style** command to set the characteristics of the multileader block.
- On the **Ribbon**, go to the **Annotate** tab. Using the **Leaders** panel, click the **Multileader Style** button:

- The following dialog box will appear:

- To create a new style, click the **New** button. The following dialog box will appear:

- Type the name of the new style, and select the existing style you want to start with. Click **Continue** to start modifying the **Multileader style**.

- You will see three tabs:
  - **Leader Format**
  - **Leader Structure**
  - **Content**
- We will review each tab in the following sections.

Leader Format

- When you click the **Leader Format** tab, you will see the following dialog box:

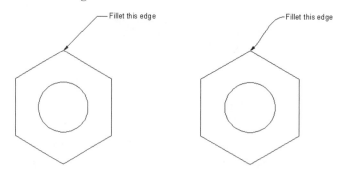

- You have three choices for the type of leader:
  - **Straight**
  - **Spline**
  - **None**
- See the following illustration:

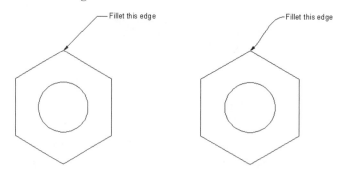

- Control the **Color**, **Linetype**, and **Lineweight** the same way you did for the **Dimension Style** command.
- Under **Arrowhead**, choose a **Symbol** from 20 different existing shapes, and select its size.
- If there is a **Leader Break**, use the **Break size** value to determine how large it will be.

Leader Structure

- When you click the **Leader Style** tab, you will see the following dialog box:

- Specify the **Maximum leader points**. As we discussed earlier, the default value is 2, but you can specify more points.
- By default, you will specify the **First segment angle** on the screen, and a small horizontal landing (**Second segment angle**) will be added. However, you can set the angle values for both in the **Multileader style**.
- If you select **Automatically include landing**, you will need to set the value of **Set landing distance**.
- Select whether the multileader will be **Annotative**. (We will leave it off for now.)

Content

- When you click the **Content** tab, you will see the following dialog box:

| Leader Format | Leader Structure | Content |

Multileader type: Mtext

Text options
Default text: Default Text   ...

Text style: Standard   ...

Text angle: Keep horizontal

Text color: ■ ByBlock

Text height: 0.1800

☐ Always left justify   ☐ Frame text

Leader connection
◉ Horizontal attachment
○ Vertical attachment
    Left attachment: Middle of top line
    Right attachment: Middle of top line
    Landing gap: 0.0900

- There are two types of **Multileaders**:
  - With **Mtext**
  - With a **Block** (either predefined or user-defined)
- See the following illustration:

- By default, **Mtext** (Multiline text) is selected. To adjust the settings:
  - If there is any text that should appear each time, type it in **Default text**.
  - Specify the **Text style**.
  - Specify the **Text angle** (**Keep horizontal**, **Right-reading**, or **As inserted**).
  - Specify **Text Color** and **Text height** (if **Text Style** height = 0).
  - Specify whether to make the text **Always left justify** and whether to **Frame text**.
  - Control the position of the text relative to the landing for both left and right leader lines.
  - Control the gap distance between the end of the landing and the text.

■ If you select the **Multileader type** to be **Block**, you will see the following dialog box:

| Leader Format | Leader Structure | Content |

Multileader type: Block

Block options

Source block: Detail Callout

Attachment: Center Extents

Color: ■ ByBlock

Scale: 1.0000

■ Control the following settings:
  • Specify the **Source block** (choose from the list) or select **User Block**. The following dialog box will appear:

Select Custom Content Block

Select from Drawing Blocks:

[   ]

[OK]   [Cancel]

  • Type the name of the desired block and click **OK**.
  • Specify the **Attachment** position.
  • Specify the **Color** of the attachment.
  • Specify the **Scale** of the attachment.

9.29 MULTILEADER COMMANDS

- After you finish creating the **Multileader Style**, you are ready to insert the multileader into your drawing.
- You will always start with the **Multileader** command to insert a single leader.
- On the **Ribbon**, go to the **Annotate** tab. Using the **Leaders** panel, click the **Multileader** button:

- The following prompts will appear:

```
Specify leader arrowhead location or [leader Landing first/
Content first/Options] <Options>: (Specify the point to which
the arrow should point.)
Specify leader landing location: (Specify the angle and the
length of the leader.)
```

- Then type the text you want to appear in the leader.
- Click the **Add Leader** button to add more leaders (arrows) to an existing single leader:

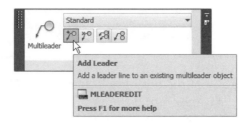

- The following prompts will appear:

```
Select a multileader:
1 found
Specify leader arrowhead location:
Specify leader arrowhead location:
```

- Click the **Remove Leader** button to remove some leaders from an existing multileader:

- The following prompts will appear:

```
Select a multileader:
1 found
Specify leaders to remove:
Specify leaders to remove:
```

- Click the **Align** button to align several multileaders in the same line:

- The following prompts will appear:

```
Select multileaders: 1 found
Select multileaders: 1 found, 2 total
Select multileaders: (Press [Enter].)
Current mode: Use current spacing
Select multileader to align to or [Options]:
Specify direction:
```

- Click the **Collect** button to collect several multileaders to a single leader. This command works only with leaders containing blocks:

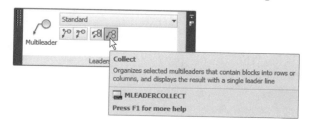

- You will see the following prompts:

```
Select multileaders:
Select multileaders: (Press [Enter] when you are done.)
Specify collected multileader location or [Vertical/
Horizontal/Wrap] <Horizontal>:
```

MULTILEADER

Exercise 9-7
1. Start AutoCAD 2011.
2. Open the file *Exercise 9-7.dwg*.
3. Create a new multileader style with the following specifications:
    a. Name = Special, start with Standard
    b. Type = Spline
    c. Multileader type = Block
    d. Source block = Circle
    e. Scale = 2
4. Make the **Dimension** layer current.
5. Using **Special** and **Standard** styles, add the following multileaders:

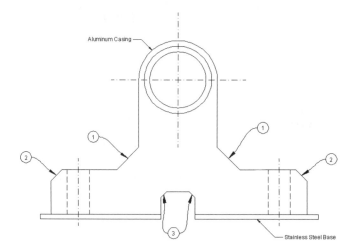

6. Save and close the file.

CREATING DIMENSION STYLES (METRIC)

 Workshop 6-M

1. Start AutoCAD 2011, and open the file *Workshop_06.dwg*.

2. Create a new dimension style and name it **Outside**, starting from **Standard**, and use for **All dimensions**. (Anything not mentioned in this Workshop should be left in the default value or setting.)

3. Under **Line** make the following changes:
   a. Extend beyond dim line = 0.25
   b. Offset from origin = 0.15

4. Under **Symbols and Arrows** make the following changes:
   a. Arrowhead, First = Oblique
   b. Arrow size = 0.25

5. Under **Text** make the following changes:
   a. Text style = Dimension
   b. Text placement, Vertical = Above
   c. Text alignment = Aligned with dimension line

6. Under **Fit** make the following changes:
   a. Use overall scale = 1000

7. Under **Primary Units** make the following changes:
   a. Linear dimension, Precision = 0.00
   b. Suffix = m
   c. Scale Factor = 0.001

8. Create a new style and name it **Inside**, starting from **Outside**, and use for **All dimensions**.

9. Under **Lines** make the following changes:
   a. Extension lines, Suppress Ext line 1 = on, Ext line 2 = on

10. Under **Symbols and Arrows** make Arrow size = 0.20.

11. Under Text make the following changes:
    a. Text style = Standard
    b. Text height = 0.25

12. Under **Fit** make the following changes:
    a. Fine tuning, Place text manually = on

13. Make a sub-style dimension style from **Outside** for **Radius dimensions**.

14. Under **Symbols and Arrows** make the following changes:
    a. Arrowheads, Second = Closed filled

15. Under **Text** make the following changes:
     a. Text alignment = ISO Standard
16. Make the **Dimension** layer the current layer.
17. Make the following layers frozen: **Furniture, Hatch**, and **Text**.
18. Using the **Outside** and **Inside** dimension styles, set the dimensions for the outer and inner dimensions as shown:

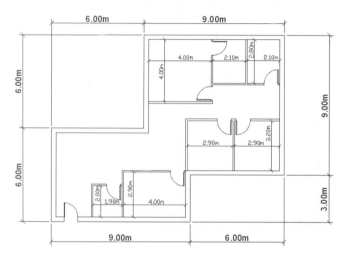

19. Save and close the file.

CREATING DIMENSION STYLES (IMPERIAL)

 Workshop 6-I

1. Start AutoCAD 2011, and open the file *Workshop_06.dwg*.
2. Create a new dimension style and name it **Outside**, starting from **Standard**, and use for **All dimensions**. (Anything not mentioned in this Workshop should be left in the default value or setting.)
3. Under **Line** make the following changes:
     a. Extend beyond dim line = 3/4"
     b. Offset from origin = 1/2"

4. Under **Symbols and Arrows** make the following changes:
    a. Arrowhead, First = Oblique
    b. Arrow size = 3/4"
5. Under **Text** make the following changes:
    a. Text style = Dimension
    b. Text placement, Vertical = Above
    c. Text alignment = Aligned with dimension line
6. Under **Fit** make the following changes:
    a. Use overall scale = 12
7. Under **Primary Units** make the following changes:
    a. Unit Format = Architectural, Precision = 0'-0"
    b. Suffix = ft
8. Create a new style and name it **Inside**, starting from **Outside**, and use for **All dimensions**.
9. Under **Lines** make the following changes:
    a. Extension lines, Suppress Ext line 1 = on, Ext line 2 = on
10. Under **Text** make the following changes:
    a. Text style = Standard (change the font to be Arial)
    b. Text height = 3/4"
11. Under **Fit** make the following changes:
    a. Fine tuning, Place text manually = on
12. Make a sub-style dimension style from **Outside** for **Radius dimensions**.
13. Under **Symbols and Arrows** make the following changes:
    a. Arrowheads, Second = Closed filled
14. Under **Text** make the following changes:
    a. Text alignment = ISO Standard
15. Make the **Dimension** layer the current layer.
16. Make the following layers frozen: **Furniture, Hatch**, and **Text**.

17. Using the **Outside** and **Inside** dimension styles, set the dimensions for the outer and inner dimensions as shown:

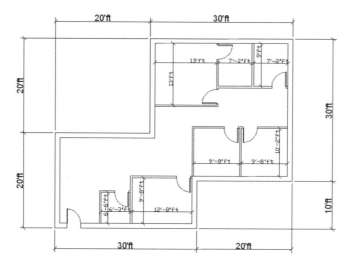

18. Save the file, and close it.

CHAPTER REVIEW

1. You can *only* create dimension styles that will affect all dimension types.
   a. True
   b. False

2. _____ and _____ are two types of dimensions that you can use with arcs.

3. Which of the following is *not* an AutoCAD dimension command?
   a. **dimlinear**
   b. **dimarc**
   c. **dimchordlength**
   d. **dimaligned**

4. The only way to add an angular dimension is to have two lines.
   a. True
   b. False

5. Which of the following is a type of **Tolerance** in AutoCAD?

    a. Deviation

    b. Symmetrical

    c. Limits

    d. All of the above

6. To make a dimension style _____, double-click the name in the **Dimension Style** dialog box.

CHAPTER REVIEW ANSWERS

1. b

2. Any two of the following: **Arc length**, **Jogged**, **Radius**, **Diameter**

3. c

4. b

5. d

6. current

10 PLOTTING YOUR DRAWING

In This Chapter

◇ **Model Space** versus **Paper Space**
◇ Creating Layouts
◇ The **Page Setup Manager**
◇ Creating and editing **Viewports**
◇ The **Plot Style Table**
◇ The **Plot** command
◇ The **Annotative** feature
◇ DWF and DWFx files
◇ The **Publish** command

10.1 INTRODUCTION

- Before AutoCAD 2000, almost all AutoCAD users plotted from **Model Space**, which is where they created their design.
- But, in AutoCAD 2000, the development of **Layouts** made it easy for everyone to shift their attention to the new method, which encompassed many new features and surpassed plotting from **Model Space**.
- Also, in AutoCAD 2000, a new feature was introduced called **Plot Style**, which allowed users to create color-independent configuration plottings.
- While AutoCAD 2000 was a flagship version in more ways than one, the improvements in the plotting process were the most important.

10.2 MODEL SPACE VERSUS PAPER SPACE

- **Model Space** is where you create the drawing using all of the modification processes.
- When you are ready to begin plotting, you should use **Paper Space**.

- There is only one **Model Space** in each drawing file.
- Before AutoCAD 2000, there was only one **Paper Space** per drawing file.
- Beginning with AutoCAD 2000, **Paper Space** was renamed **Layout**.
- You can create as many layouts as you wish in each drawing file.
- Each **Layout** is set up in **Page Setup**, where you specify at least three things:
  - Plotter to be used
  - Paper size to be used
  - Paper orientation (portrait or landscape)
- To demonstrate the importance of this feature, let's say a company owns an A0 plotter, an A2 printer, and an A4 laser printer, and the staff will use all of these printers to print a single drawing.
  - If you use **Model Space**, you will change the setup of the printer, paper size, and paper orientation, along with the drawing area to be plotted each time.
  - But if you create three layouts with **Page Setup**, printing will be easy and fast; simply go to the layout and issue the **Plot** command, and you will save time, effort, and money!

10.3 INTRODUCTION TO LAYOUTS

- Each layout consists of the following elements:
  - **Page Setup**, where you specify the printer (or plotter), the paper size, paper orientation, and other options that are covered later in this chapter.
  - **Objects**, such as blocks (e.g., the title block), text, dimensions, and any other desired object.
  - **Viewports**, which will be covered separately in the upcoming sections.

- See the following illustration:

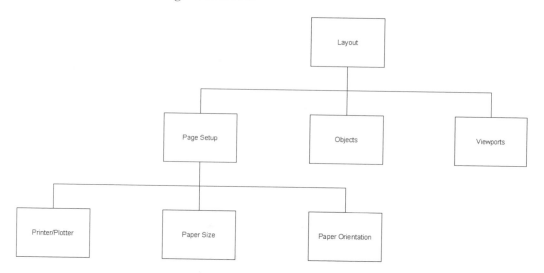

- Each layout should have a name. AutoCAD will give it a temporary name, but you can change it.
- By default, when you create a new drawing using the *acad.dwt* template, two layouts—**Layout1** and **Layout2**—are created automatically.
- You can choose to have the **Page Setup Manager** dialog box appear when you click on a layout for the first time, for the purpose of setting the printer, paper size, etc.
- **Layouts** and **Page Setup** are saved in the drawing file.
- By default, **Page Setup** has no name, but you can name it and use it in other layouts in the current drawing file or in other drawings.

10.4 SWITCHING BETWEEN MODEL SPACE AND LAYOUTS

- By default, when you start a new drawing, AutoCAD will be in the **Model Space**.
- You will see the following tabs at the lower left-hand corner of the graphical area:

Model ISO A1 Details

- Click the desired tab to go to it.

- Another method is to right-click the **Model** tab or the adjacent tab. The following shortcut menu will appear:

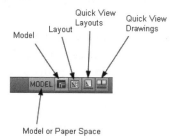

- Select the **Hide Layout and Model tabs** option. On the **Status Bar**, you will find the following:

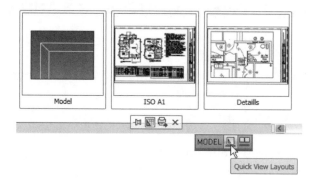

- Before you click on the **Layout** button, it is preferable to click the **Quick View Layouts** button to review the available layouts saved in your drawing. See the following illustration:

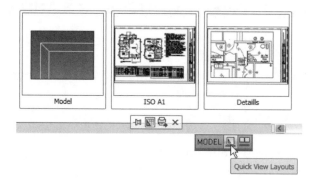

- In this illustration, you can see two layouts. You can choose which to view by clicking on the small view. You can also **Publish**, create a **New Layout**, or choose to **Pin Quick View Layouts**.
- To jump from **Model Space** to **Layout** and vice versa, click on the **Model Space** and **Layout** buttons in the **Status Bar**.
- You can also right-click, and the following shortcut menu will appear:

Display Layout and Model Tabs

10.5 CREATING A NEW LAYOUT

- There are several ways to create a new layout. You can select the **New Layout** option, use a template, or use the **Move or Copy** option.

New Layout

- **New Layout** is a very simple method. Right-click on any existing layout name and a shortcut menu will appear. Select **New Layout**:

New layout
From template...
Delete
Rename
Move or Copy...
Select All Layouts
Activate Previous Layout
Page Setup Manager...
Plot...
Import Layout as Sheet...
Export Layout to Model...
Hide Layout and Model tabs

- A new layout will be added with a temporary name. You can rename it by right-clicking and selecting **Rename**:

```
New layout
From template...
Delete
┌─────────────────────────────┐
│ Rename                      │
└─────────────────────────────┘
Move or Copy...
Select All Layouts

Activate Previous Layout

Page Setup Manager...
Plot...

Import Layout as Sheet...
Export Layout to Model...

Hide Layout and Model tabs
```

Using a Template

- You can import any layout defined inside a template and use it in your current drawing file.
- Right-click on any existing layout and a shortcut menu will appear. Select **From template**:

```
New layout
┌─────────────────────────────┐
│ From template...            │
└─────────────────────────────┘
Delete
Rename
Move or Copy...
Select All Layouts

Activate Previous Layout

Page Setup Manager...
Plot...

Import Layout as Sheet...
Export Layout to Model...

Hide Layout and Model tabs
```

- A file dialog box will appear, allowing you to pick the location and the name of the template file. Select the desired template and click **Open**. The following dialog box will appear:

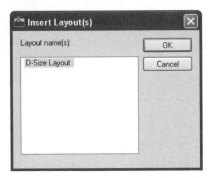

- Click on one of the listed layouts and click **OK**.

Move or Copy

- Using the **Move or Copy** option, you can move a layout from its current position to the left or to the right. You can also create a copy of an existing layout.
- Select the desired layout that you want to create a copy of and right-click. A shortcut menu will appear. Select **Move or Copy**:

New layout
From template...
Delete
Rename
Move or Copy...
Select All Layouts

Activate Previous Layout
Activate Model Tab

Page Setup Manager...
Plot...

Import Layout as Sheet...
Export Layout to Model...

Hide Layout and Model tabs

- The following dialog box will appear:

- From the upper dialog box, you can see there are two existing layouts. Select one of them and click the **Create a copy** checkbox.
- Rename the new layout.

NOTE ▶ - You can move the layout position relative to the other layouts by clicking the layout name, holding it, and dragging it to the position required without using this command.

Copying Using the Mouse

- You can also copy any desired layout by following these steps:
  - Click the name of the layout to be copied.
  - Hold [Ctrl].
  - Hold and drag the mouse to the new position of the newly copied layout.

  - Rename the new layout.

10.6 THE PAGE SETUP MANAGER

- As mentioned previously, each layout will have a **Page Setup** linked to it.
- The **Page Setup Manager** is the dialog box where you create, modify, delete, and import **Page Setups** for layouts.
- The easiest way to issue this command is to select the desired layout, right-click, and then select **Page Setup Manager**.

- The following dialog box will appear:

- At the top, you will see the **Current layout** name; at the bottom, you will see **Selected page setup details**.
- A checkbox will allow you to **Display** (the **Page Setup Manager**) **when creating a new layout**; this is highly recommended.
- To create a new **Page Setup**, click the **New** button. The following dialog box will appear:

■ Type in the name of the new **Page Setup** and click **OK**. The following dialog box will appear:

■ Specify the **Name** of the printer or plotter you want to use. (This printer should be installed and configured ahead of time.)
■ Specify the desired **Paper Size**.
■ Specify **What to plot**. You have four choices: **Display, Extents, Layout**, and **Window**. If you are printing from **Model Space** (which is discouraged), choose **Display, Extents**, or **Window**. If you are using **Layout** (which is recommended), leave **Layout** as the default setting.
■ Specify the **Plot offset**. If you are using **Layout**, **Center the plot** will be off. For the other options, **Center the plot** will be on.
■ Specify the **Plot scale**. If you want to plot from **Layout**, you will use **Viewports** (to be discussed shortly), and you will specify the plot scale for each viewport. Accordingly, you will set this plot scale to 1 = 1. Specify if you want to **Scale lineweights**.
■ Specify the **Plot style table (pen assignments)**, which will be discussed later in this chapter. Specify whether to **Display** the effects of the plot style on the layout.

- If you are plotting a 3D drawing and you want to plot it as shaded or rendered, specify the **Quality** of the shading or rendering.
- Specify the **Plot options**:
  - Plot the objects with their lineweight as specified for each object and layer. This will be available only if you specify **None** for the **Plot style** setting.
  - Let the **Plot style** control the lineweight of the objects and layers.
  - By default, **Paper Space** objects will be printed first, followed by the **Model Space** objects. Specify if you want the opposite.
  - Determine whether to show or hide the **Paper Space** objects.
- Specify the **Paper orientation**, either **Portrait** or **Landscape**. By default, the printer will start printing from top to bottom. Specify if you want the opposite.
- When you are done, click **OK**. The **Page Setup** will be available for all layouts in the current drawing file.
- To link any layout in your drawing file to a certain **Page Setup**, go to the desired layout, start the **Page Setup Manager**, select the **Page Setup** from the list, then click **Set Current**. (You can also double-click the name of the **Page Setup**.) The current layout will be linked to the **Page Setup** you select.
- To modify the settings of an existing **Page Setup**, click **Modify**.
- To use a saved **Page Setup** from an existing file, click **Import**.

CREATING LAYOUTS AND PAGE SETUP (METRIC)

Workshop 7-M
1. Start AutoCAD 2011, and open the file *Workshop_07.dwg*.
2. Make the **Viewports** layer current.
3. Right-click on the name of any existing layout and select **From template**.
4. Select the template file *Tutorial-mArch.dwt*.
5. Select the layout name **ISO A1 Layout**.
6. Go to **ISO A1 Layout** and delete the only viewport in the layout (select its frame and press [Delete]).
7. Delete **Layout2**.
8. Go to **Layout1** and rename it to **Final**. Right-click the name of the layout and select **Page Setup Manager**.
9. Create a new **Page Setup** and name it **Final**.

10. Set the following:
    a. Printer = DWF6 ePlot.pc3
    b. Paper Size = ISO A3 (420 × 297 MM)
    c. Orientation = Landscape
    d. Plot scale = 1:1
11. Make **Final** the current **Page Setup**.
12. Erase the existing viewport.
13. Make the **Frame** layer current, and insert the file named *ISO A3 Landscape Title Block.dwg* using 0,0 as the insertion point.
14. Save and close the file.

CREATING LAYOUTS AND PAGE SETUP (IMPERIAL)

Workshop 7-I
1. Start AutoCAD 2011, and open the file *Workshop_07.dwg*.
2. Make the **Viewports** layer current.
3. Right-click on the name of any existing layout, and select **From template**.
4. Select the template file *Tutorial-iArch.dwt*.
5. Select the layout name **D-Size Layout**.
6. Go to **D-Size Layout** and delete the only viewport in the layout (select its frame and press [Delete]).
7. Delete **Layout2**.
8. Go to **Layout1** and rename it to **Final**. Right-click the name of the layout and select **Page Setup Manager**.
9. Create a new **Page Setup** and name it **Final**.
10. Make the following settings:
    a. Printer = DWF6 ePlot.pc3
    b. Paper Size = ANSI B (17 × 11 Inches)
    c. Orientation = Landscape
    d. Plot scale = 1:1
11. Make **Final** the current **Page Setup**.
12. Erase the existing viewport.
13. Make the **Frame** layer current, and insert the file named *ANSI B Landscape Title Block.dwg* using 0,0 as the insertion point.
14. Save and close the file.

10.7 LAYOUTS AND VIEWPORTS

- After creating a new layout and **Page Setup** and linking the **Page Setup** to the layout, you will see the following:

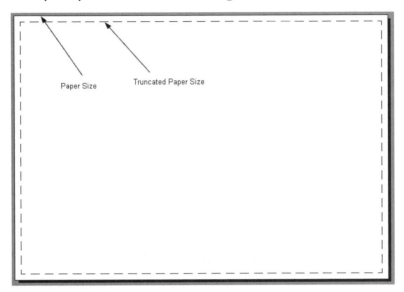

Paper Size   Truncated Paper Size

- The outer frame (solid line) is the real paper size.
- The inner frame (dashed line) is the truncated paper size, which is the paper size minus the printer margins.
  - Each printer comes with built-in margins on all sides.
  - AutoCAD can read these margins from the printer driver accordingly.
  - Thus, you should read your printer's manual to know exactly how wide the margins are on each side.
  - This will prove vital when you create the frame block of the establishment you will be working in because you should create it within the truncated paper size rather than the full size.
- Printing from layouts is WYSIWYG (what you see is what you get).
- Also, by default, you will see that a single viewport of your drawing appears at the center of the paper size.
- As stated at the beginning of this chapter, we have only one **Model Space**, but we can have as many **Layouts** as we wish. A **Viewport** is a rectangular shape (or any irregular shape) that contains a view of your **Model Space**.
- There are two types of **Viewports**:
  - **Model Space Viewports**: These are always tiled and cannot be scaled. The arrangement of viewports shown on the screen cannot be printed.

- **Layout Viewport**: These can be tiled or separated and can be scaled. The arrangement of viewports shown on the screen can be printed.
- See the following illustration:

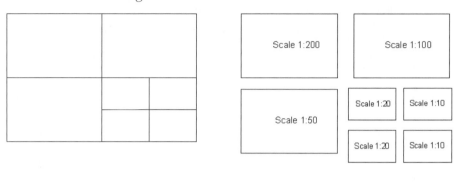

Model Space Viewports   Paper Space Viewports

10.8 ADDING VIEWPORTS TO LAYOUTS

- You can add viewports to layouts using different methods:
  - Adding a single rectangular viewport or multiple rectangular viewports.
  - Adding a single polygonal viewport.
  - Converting an object to a viewport.
  - Clipping an existing viewport.
- In the following discussion, we will review each method.

Single or Multiple Rectangular Viewports

- Use the **New Viewport** command to add as many single or multiple rectangular viewports as you wish in any layout. You must specify two opposite corners to determine the area of the viewport(s).
- On the **Ribbon**, go to the **View** tab. Using the **Viewports** panel, click the **New** button:

- The following dialog box will appear:

- From **Standard viewports**, select **Single**, then click **OK**. The following prompt will appear:

```
Specify first corner or [Fit] <Fit>:
Specify opposite corner:
```

- Just as we specify a window when we select objects, you will specify two opposite corners, a single viewport will be created accordingly.

- Use the same dialog box:

- Specify the arrangement you want. You can have two arrangements (**Horizontal** or **Vertical**), six different arrangements for three viewports, or one arrangement for four viewports.
- If you want the viewports to be tiled, leave the **Viewport Spacing** = **0.00**; otherwise, set a new value.
- Click **OK** and AutoCAD will display the following prompt:

```
Specify first corner or [Fit] <Fit>:
Specify opposite corner:
```

■ See the following illustration:

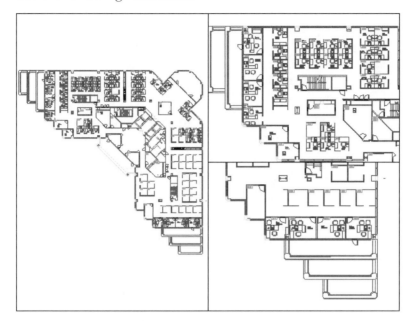

Single Polygonal Viewport

■ Use the **Create Polygonal** command to add a single viewport with any irregular shape consisting of both straight lines and arcs.
■ On the **Ribbon**, go to the **View** tab. Using the **Viewports** panel, click the **Create Polygonal** button:

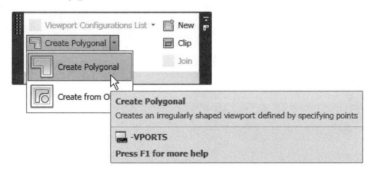

- The following prompt will appear:

```
Specify corner of viewport or
[ON/OFF/Fit/Shadeplot/Lock/Object/Polygonal/
Restore/LAyer/2/3/4] <Fit>: _p
Specify start point:
Specify next point or [Arc/Length/Undo]:
Specify next point or [Arc/Close/Length/Undo]:
```

- It is almost identical to the **Polyline** command.
- See the following illustration:

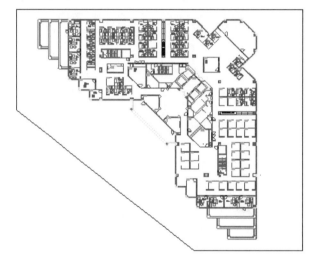

Converting an Object to a Viewport

- Use the **Create from Object** command to convert an existing object to a viewport.
- First, you must draw the object that will be converted to the viewport (e.g., a circle, polyline, ellipse).

- On the **Ribbon**, go to the **View** tab. Using the **Viewports** panel, click the **Create from Object** button:

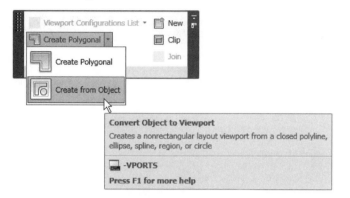

- The following prompt will appear:

```
Specify corner of viewport or
[ON/OFF/Fit/Shadeplot/Lock/Object/Polygonal/
Restore/LAyer/2/3/4] <Fit>: _o
Select object to clip viewport:
```

- See the following illustration:

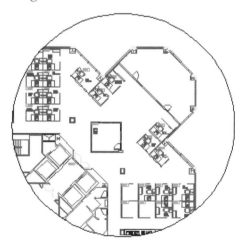

Clipping Existing Viewport

- Use the **Clip** command to change a rectangular viewport to an irregular shape.

- On the **Ribbon**, go to the **View** tab. Using the **Viewports** panel, click the **Clip** button:

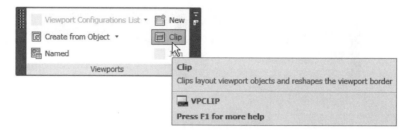

- The following prompt will appear:

```
Select viewport to clip:
Select clipping object or [Polygonal] <Polygonal>:
Specify start point:
Specify next point or [Arc/Length/Undo]:
Specify next point or [Arc/Close/Length/Undo]:
```

- Select the existing viewport first. You can draw a polyline beforehand, or you can draw any irregular shape using the **Polygonal** option, which is identical to the **Polygonal viewport**.
- See the following illustration:

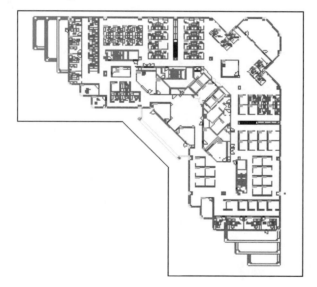

10.9 PAPER SPACE AND MODEL SPACE MODES IN LAYOUTS

- In a layout, you deal with the viewports in two modes:
  - **Paper Space** mode
  - **Model Space** mode

Paper Space Mode

- **Paper Space** is the default mode in any layout.
- In the **Status Bar**, you will see the following:

- As discussed previously, you can place the viewports in this mode.
- You can also deal with the viewports as objects, so you can copy, move, stretch, rotate, and delete them. For example:

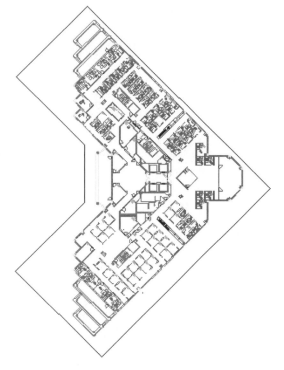

Rotated Viewport

Model Space Mode

- In the **Model Space** mode, you are *inside* the viewport. You can:
  - Zoom in, zoom out, and pan.
  - Scale each viewport.
  - Change the status of layers for the current viewports.
- There are two ways to enter this mode:
  - Double-click inside the desired viewport.
  - From the **Status Bar**, click the **Paper** button. It will switch to **Model** as shown:

- To switch from the **Model Space** mode to the **Paper Space** mode, simply double-click outside any viewport, or click the **Model** button on the **Status Bar**.

10.10 MODIFYING, SCALING, AND MAXIMIZING VIEWPORTS

- Each viewport can be modified, scaled, and maximized to fill the whole screen.

Modifying

- Each viewport is considered an object. As such, it can be copied, moved, scaled, rotated, and deleted. You must select each viewport from its border in order to select it.
- You can select viewports first and then issue the modifying command, or vice versa.

Scaling

- Each viewport should be scaled relative to the **Model Space** units.
  - Double-click inside the desired viewport; you will switch to the **Model Space** mode for this viewport.
  - At the right side of the **Status Bar**, you will see the following:

- Click the pop-up list that contains the scales. You will see a list resembling the following:

Scale to fit
1:1
1:2
1:4
1:5
1:8
1:10
1:16
1:20
1:30
1:40
1:50
1:100
2:1
4:1
8:1
10:1
100:1
1/128" = 1'-0"
1/64" = 1'-0"
1/32" = 1'-0"
1/16" = 1'-0"
3/32" = 1'-0"
1/8" = 1'-0"
3/16" = 1'-0"
1/4" = 1'-0"
3/8" = 1'-0"
1/2" = 1'-0"
3/4" = 1'-0"
1" = 1'-0"
1-1/2" = 1'-0"
3" = 1'-0"
6" = 1'-0"
1'-0" = 1'-0"
Custom...
✔ Hide Xref scales

- Select the suitable scale to be used in the viewport.

- If you did not find the desired scale, select the **Custom** option. You will see the following dialog box:

- Click the **Add** button to add a new scale. You will see the following dialog box:

- Type in the desired scale, then click **OK** twice.
- After you set the scale, you can use the **Pan** command. However, if you want to use the **Zoom** command, the scale value will be invalid, and you will have to repeat the procedure for setting the scale.
- To avoid this problem, you can lock the display of the viewport by clicking the golden opened lock in the **Status Bar** (you must be inside the viewport, or select the viewport border, for this to work). The golden lock will change to blue, and it will be locked:

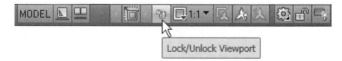

NOTE ➤ ■ There are two possible results once you have scaled a viewport:
  • The scale is perfect for the area of the viewport. Leave it as is.
  • The scale is either too small or too big. Either change the scale or change the area of the viewport.

Maximizing

■ After placing and scaling your viewports, there will be small ones and big ones.
■ For small ones, you can maximize the area of the viewport to be as large as your screen. You can do all of your work, then return it to the original size.
■ Using the **Status Bar**, click the **Maximize Viewport** button:

■ This button will become **Minimize Viewport** to restore the original size of the viewport.
NOTE ➤ ■ Another way of maximizing the viewport is to double-click the viewport's border.

10.11 FREEZING LAYERS IN A VIEWPORT

■ In Chapter 3, we learned to freeze a layer. This tool is effective in both **Model Space** and **Layouts**.
■ In **Layouts**, if you freeze a layer, it will be frozen in all viewports. If you want to freeze a certain layer(s) in one of the viewports and not the other viewports, you must freeze the layer in the current viewport.
■ Perform the following steps:
  • Make the desired viewport current by double-clicking inside it.

- On the **Ribbon**, go to the **Home** tab. Using the **Layers** panel, click the icon **Freeze or thaw in current viewport** for the desired layer, as shown:

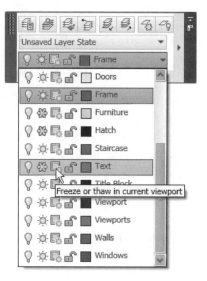

10.12 LAYER OVERRIDE IN VIEWPORTS

- **Color**, **Linetype**, **Lineweight**, and **Plot Styles** are the same for all layers in all viewports.
- You can assign different colors, linetypes, lineweights, or plot styles for each layer in each viewport. This is called **Layer Override**.
- Perform the following steps:
  - Double-click inside the desired viewport.
  - Start the **Layer Properties Manager**.
  - Under **VP Color**, **VP Linetype**, **VP Lineweight**, or **VP Plot Style**, make the desired changes.
  - You will see that changes only took place in the current viewport.

- See the following illustration:

S..	Name	O..	Fre...	L...	Color	Linetype	Lineweight	Trans...	Plot S...	P...	N..	V...	VP C...	VP Linetype	VP Linew...	VP
	0				white	Continuous	— Defa...	0	Color_7				wh...	Continuous	— Defa...	0
	Bubbles				green	Continuous	— Defa...	0	Color_3				gr...	Continuous	— Defa...	0
	Centerlines				green	DASHDOT	— Defa...	0	Color_3				gr...	DASHDOT	— Defa...	0
	Defpoints				white	Continuous	— Defa...	0	Color_7				wh...	Continuous	— Defa...	0
	Dimension				blue	Continuous	— Defa...	0	Color_5				red	Continuous	— Defa...	0
	Door_Swing				yellow	DASHED	— Defa...	0	Color_2				ye...	DASHED	— Defa...	0
	Doors				yellow	Continuous	— Defa...	0	Color_2				ye...	Continuous	— Defa...	0
	Frame				mage...	Continuous	— Defa...	0	Color_6				m...	Continuous	— Defa...	0
	Furniture				41	Continuous	— Defa...	0	Color_...				41	Continuous	— Defa...	0
	Hatch				white	Continuous	— Defa...	0	Color_7				wh...	Continuous	— Defa...	0
	Staircase				140	Continuous	— Defa...	0	Color_...				140	Continuous	— Defa...	0
	Text				cyan	Continuous	— Defa...	0	Color_4				cyan	Continuous	— Defa...	0
	Title Block				white	Continuous	— Defa...	0	Color_7				wh...	Continuous	— Defa...	0
	Viewport				blue	Continuous	— Defa...	0	Color_5				blue	Continuous	— Defa...	0
	Viewports				8	Continuous	— Defa...	0	Color_8				8	Continuous	— Defa...	0
	Walls				red	Continuous	— Defa...	0	Color_1				red	Continuous	— Defa...	0
	Windows				150	Continuous	— Defa...	0	Color_...				150	Continuous	— Defa...	0

Current layer: Frame — Search for layer

Layer Properties Manager

All: 17 layers displayed of 17 total layers

- You can see that the normal color of the **Dimension** layer is blue (which applies to **Model Space** and all other viewports), and its override color is red in the current viewport.
- Also, note that the row containing the **Dimension** layer is shaded with a different color.

INSERTING AND SCALING VIEWPORTS (METRIC)

Workshop 8-M

1. Start AutoCAD 2011, and open the file *Workshop_08.dwg*.
2. Select **ISO A1 Layout**.
3. Make the **Viewports** layer current.
4. Click **OSNAP** off.
5. On the **Ribbon**, go to the **View** tab. Using the **Viewports** panel, click the **New** button. Select the arrangement **Three: Left**, and set the **Viewport spacing** to be 5.
6. Click **OK**, and specify two opposite corners so the three viewports fill the empty space.
7. Select the big viewport at the left and set the scale to be 1:50 (make sure to go to the **Model Space** and get the right and left dimensions closer to the building). The upper viewport scale should be 1:20, and the lower viewport scale should be 1:30.

8. Double-click outside the viewports to move to the **Paper** mode.

9. Thaw **Furniture** and **Hatch**.

10. Make the big left viewport the current viewport. In this viewport, freeze only the **Hatch** layer.

11. Make the upper viewport current and pan to the master bedroom (do not use the zooming facilities). In this viewport, freeze the **Dimension** layer.

12. Make the lower viewport current and pan to the entrance and kitchen. In this viewport, freeze the **Dimension** layer.

13. Double-click outside the viewports to move to the **Paper** mode.

14. Lock the view in the three viewports.

15. Go to the **Final** layout.

16. Insert a single viewport covering the whole area.

17. Freeze the **Dimension** layer in this viewport.

18. Using **Viewport clipping**, clip the viewport around the shape of the outer wall.

19. Move the new clipped shape to the left and up a little bit.

20. In the empty space below, draw a circle and convert it into a viewport showing the kitchen.

21. Double-click inside the clipped viewport.

22. Start the **Layer Properties Manager**.

23. Change the **VP color** as follows:
    a. Furniture VP Color = Blue
    b. Door VP Color = Green
    c. Door_Swing VP Color = Green

24. Save and close the file.

INSERTING AND SCALING VIEWPORTS (IMPERIAL)

Workshop 8-I

1. Start AutoCAD 2011, and open the file *Workshop_08.dwg*.

2. Select **D-Sized Layout**.

3. Make the **Viewports** layer current.

4. Click **OSNAP** off.

5. On the **Ribbon**, go to the **View** tab. Using the **Viewports** panel, click the **New** button. Select the arrangement **Three: Left**, and set the **Viewport spacing** to be 0.35.

6. Click **OK**, and specify two opposite corners so the three viewports fill the empty space.

7. Select the big viewport at the left and set the scale to be ¼" = 1' (make sure to go to the **Model Space** and get the right and left dimensions closer to the building). Set the upper viewport and the lower viewport scale to be ½" = 1'.

8. Double-click outside the viewports to move to the **Paper** mode.

9. Thaw **Furniture** and **Hatch**.

10. Make the big left viewport the current viewport. In this viewport, freeze only the **Hatch** layer.

11. Make the upper viewport current and pan to the master bedroom (do not use the zooming facilities). In this viewport, freeze the **Dimension** layer.

12. Make the lower viewport current and pan to the entrance and kitchen. In this viewport, freeze the **Dimension** layer.

13. Double-click outside the viewports to move to the **Paper** mode.

14. Lock the view in the three viewports.

15. Go to the **Final** layout.

16. Insert a single viewport covering the whole area.

17. Freeze the **Dimension** layer in this viewport.

18. Using **Viewport clipping**, clip the viewport around the shape of the outer wall.

19. Move the new clipped shape to the left and up a little bit.

20. In the empty space below, draw a circle and convert it into a viewport showing the kitchen.

21. Double-click inside the clipped viewport.

22. Start the **Layer Properties Manager**.

23. Change the **VP color** as follows:
    a. Furniture VP Color = Blue
    b. Door VP Color = Green
    c. Door_Swing VP Color = Green

24. Save and close the file.

10.13 AN INTRODUCTION TO PLOT STYLE TABLES

- There are many colors available in AutoCAD, but will these colors print?
- There are two approaches to printing colors:
  - Using the same colors in both the soft copy and the hard copy of the drawing.

- For each color in the soft copy, assigning a different color in the hard copy.
- To translate the colors between soft copy and hard copy, you must create a **Plot Style**.
- There are two types of **Plot Style Tables**:
  - **Color-Dependent Plot Style Table**
  - **Named Plot Style Table**

10.14 THE COLOR-DEPENDENT PLOT STYLE TABLE

- This method is almost the same method used prior to AutoCAD 2000; it depends on the colors used in the drawing file.
- Each color used in the drawing file is printed with a color chosen by the user. The user will also set each color's lineweight, linetype, etc.
- This method is limited because there are only 255 colors to use.
- Also, if two layers have the same color, you will be forced to use the same output color, with the same lineweight, linetype, etc.
- Each time you create a **Color-Dependent Plot Style Table**, AutoCAD will ask you to name the file with extension *.ctb*.
- You can create **Plot Style Tables** from outside AutoCAD (using the Windows **Control Panel**), or from inside AutoCAD using the **Wizard**. These methods initiate the command, but the command works the same either way.
- From outside AutoCAD, start the Windows **Control Panel**. Double-click the **Autodesk Plot Style Manager** icon. Because this command is not available on the **Ribbon**, you can type **stylesmanager** in the **Command Window**. From the **Menu Bar**, select **Tools/Wizards/Add Plot Style Table**.

- Using the Windows **Control Panel**, you will see the following:

- Double-click **Add-A-Plot Style Table Wizard**. The following dialog box will appear, in which AutoCAD explains the next few steps to be taken:

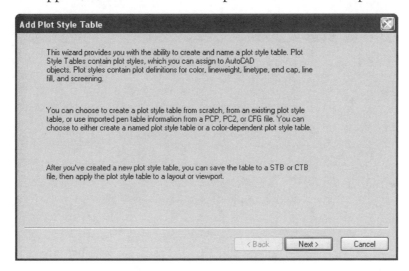

■ Click **Next** and the following dialog box will appear:

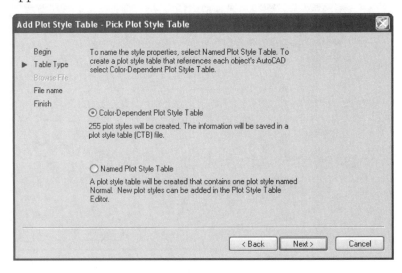

■ You have four choices:
   • Start creating your style from scratch.
   • Use an existing plot style.
   • Import the *AutoCAD R14 CFG* file and create a plot style from it.
   • Import the *PCP* or *PC2* file and create a plot style from it.
■ Select **Start from scratch** and click **Next**. The following dialog box will appear:

- Select **Color-Dependent Plot Style Table** and click **Next**. The following dialog box will appear:

```
Add Plot Style Table - File name                              [X]

    Begin                Enter a file name for the new plot style table you are creating. To
    Table Type           identify this as a plot style table file, a CTB extension will be
                         appended.
    Browse File
  ▶ File name
    Finish

                         File name :

                         [Final                                    ]


                                        [ < Back ]  [ Next > ]  [ Cancel ]
```

- Type in the name of the plot style and click **Next**. The following will appear:

```
Add Plot Style Table - Finish                                 [X]

    Begin                A plot style table named Final.ctb has been created. Plot style
    Table Type           information contained in the new table can be used to control the
                         display of objects in plotted layouts or viewports
    Browse File
    File name
  ▶ Finish

                              [    Plot Style Table Editor ...    ]

                         To modify the plot style properties in the new Plot Style Table,
                         choose Plot Style Table Editor.


                         [ ] Use this plot style table for new and pre-AutoCAD drawings.


                                        [ < Back ]  [ Finish ]  [ Cancel ]
```

■ You can select **Use this plot style table for new and pre-AutoCAD 2011 drawings**. Click the **Plot Style Table Editor** button. You will see the following:

■ At the left, select the color you used in your drawing file; at the right, change all or any of the following settings:
  • **Color**: This is the hard copy color.
  • **Dither**: This option will be dimmed if your printer or plotter does not support dithering. Dithering allows the printer to give the impression of using more colors than the limited 255 colors of AutoCAD. It is preferable to leave this option off. It should be on, however, if you want **Screening** to work.
  • **Grayscale**: You can translate the 255 colors to grayscale grades (good for laser printers).
  • **Pen #**: This option is good only for the old types of plotters—pen plotters—which are now obsolete.
  • **Virtual pen #**: This option is for non-pen plotters to simulate pen plotters by assigning a virtual pen for each color. It is preferable to leave it set on **Automatic**.

- **Screening**: This is good for trial printing. Setting numbers at less than 100 will reduce the intensity of the shading and fill hatches. You should turn **Dither** on so **Screening** will be effective.
- **Linetype**: You can use the object's linetype or you can set a different linetype for each color.
- **Adaptive**: This option changes the linetype scale to fit the current line length so it will start with a segment and end with a segment, rather than ending with a space. Turn this option off if the linetype scale is important to the drawing.
- **Lineweight**: Set the lineweight for the color selected. You can choose from a list of lineweights.
- **Line end style**: To specify the end style for lines, choose from **Butt**, **Square**, **Round**, and **Diamond**.
- **Line join style**: To specify the line join (the connection between two lines) style, choose from **Miter**, **Bevel**, **Round**, and **Diamond**.
- **Fill style**: This is used to set the fill style for the area filled in the drawing (good for trial printing).

- Click **Save & Close**, then click **Finish**.
- To link a **Color-Dependent Plot Style** to a layout, do the following:
  - Go to the desired layout and start the **Page Setup Manager**.
  - At the upper right of the dialog box, change the **Plot style table (pen assignments)** setting to the desired *.ctb* file:

  - You can click the small button at the right to edit the plot style table.
  - Click the **Display plot styles** checkbox.
- You can assign one *.ctb* file for each layout.
- To see the lineweight of the objects, you must click on the **Show/Hide Lineweight** button on the **Status Bar**:

10.15 THE NAMED PLOT STYLE TABLE

- The **Named Plot Style Table** is the method introduced in AutoCAD 2000. It does not depend on colors.
- You will create a **Plot Style Table** and give it a name. Each plot style will include different tables inside it, which you will later link with layers.
- With this method, you can have two layers of the same color that will be printed in different colors, linetypes, and lineweights.
- The **Named Plot Style Table** has the file extension **.stb*.
- The procedure for creating the **Named Plot Style Table** is identical to the **Color-Dependent Plot Style Table**, except the last step, which uses the **Plot Style Table Editor** button.
- From outside AutoCAD, start the Windows **Control Panel**. Double-click the **Autodesk Plot Style Manager** icon. Because this command is not available on the **Ribbon**, you can type **stylesmanager** in the **Command Window**.
- Double-click **Add-A-Plot Style Table Wizard**.
- Go through the dialog boxes until you reach the **Plot Style Table Editor** button. Click it and you will see the dialog box that follows.
- After you click the **Add Style** button, you will see the **Plot Style Table Editor** for the **Named Plot Style**:

- As you can see, you can make the following changes (the rest is identical to the **Color-Dependent Plot Style Table**):
  - Type in the **Name** of the style.
  - Type in any **Description** for this style.
  - Specify the **Color** that you will use in the hard copy.
- You can add as many styles as you wish in the same **Named Plot Style**.
- Click **Save & Close**, then click **Finish**.
- To link a **Named Plot Style Table** with a drawing, do the following:
  - You must first convert one of the *.ctb* files to a *.stb* file. In the **Command Window**, type **convertctb**. A dialog box with all the *.ctb* files will appear. Select one of them, keeping the same name or renaming it, then click **OK**. The following dialog box will appear:

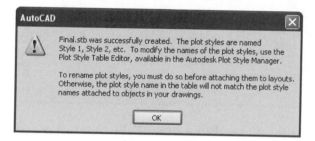

  - Convert the drawing from **Color Dependent Plot Style** to **Named Plot Style**. In the **Command Window**, type **convertpstyles**. The following warning message will appear:

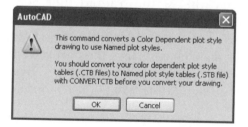

- Click **OK** and the following dialog box will appear:

- Select the **Named Plot Style Table** you just converted and click **Open**. The following message will appear in the **Command Window**:

```
Drawing converted from Color Dependent mode to Named plot
style mode.
```

- Because you will use the **Named Plot Style Table** with layers, the **Model Space** and all layouts will be assigned the same *.stb* file.
- Go to the desired layout and start the **Page Setup Manager**. At the upper right of the dialog box, change the **Plot style table (pen assignments)** setting to the desired *.stb* file. Click the **Display plot styles** checkbox and end the **Page Setup Manager** command:

- Go to the **Layer Properties Manager** and search for the desired layer in the **Plot Style** column:

S..	Name	On	Fre...	L...	Color	Linetype	Lineweight	Trans...	Plot Style	P...
✓	0	♀	☼	🔓	■ white	Continuous	—— Defa...	0	Style_1	
	Bubbles	♀	☼	🔓	■ cyan	Continuous	—— Defa...	0	Style_2	
	Centerlines	♀	☼	🔓	■ cyan	Continuous	—— Defa...	0	Style_1	
	Dimension	♀	☼	🔓	■ red	Continuous	—— Defa...	0	Style_2	
	Door	♀	☼	🔓	□ yellow	Continuous	—— Defa...	0	Style_2	
	Furniture	♀	☼	🔓	□ 51	Continuous	—— Defa...	0	Style_1	
	Hatch	♀	☼	🔓	□ 9	Continuous	—— Defa...	0	Style_2	
	Partition	♀	☼	🔓	■ blue	Continuous	—— Defa...	0	Style_2	
	Table	♀	☼	🔓	■ green	Continuous	—— Defa...	0	Style_2	
	Text	♀	☼	🔓	■ green	Continuous	—— Defa...	0	Style_1	
	Title Block	♀	☼	🔓	■ white	Continuous	—— Defa...	0	Style_2	
	Viewports	♀	☼	🔓	□ 8	Continuous	—— Defa...	0	Style_2	
	Wall	♀	☼	🔓	■ blue	Continuous	—— Defa...	0	Style_2	
	Window	♀	☼	🔓	□ yellow	Continuous	—— Defa...	0	Style_2	

Current layer: 0   Search for layer

All: 14 layers displayed of 14 total layers

- Click the name of the current style. The following dialog box will appear:

Select Plot Style

Plot styles

Style_1
Normal
Style_2

Original: Style_1
New: Style_1

Active plot style table:

Final.stb   Editor...

Attached to: Layout1

OK   Cancel   Help

- Select the desired plot style to be linked to the selected layer. When done, click **OK**.

COLOR-DEPENDENT PLOT STYLE TABLES

Exercise 10-1

1. Start AutoCAD 2011.
2. Open the file *Exercise 10-1.dwg*.
3. Go to **Layer Properties Manager** and check the colors of the different layers.
4. Notice the two layers **Centerlines** and **Centerlines-Tags**, which are using the same color but different linetypes.
5. Also, notice that there are seven layers using the same color—white (black)—that may be plotted with different lineweights.
6. Change the color of the layer **Title Block** to color = 9.
7. Click the **ISO A1 – Overall** layout.
8. Using the **Control Panel**, start a new **Plot Style Table** and choose **Color-Dependent**. Name this plot style *Arch Plan.ctb*, and make the following changes:

Drawing Color	Plotter Color	Linetype	Lineweight
Color 1	Black	Use Object linetype	0.30
Color 2	Black	Use Object linetype	0.50
Color 3	Black	Use Object linetype	0.30
Color 4	Black	Solid	0.30
Color 5	Black	Solid	0.50
Color 6	Black	Solid	0.30
Color 7	Black	Solid	0.50
Color 9	Black	Solid	0.70
Color 27	Black	Solid	0.50

9. Save the plot style and close the **Plot Style Manager**.
10. Go to the **Page Setup Manager**, and select **Plot Style Table** to be **Arch Plan.ctb**, and click **Display plot styles** on.
11. Click the **Show/Hide Lineweight** button to see the effect of the lineweight.
12. Save and close the file.

NAMED PLOT STYLE TABLES

Exercise 10-2

1. Start AutoCAD 2011.
2. Open the file *Exercise 10-2.dwg*.
3. Using the **Control Panel**, create a new **Named Plot Style Table** and name it *Arch Plan.stb*.
4. Create the following plot styles:

Style name	Color	Linetype	Lineweight
Frame	Black	Solid	0.7
Wall	Black	Solid	0.5
Annotation	Black	Solid	0.3
Centerlines	Black	Dashdot	0.3
Others	Black	Solid	0.5

5. Save and close the **Plot style editor**.
6. Go to the **ISO A1 – Overall** layout.
7. Start the **Page Setup Manager**, set **Arch Plan.stb** as your plot style, and click **Display plot styles** on.
8. Nothing will happen because we must link layers to the corresponding plot style.
9. Start the **Layer Properties Manager** and set the following plot styles for the following layers:

Layer Name	Plot Style
Title Block	Frame
A-Walls, Partition	Wall
Centerlines	Centerlines
Centerline-Tags, Dimensions, Text	Annotation
Other layers	Others

10. In the **Command Window**, type **regenall**.
11. Make sure that **Show/Hide Lineweight** is on.
12. Save and close the file.

10.16 THE PLOT COMMAND

- The final step in this process is to issue the **Plot** command, which sends your layout to the printer or plotter.
- First, go to the layout you want to plot.
- On the **Ribbon**, go to the **Output** tab. Using the **Plot** panel, click the **Plot** icon:

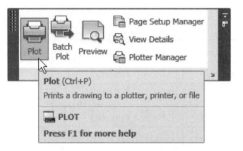

- The following dialog box will appear:

Plot - ISO A1 - Architectural Details

ⓘ Learn about Plotting

Page setup

Name: <None>   Add...

Printer/plotter

Name: DWF6 ePlot.pc3   Properties...

Plotter: DWF6 ePlot - DWF ePlot - by Autodesk

Where: File

Description:

☑ Plot to file

       ⟵ 841 MM ⟶   594 MM

Paper size   **Number of copies**

ISO A1 (841.00 x 594.00 MM)   1

Plot area   **Plot scale**

What to plot: ☐ Fit to paper

Layout   Scale: 1:1

Plot offset (origin set to printable area)   1   mm   =

X: 0.00   mm   ☐ Center the plot   1   unit

Y: 0.00   mm   ☐ Scale lineweights

Preview...   Apply to Layout   OK   Cancel   Help   ⊙

- As you can see, the settings are identical to those in **Page Setup Manager**.
- If you change any of these settings, AutoCAD will detach the **Page Setup** from the current layout.
- Click the **Apply to Layout** button if you want this plot dialog box saved with this layout for future use.
- Click the **Preview** button to see the final printed drawing on the screen before the real printout. You can decide if your choices of plot styles and other settings are correct.
- You can preview your drawing from outside this dialog box. On the **Ribbon**, go to the **Output** tab. Using the **Plot** panel, click the **Preview** button:

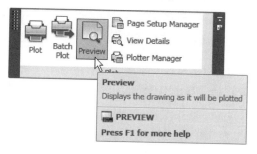

- When you are done, click **OK**. The drawing will be sent to the printer.

10.17 THE ANNOTATIVE FEATURE

- It is recommend that AutoCAD users print from layouts and not from **Model Space**. (Although you *can* print from **Model Space**!)
- It is obvious that Autodesk will not develop anything new for people who like to print from **Model Space**, and since AutoCAD 2000, Autodesk has put all of its resources toward printing from layouts.
- So, if we assume that we will print only from layouts, then we will use viewports (there is no other way), and viewports require VP scale (as discussed earlier).
- Thus, a problem lies in your annotation objects, including:
  - **Text** (**Single line** and **Multiple lines**)
  - **Dimensions** (**Dimensions** and **Multileader**)
  - **Hatching**
- The normal procedure is as follows:
  - Specify all of your annotation objects in **Model Space**.
  - Go to **Layout**, create viewports, and scale them.

- Since you may have different viewports in the same layout with different scales, annotation objects will appear clear and readable in some viewports and tiny and unreadable in others.
- Users tend to control the visibility of the layers by creating multiple styles with different sizes and by inputting different sizes in different layers.

■ To solve this problem, Autodesk invented a feature for the annotation object, called **Annotative**.

■ You will find the **Annotative** feature in different places:
  - In the **Fit** tab of the **Dimension style** box:

      Scale for dimension features
      ☑ Annotative ⓘ
      ◯ Scale dimensions to layout
      ◉ Use overall scale of: 0.75

  - In the **Leader Structure** tab of the **Multileader style** box:

      Scale
      ☑ Annotative ⓘ
      ◯ Scale multileaders to layout
      ◉ Specify scale: 1

  - In the **Text style** box:

      Size
      ☑ Annotative ⓘ   Paper Text Height
      ☐ Match text orientation   0.9000
        to layout

  - In the **Hatch** dialog box:

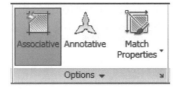

Associative   Annotative   Match Properties
Options ▾

- When using the **Block** command:

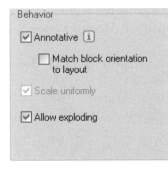

- When using the **Attribute** command:

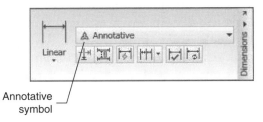

■ To differentiate an annotative style from an ordinary style, check the symbol at the left in any pop-up list:

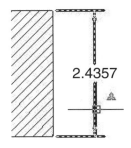

■ To know whether an object is annotative, hover over it. You will see the following:

Procedure

- To best utilize the **Annotative** feature, follow this procedure:
  - Create your drawing in **Model Space**, but without **Dimensions**, **Text**, **Hatching**, etc.
  - Go to your layout and add the desired viewports.
  - Select the desired viewport to scale (either by selecting the border or by double-clicking inside it).
  - Set the scale of the viewport using the **Status Bar**:

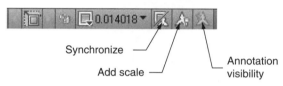

  - Click the scale pop-up list and choose the desired scale. This scale will be for both the annotation objects and the viewport.
  - Double-click inside the viewport to make it active.
  - Use your annotative style to annotate your drawing.

Important Notes

- By default, the following notes are true about annotation using annotative styles:
  - Once you input any annotation in the viewport, the annotation will appear only in this viewport and will not appear in other viewports unless they have the same scale value.
  - If you change the scale of the viewport, the annotation will disappear.
  - If you want to show the annotation in more than one viewport holding different scale values, right-click on the **Annotation Visibility** button. The following menu will appear:

  - Select between **Show Annotation Objects for Current Scale Only** and **Show Annotation Objects for All Scales**.
  - You can also control whether adding scale values to the viewport is automatic or manual. Right-click on the **Add Scale** button and the following menu will appear:

Automatically add scales to annotative objects when the annotation scale changes

- If you use the **Zoom** command inside the viewport, this will change the scale value of the viewport. To correct this issue, click the **Synchronize** button and the following message will appear:

> Annotation scale is not equal to viewport scale: Click to synchronize

- When you click this message, your viewport scale will be restored.
- At any time, you can use the lock in the **Status Bar** to lock the viewport scale.
- If you want an annotation object to appear in different viewports holding different scales, select it and right-click. When the menu appears, select **Annotative Object Scale**. The following menu will appear:

Annotative Object Scale ►	Add Current Scale
	Delete Current Scale
Clipboard ►	Add/Delete Scales...
Isolate ►	Synchronize Multiple-scale Positions

- Select the option **Add/Delete Scales**. The following dialog box will appear:

Annotation Object Scale

Object Scale List

1:1

Add...
Delete

1 paper unit = 1 drawing unit

◉ List all scales for selected objects
○ List scales common to all selected objects only

OK   Cancel   Help

- Click the **Add** button and you will see the following dialog box:

Add Scales to Object   ☒

Scale List

```
1:2
1:4
1:5
1:8
1:10
1:16
1:20
1:30
1:40
1:50
1:100
2:1
4:1
8:1
```

    [OK]   [Cancel]   [Help]

- Select the desired scale value and click **OK**; then click **OK** again to finish the command.

Before and After

■ To appreciate this feature in AutoCAD, it helps to see the before and after images:
  - When you put your dimension objects in the **Model Space** and you want to print from layout, you will get something like the following (before):

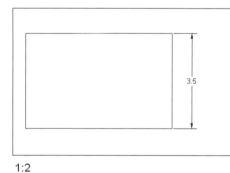

1:2   1:10

- As you can see, it is very clear in the 1:2 scale, but you cannot see it in the 1:10 scale.

- When you make your dimension style **Annotative** and you put your dimensions in the layout, you will get something like the following (after):

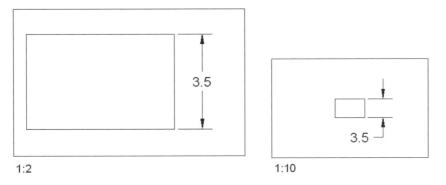

THE ANNOTATIVE FEATURE

Exercise 10-3

1. Start AutoCAD 2011.
2. Open the file *Exercise 10-3.dwg*.
3. Go to the **A4 Landscape** layout.
4. You will find three viewports, each one with its scale shown in the following illustration.
5. Make **Dimensions** the current layer.
6. Make **Annotative** the current dimension style.

7. Make sure to double-click inside each viewport before inputting the dimensions. Input the dimensions as shown:

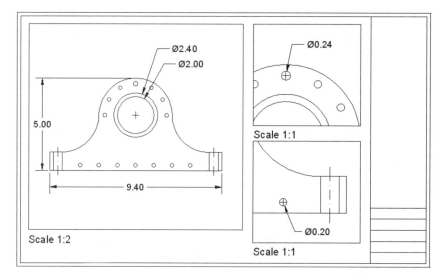

8. Make **Hatch** the current layer.
9. Double-click inside the viewport at the left and start the **Hatch** command. Be sure to switch **Annotative** on. Hatch the two holes around the center line. See the following illustration:

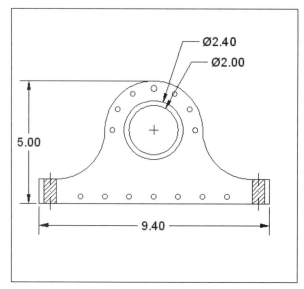

10. Notice that the hatch did not appear in the lower viewport!

11. Select the hatch, right-click, and select **Annotative Object Scale/Add Delete Scales**, and add scale 1:1. What happens?

12. Save and close the file.

10.18 WHAT IS A DWF FILE?

- Assume one or all of the following cases:
  - You want to share your design with another company, but you worry that if you send them the *.dwg* file they will mess it up.
  - Your *.dwg* file is very large (more than 10 MB), which may not be accepted by your email server.
  - The recipient does not have AutoCAD to view a *.dwg* file.
- Thus, you do not want to send your *.dwg* file, but you must share your design. How can you solve such a predicament?
- AutoCAD allows you to plot to a DWF (Design Web Format) file. This file has the following features:
  - You do not need AutoCAD to open a DWF file. Free software comes with AutoCAD, called **Autodesk Design Review**, which you can also download from the Internet free of charge.
  - You can view the file, zoom, pan, measure, mark, and print it.
  - The file is small, so you can email it.
  - The recipient cannot modify it.

10.19 WHAT IS A DWFx FILE?

- The DWFx file was introduced by both Autodesk, Inc. and Microsoft.
- It replaced the DWF as the next generation file.
- If you are using Windows Vista, you will be able to view a DWFx file without any additional viewer.
- DWFx can also be viewed using Windows Internet Explorer.

10.20 EXPORTING DWF, DWFx, AND PDF FILES

- You can export DWF, DWFx, and PDF files using AutoCAD 2011.
- On the **Ribbon**, go to the **Output** tab. Using the **Export to DWF/PDF** panel, click the **Export** button:

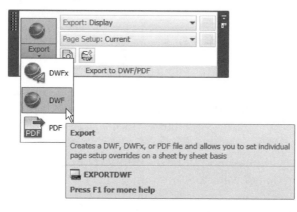

- The dialog box for the three file types is identical:

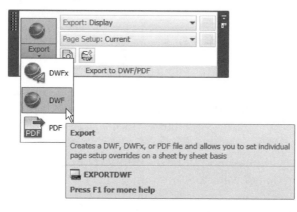

- Specify the hard disk, folder, and the name of the file.

- Review the **Current Settings** at the upper right of the dialog box:

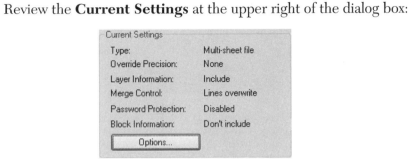

- If these settings are correct, go to the next step. If not, click the **Options** button and you will see the following dialog box:

- Change the following settings:
  - Specify the location of the file.
  - Specify if the file will be **Single sheet** (current layout) or **Multi-sheet** (all layouts). While exporting, AutoCAD will always produce a single layout, which is the current layout. This option is discussed in the next section covering the **Publish** command.
  - If you select a **Multi-sheet** file, select whether to **Prompt for name**.
  - Select whether to include the **Layer information** in the file.
  - Select whether to include a **Password** for the DWF file (not available for PDF files).
  - Select whether to include the **Block information** (such as attributes) in the file.
- Once you are done, click **OK**.

- Now set the **Output Controls**:

- Select whether to open the file in the viewer when done.
- Select whether to include a plot stamp.
- Select what to export. If you are in a layout, the choice **Current layout** will be selected automatically.
- Select the **Page Setup**. AutoCAD will make the page setup included inside the layout the selected one. You can select any other page setups that exist in the drawing, or you can create a temporary page setup for this plot only.
- When you are done, click the **Save** button.

10.21 THE PUBLISH COMMAND

- The **Publish** command produces a DWF file that contains multiple layouts from the current drawing and from other drawings.
- On the **Ribbon**, go to the **Output** tab. Using the **Plot** panel, click the **Batch Plot** button:

- The following dialog box will appear:

- You will see a list of the current file's **Model Space** and layouts.
- You can specify a previously saved **Sheet list** in the current drawing, or you can:
  - Click the open folder icon to open a previously saved **Sheet list**.

  - Click the disk icon to save a **Sheet list** for future printing.
  - Select whether you want to use the printer/plotter defined in the layout or a DWF, DWFx, or PDF file.
  - Select whether to load all open drawings automatically.
- Select one of the sheets and use the following buttons:
  - This button adds more sheets from other drawings. The **Select Drawings** dialog box will be shown to select the desired file.

  - This button removes one sheet or more from the list.

  - This button moves the sheet up in the list.

- • This button moves the sheet down in the list.

- • Use this button to preview the selected sheet (only a single sheet) as we did in **Print Preview**.

■ Click **Publish Options** and you will see the following dialog box:

Publish Options		✕
Current user: Munir		
Default output location (plot to file)		▲
Location	D:\Final Draft\	
General DWF/PDF options		▲
Type	Multi-sheet file	
Naming	Prompt for name	
Name	N/A	
Layer information	Include	
Merge control	Lines overwrite	
DWF data options		▲
Password protection	Disabled	
Password	N/A	
Block information	Don't include	
Block template file	N/A	
3D DWF options		▲
Group by Xref hierarchy	N/A	
Publish with materials	N/A	

OK   Cancel   Help

- • This dialog box was discussed in the section on DWF, DWFx, and PDF exporting.
- • Here, **Multi-sheet File** means all sheets in the current sheet list.
■ Specify the number of copies.
■ To include a **Plot Stamp** in each sheet, check the **Include plot stamp** box.
■ Select whether you want to publish in the background.
■ Select whether to open the file in the viewer when done.
■ You can see more details about the selected sheet, including **Plot device, Plot size, Plot scale**, etc.
■ When you are done with these settings, click the **Publish** button. AutoCAD will then create the sheets one by one.

■ You will see the following dialog box:

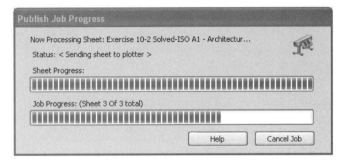

■ When AutoCAD is done, you will see the following message:

10.22 VIEWING DWF AND DWFx FILES

■ AutoCAD 2011 comes with a free viewer called **Autodesk Design Review** to view DWF and DWFx files.
■ To open a DWF or DWFx file, double-click it and the software will open it.
■ In **Autodesk Design Review**, you can make measurements and insert comments.

- See the following illustration:

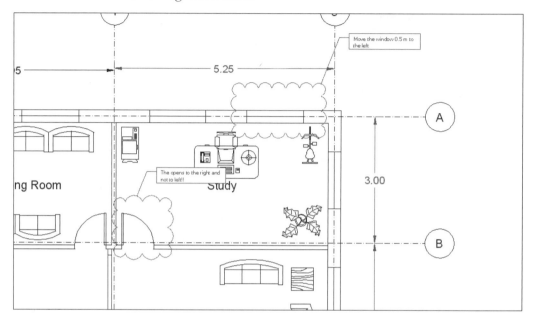

DWF AND THE PUBLISH COMMAND

Exercise 10-4

1. Start AutoCAD 2011.
2. Open the file *Exercise 10-4.dwg*.
3. Start the **Batch Plot** command.
4. From the **Sheet list**, remove **Exercise 10-4-Model** from the list.
5. Using the **Add Sheets** button, select **First Floor Plan.dwg**.
6. From the **Sheet list**, remove **First Floor Plan-Model** from the list.
7. Under **Publish to**, select DWF.
8. Make sure to include the layer information with the DWF.
9. Switch **Publish in background** off.
10. Save the file in your Exercises folder under the same name.
11. **Autodesk Design Review** should start automatically; if not, double-click the file to start the software.
12. View it and test the software.
13. Exit **Autodesk Design Review**.

CHAPTER REVIEW

1. Which of the following do you control in **Page Setup**?
   a. Paper size
   a. Which plotter to send to
   a. Viewports
   a. A and B
2. Layouts contain _____, and each one can be set to its own scale.
3. DWF files can be single sheet or multiple sheets.
   a. True
   a. False
4. You can choose to include or not include layers in a DWF file.
   a. True
   a. False
5. The **Named Plot Style Table** file extension is:
   a. *filename.ctb*
   a. *filename.stb*
   a. *filename.sbt*
   a. *filename.bct*
6. In a **Named Plot Style Table**, if you assign a plot style to a layer, you must click the _____ button from **Status Bar** to see this lineweight in the layout.

CHAPTER REVIEW ANSWERS

1. d
2. viewports
3. a
4. a
5. b
6. **Show/Hide Lineweight**

Chapter **11** **ADVANCED OBJECTS**

In This Chapter
◇ The **Polyline** command
◇ **Polyline** editing commands
◇ The **Construction Line** and **Ray** commands
◇ The **Point** command, including **Divide** and **Measure**
◇ The **Spline** and **Ellipse** commands
◇ The **Boundary** and **Region** commands, including Boolean operations

11.1 INTRODUCTION

- So far, we have covered the basic objects in AutoCAD, including the **Line, Arc, Circle**, and **Polyline** commands.
- In the remaining chapters, we will cover almost all the other 2D objects. At the end of this chapter, you should have a better understanding of the AutoCAD 2D drafting commands.
- Because the **Polyline** command is a very important drafting command, it will be covered again with more emphasis on the **PEDIT** command, which is the command used to edit any polyline. We will also discuss the other drafting commands that are based on polylines. **Rectangle, Polygon**, and **Donut**. Then we will cover what is special about polylines in some editing commands, such as the **Fillet** and **Chamfer** commands.
- The **Spline** and **Ellipse** commands are exact curves that help drafters draw real and mathematically accurate curved shapes.
- Other drafting commands include the **Point, Revision Cloud**, and **Wipeout** commands.
- This chapter ends with a discussion on the **Boundary** command, which helps create areas out of intersecting areas. Finally, we will discuss the unique 2D command **Region**.

11.2 THE POLYLINE COMMAND: A REVISION

- Let's begin by reviewing how to issue the **Polyline** command. On the **Ribbon**, go to the **Home** tab. Using the **Draw** panel, click the **Polyline** button:

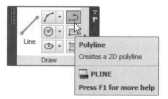

- The following prompts will appear:

```
Specify start point: (Specify the starting point.)
Current line-width is 0.9000
Specify next point or [Arc/Halfwidth/Length/Undo/ Width]:
(Specify the next point or choose one of the options
available.)
```

- After you have specified the first point, the **Polyline** command will respond with the current polyline width (in our example it is 0.90). You will then be asked to specify the next point. You can use all the methods we learned in the **Line** command.
- If you do not want to specify the second point, you can choose from the **Arc, Halfwidth, Length**, and **Width** options.

Arc

- By default, the **Polyline** command will draw lines.
- You can change the mode to draw arcs by selecting the **Arc** option. The following prompt will appear:

```
Specify endpoint of arc or
[Angle/CEnter/CLose/Direction/Halfwidth/Line/Radius/Second
pt/Undo/Width]:
```

- We learned in the **Arc** command that AutoCAD needs three pieces of information to draw an arc.
- AutoCAD already knows the starting point of the arc, which is the starting point of the polyline or the endpoint of the last line segment.
- AutoCAD will make another assumption regarding the direction of the arc, and will use the same angle as the last line segment. You can accept or reject this assumption.
- If you accept this assumption, then AutoCAD will ask you to specify the endpoint of the arc.

- If you reject this assumption, then specify the second piece of information from the following:
    - **Angle** then **Center** or **Radius**
    - **Center** then **Angle** or **Length**
    - **Direction** then **End**
    - **Radius** then **End** or **Angle**
    - **Second** then **End**

Halfwidth

- **Halfwidth** is the first method used to specify the width of the polyline.
- Specify the halfwidth of the polyline from the center to one of its edges, which will resemble the following:

- When you select this option, AutoCAD will show the following prompt:

```
Specify starting half-width <1.0000>:
Specify ending half-width <1.0000>:
```

- In this example, the halfwidth is 1.0 for both the start and end.

Length

- In the **Polyline** command, select the **Length** option if you draw an arc, then switch to a line, and you want the line to be tangent to the arc.
- This option will assume the angle is the same as the last segment. Hence, AutoCAD will ask you only for the length. The following prompt will appear:

```
Specify length of line:
```

Width

- The **Width** option is the same as **Halfwidth**, but instead you must input the full width of the polyline. See the following illustration:

- **NOTE** The **Undo** and **Close** options are the same options as in the **Line** command.
- If you choose to close in the **Arc** option, it will close the shape with an arc.

DRAWING POLYLINES

Exercise 11-1
1. Start AutoCAD 2011.
2. Open the file *Exercise 11-1.dwg*.
3. Using the **Ortho** command and the **Direct Distance Entry** option, draw the following shape (without dimensions) using the **Polyline** command with **Width** = 0.1.

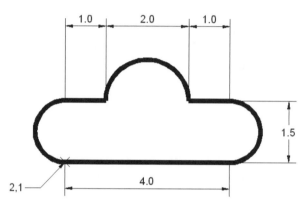

4. Save and close the file.
5. Note the following tips:
   - Start from point 2,1 and go to the right.
   - To draw the large arc, use **Angle** = 180.
   - Before you draw the last arc, change the mode to **Arc**, and select **Close**.

11.3 THE RECTANGLE COMMAND

- The **Rectangle** command is a **Polyline** command.
- On the **Ribbon**, go to the **Home** tab. Using the **Draw** panel, click the **Rectangle** button:

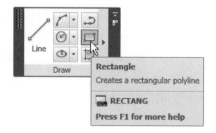

- The following prompts will appear:

```
Specify first corner point or [Chamfer/Elevation/Fillet/
Thickness/Width]: (Specify the first corner.)
Specify other corner point or [Area/Dimensions/ Rotation]:
(Specify the second corner.)
```

- This is the default method, in which the user specifies two opposite corners.

Chamfer

- You can draw a rectangle with chamfered edges.
- When the first prompt appears, type **c** and press [Enter]. You will see the following prompts:

```
Specify first chamfer distance for rectangles <0.0000>:
(Specify the first chamfer distance.)
Specify second chamfer distance for rectangles <0.2000>:
(Specify the second chamfer distance.)
```

- The command then continues normally.

Elevation and Thickness

- The **Elevation** and **Thickness** options are for 3D drawings, not 2D.

Fillet

- You can draw a rectangle with filleted edges.
- When the first prompt appears, type **f** and press [Enter]. You will see the following prompt:

```
Specify fillet radius for rectangles <0.0000>:
```

- The command then continues normally.

Width

- As with the **Polyline** command, you can draw a rectangle with the **Width** option.
- When the first prompt appears, type **w** and press [Enter]. You will see the following prompt:

```
Specify line width for rectangles <0.0000>:
```

- The command then continues normally.
- After you specify the first corner, the following prompt will appear:

```
Specify other corner point or [Area/Dimensions/Rotation]:
```

- The options are **Area, Dimension**, and **Rotation**.

Area

- Using the **Area** option, you can draw a rectangle with a predefined area value.
- Specify the first corner. When the second prompt appears, type **a** and press [Enter]. You will see the following prompts:

```
Enter area of rectangle in current units <25.0000>: (Type in
the desired Area value.)
Calculate rectangle dimensions based on [Length/Width]
<Length>: (Select the known dimension. Length is always in x
direction.)
Enter rectangle length <10.0000>: (Type in the value.)
```

- The rectangle will always be above and to the right of the first corner.

Dimensions

- The **Dimensions** option allows you to type in the values of the length and the width.
- Specify the first corner. When the second prompt appears, type **d** and press [Enter]. You will see the following prompts:

```
Specify length for rectangles <10.0000>:
(Input the dimension in X.)
Specify width for rectangles <10.0000>:
(Input the dimension in Y.)
Specify other corner point or [Area/Dimensions/ Rotation]:
(Specify where the rectangle will be drawn X [+ve], and Y
[-ve], or X [+ve] and Y [+ve], etc.)
```

Rotation

- The **Rotation** option allows you to draw a rotated rectangle.
- Specify the first corner. When the second prompt appears, type **r** and press [Enter]. You will see the following prompt:

```
Specify rotation angle or [Pick points] <0>:
```

- Then specify the second corner.
- **NOTE** ➤ If you change any or all of these options, the next time you issue the **Rectangle** command, you will see something like the following:

```
Current rectangle modes:  Fillet=0.5000  Rotation=45
```

11.4 THE POLYGON COMMAND

- The **Polygon** command is a **Polyline** command.
- Using it, you can draw an equilateral polygon starting from 3 sides up to 1024 sides.
- On the **Ribbon**, go to the **Home** tab. Using the **Draw** panel, click the **Polygon** button:

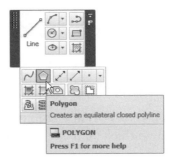

- The following prompt will appear:

`Enter number of sides <6>:` (**Specify the number of sides.**)

- You have two options. Either you know the center of the polygon or you know the length of one of the sides.
- If you know the center, specify it when you see the following prompt:

`Specify center of polygon or [Edge]:`

- If you know the center of the polygon, again you have two choices. Either the polygon is **Inscribed** inside an imaginary circle or the polygon is **Circumscribed** about this imaginary circle. See the following illustrations:

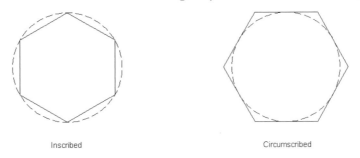

Inscribed   Circumscribed

- After you specify the method you want to use with, specify the radius of the imaginary circle. The following prompts will appear:

`Enter an option [Inscribed in circle/Circumscribed about circle] <I>:` (*Specify whether I or C.*)
`Specify radius of circle:` (*Type the value of the Radius.*)

- Another way to draw a polygon is to know the length of one of the sides and AutoCAD will draw the other sides. To do that you have to specify two points; this will tell AutoCAD the length and the angle of the first side, and then AutoCAD will know the position of the resulting polygon. The following prompts will appear:

```
Enter number of sides <4>: (Specify the number of sides.)
Specify center of polygon or [Edge]: E
Specify first endpoint of edge: (Specify the first point.)
Specify second endpoint of edge: (Specify the second point.)
```

11.5 THE DONUT COMMAND

- The **Donut** command is a **Polyline** command.
- You can use it to draw a thickened circle by specifying two diameters: inside and outside.
- On the **Ribbon**, go to the **Home** tab. Using the **Draw** panel, click the **Donut** button:

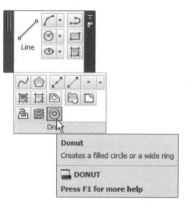

- The following prompts will appear:

```
Specify inside diameter of donut <0.5000>: (Type the value
of the inside diameter.)
Specify outside diameter of donut <1.0000>: (Type the value
of the outside diameter.)
Specify center of donut or <exit>: (Specify the center for
as many times as you wish.)
```

DRAWING RECTANGLES, POLYGONS, AND DONUTS

Exercise 11-2
1. Start AutoCAD 2011.
2. Open the file *Exercise 11-2.dwg*.
3. Draw two polygons using the information shown in the illustration.
4. Using the two points (turn on **Node** in **OSNAP**), draw the rectangle using **Angle** = 45 and **Chamfer distance** = 0.1.

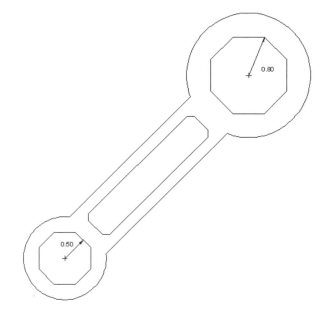

5. Save and close the file.

11.6 EDITING POLYLINES USING THE PEDIT COMMAND

- Although polylines respond to the same editing commands that lines do, the **PEDIT** command was created specifically to edit polylines.
- It can open a closed polyline and close an opened polyline.
- It can create curves from straight lines, and vice versa.

- On the **Ribbon**, go to the **Home** tab. Using the **Modify** panel, click the **Edit Polyline** button:

- The following prompts will appear:

```
Select polyline or [Multiple]: (Select the desired single
polyline to edit.)
Enter an option [Close/Join/Width/Edit vertex/Fit/Spline/
Decurve/Ltype gen/Reverse/Undo]:
```

Open

- The **Open** option appears only if the selected polyline is closed.
- To open a closed polyline, AutoCAD remembers the last segment and erases it.

Close

- The **Close** option appears only if the selected polyline is open.
- To close an opened polyline, AutoCAD remembers the first and last points and connects them.

Join

- When the first prompt appears, if you select a line or arc for the purpose of joining them together to become a polyline, AutoCAD will issue the following prompt:

```
Object selected is not a polyline
Do you want to turn it into one? <Y>
```

- You can select the **Join** option to connect this converted object to all the other lines and arcs.

Width

- The **Width** option allows you to give the selected polyline a uniform width for all its segments.

- The following prompt will appear:

Specify new width for all segments: *(Specify the uniform width.)*

Edit Vertex

- The **Edit Vertex** option allows you to edit the vertices of the selected polyline.
- It is used to add a new vertex, delete an existing vertex, etc.
- This option is very complicated. It is more productive to explode the polyline, make all the necessary adjustments, then join it again than it is to spend valuable time searching for the right option.
- If you select the **Edit Vertex** option, the following prompt will appear:

[Next/Previous/Break/Insert/Move/Regen/Straighten/Tangent/ Width/eXit] <N>:

Fit/Spline/Decurve

- These three options are primarily used to achieve the same results.
- To straight lines of a selected polyline to curves, you can use one of two options:
  - **Fit**, which creates an arc connecting the vertices.
  - **Spline**, which uses the vertices as controlling points to draw an approximation of a B-spline curve.
- To return curves to straight segments, you can use the **Decurve** option.
- See the following illustration:

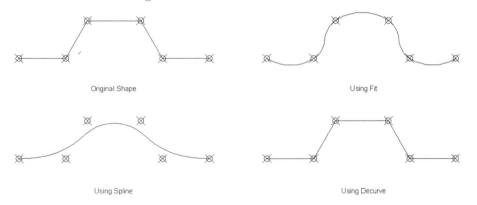

Original Shape   Using Fit

Using Spline   Using Decurve

Ltype gen

- When you are converting straight line segments using the **Spline** option and the lines were dashed, the output of the function will be either a continuous curve or a semicontinuous curve. See the following illustration:

Before   After

- To return to the original specifications, use the **Ltype gen** option. See the following illustration:

Before   After

- The following prompt will appear:

```
Enter polyline linetype generation option [ON/OFF] <Off>: ON
(Type ON if you want to activate it.)
```

Reverse

- The **Reverse** option allows you to reverse the order of vertices in a polyline:

First Vertex   First Vertex

Before Reverse   After Reverse

Undo

- The **Undo** option allows you to undo the last operation that took place in the **PEDIT** command.

Multiple

- The **Multiple** option allows you to edit multiple polylines in one command.
- The options available for single polyline editing are the same for multiple polyline editing.

- One of the advantages of this option is the ability to join two polylines or more together. (Single polyline editing allows you to join lines and arcs to create polylines. This option allows you to join two or more polylines together to create one object.)
- To successfully join two polylines, you must set two factors:
    - **Fuzz distance**: This is the maximum distance between the endpoints of the two polylines to be joined. If the actual distance is more than the **Fuzz distance**, the joining process will not be completed.
    - **Join Type**: This dictates the method of joining (i.e., **Add, Extend**, or **Both**).
- The following illustration demonstrates the difference between **Add** and **Extend**:

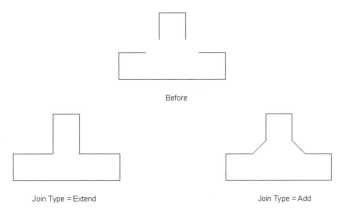

Before

Join Type = Extend   Join Type = Add

 NOTE
- If you are joining lines and arcs to make them polylines, you may receive the following prompt:

```
Object selected is not a polyline
Do you want to turn it into one? <Y>
```

- If you do not want to receive this prompt, you can use the system variable **PEDITACCEPT** and set it to 1. AutoCAD will make the conversion of the first object selected without asking you each time to turn it into one.

EDITING POLYLINES

Exercise 11-3
1. Start AutoCAD 2011.
2. Open the file *Exercise 11-3.dwg*.

3. In the **Command Window**, type **PEDITACCEPT** to make sure that each time you use the **PEDIT** command, AutoCAD will convert lines into polylines automatically. Enter the value of 1.

4. The following illustration starts with lines. Using the **PEDIT** command, convert each closed shape to a polyline.

5. Using the **Multiple** option, convert all polylines to splines.

6. Using the **Multiple** option and the **Ltype gen** option, restore the linetype of the polylines.

7. You should have something like the following:

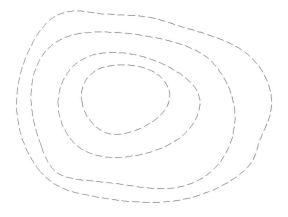

8. Save and close the file.

EDITING POLYLINES

Exercise 11-4

1. Start AutoCAD 2011.

2. Open the file *Exercise 11-4.dwg*.

3. Make sure that all of the objects in this file are polylines (click on any object and **Quick Properties** will show that it is a polyline).

4. Using the **PEDIT** command and the **Multiple** option, do the following:

    *   Using the shapes at the right, join the two polylines as shown (enter a proper **Fuzz Distance**, since you know that the length of the opening is 0.5657).

- Using the shapes at the left, join the two polylines as shown:

5. Save and close the file.

11.7 POLYLINE EDITING COMMANDS

- Because a polyline is a unique object, some of its editing commands are unique as well.
- These commands are:
  - **Offset**
  - **Fillet** and **Chamfer**
  - **Area**
  - **Quick Properties**
  - **Properties**

Offset

- Because a polyline is one object, when you offset, it will be offset as one object.
- Therefore, if you want to draw a plan of a wall, using a polyline is suggested because it will offset it quickly and easily.
- See the following illustration:

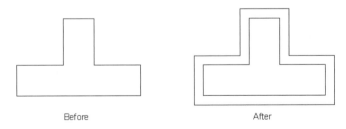

Before   After

Fillet and Chamfer

- There is a special option in the **Fillet** and **Chamfer** commands used for working with polylines.

- In the **Fillet** command, the following prompt appears:

```
Current settings: Mode = TRIM, Radius = 0.4000
Select first object or [Undo/Polyline/Radius/Trim/Multiple]: P
Select 2D polyline: (Select the desired polyline.)
```

- All of the edges of the plotline will be rounded in one step using the radius specified. See the following illustration:

Before   After

- In the **Chamfer** command, the following prompt appears:

```
(TRIM mode) Current chamfer Dist1 = 0.5000, Dist2 = 0.5000
Select first line or [Undo/Polyline/Distance/Angle /Trim/
mEthod/Multiple]: P
Select 2D polyline: (Select the desired polyline.)
```

- All of the edges of the plotline will be chamfered in one step using the distances specified. See the following illustration:

Before   After

Area

- The **Area** command is an easy one-step way to get the area of a closed (or even an open) polyline containing line segments or even lines and arcs.
- Start the **Area** command and type **O** (for Object), then select the polyline. The area will be shown right away.

- The following prompts will appear:

```
Specify first corner point or [Object/Add/Subtract]: O
Select objects: (Select the desired polyline.)
Area = 70.6318, Length = 40.1690
```

Quick Properties

- Without issuing a command, select any polyline you want to edit. The **Quick Properties** window will appear, as follows:

Polyline	
Color	■ ByLayer
Layer	0
Linetype	———— ByLayer
Global width	0.0000
Closed	Yes

- You can change the following:
  - **Color**
  - **Layer**
  - **Linetype**
  - **Global width**
  - **Closed** (**Yes/No**)

Properties

- You will find the **Properties** command very useful for editing almost all AutoCAD objects.
- It will not replace the editing commands, but it will make editing objects much easier.

■ If you select a polyline and right-click and then select **Properties** from the list, you will see a panel resembling the following:

Polyline	
General	
Color	■ ByLayer
Layer	0
Linetype	——— ByLayer
Linetype scale	1.0000
Plot style	ByColor
Lineweight	——— ByLayer
Transparency	ByLayer
Hyperlink	
Thickness	0.0000
3D Visualization	
Material	ByLayer
Geometry	
Vertex	1
Vertex X	9.0544
Vertex Y	11.7162
Start segment width	0.0000
End segment width	0.0000
Global width	0.0000
Elevation	0.0000
Area	58.2130
Length	31.1791
Misc	
Closed	Yes
Linetype generation	Disabled

■ You can do the following:
   • Move through the vertices (**PEDIT/Vertex**).
   • Change the width of the beginning of the segment, the endpoint of the segment, or the whole polyline.
   • Close and open polylines, and vice versa.
   • Use **Linetype** generation just as in the **PEDIT** command.
■ As you can see, the **Area** and total **Length** are already there without using the **Area** command.

POLYLINE EDITING COMMANDS

Exercise 11-5
1. Start AutoCAD 2011.
2. Open the file *Exercise 11-5.dwg*.
3. Using the existing polyline, create a fillet with **Radius** = 6".

4. Offset the new polyline to the inside using **Offset distance** = 3".
5. Using the **Area** command, calculate the inner area. (*Answer: 43.4110 sq. ft.*)
6. Using the **Properties** command, what is the total length of the outer polyline?
7. Using the **Quick Properties** command, change the **Global Width** to 1".
8. You will get the following picture:

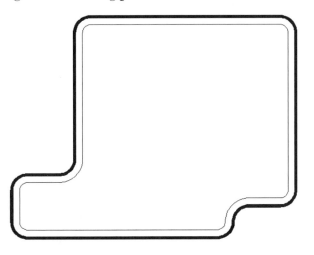

9. Save and close the file.

11.8 THE CONSTRUCTION LINE AND RAY COMMANDS

- The **Construction Line** command draws an infinite line that extends beyond the screen in two directions using different angle methods.
- The **Ray** command draws a line with a known starting point and an infinite endpoint.
- You can use commands such as **Offset, Trim**, and **Break** on the two objects.

Construction Line

- To use the **Construction Line** command, go to the **Home** tab on the **Ribbon**. Using the **Draw** panel, click the **Construction Line** button:

- The following prompt will appear:

```
Specify a point or [Hor/Ver/Ang/Bisect/Offset]:
```

- The following sections explain these options.

Hor

- The **Hor** option allows you to draw a horizontal construction line. The following prompt will appear:

```
Specify through point:
```

- This prompt will be repeated as many times as you wish. When you are done press [Enter].

Ver

- The **Ver** option allows you to draw a vertical construction line. The following prompt will appear:

```
Specify through point:
```

- This prompt will be repeated as many times as you wish. When you are done press [Enter].

Ang

- The **Ang** option allows you to draw a construction line with an angle. The following prompts will appear:

```
Enter angle of xline (0) or [Reference]:
(Type the desired angle)
Specify through point:
```

- First, type in the desired angle, then specify the point the construction line will go through. This prompt will be repeated as many times as you wish. When you are done press [Enter].

Bisect

- The **Bisect** option will ask for three points:
  - The construction line will pass through the first point.
  - The second and third points will form an angle, and the construction line will bisect this angle.
- The following prompts will appear:

```
Specify angle vertex point:
Specify angle start point:
Specify angle end point:
```

- The last prompt will be repeated as many times as you wish. When you are done, press [Enter].

Offset

- Use the **Offset** option if you have an existing line or polyline in your drawing and you want to draw a construction line parallel to it. The following prompts will appear:

```
Specify offset distance or [Through] <Through>:
Select a line object:
Specify side to offset:
```

- As you can see, these prompts are identical to those in the **Offset** command.
- All of the preceding options can be found by right-clicking, which will show the following menu:

Ray

- To use the **Ray** command, go to the **Home** tab on the **Ribbon**. Using the **Draw** panel, click the **Ray** button:

- The following prompt will appear:

```
Specify start point:
Specify through point:
```

- This simple command requires only two points. Specify the starting point and then the second point, which will determine the angle of the ray.
- The last prompt will be repeated as many times as you wish. When you are done, press [Enter].
- If you break a construction line, it will become a ray.
- If you trim a construction line from one side, it will become a ray; if you trim it from two sides, it will become a line.
- If you trim a ray, it will become a line.

THE CONSTRUCTION LINE AND RAY COMMANDS

Exercise 11-6

1. Start AutoCAD 2011.
2. Open the file *Exercise 11-6.dwg*.
3. Make sure you are in the **Construction** layer; if not, make it current.
4. Using the **Construction Line** command and the **Offset** option, create two construction lines parallel to the two vertical lines on the inside with **Offset distance** = 1.
5. Do the same to the lower and upper horizontal lines.
6. Using the **Construction Line** command and the **Vertical** option, create one construction line in the middle of the top horizontal line.

7. Make sure that **Intersection** in **OSNAP** is on.

8. Draw an arc (one-half of a circle) using the lower three points (**Start/Center/End**).

9. You should have the following picture:

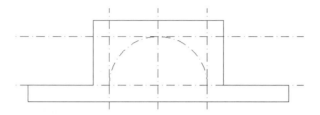

10. Draw four rays with angles (25, 40, 55, and 75) starting at the center point of the arc.

    Use **Dynamic Input** to get the angles right.

11. Make the **Openings** layer current. Draw four circles (D = 0.5) using the intersection of the rays with the arc, and draw one circle using the intersection of the middle construction line with the arc.

12. Freeze the **Construction** layer.

13. Mirror the existing four circles (excluding the one with **Angle** = 90) to the left.

14. You should have the following picture:

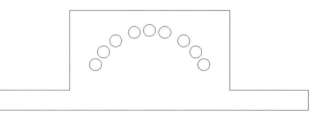

15. Save and close the file.

11.9 THE POINT COMMAND: INTRODUCTION

- The **Point** command helps you draw points, either by typing coordinates or by using **OSNAP**.
- The shape of the point is specified before you insert the point using the **Point Style** command.

Point Style

- To issue the **Point Style** command, go to the **Home** tab on the **Ribbon**. Using the **Utilities** panel, click the **Point Style** button:

- The following dialog box will appear:

- In this dialog box, you have 20 different shapes to choose from.
- Set the size of the point. You have two choices:
  - The point size can be relative to the screen size. You must specify a percentage of the screen size.
  - The point size can be an absolute value regardless of the screen size.
- After inserting points in the drawing, you can go to the **Point Style** command and change the shape and size. All the inserted points will change accordingly.
- There will be only one **Point Style** per file.

The Point Command

- The **Point** command allows you to place a point in the X, Y, Z space.
- On the **Ribbon**, go to the **Home** tab. Using the **Draw** panel, click the **Multiple Points** button:

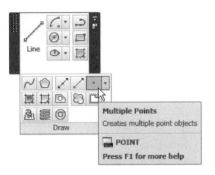

- AutoCAD will show the following prompt:

```
Specify a point:
```

- Click on the desired point. This prompt will be repeated as many times as you wish. When you are done, press [Esc].
- After inserting points in the drawing, you can use the **OSNAP Node** to catch the exact point.

11.10 THE POINT COMMAND: DIVIDE AND MEASURE

- Both the **Divide** and **Measure** commands use points to cut objects into segments.
- The **Divide** command uses points to cut any object into equal-length segments specified by the user.
- The **Measure** command uses points to cut any object into lengths specified by the user.

The Divide Command

- To issue the **Divide** command, go to the **Home** tab on the **Ribbon**. Using the **Draw** panel, click the **Divide** button:

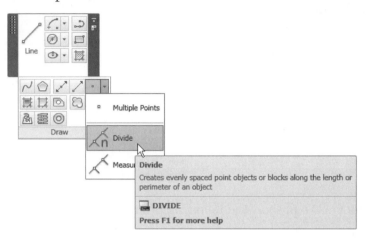

- AutoCAD will show the following prompts:

```
Select object to divide: (Select the desired object)
Enter the number of segments or [Block]: (Type in the number
of equal spaced segments.)
```

The Measure Command

- To issue the **Measure** command, go to the **Home** tab on the **Ribbon**. Using the **Draw** panel, click the **Measure** button:

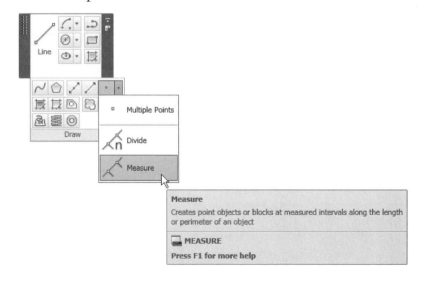

- AutoCAD will show the following prompts:

```
Select object to measure: (Select the desired object.)
Specify length of segment or [Block]: (Type in the length of
the segments.)
```

NOTE ▶
- It is important to know from which end you want to start measuring; choose the object from a point near the desired end.
- AutoCAD will start inserting points measuring from that end until the remaining distance is less than the specified distance.

NOTE ▶
- In both commands, you can use a **Block** instead of a point. The following prompts will appear:

```
Enter the number of segments or [Block]: B
Enter name of block to insert: chair (Type in the name of
the block.)
Align block with object? [Yes/No] <Y>: (Select Yes or No.)
Enter the number of segments: (Type in the number of
segments for Divide and the Length of the segment for
Measure.)
```

- The following illustration demonstrates how to align a block.

Align = Yes

- The block will move with the shape of the object, as shown:

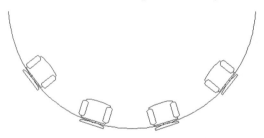

Align = No

- The block will maintain its original angle, as shown:

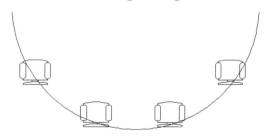

POINT AND POINT STYLE COMMANDS

Exercise 11-7

1. Start AutoCAD 2011.
2. Open the file *Exercise 11-7.dwg*.
3. Set the **Point Style** to ☒.
4. Explode the inner polyline.
5. Using the **Divide** command, divide the upper horizontal line into four equal segments.
6. Using the **Measure** command, measure the lower horizontal line with 13' distance, starting from the right of the line.
7. Erase the last point at the left of the line.
8. You should have the following shape:

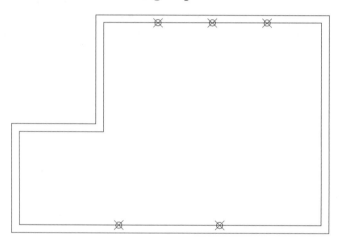

9. Make sure that **Node** in **OSNAP** is on.
10. Make the **A-Windows** layer current.
11. Insert the **Window** block at the location specified by the points (for the lower ones, use **Angle** = 180).

12. You will get the following picture:

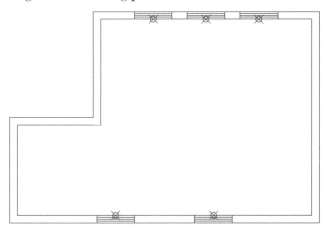

13. Freeze layer **Points**.
14. Save and close the file.

POINT AND POINT STYLE COMMANDS

Exercise 11-8
1. Start AutoCAD 2011.
2. Open the file *Exercise 11-8.dwg*.
3. Divide the two offset arcs using the block named **Chair**.
4. You can get the rest of the information from the following picture:

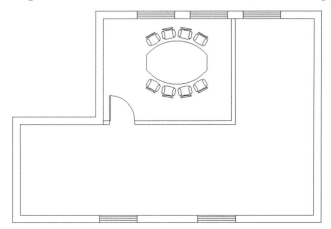

5. Save and close the file.

11.11 THE SPLINE COMMAND

- The **Spline** command allows you to draw a smooth curve using a series of points based on an exact mathematical method.
- On the **Ribbon**, go to the **Home** tab. Using the **Draw** panel, click the **Spline** button:

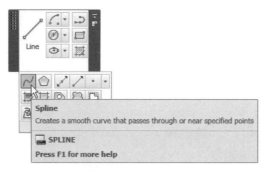

- The following prompts will appear:

```
Specify first point or [Object]: (Specify the first point.)
Specify next point: (Specify the second point.)
Specify next point or [Close/Fit tolerance] <start tangent>:
(Specify the third point, or select one of the options.)
```

- AutoCAD will draw a curve connecting the points you select. The other available options help you close the spline the right way.

Object

- If you edit the polyline to be a spline, it will stay a polyline. You can convert it to be a full spline using the **Object** option.
- The following prompt will appear:

```
Select objects:
```

- Select the polyline that has been edited to be a spline. AutoCAD will transform it to be a real spline. See the following illustration:

Before   After

Close

- To use the **Close** option, you must specify an angle of the tangent that will pass through the starting point.
- The following prompt will appear:

```
Specify tangent:
```

Fit Tolerance

- By default, a spline will pass through the specified points. However, you can make the spline pass *near* the points, rather than through them, by specifying the **Fit Tolerance** distance.
- The following prompt will appear:

```
Specify fit tolerance <0.0000>:
```

Start Tangent

- If you would like to stop after specifying a series of points, but without closing the shape, press [Enter] and the **Start Tangent** option will be selected.
- You must specify two tangents—one that passes through the first point and a second that passes through the endpoint.
- The following prompts will appear:

```
Specify start tangent:
Specify end tangent:
```

THE SPLINE COMMAND

Exercise 11-9

1. Start AutoCAD 2011.
2. Open the file *Exercise 11-9.dwg*.
3. Using the **Spline** command, draw the inner contour starting from point 1 and moving to the left.
4. When you want to close, use **Angle** = 345.
5. Freeze the layers **Points** and **Text**.

6. You should get the following picture:

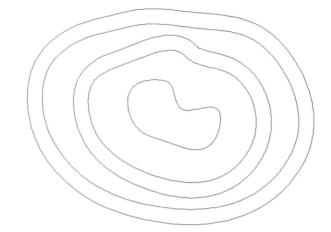

7. Save and close the file.

11.12 THE ELLIPSE COMMAND

- The **Ellipse** command allows you to draw an elliptical shape or elliptical arc.
- On the **Ribbon**, go to the **Home** tab. Using the **Draw** panel, click the **Ellipse** button:

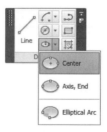

- There are two ways to draw an ellipse in AutoCAD:
  - **Axis/End**
  - **Center**

Axis/End

- You must specify three points for this method:
  - Two points to specify one of the two axes.
  - One point on the other axis.

- See the following illustration:

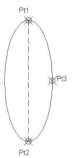

- The following prompts will appear:

```
Specify axis endpoint of ellipse or [Arc/Center]:
Specify other endpoint of axis:
Specify distance to other axis or [Rotation]:
```

Center

- For this method, you must also specify three points:
  - The first point is the center point of the ellipse.
  - The second point is the endpoint of one of the two axes.
  - The third point is the endpoint of the other axis.
- See the following illustration:

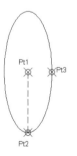

- The following prompts will appear:

```
Specify axis endpoint of ellipse or [Arc/Center]: C
Specify center of ellipse:
Specify endpoint of axis:
Specify distance to other axis or [Rotation]:
```

NOTE
- For these two methods, you can use the **Rotation** option as the last piece of information (the third point).
  - When you define the first axis using either method, you are drawing a circle. Imagine that the circle is rotating around this axis.

- If the rotation angle is equal to 0 or 180, the output will be a circle.
- If the rotation angle is equal to 90 or 270, the output is nothing.
- If the rotation angle is equal to any other value, the output is an ellipse.

Elliptical Arc

- To draw an elliptical arc, you must specify the following:
  - Draw an ellipse using one of the two methods discussed in the **Ellipse** command section.
  - Specify two angles. AutoCAD will draw an elliptical arc counterclockwise between the two angles (it is better to have **Polar Tracking** turned on to control the arc graphically rather than type angles).
- The following prompts will appear:

```
Specify axis endpoint of ellipse or [Arc/Center]: A
Specify axis endpoint of elliptical arc or [Center]:
Specify other endpoint of axis:
Specify distance to other axis or [Rotation]:
Specify start angle or [Parameter]:
Specify end angle or [Parameter/Included angle]:
```

NOTE ➤ ■ The elliptical arc is not really a separate command because it is part of the **Ellipse** command.

THE ELLIPSE COMMAND

Exercise 11-10
1. Start AutoCAD 2011.
2. Open the file *Exercise 11-10.dwg*.
3. Make sure that **Node** in **OSNAP** is turned on.
4. Using the points available, draw the ellipse needed to complete the shape of the toilet.
5. Draw an elliptical arc to complete the shape of the window using the following:
   - The first axis of the ellipse is the width of the window.
   - From the center to other axis **Distance** = 2.
   - **Start Angle** = 0, **End Angle** = 180.
6. Make an offset for the new arc, where **Offset distance** = 0.2 to the inside.

7. Make the necessary trimming to create the following shape:

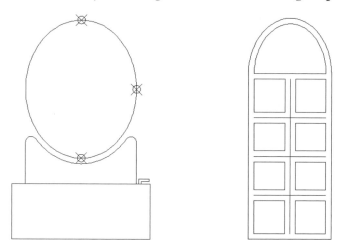

8. Save and close the file.

11.13 THE REVISION CLOUD COMMAND

- The **Revision Cloud** command allows you to draw a revision cloud in your drawing.
- This command is a polyline with arcs that connect to each other. Simply click on the desired points and the shape will close automatically.
- On the **Ribbon**, go to the **Home** tab. Using the **Draw** panel, click the **Revision Cloud** button:

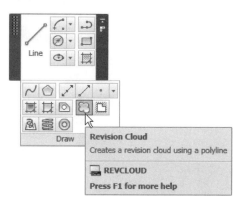

- You will see the following prompt:

```
Minimum arc length: 15    Maximum arc length: 15
Style: Normal
Specify start point or [Arc length/Object/Style] <Object>:
```

- Before you start drawing any revision clouds, check the information given to you. The first prompt tells us the following:
  - **Minimum arc length** = 15
  - **Maximum arc length** = 15
  - **Style** = Normal

Arc Length

- You can change the first two settings using this option. The following prompts will appear:

```
Specify minimum length of arc <15>: 30
Specify maximum length of arc <30>: 50
```

- This means the lengths of the arcs of the revision clouds will be between 30 and 50.

Style

- This option allows you to change the line style from **Normal** to **Calligraphy**. The following prompt will appear:

```
Specify start point or [Arc length/Object/Style] <Object>: S
Select arc style [Normal/Calligraphy] <Normal>:C
Arc style = Calligraphy
```

- See the following illustration:

Normal   Calligraphy

Object

- This option allows you to convert any existing object to a revision cloud. The following prompt will appear:

```
Specify start point or [Arc length/Object/Style] <Object>: O
Select object:
Reverse direction [Yes/No] <No>: (Specify Yes or No.)
```

- See the following illustration:

Before   After

THE REVISION CLOUD COMMAND (GENERIC)

Exercise 11-11

1. Start AutoCAD 2011.
2. Open the file *Exercise 11-11.dwg*.
3. You will notice two things about this drawing:
    - The bathroom furniture is larger than it should be.
    - The dimension at the left is incorrect.
4. Do the following two things:
    - Using the **Revision Cloud** command, draw a revision cloud around the toilet making the maximum and minimum **Arc Length** = 15.
    - Convert the rectangle around the dimension to a revision cloud.

5. You should have something resembling the following:

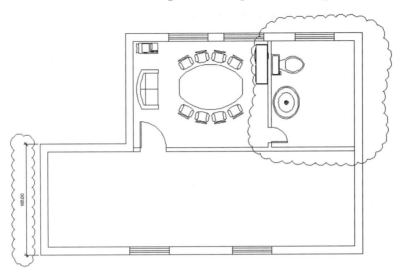

6. Save and close the file.

11.14 THE BOUNDARY COMMAND

- The **Boundary** command allows you to create a polyline (or **Region**—the subject of the next command) from intersecting areas of different objects.
- On the **Ribbon**, go to the **Home** tab. Using the **Draw** panel, click the **Boundary** button:

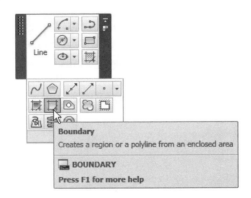

- The following dialog box will appear:

- The **Pick Points** button is the only way to click inside the area you want to create a polyline in.

Island Detection

- **Island detection** is used to detect any object (such as a circle) within the area and consider it a boundary.

Object Type

- Select **Object type** if you want to create a **Polyline** or **Region** (we will discuss regions shortly).

Boundary Set

- The **Boundary set** option provides you with two choices:
  - **Current viewport**: All of the objects in the current viewport will be taken into consideration when AutoCAD creates the polyline.
  - **New**: Only the objects you select will be considered when AutoCAD creates the polyline.

THE BOUNDARY COMMAND

Exercise 11-12

1. Start AutoCAD 2011.
2. Open the file *Exercise 11-12.dwg*.
3. Start the **Boundary** command and click inside the area.
4. Move the magenta objects to the left. (Select the two slots and the circle at the center of the area by clicking; do not use the **Crossing** or **Window** mode.)
5. Start the **Boundary** command again. This time, click off **Island detection**, then click inside the area.
6. Compare the two results.
7. Start the **Boundary** command for the third time.
8. Under **Boundary set**, click **New** and select the outer shape (it is red and has two slots and a circle in the middle). Make sure that **Island detection** is on, click **Pick points**, and click inside the area.
9. Move the resulting shape up.
10. Compare the four shapes.
11. Save and close the file.

11.15 THE REGION COMMAND: INTRODUCTION

- All of the 2D objects we learned previously are considered *wireframes*. A region is the only 2D object considered to be different.
- A region is a very *thin-shelled* object. Hence, any holes inside the region are considered part of the object rather than being considered isolated objects (as they would be in polylines).
- On the **Ribbon**, go to the **Home** tab. Using the **Draw** panel, click the **Boundary** button:

- There are two ways to create a region in AutoCAD:
  - Using the **Region** command
  - Using the **Boundary** command

Region Command

- This command converts any 2D *closed* shape to a region. For example, this command will convert any combination of lines, arcs, polylines, splines, or closed shapes such circles or ellipses.
- The following prompt will appear:

```
Select objects:
```

- Select the objects that will form a closed shape. Once you are done, press [Enter]. Objects will be transformed to regions.

Boundary Command

- Using this command, select **Object type** to be **Region**.
- When you click inside the desired area, the object created will be a region.

11.16 THE REGION COMMAND: BOOLEAN OPERATIONS

- Region objects are the only 2D objects that will accept **Boolean Operation** commands. These commands are:
  - **Union**, which is used to combine two or more regions to create a new single region.
  - **Subtract**, which is used to subtract a group of regions from another group of regions.
  - **Intersect**, which is used to produce an intersecting area from a group of regions.
- NOTE ▸ Note that before selecting these commands *you must change the workspace to 3D Basics*.
- On the **Ribbon**, go to the **Home** tab. Using the **Edit** panel, select one of the three commands:

- NOTE ▸ The **Union** command and **Intersect** command will both have the same prompt:

```
Select Objects:
```

- You can select the objects in any order.
- The **Subtract** command has the following prompts:

```
Select solids and regions to subtract from...
Select objects:
Select objects:   Select solids and regions to subtract...
Select objects:
```

- First, select the region(s) you want to subtract from and press [Enter]. Then select the region(s) to be subtracted.
- One of the unique things about regions is that you can get physical information about your 2D object.
- To issue this command, type **massprop** in the **Command Window**.
- You will see a listing resembling the following:

```
Area:                      803004.1226
Perimeter:                 5347.2674
Bounding box:         X: 1360.1537   --   2511.5395
                      Y: 324.3740   --   1475.7599
Centroid:             X: 1935.8466
                      Y: 900.0670
Moments of inertia:   X: 7.3228E+11
                      Y: 3.0910E+12
Product of inertia:  XY: 1.3991E+12
Radii of gyration:    X: 954.9506
                      Y: 1961.9664
Principal moments and X-Y directions about centroid:
                      I: 81753968390.5518 along [1.0000
                      0.0000]
                      J: 81753968390.5518 along [0.0000
                      1.0000]
```

THE REGION COMMAND

Exercise 11-13

1. Start AutoCAD 2011.
2. Open the file *Exercise 11-13.dwg*.
3. Using the **Region** command, convert all shapes to regions.
4. To make sure the objects are converted, click one of the objects and check its type using **Quick Properties**.
5. Using the **Union** command, unite the upper two circles and the rectangle.

6. Repeat the previous step for the lower circles.
7. Using the **Subtract** command, subtract all the shapes from the outer shape.
8. Using **Properties**, what is the net area of the shape? (*Answer: 22.4 sq. in.*)
9. Using the **massprop** command, provide the values for following:
   - Moments of inertia in X
   - Moments of inertia in Y
   - Radius of gyration in X
   - Radius of gyration in Y
10. Save and close the file.

CHAPTER REVIEW

1. The object type that is different from all other 2D objects is:
   a. Boundary
   b. Polyline
   c. Region
   d. All of the above
2. **Axis/End** is one method used to draw _____.
3. If you convert a polyline from line segments to curves, you may lose the **Linetype** of the polyline.
   a. True
   b. False
4. The **Island detection** option in the **Boundary** command allows the user to pick the objects that will be taken into consideration when AutoCAD creates a polyline.
   a. True
   b. False
5. When using the **Divide** and **Measure** commands, you can:
   a. Distribute points along a selected object.
   b. Distribute blocks along a selected object.
   c. Align blocks over a selected object.
   d. All of the above.
6. In the **Fillet** and **Chamfer** commands, there is a special option for _____.

CHAPTER REVIEW ANSWERS

1. c
2. an ellipse
3. a
4. b
5. d
6. polylines

Chapter 12 ADVANCED TECHNIQUES

In This Chapter

◊ Advanced options in the **Offset, Trim**, and **Extend** commands
◊ Using **Cut, Copy**, and **Paste** when opening more than one file
◊ Importing AutoCAD objects from other software
◊ The **Hyperlink, View**, and **Viewport** commands
◊ Using Fields
◊ Formulas and Tables, including advanced Table functions
◊ The **Quick Select, Select Similar**, and **Add Selected** commands
◊ The **Partial Open** and **Partial Load** features
◊ The **Object Visibility** command

12.1 ADVANCED OPTIONS IN THE OFFSET COMMAND

■ Many AutoCAD users use the default settings for the **Offset, Trim**, and **Extend** commands without looking at the other options—options that would help them do their job faster and better.

■ In this section, we will focus on the overlooked options of these three commands.

■ When you start the **Offset** command, you will see the following prompt:

```
Current settings: Erase source=No Layer=Source OFFSETGAPTYPE=0
Specify offset distance or [Through/Erase/Layer] <Through>:
```

First line states:

- **Erase source** = No
- **Layer** = Source
- **OFFSETGAPTYPE** = 0

- In the second line, you will see the following options:
  - Erase
  - Layer

Erase

- If you select the **Erase** option, AutoCAD will show the following prompt:

```
Erase source object after offsetting? [Yes/No] <No>:
```

- If you answer **No**, your original object will remain intact, along with the parallel object generated.
- If you answer **Yes**, your original object will be deleted, while the parallel object generated will remain.

Layer

- By default, the offset object will reside in the same layer as the original object, regardless of the current layer.
- Using the **Layer** option, you can send the duplicate object to the current layer and not to the original object's layer.
- You will see the following prompt:

```
Enter layer option for offset objects [Current/Source]
<Source>:
```

- As you can see, the default option is **Source**, but you have the choice to input **Current**.

OFFSETGAPTYPE

- **OFFSETGAPTYPE** is a **System Variable** that controls how AutoCAD treats polylines when they are offset to bigger polylines and how the gaps generated from the offset are treated.
- There are three options:
  - **OFFSETGAPTYPE** = 0, which means lines will be extended.
  - **OFFSETGAPTYPE** = 1, which the means angles will be filleted (fillet radius will equal the value of the offset distance).
  - **OFFSETGAPTYPE** = 2, which means the angles will be chamfered.
- See the following illustration:

 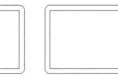

OFFSETGAPTYPE = 0   OFFSETGAPTYPE = 1   OFFSETGAPTYPE = 2

NOTE
- These settings will affect all of the files, so be cautious.

ADVANCED OPTIONS IN THE OFFSET COMMAND

Exercise 12-1

1. Start AutoCAD 2011.
2. Open the file *Exercise 12-1.dwg*.
3. The shape was drawn in layer 0 (zero).
4. Using the **Command Window**, type the **OFFSETGAPTYPE** command and set the value to 1.
5. Start the **Offset** command and set the following:
   - **Layer** = Current
   - **Erase** = Yes
6. Offset the shape to the outside using **Offset Distance** = 1'.
7. What is the area of the new polyline? (*Answer: 2019.1094 sq. ft.*)
8. Save and close the file.

12.2 ADVANCED OPTIONS IN THE TRIM AND EXTEND COMMANDS

- We covered most of the **Trim** and **Extend** options in earlier chapters, but two options remain to be discussed:
  - **Project** (which is applicable in 3D drawings only)
  - **Edge**

Edge

- By default, for the **Trim** command to be successful, the cutting edge(s) and the objects to be trimmed need to intersect.
- Also by default, for the **Extend** command to be successful, the boundary edge(s) and the objects to be extended should have proposed intersecting points.
- With the **Edge** option, you can trim objects based on extrapolated cutting edges, and you can extend objects based on extrapolated boundary edges.
- If you select the **Edge** option, you will see the following prompt:

```
Enter an implied edge extension mode [Extend/No extend] <No
extend>: E
```

- By default, the mode is **No extend**. Select the **Extend** mode by typing **E** or by right-clicking and selecting the **Extend** option.

- See the following example:

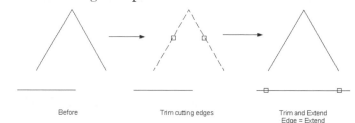

 - In this example, we used the **Trim** command and [Shift] to change the mode from **Trim** to **Extend**.
- These settings will affect all of the files.

ADVANCED OPTIONS IN THE TRIM AND EXTEND COMMANDS

Exercise 12-2

1. Start AutoCAD 2011.
2. Open the file *Exercise 12-2.dwg*.
3. Start the **Trim** command and select the arc as the cutting edge.
4. Set the **Edge** to **Extend**.
5. Trim the upper two horizontal lines.
6. Extend the lower two horizontal lines using [Shift] to flip the command to **Extend**.
7. Draw an arc using the **3-Point** method, given the following points:
    - **Point 1** = endpoint of the upper horizontal line at the right.
    - **Point 2** = endpoint of the lower horizontal line at the right.
    - **Point 3** = endpoint of the upper horizontal line at the left.
8. You should have the following picture:

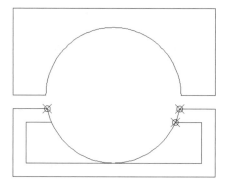

9. Save and close the file.

12.3 OPENING MORE THAN ONE AUTOCAD FILE

- Earlier we covered the **Design Center**, which allows us to share **Blocks, Layers, Text Styles**, etc., between files. However, we did not cover sharing objects between files.
- Because AutoCAD allows us to open more than one file at a time, we can copy and paste objects between files.
- Using the **Open** command, you can select more than one file at the same time using the [Ctrl] key (you can also open files one by one). See the following illustration:

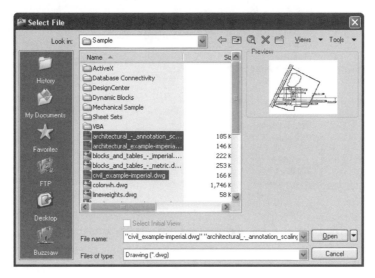

- When you open more than one file, you can use the **View** tab and the **Window** panel to control these files:

- All of these commands are common to all Windows applications.
- You can see a list of the opened files using the **Switch Windows** button:

D:\Program Files\Autodesk\AutoCAD 2011\Sample\civil_example-imperial.dwg
D:\Program Files\Autodesk\AutoCAD 2011\Sample\architectural_-_annotation_scaling_and_multileaders.dwg
✓ D:\Program Files\Autodesk\AutoCAD 2011\Sample\architectural_example-imperial.dwg

- We must differentiate between two AutoCAD commands:
  - **Modify/Copy** will copy objects within a single file.
  - **Edit/Copy** will copy objects from one file to another.
- To copy from one drawing to another, do the following:
  - Without issuing any command, select the desired object from the source file.
  - Right-click and a menu will appear. Select the **Clipboard** option. You will see the following:

  - Select either **Cut, Copy**, or **Copy with Base Point**.

Cut

- The **Cut** option allows you to cut (move) selected objects from the source to the destination file.

Copy

- The **Copy** option allows you to copy selected objects from one file to another file without specifying a base point.

Copy with Base Point

- The **Copy with Base Point** option allows you to copy selected objects from one file to another file by specifying a base point.
- The following prompt will appear asking you for a base point:

```
Specify base point:
```

- To paste from one drawing to another, do the following:
  - Go to the destination file.

- Right-click and a menu will appear. Select the **Clipboard** option. You will see the following:

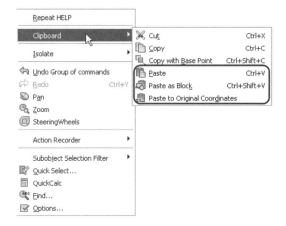

Paste

- The **Paste** option allows you to paste objects in the current drawing.

Paste as Block

- Although you selected objects, the **Paste as Block** option allows you to paste these objects in the current file as a block. AutoCAD will give it a random name. You can use the **Rename** command to give it the desired name.

Paste to Original Coordinates

- The **Paste to Original Coordinates** option allows you to paste the selected objects using the coordinates from the source file.
- This feature can also be found from the **Ribbon** by using the **Home** tab and the **Clipboard** panel:

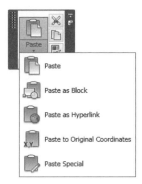

Paste as Hyperlink

- The **Paste as Hyperlink** option is only applicable when copying objects from other applications to AutoCAD; it does not allow you to copy objects from one AutoCAD file to another AutoCAD file.

Paste Special

- The **Paste Special** option is also only applicable for objects copied from other applications (we will discuss it shortly).

NOTE ▶
- Earlier we used the **Match Properties** command. You can use this command across files.
  - If you match an object that resides in a particular layer with an object in a file in which this layer does not exist, AutoCAD will create the same layer in the destination file.
  - The same applies for all types of styles: **Dimension, Text, Multileader, Table**, etc.

NOTE ▶
- You can select objects and drag and drop them (avoiding grips) to the other file using the left button or right button of your mouse.
  - Using the left button, you can paste the selected objects in your destination drawing with no extra prompts or menu.
  - Using the right-click between files, and after dragging the objects to the destination drawing, you will see the following menu:

```
Copy Here
Paste as Block
Paste to Orig Coords
Cancel
```

  - All of these options were discussed previously.

OPENING MORE THAN ONE AUTOCAD FILE

Exercise 12-3

1. Start AutoCAD 2011.
2. Open the file *Exercise 12-3.dwg*.
3. In *Exercise 12-3.dwg*, make sure there is a layer called "Furniture."
4. Open the file *Previous Project.dwg*.
5. Click one of the chairs. What is the name of the chair's layer?
6. Tile both files vertically.
7. In *Previous Project.dwg*, copy the table and chairs. Specify a base point using the upper left-hand corner of the room.

8. In *Exercise 12-3.dwg*, paste the objects as a block.
9. Type **Rename** in the **Command Window**. You will find a block with a random name—something like A$C4A1D2F06. Rename it "Table and Chairs."
10. Now check again: Is there a layer called "Furniture"?
11. Save and close the files.

OPENING MORE THAN ONE AUTOCAD FILE

Exercise 12-4
1. Start AutoCAD 2011.
2. Open the file *Exercise 12-4.dwg*.
3. Check for the following:
   • Is there a layer called "text"?
   • Is there a **Text Style** called "Georgia_09"?
4. Open the file *My Source.dwg*.
5. Tile both files vertically, and make sure that *My Source.dwg* is the current file.
6. Using the **Match Properties** command, select the text as the **Source** object.
7. Click on *Exercise 12-4.dwg* and select the text as the **Destination**.
8. Check *Exercise 12-4.dwg* again:
   • Is there a layer called "text"?
   • Is there a **Text Style** called "Georgia_09"?
9. Save and close the file.

12.4 IMPORTING OBJECTS FROM OTHER APPLICATIONS

- "Instead of writing text in AutoCAD, I'll let my assistant type up the notes in Microsoft Word and import them into my AutoCAD drawing," said one engineer.
- "Instead of creating tables in AutoCAD, I'll ask one of my company's computer wizards to create them in Microsoft Excel and paste them into my drawing," said another engineer.

- Both of these engineers are 100% correct. You can import any object from any application to AutoCAD, and vice versa.
- **OLE** (Object Linking and Embedding) is a Windows feature, and all applications that work under Windows can use it.
- Linking means there is a *connection* between the source application data and the image in the destination application; hence, if any change takes place in the original file, the image will reflect this change.
- Embedding means there is *no connection* between the source application data and the image in the destination application; hence, if any change takes place in the original file, the image will not reflect this change.
- We will use the same commands we used in the previous pages: **Cut, Copy**, and **Paste**.
- If you want to copy objects from other applications into AutoCAD, do the following:
  - Start the desired application and open the desired file.
  - Select the objects to be copied.
  - If you want to copy and delete them, use **Edit/Cut**; if you want to keep the original objects, use **Edit/Copy**.
  - Start AutoCAD and open the file in which you would like to import the objects.
  - You can use the **Paste** command if you do not want any link to be established. You can use the **Paste Special** command if you want to establish a link.

Edit/Paste

- When using the **Paste** command, the following prompt will appear:

`Specify insertion point:` *(Specify an insertion point.)*

- The following dialog box will appear:

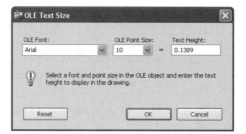

- The dialog box will list the font and font size used in the Windows application. You must specify the AutoCAD text height. Once you are done, click **OK**.

- If the pasted object is simple ASCII (text coming from a Notepad application or something similar), the object will be pasted as an **MTEXT** object. Other types of objects will be pasted as **OLE** objects.

OLE Editing

- To edit an **OLE** object, select it and right-click. The following menu will appear:

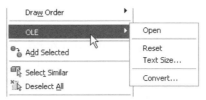

- If you want to open the source application, double-click on the **OLE** object or right-click and select **OLE/Open**.
- Select **OLE/Reset** to change the font and font size to the original source font and font size.
- Select **OLE/Text Size** to change the text size to a new value (just like the dialog box that appears with the **Edit/Paste** command).
- Select **OLE/Convert** to change the nature of the **OLE** object.

Edit/Paste Special

- When using the **Paste Special** command, you must choose between two options:
  - **Paste**
  - **Paste Link**

Paste

- The **Paste** option allows you to paste an object without linking it.
- See the following two examples for MS Word and Excel:

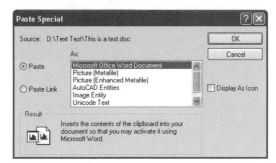

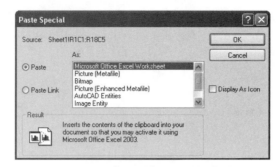

- You can select the type of pasting you need:
  - As its source format (e.g., Word, Excel)
  - As different types of pictures (e.g., Metafile, Enhanced Metafile)
  - As **AutoCAD Entities**
- Select the desired type and click **OK**.
- If you copied MS Word objects, then you select **Paste Special** in the AutoCAD drawing and select the **Paste** option and **AutoCAD Entities**. The objects will be pasted as **Single Line Text** objects.
- If you copied MS Excel objects, then you select **Paste Special** in the AutoCAD drawing and select the **Paste** option and **AutoCAD Entities**. The objects will be pasted as a table. If the Excel table has any formulas inside the cells, AutoCAD will preserve the same formulas to be used in the drawing.

Paste Link

- The **Paste Link** option allows you to paste an object and link it.
- See the following two examples for MS Word and Excel:

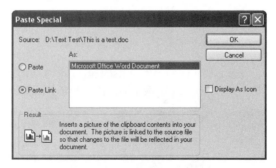

- MS Word has only one option—to paste links as MS Word entities, which will make them exactly like **OLE**.
- MS Excel has two options—either to paste as Excel entities (**OLE**) or to paste as **AutoCAD Entities** (i.e., as a table).
- If you choose to paste an Excel sheet as **AutoCAD Entities**, then when you select it and hover over it, two symbols will appear: *locked* and *linked*.
- You can unlock any number of cells in the table; therefore, you will be able to change the values and and those changes will be reflected in the original Excel sheet.
- Consequently, you can do two things:
  - Change the values in Excel and then update them in AutoCAD.
  - Change the values in AutoCAD and then update them in Excel.
- Perform the steps in the following example:
  - Copy a part of a sheet in Excel.
  - Using the **Paste Special** command with the **Paste Link** option, paste what you copied in AutoCAD as **AutoCAD Entities**.
  - Select the table (from the outside frame), then hover over it. You will see the locked and linked symbols, as shown:

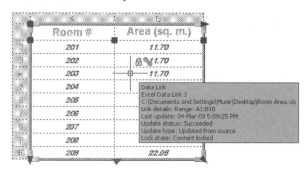

- On the **Ribbon**, go to the **Insert** tab. Using the **Linking & Extraction** panel, click the **Data Link** button:

- You will see the following dialog box:

- In the **Data Link Manager**, you will see that Excel established a link automatically between your file and the Excel file and gave it a temporary name: **Excel Data Link 1**.

- When you click the link, you will see the following:

- You can see **Details** of the link (name, source file name, and the cell range in Excel). You can also see a **Preview**.
- If you right-click the link name, you will see the following:

- You can open the source file, edit the link (more details will follow), rename the link, and delete the link.
- Deleting the link will only work when you erase the table. AutoCAD will display the following message:

- When you select the **Edit** option, the following dialog box will appear:

Modify Excel Link: Excel Data Link 1

File
Choose an Excel file:

`D:\AutoCAD 2011 Courseware\AutoCAD 2011 Ad` `[...]`

Path type:
`Full path`

Link options

Select Excel sheet to link to:
`Sheet1`

○ Link entire sheet

○ Link to a named range:

⦿ Link to range:
`A1:B10` [Preview]

Cell contents
○ Keep data formats and formulas
○ Keep data formats, solve formulas in Excel
⦿ Convert data formats to text, solve formulas in Excel
☐ Allow writing to source file

Cell formatting
☑ Use Excel formatting
   ○ Keep table updated to Excel formatting
   ⦿ Start with Excel formatting, do not update

☑ Preview

Room #	Area (sq. m.)
101	11.19
102	11.79
103	11.79
104	12.99
105	26.83
106	19.05
107	10.18
108	24.04
109	22.90

[OK]   [Cancel]   [Help]   ◀

ⓘ Learn about linking to Excel

- It presents the following:
  - The Excel file path and path type.
  - The Excel sheet name and the cell range.
  - Options for the cell content (i.e., whether to keep the data format and formulas).
  - An option to allow writing to the source file (keep this on if you want your edits in AutoCAD to be reflected in the Excel sheet).
  - Options for updating (or not) the Excel formatting.
- When done, click **OK**; click **OK** again for the following menu.
- Select the first two cells (for example), then right-click. A long menu will appear. Select **Locking** and then **Unlocked**:

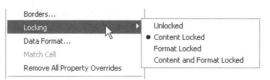

- Select one of the unlocked cells and change the value.
- Select the whole table.
- On the **Ribbon**, go to the **Insert** tab. Using the **Linking & Extraction** panel, click the **Upload to Source** button:

- You should see the following prompt in the **Command Window**:

```
1 object(s) found.
1 data link(s) written out successfully.
```

- Your Excel sheet should be closed when you **Upload to Source**.
- If you make a change in the Excel sheet and you want it reflected in the AutoCAD drawing, do so as follows: On the **Ribbon**, go to the **Insert** tab. Using the **Linking & Extraction** panel, click the **Download from Source** button:

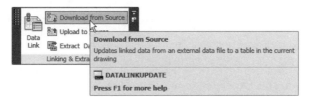

- This option will make the data in the AutoCAD drawing match the latest version of the Excel sheet.

IMPORTING OBJECTS FROM OTHER APPLICATIONS

Exercise 12-5
1. Start AutoCAD 2011.
2. Open the file *Exercise 12-5.dwg*.
3. Make sure you are at the **ISO A1 Layout**.
4. Start MS Word and open the file *General Notes.doc*.
5. Press [Ctrl] + A to select all text, then select **Edit/Copy**.
6. Return to AutoCAD 2011. Make sure you are at the **Text** layer and select **Edit/Paste**.

7. Place the text in the upper right-hand corner of the layout.

8. Change the font to 12 = 6 and check the content of the object.

9. Look at the object that landed in your drawing. What is it?

 Select it and the **Quick Properties** will tell you.

10. Start MS Excel and open the file *Room Area.xls*.

11. Select the existing table and copy it.

12. Return to AutoCAD. Select the **Paste Special** command and the **Paste Link** option; then select **AutoCAD Entities**.

13. Place the table below the text.

14. Close the Excel sheet (*very important*).

15. Select the table and hover over it. You will notice the locked and linked symbols.

16. Using the **Data Link Manager**, select **Excel Data Link 1**, right-click, and select the **Edit** option. Turn on **Allow writing to source file** and click **OK** twice.

17. Select the row containing Room 205 (the two cells), then right-click and select **Locking/Unlock**.

18. Change the value of the area from 24.82 to 24.92.

19. Click the table again and select **Upload to Source**.

20. You should see the following message in the **Command Window**:

```
1 object(s) found.
1 data link(s) written out successfully.
```

21. If so, open the Excel sheet again and you will see that the value has changed.

22. Save and close the file.

12.5 THE HYPERLINK COMMAND

- AutoCAD continues to grow more sophisticated. It is no longer composed of only simple graphical objects; it is full of data and information.
- Using the **Hyperlink** command, you can link any object(s) with any type of data, such as websites, email addresses, other AutoCAD drawings, and other Word, Excel, and PowerPoint® files.

- The procedure for adding a hyperlink is very simple:
  - Select the desired object(s) in AutoCAD.
  - On the **Ribbon**, go to the **Insert** tab. Using the **Data** panel, select the **Hyperlink** button:

  - The following dialog box will appear:

  - In the **Text to display** window, type in the tip you want the user to see when he/she gets close to the object(s).
  - In the **Type the file or Web page name** window, type the website address or the file path.
  - Click **OK** when done.
- You can also do this in reverse order: Select the objects from the application you want and select **Edit/Copy**. Go to the AutoCAD drawing and select **Edit/Paste as Hyperlink**, then select the objects in AutoCAD to be linked. Your AutoCAD objects will be hyperlinked.

THE HYPERLINK COMMAND

Exercise 12-6

1. Start AutoCAD 2011.
2. Open the file *Exercise 12-6.dwg*.
3. Select the 3D shape and press [Ctrl] + K. The **Hyperlink** dialog box will appear.
4. In the **Text to display** window, type PART DETAIL.
5. Click the **File** button and select the file *PART DETAIL.dwg*.
6. Click **OK**.
7. Test the hyperlink.
8. Save and close the file.

12.6 THE VIEW AND VIEWPORT COMMANDS

- A view in AutoCAD is any portion of the drawing saved under a name.
- There are two ways to define a view in AutoCAD:
  - Zoom to the required area using the **Zoom** and **Pan** commands, issue the **View** command, and create and name a new view.
  - Issue the **View** command to create a new view. In the dialog box, specify two opposite corners (i.e., create a window). Whatever is inside the window will be created and named as the view.
- On the **Ribbon**, go to the **View** tab. Using the **Views** panel, click the **Named Views** button:

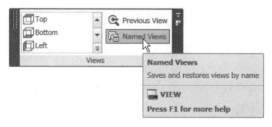

- The following dialog box will appear:

- Click the **New** button and you will see the following dialog box:

- Specify the **View name**.
- Specify a **View category**, which is a user-defined field. You can type a name for the category or you can leave it empty. Then specify the **View type** (AutoCAD 3D).
- From **Boundary**, select either **Current display** if you are already zoomed to the desired area of the drawing or **Define window** if you want to now zoom to the desired area. Then, click on the small button at the right.
- Under **Settings**, choose to **Save layer snapshot with view**, which means you will save the current status of the layers with the view so when you retrieve it you will restore this layer status with it. The other three options related to the 3D functions of AutoCAD 2011 are **UCS, Live Section**, and **Visual Style**.
- Under **Background**, select the background of the view. You can select the default color (the current background color), or you can select **Solid**, **Gradient**, **Image**, or **Sun & Sky** (which are also related to the 3D functions of AutoCAD 2011).
- Click **OK** to save the view.
- After you save several views, you will see the following dialog box:

- Select the name of the view and click the **Set Current** button to restore the selected view.
- Click the **Update Layers** button if you want to restore the layer status saved with the view.
- Click the **Edit Boundaries** button if you want to change the window containing the view.
- To remove the view from your drawing, select the name of the view from the list and click the **Delete** button.

View and Viewport

- You can use the views you created in the **Viewport** dialog box.
- Start the **Viewport** dialog box:

- As you can see in the **Preview** area, you can select each part of the screen.
- After making your selection, look at the lower part of the dialog box where it says **Change view to** and select the saved view that you wish to show in the selected viewport.

Named Viewport

- You can also show viewports while in the **Model Space** mode.
- These viewports cannot be printed together or scaled; however, you can create arrangements other than the saved ones in AutoCAD, name them, and save them. You can then recall them in the **Paper Space** mode.
- First, make sure you are in the **Model Space** mode. On the **Ribbon**, go to the **View** tab. Using the **Viewports** panel, click the **New** button:

■ You will see the following dialog box:

■ Select the arrangement that you wish to use from the **Standard viewports** list (let's select **Three: Left**).
■ Select one of the viewports from the **Preview** area (let's select the upper one).
■ Start the **Viewport** command again and select another arrangement (let's select **Two: Horizontal** this time). Under **Apply to**, select **Current Viewport**:

- Click inside the viewport at the lower right. On the **Ribbon**, using the **View** tab and the **Viewports** panel, click the **Join** button:

- You will see the following prompts:

```
Select dominant viewport <current viewport>:
Select viewport to join:
```

- Click inside the dominant viewport (its view will be the one used in the viewport you are creating), then select the viewport to join.
- You now have a new arrangement that you can save.
- Start the **Viewport** command again. You will see something resembling the following:

- Type in the name of the new arrangement and click **OK**.
- This new arrangement can be used in **Layouts** as well.

THE VIEW AND VIEWPORT COMMANDS

Exercise 12-7

1. Start AutoCAD 2011.
2. Open the file *Exercise 12-7.dwg*.
3. Create four new views (selecting **Save layer snapshot with view**) as well as an **Overall** view that includes the whole plan. The four new views are:
   - **Living Room**
   - **Study**
   - **Sitting Room**
   - **Kitchen and Toilet**
4. On the **Ribbon**, go to the **View** tab. Using the **Views** panel, click on the name of the view to zoom to it.
5. Go to the **Layer Properties Manager** dialog box and thaw the three frozen layers.
6. On the **Ribbon**, go to the **View** tab. Using the **Views** panel, select the names of the views again. Notice that the layers that used to be frozen when you saved the views are not shown.
7. Go to the **ISO A1 Overall** layout.
8. Make the **Viewport** layer current.
9. Using the **Viewport** command, insert a single viewport showing the **Overall** view.
10. Go to **ISO A1—Architectural Details** and insert four viewports showing four different views, setting the **Viewport Spacing** to 10:
    - Top left = **Living Room**
    - Top right = **Study**
    - Bottom left = **Kitchen and Toilet**
    - Bottom right = **Sitting Room**
11. Return to the **Model Space**.
12. Using the **Viewport** command, set the viewports to **Three: Left**, showing at the left **Overall** view. At the top right, select **Living Room**, and at the lower right, select **Sitting Room**.

13. Select the upper right viewport and start the **Viewport** command again. Select **Two: Horizontal**. At **Apply to**, select **Current Viewport**.
14. Join the two lower right viewports, selecting the one at the bottom first.
15. Save the new arrangement as "Three Unequal."
16. Go to the **ISO A1 Three Unequal** layout.
17. Start the **Viewport** command and select **Named Viewports**. You will see the **Three Unequal** viewport arrangement there. Select it and specify the area you want to occupy.
18. Save and close the file.

12.7 USING FIELDS

- Fields are data stored in AutoCAD that can be changed throughout the course of building your drawing. AutoCAD will update these whenever the field values changes.
- You can use fields through:
  - The **Field** command
  - The **Table** command
  - The **Attribute Definition** command
  - The **MTEXT** and **TEXT** commands
- On the **Ribbon**, go to the **Insert** tab. Using the **Data** panel, click the **Field** button:

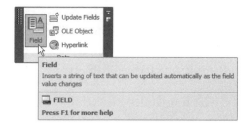

- You will see the following dialog box:

- By default, **Field category** is **All**, but you can select the desired field category from the following:
    - **Date & Time**, which includes everything related to the date and time of the drawing.
    - **Document**, which includes everything related to the AutoCAD file.
    - **Linked**, which includes everything related to hyperlinks.
    - **Objects**, which includes everything related to AutoCAD objects.
    - **Other**, which includes everything related to AutoCAD programming languages or system variables.
    - **Plot**, which includes everything related to the plotting process in AutoCAD.
    - **Sheet Sets**, which includes everything related to the Sheet Sets.

Example 1

- The following is the **Field** dialog box:

- The selections made in this box are as follows: the **Field category** is **Objects**, the **Field name** is **Object**, and **Polyline** is the **Object type**. AutoCAD lists the **Properties** of this specific object. From these properties, we selected **Area**, and AutoCAD gave us a **Preview** for the area. We then changed the **Format** of the area to be **Decimal** and the **Precision** to be **0.00**.

NOTE ➤
- The field will be displayed using the current text style and current text height.

Example 2

- From the **Application Menu**, select **Drawing Utilities/Drawing Properties**. You will see the following dialog box:

Ground Floor Plan.dwg Properties

General | Summary | Statistics | Custom

Title: Ground Floor Plan

Subject: Architectural Design

Author: M. H.

Keywords: New York, Paris, Industrial

Comments:

Hyperlink base:

OK   Cancel   Help

- Go to the **Summary** tab and fill in the required data, including **Title, Subject, Author**, etc.
- Click the **Custom** tab. You will see the following:

Ground Floor Plan.dwg Properties

General | Summary | Statistics | Custom

Custom properties:

Name	Value
Checked By	M.H.

Add...

Delete

OK   Cancel   Help

- Click the **Add** button and you will see the following dialog box:

- Type in the name of the new information you want to include and the desired value.
- Go to the **Field** command and select **Document** from the list. You will see something resembling the following:

- If you are inside the **MTEXT** editor, you can use the **Insert Field** button in the **Insert** panel, which appears with the **MTEXT** command:

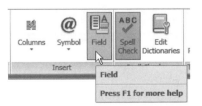

- Or you can simply right-click inside the **MTEXT** editor and select **Insert Field** from the menu. (You can also use [Ctrl] + F.)
- You can do the same thing in the **TEXT** command.
- In the **Attribute Definition** dialog box, there is a button to insert a field (this command will be discussed in later chapters).
- Also, in the **Table** command, you can double-click inside a cell and right-click to select the **Insert Field** option.

NOTE ▶
- By default, a field similar to the following will be inserted with a background:

- If you do not want a background, click the **Options** button at the bottom of the **Application Menu**. Select the **User Preferences** tab and click off the **Display background of fields** option:

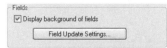

- While here, you can also click **Field Update Settings**, which will show the following dialog box:

- By default, a field will be updated when you open the file or when you save, use **Regen**, plot, or use **eTransmit** (this command will be discussed in later chapters).

USING FIELDS

Exercise 12-8
1. Start AutoCAD 2011.
2. Open the file *Exercise 12-8.dwg*.

3. Make sure of the following:
   - You are in the **Model Space** mode.
   - **Text** is the current layer.
   - **Standard** is the current text style.
4. Using **Multiline Text** in the room at the upper left, type the following:
   - **Room #201** (in the first line)
   - **Area** = (in the second line)
5. After the equal sign, right-click and select the **Insert Field** option.
6. In the **Field category**, select **Objects**. From the **Field names**, select **Object**, and then select the *cyan polyline* around the room. Select **Area** and change the **Precision** to be 0.00, and then click **OK**. Finally, select the **Close Text Editor** button.
7. Do the same for any other room in the drawing.
8. From the **Application Menu**, select **Drawing Utilities/Drawing Properties** and change the following:
   - **Title** = 2nd Floor Plan
   - **Author** = M. H.
   - Go to **Custom**, define a new field **Checked By**, and enter its value as **A. A.**
9. Go to **ISO A1 Layout**, and using the **Field** command, do the following:
   - Using the text style **TitleBlock_Regular**, insert the title of the drawing in the right place.
   - Using the text style **ISO Proportional**, insert the **Designed By** (**Author**) and **Checked By**.
10. Remove the background of the fields.
11. You should have something resembling the following:

Itemref	Quantity	Title/Name, designation, material,
Designed by M. H.	Checked by A. A.	Approved by - da APPROVED_BY_

2nd Floor Plan

14

12. Save and close the file.

12.8 FORMULAS AND TABLES

■ Earlier, we covered how to create a table style and how to insert a table in your drawing.
■ Here we will discuss how to create formulas, imitating MS Excel.
■ We will also cover some advanced functions in **Tables**.

Formulas

■ For our purposes, we will assume you do not have any MS Excel experience so we will begin with some basic rules:
   • Each cell has an address linking it to its column and row. For example, A3 refers to the cell in column A, row 3.
   • To start a formula in any cell, double-click inside the cell, and always start your input with an equals sign (=). Input a cell address along with a basic math function, such as +, − ,*, or /. For example, the following is a valid formula: =A3+B3–C3 (this formula will be evaluated from left to right unless there are brackets, which will be evaluated first).
   • You can also use predefined functions, such as **SUM(range of cells)**, **AVERAGE(range of cells)**.
   • For convenience, the cell address is always relative. Assume we have the following formula in cell E14: =(A14+B14)–(C14/D14). If you copy the contents of the cell to E15, what will happen? The formula will be =(A15+B15)–(C15/D15). This is because the formula is showing relative addresses.
   • You can add a dollar sign ($) if you want to make the address absolute. For example, $A3 means column A will always be the column to copy from, but the row will change with the copying. A$3 means row 3 will always be copied from and the column will change. A3 means you will always go to cell A3.
   • If you select the cell (by clicking inside its border), there will be a handle (**Autofill grip**) at the lower right-hand corner, which allows us to copy the contents of the cell to the other cells. See the following example:

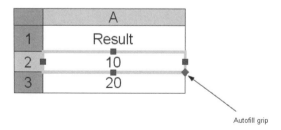

Autofill grip

- Click on the handle and drag it downward (or upward), and the formula will be copied accordingly.
- You can add an **Autofill grip** to increment the numbers by one.
- Also, if you typed two numbers, select both cells and drag the **Autofill grip**. AutoCAD will take the difference between the two numbers and consider it as an increment; thus, if you drag the handle of the two cells, an incremental number will always be shown.

12.9 ADVANCED TABLE FEATURES

- If you double-click inside a cell, you will be able to input data or edit existing data. If you click on one cell, you will see four grips and the handle (**Autofill grip**). You will also see a new tab called **Table** and panels that contain some advanced functions.

Rows

- The **Rows** panel appears as follows:

- **Insert Above** means a new row will be added above the selected row.
- **Insert Below** means a new row will be added below the selected row.
- **Delete Row(s)** will delete the selected row(s).

Columns

- The **Columns** panel appears as follows:

- **Insert Left** means a new column will be added to the left of the selected column.
- **Insert Right** means a new column will be added to the right of the selected column.
- **Delete Columns(s)** will delete the selected column(s).

Merge

- The **Merge** panel appears as follows:

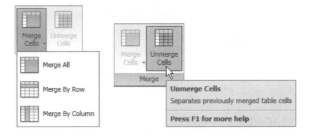

- For this command to be active, you must select more than one cell. This function is used to merge cells. If you select many cells, AutoCAD will give you three options: **All** (to merge all cells into a single cell), **By Row** (to merge all cells into the same row while retaining the columns), or **By Column** (to merge all cells into the same column while retaining the rows). In all cases, the following message will appear before the merging process:

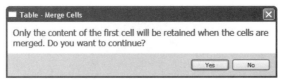

- **Unmerged Cells** is the opposite of the **Merge** function. You can unmerge merged cells whenever you want, even after closing the file.

Cell Styles

- The **Cell Styles** panel appears as follows:

- **Match Cell** means the user will select the cell that AutoCAD will copy the properties from and will then select as many cells as he or she wishes it to match with.

- Select the **Alignment** button (the button in the center of the panel). You will see the following list:

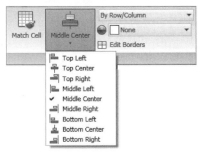

- This list refers to the **Alignment** of the text related to the borders of the cell. There are nine choices: Top Left, Top Center, Top Right, Middle Left, Middle Center, Middle Right, Bottom Left, Bottom Center, and Bottom Right (the shape of the button will change depending on your alignment choice).
- Select the desired cell style for the selected cells:

- Select the desired background color for the selected cells:

- Select **Edit Borders**. You will see the following dialog box:

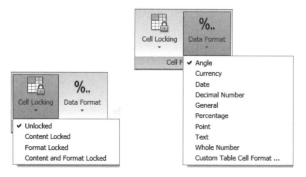

- You can specify **Lineweight**, **Linetype**, and the **Color** of the borders. By default, the border is single line, but you can make it double line. If you do, specify the **Spacing** of the double line. Select to make the lines for **All Borders, Outside Borders, Inside Borders**, or **No Borders**.

Cell Format

- The **Cell Format** panel appears as follows:

- The **Cell Locking** function allows you to lock the cell so it cannot be changed. There are four locking options: lock the **Content** of the cell, lock the **Format** of the cell, lock the **Content and Format** of the cell, or leave the cell **Unlocked**.

- To control the **Data Format**, you can choose from nine options (as shown in the illustration) or create a custom format.

Insert

- The **Insert** panel appears as follows:

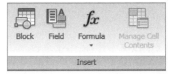

- When you click the **Block** button, you will see the following dialog box:

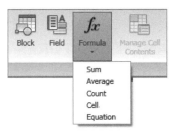

- Specify the **Name** of the block, **Scale** or **AutoFit**, the **Rotation angle**, and the **Alignment** of the block reference to the desired cell.
- The **Field** button is used to insert a field in the cell (as was discussed earlier).
- When using the **Formula** button, you will see the following list:

- You will insert one of the predefined formulas from the five choices shown in the illustration.

Data

- The **Data** panel appears as follows:

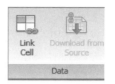

- If you click the **Link Cell** button, you will see the following dialog box:

- This box is the same dialog box we discussed when we introduced the concept of importing Excel objects into an AutoCAD drawing. You will create the link with an Excel sheet cell.
- You can then use **Download from Source** to import the data from this link.

FORMULAS AND ADVANCED FEATURES IN TABLES

Exercise 12-9
1. Start AutoCAD 2011.
2. Open the file *Exercise 12-9.dwg*.
3. Check the preexisting table.
4. Select all the **Data cells** and make the **Alignment** = Middle Center.
5. Select the rightmost column.
6. Insert a new column to its right.

7. Make the **Header of the column** = Area.

8. In the first cell, below the header, type the following formula: **=C3*D3**.

9. Copy the formula to the cells beneath.

10. Select the lower row.

11. Insert a new row beneath it.

12. Select all cells of the new row except the rightmost cell.

13. Merge the cells by row.

14. In the merged cells, type **Total Area**. If it asks you, select **Change the data type**, and make its **Alignment** = Middle Right.

15. Click the rightmost cell, then click the **Formula** button and select the **Sum** function.

16. Select the range of the areas (from E3 to E6).

17. Select the **Area** column and change the background color to yellow.

18. Lock both the content and the format for the **Area** column (now when you hover over these cells, you will see the lock symbol).

19. Try to double-click one of these cells. What message do you receive?

20. Using the **Options** dialog box and the **User Preferences** tab, click off the **Display background of fields** option.

21. Save and close the file.

12.10 THE QUICK SELECT COMMAND

- The selecting methods covered earlier in the book are all visual methods, which means you must click on an object or specify some sort of window to select a group of objects.
- The **Quick Select** method helps you select objects based on their properties, even if these objects are not easily seen throughout the drawing.
- **Quick Select** works closely with **Properties** as it supplies the objects.
- On the **Ribbon**, go to the **Home** tab. Using the **Utilities** panel, click the **Quick Select** button:

- Another way to reach the command is to right-click while in the graphical area and select **Quick Select** from the displayed menu.
- Either method will produce the following dialog box:

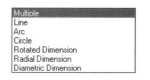

- In the **Apply to** section, select whether to search in the **Entire drawing** or a specific window.
- By default, AutoCAD knows all of the types of objects in any file. Hence, in the **Object type**, select **Multiple** or any specific object type that exists in your drawing. See the following illustration:

> Multiple
> Line
> Arc
> Circle
> Rotated Dimension
> Radial Dimension
> Diametric Dimension

- **Properties** differ according to the object type:
  - If you choose **Multiple**, then you will only see the general properties listed.
  - If your drawing contains a polyline, for example, then you will see the general properties as well as the specific properties of polylines.
- Specify the **Operator** (**Equals, Not Equal, Greater than, Less than**, or **Select All**) and its **Value**.
- Under **How to apply**, you have two choices:
  - Create a new selection set based on the objects that fit the criteria mentioned in the **Quick Select** dialog box.
  - Select all of the objects that do not fit the criteria.

- You can also select to **Append** the selected objects to an existing selection set (the selection set must be created before issuing the **Quick Select** command).

 ▶ - You can also issue the **Quick Select** command from the **Properties** palette. See the following illustration:

THE QUICK SELECT COMMAND

Exercise 12-10

1. Start AutoCAD 2011.
2. Open the file *Exercise 12-10.dwg*.
3. The people who drafted this drawing made the following mistakes:
   - All circles should have a **Diameter** = 0.24, but only 1 of 14 has the correct diameter; the others are all wrong.
   - The dimensions **Rotated** (which is Linear), **Diameter**, and **Radial** are all in layer 0 (zero).
   - All center marks are in layer 0 (zero).
4. To correct the first problem: use the **Quick Select** command and the **Properties** command and select all circles with **Diameter** < 0.24 and set the **Diameter** = 0.24.

5. To correct the second problem, perform the following steps:
    - Start the **Properties** command and click the **Quick Select** button.
    - At **Object type**, select **Rotated Dimension**; at **Operator**, choose **Select All**. Click **OK**. AutoCAD should find three of these.
    - Click the **Quick Select** button in the **Properties** palette, and select **Radial Dimension**. At **Operator**, choose **Select All**. This time use **Append to current selection set** and click **OK**. AutoCAD should find two of these.
    - Repeat the preceding step for **Diameter Dimension**. AutoCAD should find three of these, bringing the total to eight.
    - Move all dimension objects to the **Dimensions** layer.
6. All center marks (center marks are lines, not blocks) are in layer 0 (zero). Select all objects (**Multiple**) in layer 0 and send them to the **Dimensions** layer.
7. Save and close the file.

12.11 THE SELECT SIMILAR AND ADD SELECTED COMMANDS

- These two commands will help you select and draw objects faster.
- The **Select Similar** command will select objects with similar properties.
- The **Add Selected** command will allow you to select an object and use its properties when drawing objects.

Select Similar

- The **Select Similar** command is only accessible by typing and right-clicking.
- Simply select an object (or multiple objects) and right-click.
- You will see the following menu. Choose **Select Similar**.

- AutoCAD will automatically select similar objects with the same properties.

- Without selecting any object, if you type **SELECTSIMILAR** in the **Command Window**, you will see the following prompt:

```
Select objects or [SEttings]:
```

- Choose the **Settings** option and the following dialog box will appear:

- By default, AutoCAD will select similar objects based on the **Layer**.
- You can select more criteria, including **Color, Linetype**, etc.
- **Object style** is for any object created using a style, including **Mtext, Single Line Text, Table, Dimension**, etc.
- **Name** refers to reference names, such as blocks, Xref dwg, image, pdf, etc.
- If you select more than one object—for example, polyline and line—while each object is in a different layer, and if the similarity is based on the layer, then AutoCAD will select all lines in the same layer and all polylines in the same layer.

Add Selected

- The **Add Selected** command is accessible by right-clicking.
- Select an object, then right-click and choose the **Add Selected** option:

- Depending on the object you select, AutoCAD will start the command and will draw the new objects with the same properties as the selected object.

THE SELECT SIMILAR AND ADD SELECTED COMMAND

Exercise 12-11

1. Start AutoCAD 2011.
2. Open the file *Exercise 12-11.dwg*.
3. While you are not selecting any object, type **SELECTSIMILAR** in the **Command Window**. Using **Settings**, make sure that the **Layer** option is turned on.
4. Select one of the small green circles and press [Enter].
5. How many circles have been selected? (*Answer: 14*)
6. Press [Esc] to remove the selection.
7. While you are not selecting any object, type **SELECTSIMILAR** in the **Command Window**. Using **Settings**, turn off the **Layer** option.
8. Select one of the small green circles and press [Enter].
9. How many circles have been selected? (*Answer: 16*)

   Why is this number different than the number of circles selected with the **Layer** option turned on?
10. Select one of the two yellow lines, and right-click and select the **Add Selected** option. Draw two vertical and horizontal centerlines with **Length** = 6.
11. Select the horizontal dimension measuring 9.4, and right-click and select the **Add Selected** option. Add a vertical distance between the center of the big circle and lower right edge of the shape (measurement should be 3.0).
12. Save and close the file.

12.12 THE PARTIAL OPEN AND PARTIAL LOAD FEATURES

- Sometimes you have a massive drawing that contains many views and layers, and you do not want to open the whole drawing, only part of it. In this case, you can use the **Partial Open** feature.
- Once you have opened a file partially, you can load additional views and layers.

Procedure

- Using the **Open** command, select the file name; then, instead of clicking on the **Open** button, click the small arrow to its right and select **Partial Open**. See the following illustration:

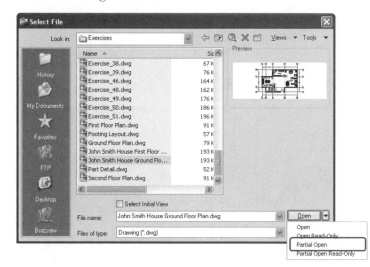

- Once you select **Partial Open**, the following dialog box will appear:

- You can select layers to be loaded for the **Extents** of the drawing.
- You can select layers to be loaded only in one of the saved views.
- Once you have partially loaded a file, you can type **partiaload** in the **Command Window**. The following dialog box will appear:

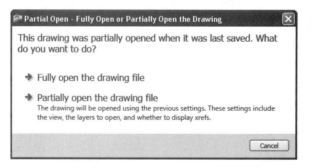

- This dialog box is identical to the **Partial Open** dialog box, except for the small button at the left. By default you can partially load the layers in the entire drawing or you can specify a window in the drawing to load the extents of objects.
- If you save your file and close it while it was partially opened (or loaded), AutoCAD will display the following message when you try to open the file again:

- Select whether you want it fully opened or want to restore the status as it was the last time you saved it.

THE PARTIAL OPEN AND PARTIAL LOAD FEATURES

 Exercise 12-12

1. Start AutoCAD 2011.
2. Using the **Open** dialog box, select *Exercise 12-12.dwg* (*do not double-click it*).
3. From the **Open** button, select **Partial Open**.
4. Select the following layers:
   - **A-Walls**
   - **A-Doors**
   - **Partition**
5. Make sure that **Extents** is selected in the list on the left. Click **OK** to open the file with these layers only.
6. Start the **Partial Load** command.
7. Select the view named **Study** and the layers **A-Windows, Furniture**, and **Text**.
8. Start the **Partial Load** command again.
9. Click the **Pick a window** button and create a window around the Kitchen and Toilet, then select the layers **Furniture** and **Centerlines**.
10. Save and close the file.
11. Try to open it again. What is AutoCAD's response?
12. Select to open it fully.
13. Save and close the file.

12.13 THE OBJECT VISIBILITY COMMAND

- The **Object Visibility** command allows you to show and hide objects in just a few quick clicks.
- This command is available by right-clicking.
- There are three options in it:
  - **Isolate Objects**
  - **Hide Objects**
  - **End Object Isolation**

Isolate Objects

- Use the **Isolate Objects** option if you want to hide all objects except the selected ones.
- Select the desired object(s).
- Right-click and select the **Isolate** option, then select **Isolate Objects**.

- Everything will disappear except the selected objects:

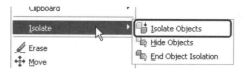

Hide Objects

- Use the **Hide Objects** option if you want to show all objects except the selected ones.
- Select the desired object(s).
- Right-click and select the **Isolate** option, then select **Hide Objects**.
- Everything will be shown except the selected objects:

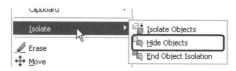

End Object Isolation

- Use the **End Object Isolation** option to restore the visibility of the isolated objects.
- Without selecting any objects, right-click and select the **Isolate** option, then select **End Object Isolation**.
- All objects will be restored to their normal visibility:

- If you open a file (created by others), you can determine if there are isolated objects.
- At the **Status Bar**, there is a lightbulb that will be either on or off:

- In the illustration, there are isolated objects in the drawing. You need to click **Unisolate Objects** to see them.

THE OBJECT VISIBILITY COMMAND

Exercise 12-13

1. Start AutoCAD 2011.
2. Open the file *Exercise 12-13.dwg*.
3. You need to work in the Kitchen and Toilet areas, so you want to hide everything else.
4. In the window, select the area covering the Kitchen and Toilet.
5. Right-click and select the **Isolate** option, then click **Isolate Objects**.
6. Everything will be hidden except the objects you selected.
7. Right-click and select the **Isolate** option, then click **End Object Isolation**.
8. Select the hatch (all hatches are one object). Right-click and select the **Isolate** option, then click **Hide Objects**.
9. Only hatched objects disappear, and the rest are shown.
10. Right-click and select the **Isolate** option, then click **End Object Isolation**.
11. Save and close the file.

CHAPTER REVIEW

1. Which of the following statements is false?
   a. You can offset objects and fillet them at the same time.
   b. You can access **Quick Select** from the **Properties** palette.
   c. You can open more than one file in AutoCAD, but you cannot use the drag-and-drop technique to copy objects from one file to anther.
   d. **Partial Load** can be used only if the file was opened in **Partial Open**.
2. In **Quick Select** command, in order to select all objects of a certain type, at _____, use the **Select All** option.
3. Which of the following statements about tables in AutoCAD is false?
   a. You can insert a new column to the right of an existing column.
   b. You can add a formula with relative or absolute references.
   c. You can insert a field inside one of the cells.
   d. You cannot lock a cell(s) in a table in order to prevent editing.

4. The total length of a polyline can be a field that you can insert in your drawing.

   a. True

   b. False

5. Using the **Edge** option in the **Trim** command, you can trim objects based on an extrapolated cutting edge.

   a. True

   b. False

6. Using _____, you can link any object in any drawing to another file.

CHAPTER REVIEW ANSWERS

1. c
2. **Operator**
3. d
4. a
5. a
6. **Hyperlink**

Chapter 13

PARAMETRIC CONSTRAINTS AND DYNAMIC BLOCKS

In This Chapter

◊ An introduction to **Parametric Constraints**
◊ **Geometric Constraints**
◊ **Dimensional Constraints**
◊ The **Dynamic Blocks** feature
◊ **Dynamic Blocks** and **Constraints**

13.1 PARAMETRIC CONSTRAINTS: AN INTRODUCTION

- Using **Parametric Constraints** in AutoCAD allows you to do two things:
  - Assign a geometric relationship between two objects that will not be altered by normal modifying commands.
  - Assign a size for an object that will not be changed by normal modifying commands.
- This feature used to be available only in the vertical products, but now it is available in AutoCAD as well.
- This feature will help any engineer draw his or her design exactly as intended.
- With the power of parametric constraints, the designer can limit mistakes made in later stages of the design process.
- There are two types of parametric constraints:
  - **Geometric**
  - **Dimensional**
- These are discussed in the following sections.

13.2 GEOMETRIC CONSTRAINTS

- To reach the geometric constraints menu, do as follows: On the **Ribbon**, go to the **Parametric** tab. Using the **Geometric** panel, select from the options shown:

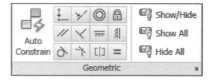

- As you can see, there are 13 geometric constraints: **Coincident, Collinear, Concentric, Fix, Parallel, Perpendicular, Horizontal, Vertical, Tangent, Smooth, Symmetric, Equal**, and **AutoConstrain**.

Coincident

- Using the **Geometric** panel, click the **Coincident** button:

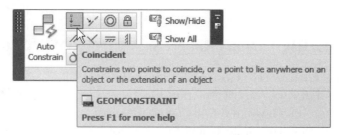

- The **Coincident** feature allows you to constrain two points to coincide.
- For example, assume we have the following two lines:

  - Start the **Coincident** command. The following prompt will appear:

  ```
  Select first point or [Object/Autoconstrain] <Object>:
  ```

- Click a point on the first object as shown:

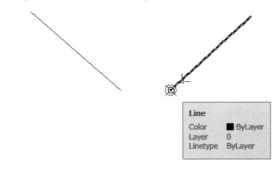

- The following prompt will appear:

```
Select second point or [Object] <Object>:
```

- Click the coincident point in the second object as shown:

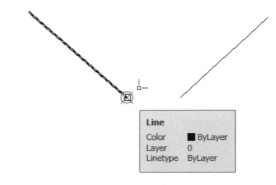

- The result will be as follows:

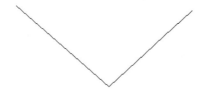

NOTE ■ Because these two lines are constrained at the endpoint, the lines will stay connected. See the following illustration:

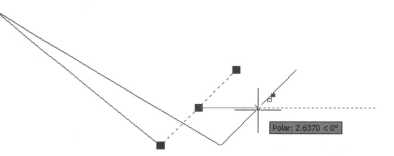

• If you hover over one of the two lines, you will see the following:

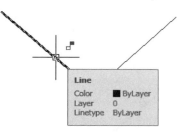

• This means that these two objects have parametric constraints placed on them.

Collinear

■ Using the **Geometric** panel, click the **Collinear** button:

■ The **Collinear** feature allows you to constrain two lines to lie on the same infinite line.
■ See the following illustration:

Before   After

Concentric

- Using the **Geometric** panel, click the **Concentric** button:

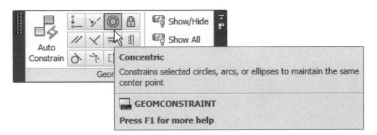

- The **Concentric** feature allows you to constrain selected circles, arcs, or ellipses to maintain the same center point.
- See the following illustration:

Before   After

Fix

- Using the **Geometric** panel, click the **Fix** button:

- The **Fix** feature allows you to constrain a point or a curve to a fixed point relative to the World Coordinate System.

■ See the following illustration:

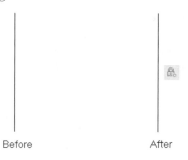

Before   After

Parallel

■ Using the **Geometric** panel, click the **Parallel** button:

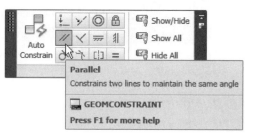

■ The **Parallel** feature allows you to constrain two lines to maintain the same angle.

■ See the following illustration:

Before   After

Perpendicular

- Using the **Geometric** panel, click the **Perpendicular** button:

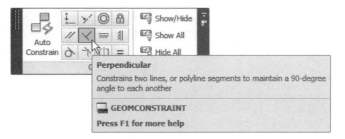

- The **Perpendicular** feature allows you to constrain two lines or polyline segments so they maintain a 90° angle to each other.
- See the following illustration:

Before   After

Horizontal

- Using the **Geometric** panel, click the **Horizontal** button:

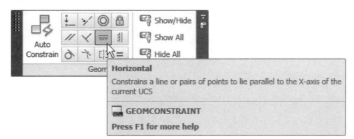

- The **Horizontal** feature allows you to constrain a line to lie parallel to the x-axis.

- See the following illustration:

Before   After

Vertical

- Using the **Geometric** panel, click the **Vertical** button:

- The **Vertical** feature allows you to constrain a line to lie parallel to the *y*-axis.
- See the following illustration:

Before   After

Tangent

- Using the **Geometric** panel, click the **Tangent** button:

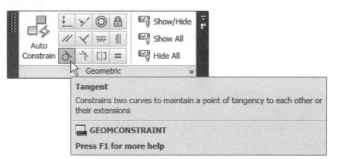

- The **Tangent** feature allows you to constrain two curves to maintain a point of tangency to each other.
- See the following illustration:

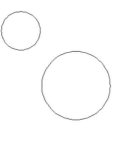
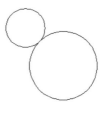

Before   After

Smooth

- Using the **Geometric** panel, click the **Smooth** button:

- The **Smooth** feature allows you to constrain a spline to be contiguous and maintain G2 continuity with another spline, line, arc, or polyline.

NOTE ▶ - Before you apply the **Smooth** constraint, you should first apply the **Coincident** constraint on the two curves.

- See the following illustration:

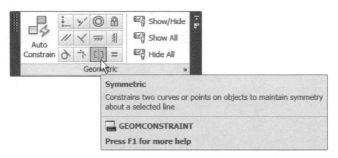

Before   Apply Coicident constraint   After

Symmetric

- Using the **Geometric** panel, click the **Symmetric** button:

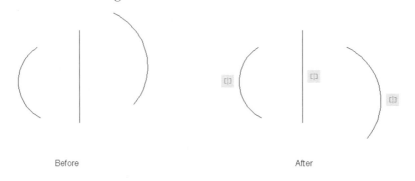

- The **Symmetric** feature allows you to constrain two curves to maintain symmetry around a selected line.

- See the following illustration:

Before   After

Equal

- Using the **Geometric** panel, click the **Equal** button:

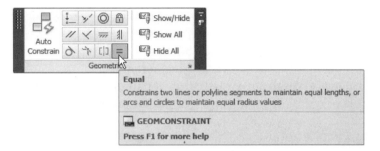

- The **Equal** feature allows you to constrain two lines or polyline segments to maintain equal lengths, or to constrain arcs and circles to maintain equal radius values.
- See the following illustration:

Before   After

AutoConstrain

- Using the **Geometric** panel, click the **AutoConstrain** button:

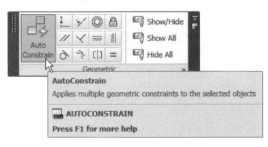

- The **AutoConstrain** feature allows you to apply multiple geometric constraints to selected objects. This feature depends on two things:
  - The objects selected.
  - The order of the geometric constraints in the **Constraint Settings** dialog box.
- You can reach the **Constraint Settings** dialog box by selecting the **Settings** option from the **AutoConstrain** command.
- You can also reach the **Constraint Settings** dialog box by clicking the arrow in the lower right-hand corner of the **Geometric** panel:

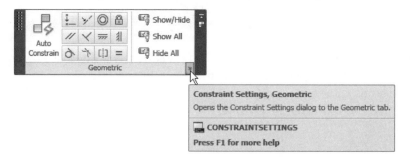

- You will see the following dialog box. Select the **AutoConstrain** tab:

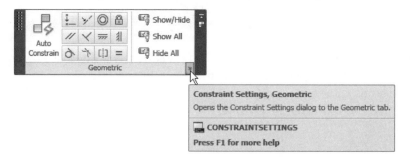

  - You can set the priority for each constraint. Select the constraint with more priority and click **Move Up**; select the constraint with less priority and click **Move Down**.

- You can turn off any undesired constraint by clicking the checkmark ($\checkmark$) at the right.
  - At any time, you can click **Reset** to return to the default settings.
  - You can also set the rules for **Tangent** and **Perpendicular**.
- Consider the following example.

- Begin with the following rectangle:

- Start the **AutoConstrain** command. The following prompt will appear:

```
Select objects or [Settings]:
```

- Select the desired object (the rectangle) and press [Enter]. The following message will appear:

```
8 constraint(s) applied to 4 object(s)
```

- You will see the following picture:

- The eight constraints are **Parallel** (2), **Horizontal, Perpendicular**, and **Coincident** (4).
- There are three constraints that **AutoConstrain** will not insert: **Symmetric, Fix**, and **Smooth**.

NOTE

Show and Hide

- You can show or hide the geometric constraints using three functions:

- Using **Show**, you can show the constraints for some of the objects.
- Using **Show All**, constraints will be shown for all objects.
- Using **Hide All**, constraints will be hidden for all objects.

13.3 CONSTRAINT BARS

- When you place a geometric constraint on an object, a small bar will appear in the drawing.
- When you hover over the bar, the objects involved in this constraint will be highlighted:

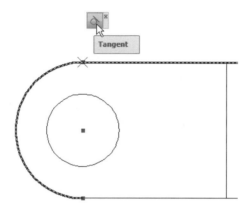

- Conversely, when you hover over an object with a geometric constraint attached to it, the corresponding **Constraint Bar** will be highlighted.
- For example, the following illustration shows an object with three geometric constraints attached to it:

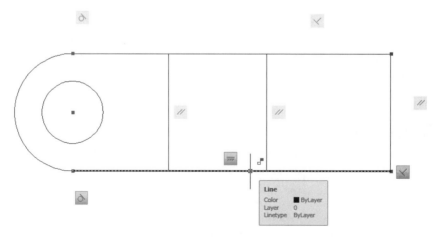

- Sometimes, the bar contains multiple similar constraints.
- The following example shows three parallel constraints on the same line:

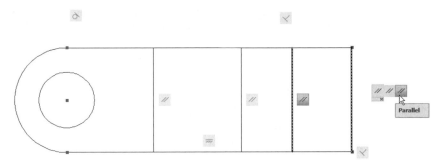

- If you right-click the **Constraint Bar**, you will see the following menu:

- It includes the following options:
  - **Delete**, which will delete the geometric constraint (another way is to hover over the constraint and press [Delete]).
  - **Hide**, which will hide this specific constraint.
  - **Hide All Constraints**, which will hide all the constraints placed on this drawing.

- **Constraint Bar Settings**, which will produce the following dialog box if clicked:

NOTE
- The **Constraint Bar** is not affected by zooming; it will maintain its size regardless of how much you zoom in or out.
- This dialog box allows you to show or hide a specific type of constraint.
- You can also control the transparency of the **Constraint Bar**; by default, it is 50%.
- You can switch on/off the following two choices:
  - **Show constraint bars after applying constraints to selected objects**
  - **Show constraint bars when objects are selected**

NOTE
- You can move constraint bars to any location you want in the drawing. Click the bar, hold it, and drag it to the new location.

13.4 INFER CONSTRAINTS

- By default, you draw objects first and then apply geometric constraints to them.
- Using **Infer Constraints**, you can apply geometric constraints while you are drafting.

- Using the **Status Bar**, click **Infer Constraints** to turn it on:

- Now when you start drawing objects, they will be constrained right away.
- To control which constraints are applied, right-click the **Infer Constraints** button. You will see the following menu:

- Select **Settings** and you will see the following dialog box:

- This is the same box we used for the **Constraint Bar Settings**.
- Here, we can select which constraints will not be applied when **Infer Constraint** is on.

13.5 RELAXING AND OVERCONSTRAINING

- If, for example, you apply the **Horizontal** constraint to a line and then try to rotate it, you will receive the following message:

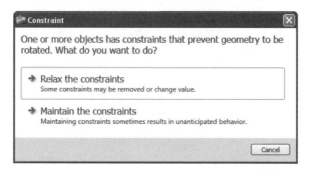

- In this case, relaxing means that some of the constraints will be removed to allow the command to be effective (in our example, a line will be allowed to rotate).
  - If you select **Relax the constraints**, then AutoCAD will permanently remove the constraint that keeps the commands from performing.
  - If you select **Maintain the constraints**, then objects will keep their current constraints.
- Sometimes, when you apply too many constraints on an object and/or apply contradicting constraints, you will receive the following message:

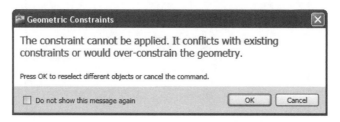

- You will have to change your existing constraints if you still wish to apply the new constraint.

PARAMETRIC CONSTRAINTS: GEOMETRIC (GENERIC)

Exercise 13-1
1. Start AutoCAD 2011.
2. Open the file *Exercise 13-1.dwg*.

3. On the **Ribbon**, go to the **Parametric** tab. Using the **Geometric** panel, select the **Horizontal** constraint and select the lower horizontal line at the middle.

4. Using the **Parallel** constraint, select all of the other horizontal lines in the drawing (you must select them one at a time).

5. Using the **Tangent** constraint, set the two vertical lines with the arc to be tangent (you must select them one at a time, selecting the arc first).

6. Using the **Coincident** constraint and **AutoConstrain**, select the whole shape.

7. Using the **Concentric** constraint, select the inner circle and the outer arc.

8. Using the **Vertical** constraint, select the right vertical line (which is tangent to the arc).

9. Using the **Parallel** constraint, select the right vertical line and all the other vertical lines (you must select them one at a time).

10. Go to the **Constraint Bar** which shows **Parallel** at the right of the right vertical line.

11. You will see five icons. Hover over each one to make sure you created the right relationship with all vertical lines.

12. If you have any overlapping bars, move them away from each other.

13. Save the file as *Exercise 13-1-1.dwg* and close it.

14. Open the file *Exercise 13-1.dwg* again.

15. Start the **AutoConstrain** command. Using **Settings**, turn off the **Collinear** and **Perpendicular** constraints.

16. Select the whole shape and press [Enter].

17. How many constraints have been applied? (*Answer: 31*) On how many objects? (*Answer: 13*)

18. Undo the **AutoConstrain** command.

19. Start the **AutoConstrain** command again. Using **Settings**, click the **Reset** button. As you can see, all constraints are turned on except **Equal**. Switch **Equal** on.

20. How many constraints have been applied? (*Answer: 28*) On how many objects? (*Answer: 13*)

21. Using the **Status Bar**, switch on **Infer Constraints**.

22. Draw a rectangle (in any space at the right of the shape): **Length** = 6, **Width** = 10.

23. Because we had **Infer Constraints** on, the constraints were applied automatically.

24. Using the **Collinear** constraint, select the small horizontal line in the original shape, then select the lower horizontal line of the rectangle.

25. The rectangle will be the side view of the shape, so we want to draw hidden lines representing the hole and base.

26. Make the **Hidden** layer current and switch on **OSNAP**. Make sure that **Quadrant** and **Intersection** are both on.

27. Using **OSNAP** and **OTRACK**, draw lines in the rectangle representing the hole and the base.

28. Using the **Coincident** constraint and **AutoConstrain**, select the rectangle and the lines inside it. Press [Enter].

29. Using the **Geometric** panel, click **Hide All**.

30. Start the **Move** command, select the rectangle and the lines inside it, and move them upward. Notice how the shapes moved together.

31. Save the file as *Exercise 13-1-2.dwg* and close it.

13.6 DIMENSIONAL CONSTRAINTS

- Dimensional constraints constrain the length of a line (linear or aligned), the radius or diameter of a circle or an arc, or the angle between two lines, including the angle of an arc.

- To reach these constraints, do as follows: On the **Ribbon**, go to the **Parametric** tab. Using the **Dimensional** panel, select from the options shown:

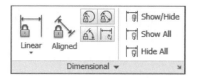

- There are eight different dimensional constraints: **Linear, Horizontal, Vertical, Aligned, Radial, Diameter, Angular**, and **Convert**.

Linear, Horizontal, and Vertical

- Using the **Dimensional** panel, click the **Linear** button. You will have three options:

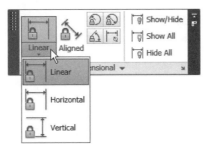

- The **Linear** option will constrain either horizontally or vertically.
- The **Horizontal** option will constrain the x-axis distance between two points.
- The **Vertical** option will constrain the y-axis distance between two points.
- See the following illustration:

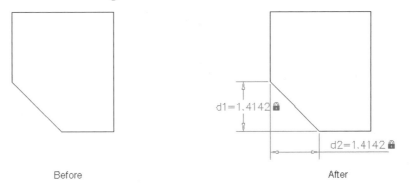

Before   After

Aligned

- Using the **Dimensional** panel, click the **Aligned** button:

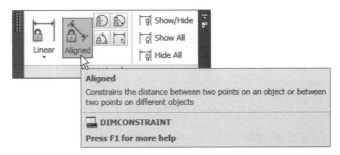

- The **Aligned** feature allows you to constrain the distance between two points.
- See the following illustration:

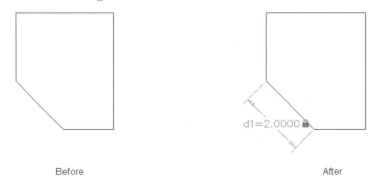

Before   After

Radial and Diameter

- Using the **Dimensional** panel, click the **Radial** or **Diameter** button:

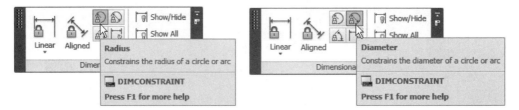

- The **Radial** and **Diameter** features allow you to constrain the radius or the diameter of a circle or an arc.
- See the following illustration:

Before   After

Angular

- Using the **Dimensional** panel, click the **Angular** button:

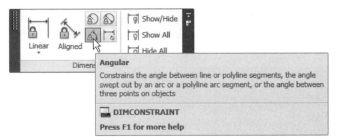

- The **Angular** feature allows you to constrain the angle between two lines or polyline objects.
- See the following illustration:

Before   After

Convert

- Using the **Dimensional** panel, click the **Convert** button:

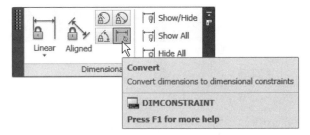

- The **Convert** feature allows you to convert dimensions to dimensional constraints.

- See the following illustration:

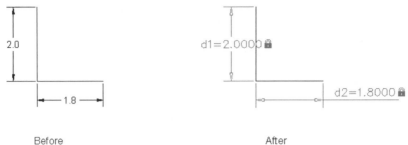

Before   After

Show Dynamic Constraints

- Using the **Dimensional** panel, click the **Show Dynamic Constraints** button:

- You will have the following options:
  - **Show/Hide** the dimensional constraints that you select.
  - **Show All** of the dimensional constraints in the drawing.
  - **Hide All** of the dimensional constraints in the drawing.

Constraint Settings

- Using the **Parametric** tab and the **Dimensional** panel, click the arrow at the lower right to see the **Constraint Settings** for the dimensional constraints:

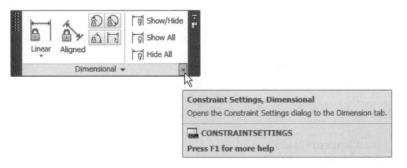

- You will see the following dialog box:

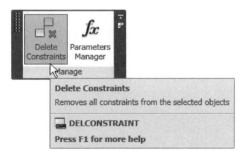

- In this dialog box, you can control the **Dimension name format**. You have three choices:
  - **Name**
  - **Value**
  - **Name and Expression**
- Select whether to show the lock symbol.
- Select whether to show (when the dimensional constraints are hidden) the dimensional constraint for any object you select.

Delete Constraints

- You can delete both geometric and dimensional constraints. On the **Ribbon**, go to the **Parametric** tab. Using the **Manage** panel, click the **Delete Constraints** button:

- The following prompt will appear:

```
All constraints will be removed from selected objects...
Select objects:
```

- Constraints will be deleted after pressing [Enter].
- Dimensional constraints will not be printed.
- Dimensional constraint will not be affected by zooming.

13.7 THE PARAMETERS MANAGER

- You can create relationships between dimensional constraints by creating equations using the **Parameters Manager**.
- You can create user-defined parameters that will help define more complex equations.
- Additionally, if you have many parameters, you can create parameter groups.
- On the **Ribbon**, go to the **Parametric** tab. Using the **Manage** panel, click the **Parameters Manager** button:

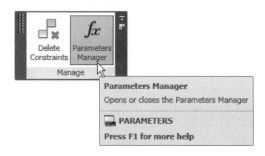

- You will see a palette resembling the following:

- You will see the dimensional constraints already added in your drawing.
- In this example, the constraints are named **rad1** and **rad2**.
- You can rename them by clicking the current name and typing a new name:

- In the **Expression** column, you can enter any equation you want:

- In this example, we created an equation to make **outside_radius** = **hole1+0.75**.
- Whenever the **hole1** value changes, the **outside_radius** will be updated automatically.
- Using the same palette, you can create user-defined parameters:

Name	Expression	Value
Dimensional Constraint Parameters		
d1	basic_length+d2	9.7500
d2	2	2.0000
hole1	1.5	1.5000
outside_radius	hole1+0.75	2.2500
User Parameters		
basic_length	7.75	7.7500

Creates a new parameter group (Alt+G)
All Used in Expressions
Invert filter
All: 5 of 5 parameters displayed
Parameters Manager
Search for parameter

- When you click on the button indicated in the previous illustration, the following menu will appear. Type in the name of the user-defined parameter:

Name	Expression	Value
Dimensional Constraint Parameters		
d1	9.75	9.7500
d2	2	2.0000
hole1	1.5	1.5000
outside_radius	hole1+0.75	2.2500
User Parameters		
basic_length	7.75	7.7500

- The user-defined parameter in this example is **basic_length**. We did not define reference in the drawing and gave it a basic value of 7.75.

- You can now include it in the expression of the dimensional constraints. We will make the **Expression** of the **d1** paramether = **basic_length+d2**:

Name ▲	Expression	Value
⊟ **Dimensional Constraint Parameters**		
🔒 d1	basic_length+d2	9.7500
🔒 d2	2	2.0000
hole1	1.5	1.5000
outside_radius	hole1+0.75	2.2500
⊟ **User Parameters**		
basic_length	7.75	7.7500

- Thus, whenever we change **basic_length** and/or **d2, d1** will be updated to the new value.
- If you have many parameters, you can create filters to focus on a group of related parameters.
- First, using the left pane, create a new filter:

	e ▲	Expression	Value
Creates a new parameter group (Alt+G)	⊟ **Dimensional Constraint Parameters**		
All Used in Expressions	🔒 d1	basic_length+d2	9.7500
	🔒 d2	2	2.0000
	hole1	1.5	1.5000
	outside_radius	hole1+0.75	2.2500
	⊟ **User Parameters**		
	basic_length	7.75	7.7500

Search for parameter

☐ Invert filter   «

All: 5 of 5 parameters displayed

- Type in the name of the filter.
- Drag and drop the desired parameter to the appropriate group.

- You will see a palette resembling the following:

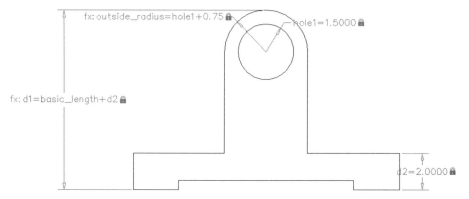

(Parameters Manager palette showing:)

Name ▲	Expression	Value
Dimensional Constraint Parameters		
hole1	1.5	1.5000
outside_radius	hole1+0.75	2.2500

Filters
- fx All
  - All Used in Expressions
  - Radial
  - Length

☐ Invert filter

Radial: 2 of 5 parameters displayed

- In this example, we created two filters, **Radial** and **Length**. We dragged and dropped the two radial parameters into the **Radial** filter, and we dragged and dropped the three length parameters into the **Length** filter.
- In the graphical area, you will see an illustration resembling the following:

fx: outside_radius=hole1+0.75

hole1=1.5000

fx: d1=basic_length+d2

d2=2.0000

- You can see in this example that the equation begins with **fx:** to differentiate it from the normal parameter.
- If you double-click the equation and input a value, the new value will replace the equation.

13.8 DIMENSIONAL VERSUS ANNOTATIONAL CONSTRAINTS

- By default, dimensional constraints are not plotted and are not affected by zooming.
- If you want the constraint to serve as a dimensional constraint and also a dimension block, you can convert it to an annotational constraint.
- Annotational constraints are plotted and use the current dimensional style.
- To convert dimensional constraints to annotational, do the following:
  - Select the desired dimensional parameter.
  - Right-click and select the **Properties** option.
  - At **Constraint Form**, change the value from **Dynamic** to **Annotational**:

- Using this method, you will first insert the dimensional parameter, then convert it. However, you can also set the mode before inserting, thus allowing you to insert annotational parameters right away.

- On the **Ribbon**, go to the **Parametric** tab. Using the **Dimensional** panel, click the small triangle beside the title **Dimensional**. Select the mode you wish to use, either **Dynamic Constraint Mode** or **Annotational Constraint Mode**:

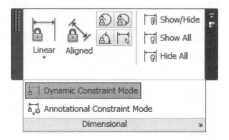

13.9 DIMENSIONAL GRIPS

- Dimensional parameters have their own grips, which vary depending on the type of parameter.
- If you click a linear, horizontal, vertical, or aligned parameter, you will see something similar to the following:

- The middle grip is used to relocate the parameter.
- The two grips at either end are used to increase or decrease the length to the right or to the left.
- If you click an angular parameter, you will see the following:

- The middle grip is used to relocate the parameter, and the two arrows are used to increase or decrease the angle.

- If you click the radial or diametric parameter, you will see the following:

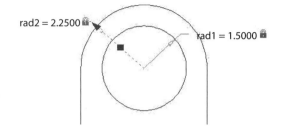

- The middle grip is used to relocate the parameter, and the arrow is used to increase or decrease the radius or diameter.

DIMENSIONAL CONSTRAINTS

Exercise 13-2

1. Start AutoCAD 2011.
2. Open the file *Exercise 13-2.dwg*.
3. You should see the geometric constraints; if not, go to the **Geometric** panel and click **Show All**.
4. As you can see, the two shapes are fully constrained geometrically. Click **Hide All**.
5. Input the linear and radial parameters shown in the following illustration, accepting the default values (make sure the names you see—d1, d2, rad1, etc.—match those in the illustration):

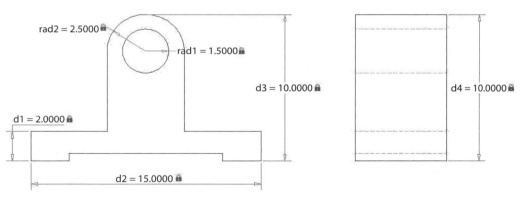

6. Using the **Parameters Manager**, rename the parameters as follows:
    a. rad1 = hole1
    b. rad2 = outside_radius
    c. d2 = total_width

7. Create a user-defined parameter and call it **basic_length**, with value = 8.
8. Create the following equations:
   a. outside_radius = hole1+0.75
   b. d3 = d1+basic_length
   c. d4 = d3
   d. total_width = d3×1.5
9. After testing, you discover you need more dimensional constraints. Add another linear parameter as follows:

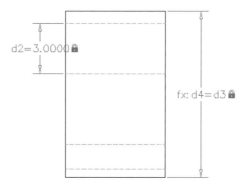

10. Notice how AutoCAD reassigned the name d2.
11. Set the following equation: d2 = hole1×2.
12. Test the model, making sure that the side view is fully aligned with the front view. When hole1 changes, what will happen to the lines representing the hole in the side view? Are they are aligned? Try to change the **basic_length** value. How do both sides react? To make sure that the equation will not be removed, only use the **Parameters Manager**.
13. Create two filters. Call the first **Radial** and the second **Linear**. Drag and drop each parameter into its logical filter.
14. You can now click on **All** to see all parameters or **Radial** to see only the radial parameters.
15. Convert **d1** to annotational. What happened?
16. Undo the previous step.
17. Start the **Constraint Settings** dialog box. Using the **Dimensional** tab, change the **Dimension name format** to **Name**, then **Value**, and finally **Name and Expression** (you can do the same for selected parameters by right-clicking and selecting **Dimension Name Format**, then selecting the desired value).
18. Save and close the file.

13.10 DYNAMIC BLOCKS: AN INTRODUCTION

- The **Dynamic Blocks** feature was introduced in AutoCAD 2006.
- It allows users to work with blocks that have multiple features, (e.g., different sizes, different views, and different shapes) and combine them into a single block.
- Before AutoCAD 2006, the only types of blocks available were static blocks. With static blocks, users had only one shape, one size, one view, etc., to work with.
- The **Dynamic Blocks** feature offers the following benefits:
  - Users work with fewer blocks. Big companies that deal with thousands and thousands of static blocks can downsize them to just hundreds of blocks.
  - Fewer mistakes will occur when dealing with the different shapes and sizes of a certain block. For example, the **Door** block for size 1' will include the plan view and the elevation view; hence, users will always drag the same block, whether they are in a plan drawing or in an elevation or section drawing. All they have to do is change the view of the block.
  - Intelligent features are included. For example, the **Alignment** command allows users to align a block based on an existing object, and the **Flip** command offers users the mirror image of the block.
  - If we assume that blocks occupy 30% of any drawing, then using **Dynamic Blocks** will speed up the process of inserting blocks, thereby speeding up the creation of the drawing.

13.11 IDENTIFYING A DYNAMIC BLOCK

- If you are using **Tool Palettes**, you will see the following:

- If you are using the **Insert** command, you will see the following:

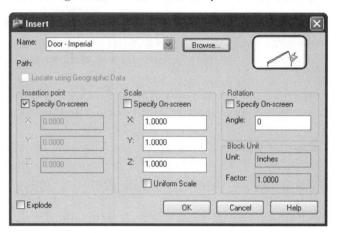

- If you click on a block, you will see something like the following:

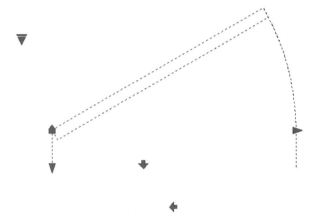

- Using any of these three methods, you can tell when you are dealing with a dynamic block.

13.12 CREATING A DYNAMIC BLOCK

- There are several ways to create a dynamic block in AutoCAD:
  - While creating a static block.
  - By double-clicking an inserted block.
  - By using the **Block Editor** command.

Creating a Static Block

- When you want to create a static block, you must issue the **Block** command. The following dialog box will appear:

- Notice the **Open in block editor** option in the lower left-hand corner of this dialog box.
- If you check this box, AutoCAD will create a static block and will open the **Block Editor**, enabling you to add the features needed to make it a dynamic block.

Double-Clicking an Inserted Block

- If you double-click an existing block, the following dialog box will appear:

- In this example, we will open the **Door-Imperial** block in the **Block Editor** to add some dynamic features to it.

Using the Block Editor Command

- To issue this command, do as follows: On the **Ribbon**, go to the **Insert** tab. Using the **Block** panel, click the **Block Editor** button:

- You will see the following dialog box:

- Here, you can select an existing block and edit it, or you can create a new block from scratch.

13.13 THE BLOCK AUTHORING TOOL PALETTE

- When you are inside the **Block Editor**, you will see a tool palette resembling the following:

- **The Block Authoring Palette** contains four tabs:
  - **Parameters**
  - **Actions**
  - **Parameter Sets**
  - **Constraints**
- Each parameter and action has properties that can be modified.
- NOTE ▶ The properties of parameters and actions play a pivotal role in controlling dynamic blocks.

Parameters

- A **Parameter** is a geometrical definition of a block (e.g., **Linear, Polar, XY, Rotation**).
- A description of each available parameter follows.
  - The **Point** parameter allows you to add a point definition to the dynamic block. **Stretch** and **Move** actions will work with this parameter.

- The **Linear** parameter allows you to add a linear dimension to the geometry of a dynamic block. This distance can have any angle. When you apply an action, users cannot change this angle. The **Move, Stretch, Scale**, and **Array** actions work with this parameter.

- The **Polar** parameter is just like the **Linear** parameter, except users are allowed to change the angle while using this dynamic block. The **Move, Stretch, Polar Stretch, Scale**, and **Array** actions work with this parameter.

- The **XY** parameter allows you to define two associated dimensions (when the first changes, the second will change as well). The **Move, Stretch, Scale**, and **Array** actions work with this parameter.

- The **Rotation** parameter allows you to add a rotation parameter to the block definition. Only the **Rotate** action will work with this parameter.

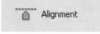

- The **Alignment** parameter allows the block to align itself with any object in the drawing. No action is needed for this parameter.

- The **Flip** parameter allows the block to create its mirror image around a selected axis. Only the **Flip** action will work with this parameter.

- The **Visibility** parameter allows you to convert several blocks into a single dynamic block. You can choose which objects will be visible. No action is needed for this parameter.

- The **Lookup** parameter allows you to create tables of other parameters and arrange them as a list of views, sizes, etc. Only the **Lookup** action will work with this parameter.

- The **Basepoint** parameter allows you to define another basepoint for the block. No action is needed for this parameter.

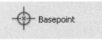

Actions

- **Actions** are commands implemented over a parameter. Almost all actions require you to select an already defined parameter.
- A description of each available action follows:
  - The **Move** action is similar to the **Move** command. You must select the parameter, specify the parameter point (basepoint), then select the objects to be moved.

  - The **Scale** action is similar to the **Scale** command. You must select the parameter, then select the objects to be scaled.

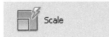

- The **Stretch** action is similar to the **Stretch** command. You must select the parameter first, specify the parameter point (basepoint), specify the stretch frame (crossing concept in the **Stretch** command), and finally select the objects to be stretched. The **Stretch** action will act only on the angle specified in the parameter.

- The **Polar Stretch** action is identical to the **Stretch** action, except it has an angle option.

- The **Rotate** action is similar to the **Rotate** command. You must select the parameter first, then select the objects to be rotated.

- The **Flip** action will produce a mirror image around an axis specified in the **Flip** parameter. You must select the parameter first, then select the objects to be flipped.

- The **Array** action is similar to the **Rectangular Array** command. You must select the parameter first, then select the objects to be arrayed. If the **Linear** parameter is selected, you must specify the number of columns. If the **XY** parameter is selected, you must specify the number of rows and columns.

- The **Lookup** action works on the **Lookup** parameter to create a table of parameters and show them as a list when you use the **Dynamic Block** command.

- The **Block Properties Table** creates and defines a new user parameter to be added to the **Properties Table**.

Parameter Sets

- **Parameter Sets** consist of both parameters and actions.
- They contain preset parameters and actions, with the following two exceptions:
  - **Pairs** associates two actions with one parameter. For example, the **Linear Stretch Pair** includes two **Stretch** commands, one at each end of the **Linear** parameter.
  - **Box Set** associates four actions with one parameter. For example, the **XY Stretch Box Set** includes four **Stretch** actions, one at each corner of the **XY** parameter.

Constraints

- These are the geometric and dimensional constraints discussed in the preceding sections. **Constraints** can be integrated inside a dynamic block.
- NOTE ► In the **Block Editor**, you will see a panel called **Actions Parameters**. It includes all the parameters and actions we have discussed.

13.14 PARAMETER PROPERTIES

- All parameters have properties the user can control.
- Select the desired parameter and right-click, then select **Properties**. You will see a panel resembling the following:

- Under **Property Labels**, you can change the **Distance name** (by default it will be **Distance 1**), which will reflect the real name of the distance. See the following example:

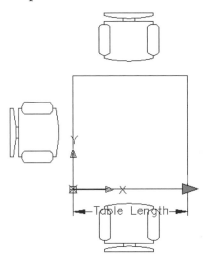

- For **Dist type** under **Value Set**, you will have three choices: **None, Increment**, and **List**.

None

- **None** means the distance will have two values—the minimum value and the maximum value:

Value Set	
Dist type	None
Dist minimum	15.0000
Dist maximum	30.0000

Increment

- **Increment** means there will be different values for this distance, with a constant increment:

Value Set	
Dist type	Increment
Dist increment	15.0000
Dist minimum	15.0000
Dist maximum	60.0000

List

- **List** means there will be different values for this distance, but the values will be random:

- You can either input the values with a comma between values or you can click the small button with the three dots, in which case you will see the following dialog box:

- This box allows you to add or delete distance values. To add, type in the value and click the **Add** button. To delete, select any undesired value and click the **Delete** button.
- Under **Misc**, you will find **Number of Grips**. To understand this option, see the following example:

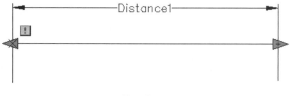

Two Grips

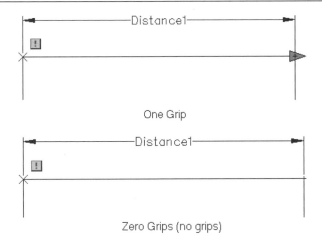

One Grip

Zero Grips (no grips)

13.15 THE BLOCK EDITOR TAB

- When you are inside **Block Editor**, a new tab called **Block Editor** will be added to the **Ribbon**.
- This tab includes the following panels:
  - **Open/Save**
  - **Geometric** (identical to the **Geometric** panel in the **Parametric** tab)
  - **Dimensional** (identical to the **Geometric** panel in the **Parametric** tab)
  - **Manage**
  - **Action Parameters**
  - **Visibility**
  - **Close**

Open/Save

- The **Open/Save** panel appears as follows:

- It includes three buttons:
  - **Edit Block**, which opens the **Block Definitions** in the **Block Editor**.
  - **Save Block**, which saves the block with the newly added dynamic features.
  - **Test Block**, which allows you to test the block without the need to save and leave the **Block Editor**.

Geometric

■   The **Geometric** panel is identical to the options in the **Parametric** tab.

Dimensional

■   The **Dimensional** panel is identical to the options in the **Parametric** tab, except this panel has a **Block Table** button (which will be discussed later in this chapter).

Manage

■   The **Manage** panel appears as follows:

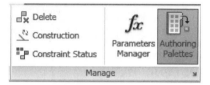

- You can switch the **Authoring Palettes** on/off.
- The **Parameters Manager** button offers the same options we discussed in the **Parametric** tab.
- The other three buttons will be discussed later in this chapter.

Action Parameters

■   The **Action Parameters** panel appears as follows:

- The first two buttons are **Parameters** and **Actions** the same as in the **Authoring Palettes**.
- **Attribute Definition** allows a dynamic blocks to include attributes (which will be discussed in the next chapter).

Visibility

- The **Visibility** panel appears as follows:

- If you have a **Visibility** parameter in the **Block Editor**, this panel will be active; otherwise, it will be inactive.
- Click the **Visibility States** button. You will see the following:

- In this dialog box, you can define a new visibility state or rename an existing one.
- In each state, you can select **Make Visible** or **Make Invisible** to control each object's visibility. You can also control whether you see or don't see the invisible objects using the **Visibility Mode** button.

Close

- The **Close** panel has a single button called **Close Block Editor**.
- If you did not use the **Save Block** command in the **Open/Save** panel, AutoCAD will warn you to save (or discard) the changes you made.

DYNAMIC BLOCKS: PART 1

Exercise 13-3

1. Start AutoCAD 2011.
2. Open the file *Exercise 13-3.dwg*.
3. You will find a table with three chairs.
4. Start the **Block** command to define a new block using the following information:
    - **Block name** = Meeting table.
    - **Base point** = Lower left-hand corner of the table.
    - **Objects** = Select all objects and select **Delete** to delete the objects after creating the block.
    - Make sure that the **Open in Block Editor** option is turned on.
    - You are now inside the **Block Editor**.
    - Using the **Block Authoring Palette**, select the **Parameters** tab, and then select the **Linear** parameter. Select two points representing the length of the table (lower horizontal line). Make sure to select the left point before the right point.
    - Select the **Linear** parameter, right-click, and select **Properties**.
    - Change the **Distance** label to **Table Length**.
    - **Under Misc**, change **Number of Grips** to 1. (This change prevents the table from being stretched to the left, which is also why we chose the points from left to right.)

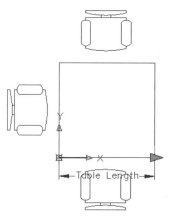

- Using the **Block Authoring Palettes**, select the **Actions** tab, and then select the **Stretch** action:
    - Select the defined parameter.
    - Select the lower right-hand corner to associate this point with the action.

- Because we know how to use the normal **Stretch** command, select the **Crossing Window**, which will stretch the table to the right side, as shown:

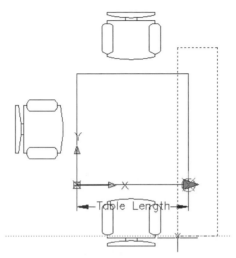

- When you are prompted to **Select objects**, specify the same **Crossing Window** (avoid selecting the chairs).
- The command will end.

■ To avoid leaving it to the user to specify the length of the stretch, select the parameter again and right-click. Select **Properties** under **Value Set** and specify the following:
  - **Dist type** = Increment
  - **Dist increment** = 40
  - **Dist minimum** = 40
  - **Dist maximum** = 120

■ Using the **Block Authoring Palette**, select the **Actions** tab, and then select the **Array** action:
  - Select the defined parameter.
  - Select the two chairs.
  - Set the **Distance between columns** = 40.

■ Save the block.
■ Click **Close Block Editor**.
■ Insert the block **Meeting Table** and test it.
■ Save and close the file.

DYNAMIC BLOCKS: PART 2

Exercise 13-4

1. Start AutoCAD 2011.
2. Open the file *Exercise 13-4.dwg*.
3. You will find an empty file.
4. Start the **Block Editor** command and create a new block named **Chairs and Sofas**.
5. Insert the following existing blocks always using the insertion point of 0,0:
   • **Chair – Desk**
   • **Chair – Rocking**
   • **Sofa Roundback 7 ft**
   • **Sofa Roundback Loveseat 5 ft**
6. Double-click the mouse wheel to see all the blocks.
7. Although there are four blocks on top of each other, it is easy to select just one of them.
8. Turn the **Visibility Mode** button on.
9. Using the **Block Authoring Palette** and the **Parameters** tab, click the **Visibility Parameter** and insert it in a suitable place.
10. Using the **Visibility** panel, click the **Visibility States** button and **Rename** the existing state as **Chair – Desk**.
11. Using the **Visibility** panel, click the **Make Visible** button and click the block **Chair – Disk**. Then click the **Make Invisible** button and make the other three blocks invisible—only in the current visibility state.
12. You can click the button **Visibility Mode** to make the blocks gray rather than totally invisible.
13. Using the **Visibility** panel, click the **Visibility States** button and **New**. Create a new state as **Chair – Rocking**.
14. Click the **Make Visible** button and make the **Chair – Rocking** visible. Click the **Make Invisible** button and make the **Chair – Desk** invisible.
15. Repeat the same procedure for the other two sofas.
16. Before saving and closing, test your block using the small list in the **Open/Save** panel.
17. Save and close the **Block Editor**.
18. Insert the new block and test it.
19. Save and close the file.

DYNAMIC BLOCKS: PART 3

 Exercise 13-5

1. Start AutoCAD 2011.
2. Open the file *Exercise 13-5.dwg*.
3. You will find a preexisting block called **Window**.
4. Double-click the block, then select the block **Window** and click **OK**. The **Block Editor** will open.
5. Add an **XY** parameter, selecting the lower left-hand corner and the upper right-hand corner of the shape.
6. Add a **Scale** action to the **XY** parameter, selecting all the objects.
7. Click the **XY** parameter and right-click, then select **Properties**. Specify the following:
   - **Number of Grips** = 0
   - Under **Value Set**, set **Hor type** to **List**, and input the new values 3'-6", 4'-6".
   - Set the **Ver type** to **List** and input the new values 1'-9", 2'-3".
8. Add a **Lookup** parameter and **Lookup** action.
9. In the **Lookup** action, click the **Add Properties** button. Select the two available parameters.
10. In the table, add the proper Y value for each X value, and add a suitable lookup value, such as **Window** 3'-6"×1'-9".
11. Complete the values for the three windows.
12. Save and close the **Block Editor**.
13. Test the block.
14. Save and close the file.

13.16 DYNAMIC BLOCKS AND CONSTRAINTS

- You will sometimes need several parameters and actions to perform a job.
- But working with too many parameters and actions can become confusing.
- You can use constraints (both geometric and dimensional) to create dynamic blocks, thus reducing the steps needed to make your block more intelligent.
- Some parameters and actions cannot be replicated using constraints, such as the **Visibility** parameter and the **Array** action.

- You can use the geometric and dimensional constraints as shown earlier. However, with the **Block Editor**, you can select a dimensional constraint, right-click and select **Properties**, and set the **Value Set** as we did for the **Linear** parameter.
- You can also use the **Parameters Manager** as we described earlier.
- For geometric and dimensional constraints, there are mainly three differences in the **Block Editor**:
  - **Block Table** (in the **Dimensional** panel)
  - **Construction** (in the **Manage** panel)
  - **Constraint Status** (in the **Manage** panel)

Block Table

- The **Block Table** feature looks and acts like the **Lookup Table** parameter and action.
- It will sum up some or all of the dimensional parameters used to form a drop-down menu and show different sizes.
- On the **Ribbon**, go to the **Parametric** tab. Using the **Dimensional** panel, click the **Block Table** button:

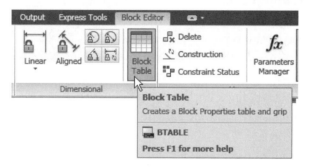

- You will see the following prompts:

```
Specify parameter location or [Palette]:
Enter number of grips [0/1] <1>:
```

■ You will then see the following dialog box:

■ You must add the dimensional parameters first, using the following button:

■ You will see the following dialog box, which contains all the defined dimensional parameters:

- You can select some or all of the parameters, then click **OK**.
- Next, fill in the different values of the different parameters.
- You will see a dialog box resembling the following:

- You can use the second button in the top left-hand corner to add user-defined parameters (just like we did in the **Parameters Manager**):

- You can select the **Audit** option to compare the values input in the **Block Table** to the properties of the block:

- While you are in the **Block Properties Table**, if you select a row and right-click, you will see the following menu:

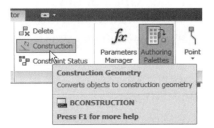

- Using this menu, you can:
  - **Cut, Copy**, or **Paste**
  - **Delete** a cell
  - **Insert, Delete**, or **Clear** a row, or move a row up or down
- After you finish, you will see something like the following in the **Block Editor**:

Construction

- If you draw an object in the block to help locate points or draw objects and you do not want this object to be seen by the user of the block, you can convert it to **Construction**.
- On the **Ribbon**, go to the **Parametric** tab. Using the **Manage** panel, click the **Construction** button, then select the desired object:

- The object will be dashed. Once you finish working with the **Block Editor**, users will not see it.

Constraint Status

- While you are using geometric constraints in the **Block Editor**, you can make sure that you are fully constraining the block, not partially.
- Click on the **Constraint Status** button to see the color. If it is blue, then the block is partially constrained; if it is magenta, then it is fully constrained. (AutoCAD will ask for one **Fix** constraint to consider the object fully constrained.)
- On the **Ribbon**, go to the **Parametric** tab. Using the **Manage** panel, click **Constraint Status** button:

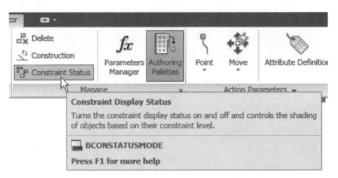

DYNAMIC BLOCKS AND CONSTRAINTS

Exercise 13-6

1. Start AutoCAD 2011.
2. Open the file *Exercise 13-6.dwg*.
3. Using the existing shape, create a new block with the following information:
   - **Name** = Window
   - **Base point** = Lower left-hand corner
   - **Objects** = All objects (with **Delete** option)
   - Make sure to click on **Open in Block Editor**
4. Using the **Geometric** panel and the **AutoConstrain** command, select all the objects to constrain them in one step.
5. Hide all geometric constraints.

6. Using **Linear** in the **Dimensional** panel, input the constraints shown in the following illustration:

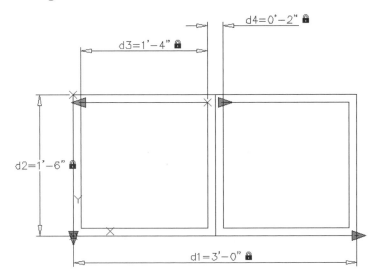

7. Using the **Parameters Manager**, set the following equations:
   - **d2** = d1/2
   - **d3** = d2–d4
8. Select **d1**, and right-click then select **Properties**. At the **Value Set**, select the type to be **Increment**. Set **Increment** = 6", **Dist minimum** = 3', and **Dist maximum** = 4'-6", then close the **Properties** palette.
9. Use the **Test Block** to test the block. You will find it flawed; the objects enlarge in different directions. This is due to not defining the relationship between the outer frame and the inner frame. Also, you can see more than one grip for other lines.
10. Close the **Test Block**.
11. Define two more **Dimensional Linear** parameters, as shown:

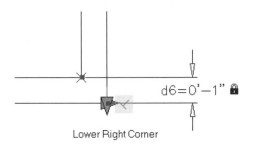

Lower Right Corner

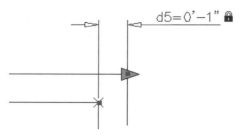

Upper Right Corner

12. Select all dimensional constraints except **d1**, and set **Grips** = 0 (zero).
13. Test the block again. It is now neater.
14. To make it more professional, we will create a **Block Table**.
15. Close the **Test Block**.
16. Start the **Block Properties Table** command and specify the location of the table at the upper left-hand corner of the window. Set the number of grips = 1.
17. Click **Add Properties** and select only **d1** and **d2**.
18. Set the values as shown in the following illustration, then click on **Block properties must match a row in the table**:

Block Properties Table	
d1	d2
3'	1'-6"
3'-6"	1'-9"
4'	2'
4'-6"	2'-3"

☑ Block properties must match a row in the table

| OK | Cancel | Help |

19. Click **OK** to end the command.
20. Test the block again.
21. Close **Test Block**.
22. Save changes and close the **Block Editor**.
23. Insert the block **Window**. Notice the different sizes of the window using the **Block Table**.
24. Save and close the file.

CHAPTER REVIEW

1. Which of the following is not a method used to create a dynamic block?
   a. Double-clicking an existing block
   b. Using the **Block** command
   c. Right-clicking an existing block and selecting the option **Convert to Dynamic**
   d. Using the **Block Editor** command
2. There are two types of constraints: _____ and _____.
3. Which of these is not an action in **Block Editor**?
   a. **Stretch**
   b. **Scale**
   c. **Fillet**
   d. **Array**
4. To make a block fully constrained, you must add a minimum of one **Fix** constraint.
   a. True
   b. False
5. You cannot create equations from different dimensional constraints.
   a. True
   b. False
6. _____ are parameters and actions together.
7. You can convert any dimensional constraint to become _____ using the **Properties** palette.

CHAPTER REVIEW ANSWERS

1. c
2. **Geometric, Dimensional**
3. c
4. a
5. b
6. **Parameter Sets**
7. annotational

Block Attributes and External Referencing (XREF)

Chapter **14**

In This Chapter

◊ An Introduction to **Block Attributes**
◊ Defining and editing **Block Attributes**
◊ Extracting attribute values from drawings
◊ Using **External Reference (XREF)** files
◊ The **Clip** command
◊ Using the **eTransmit** command

14.1 BLOCK ATTRIBUTES: AN INTRODUCTION

- A **Block Attribute** is information inside a block.
- There is no new command to create a block with attributes. You still use the **Block** command. The only difference is that when you are done drafting the desired shape, you can add the attributes inside or outside that shape and use the **Block** command to define the new block.
- There are two phases in using **Block Attributes**:
  - Phase I: Create the attribute definitions. This phase occurs while you are defining the block. At this time, attributes are considered queries to you (e.g., **Door number, Door Material, Door Model**).
  - Phase II: Insert blocks with attributes. You will input the values (answers) for the attributes for this specific block (e.g., **D12, Wood, DW-01-201**).
- You can control the visibility of the attributes with the blocks, and you can show them or hide them as you wish.

- Once you have added the attribute values to the different blocks inserted in your drawing, you will have two editing options:
  - Modify the values of the attributes.
  - Modify the attribute definitions themselves.
- If all of the data was added correctly to the drawing, you can either extract this data as a table in the drawing or export it to MS Excel or another database engine.

14.2 DEFINING BLOCK ATTRIBUTES

- The first step in the attribute workflow process is to create the attributes.
- Creating the text style(s) prior to creating the attributes is highly recommended.
- On the **Ribbon**, go to the **Insert** tab. Using the **Attributes** panel, click the **Define Attributes** button:

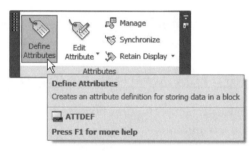

- You will see the following dialog box:

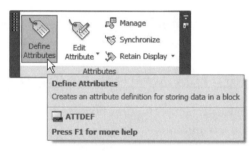

Tag

- The **Tag** is the name of the attribute. If you are familiar with any programming language, this is identical to a *variable*. **DOORMAT** is an example.

Prompt

- The **Prompt** is the query that will appear asking you for the data after you insert a block (optional). **Door Material** is an example.

Default

- The **Default** is the value that will appear to users (optional). **Wood** is an example.
  - This option allows the insertion of a field to be the default value of the attribute.
  - It is the only way to link stored data in AutoCAD to attributes.

Invisible

- The **Invisible** option allows you to create an invisible attribute. Once the block is inserted, the attribute value will not appear.

Constant

- The **Constant** option allows you to create a constant value for all of the insertions.

Verify

- The **Verify** option will ask you to enter the value twice (only applicable with non-dialog box input).

Preset

- The **Preset** option equalizes the attribute to the default value.

Lock Position

- The **Lock position** option allows you to lock the position of the attribute reference in the block geometry. If it is off, the attribute position can be changed later.

Multiple Lines

- By default, the attribute is single line text. However, with attributes such as **Address**, you may need to input multiple lines. The **Multiple lines** option allows you to do so.

Justification

- The **Justification** option allows you to justify the text reference to the insertion point. This option is identical to the single line text **Justification** options.

Text Style

- The **Text style** option allows you to choose a premade text style that will dictate the characteristics of the attribute text.

Text Height

- If the text style specified in the preceding step does not have a value assigned for the height, the **Text height** option allows you to to do so. Otherwise, the height will default to the height specified in the text style.

Rotation

- The **Rotation** option allows you to control the rotation angle of the attribute text.

Boundary Width

- The **Boundary width** option is available only when the **Multiple lines** option is on. This option specifies the maximum line length for multiple lines before the editor wraps the text.

Insertion Point

- The **Insertion Point** option allows you to specify the location of the attribute text reference in the block geometry. You have two choices: either type in the **X, Y, Z** of the attribute location or choose **Specify on-screen**.
- NOTE ▸ If you already inserted one attribute and you want the second one to be aligned below the first, then select the following option:

☑ Align below previous attribute definition

- Once you select this option, all the text settings and insertion points will be dimmed to indicate that they are all preset.
- NOTE ▸ After you define the attributes near/within the objects that will be blocks, use the **Block** command to define the block with attributes. It is preferable to select the attributes in the same order that you wish to show the user.

DEFINING ATTRIBUTES

 Exercise 14-1

1. Start AutoCAD 2011.
2. Open the file *Exercise 14-1.dwg*.
3. Make the **Text** layer current.
4. Zoom to the door at the right side.
5. Define the following parameters:

Tag	DOORNO	DOORH	DOORW
Prompt	Door Number	Door Height	Door Width
Default	—	2.00	Field
Mode	—	Invisible, Preset	Invisible
Text Style	Arial_010	Arial_010	Arial_010
Justification	Middle Center	Left	Left
Insertion Point	At the center of the circle	Below the Door	Align below previous attribute

6. Specify the **Field** information as follows:
   - Object
   - Select the outside vertical line
   - Select **Length**
   - **Decimal** = 0.00
7. Define a block from the shape and attribute, specifying the following:
   - Block name = **Door – New**.
   - **Insertion point** = Lower left-hand corner of the door.
   - **Select objects** = Select all objects first without the attributes. Next, select the attributes from top to bottom, one by one, and select **Delete**.
8. Save and close the file.

14.3 INSERTING BLOCKS WITH ATTRIBUTES

- The first step to inserting a block with attributes is to choose the way the attribute definitions will be displayed to you for filling in the values.

■ System variable **ATTDIA** controls this:
  • If **ATTDIA** = 0, then the attribute definitions will be shown in the **Command Window**.
  • If **ATTDIA** = 1, then a dialog box will appear for you to fill.
■ If you select the second choice and insert a block with attributes, the following dialog box will appear:

Edit Attributes	☒

Block name: Door - New

Door Number	01
Door Height	2.00
Door Width	1.00

[OK]   [Cancel]   [Previous]   [Next]   [Help]

14.4 CONTROLLING THE VISIBILITY

■ There are three visibility modes for attributes:
  • **Retain Display** means all attributes will be "as defined."
  • **Display All** means all attributes will be visible regardless of their original definitions.
  • **Hide All** means all attributes will be invisible regardless of their original definitions.
■ To issue these three options, do as follows: On the **Ribbon**, go to the **Insert** tab. Using the **Attributes** panel, click the **Visibility** button:

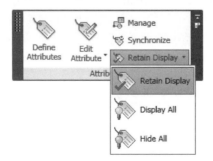

INSERTING BLOCKS WITH ATTRIBUTES

Exercise 14-2
1. Start AutoCAD 2011.
2. Open the file *Exercise 14-2.dwg*.
3. Make the **Door** layer current.
4. As you can see, there are three openings—from left to right, 1.00, 0.90, 0.80.
5. Insert block **Door – New**, specifying the following:
   - **Door Number** = 01 for all three blocks
   - For the first opening, **X Scale** = 1.0
   - For the second opening, **X Scale** = 0.9, **Scale Uniform** = on
   - For the third opening, **X Scale** = 0.8, **Scale Uniform** = on
   - Notice how the **Door Width** changes automatically, as the default value is a *field*.
6. Using **Attribute Visibility**, adjust the visibility as you wish.
7. Save and close the file.

14.5 EDITING VALUES (ONE BY ONE)

- After inserting blocks with attributes, you may need to edit the values (we are not talking about the attribute definitions).
- You can edit the values of a single block one at a time.
- On the **Ribbon**, go to the **Insert** tab. Using the **Attributes** panel, click the **Edit Attribute** button, then select **Single**:

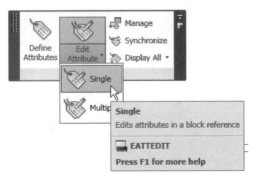

- The following prompt will appear:

Select a block: *(Select the desired block with attributes.)*

- Once you select the desired block, the following dialog box will appear:

- At the top of the dialog box, you will see the name of the block selected.
- There are three tabs in this dialog box:
  - **Attribute**
  - **Text Options**
  - **Properties**

Attribute

- In this tab, you will see a list of the attributes and their respective values. You can edit any of the values.
- Select the desired attribute and input the desired value in the **Value** field.

Text Options

- If you click on this tab, you will see the following dialog box:

- You can change any of the following (all of these options also exist in the **Text Style** dialog box):
  - **Text Style**
  - **Justification**
  - **Backwards** and **Upside down**
  - **Height**
  - **Width Factor**
  - **Rotation** (angle)
  - **Oblique Angle**
  - **Boundary width** (for multiple line attributes)
  - **Annotative**

Properties

- If you click on this tab, you will see the following dialog box:

- You can change any of the following:
  - **Layer**
  - **Linetype**
  - **Color**
  - **Lineweight**
  - **Plot style**
- NOTE ▶ You can also reach the **Enhanced Attribute Editor** dialog box by double-clicking the block.

14.6 EDITING VALUES (GLOBALLY)

- On the **Ribbon**, go to the **Insert** tab. Using the **Attributes** panel, click the **Edit Attribute** button, then select **Multiple**:

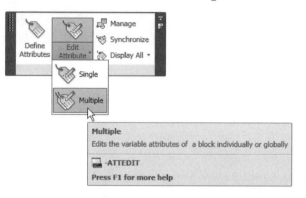

- The **Multiple** command allows you to edit the values of attributes for all blocks in the same drawing.
- This command is somewhat lengthy and tedious. It is highly recommended that you use the **Find** command instead. It will do the same thing but in fewer steps.
- On the **Ribbon**, go to the **Annotate** tab. Using the **Text** panel, type the text you want (in this case, it is the attribute value) in the *Find text* line:

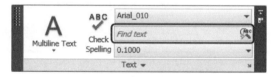

- When you have entered your text, click the small button at the right. The following dialog box will appear:

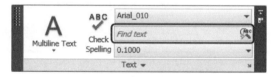

- If you click the small button in the lower left-hand corner, the following dialog box will appear:

- Under **Find what**, type in the current value of the text you want to change, and under **Replace with**, type in the new value. You can also specify to search for this string either in the **Entire drawing** or in a specified window.
- Under **Search Options**, make sure to select **Search blocks**. Under **Text Types**, make sure to select **Block attribute value**.
- Select one of the following choices:
  - **Find** allows you to find the text only without replacing it.
  - **Replace** allows you to find and replace the text one by one.
  - **Replace All** allows you to replace all text in this drawing at once.
- If your desired attributes are invisible, then turn **Ignore hidden items** off.

EDITING ATTRIBUTE VALUES

Exercise 14-3
1. Start AutoCAD 2011.
2. Open the file *Exercise 14-3.dwg*.
3. Using the **Find** command, do the following:
   - Make sure that **Ignore hidden items** is off.
   - Replace **ABC Wood** with **Acme Wood Works**.
   - Replace **199.99** with **149.99**.
4. Select any door, double-click it, and change the color of **DOORNO** to cyan.

5. Select another door, double-click it, select the **DOORNO** attribute, and make the **Text style** = ISO Proportional, and **Height** = 0.2.

6. Save and close the file.

14.7 REDEFINING ATTRIBUTES

■   The **Redefining Attributes** command will help you change the attribute definitions (not the values).

■   This command will not help you add new attributes to an existing block. If you want to add a new attribute to an existing block, you must explode it first, define a new attribute, and redefine it under the same name.

■   On the **Ribbon**, go to the **Insert** tab. Using the **Attributes** panel, click the **Manage** button:

■   The following dialog box will appear:

NOTE   This command is used to change the definition of an existing attribute, *not* the value of this attribute.

■   As a first step, you must select an existing block. There are two methods:
    •   If you do not know the name of the block, click the button at the top left-hand side of the dialog box and select the desired block.

537

- If you know the name of the desired block, select the block name from the list beside the button, as shown:

- Accordingly, a list of the attributes associated with this block will appear.
- Next, you must select the desired attribute to make one of the following modifications:

[Move Up]
- Select **Move Up** to move the selected attribute one position up.

[Move Down]
- Select **Move Down** to move the selected attribute one position down.

[Remove]
- Select **Remove** to delete the selected attribute.

[Edit...]
- Select **Edit** to change the settings of the selected attribute. When you click **Edit**, the following dialog box will appear:

- You can edit all attribute-defined information (i.e., **Tag**, **Prompt**, **Default** value, **Mode**).
- **Text Options** and **Properties** have already been covered in this text.

14.8 SYNCHRONIZING ATTRIBUTES

- If a user explodes a block with attributes, adds a new attribute, and then redefines the new block with the same name, all the new insertions will show the new attribute(s). But what about the already-inserted blocks?
- The **Synchronize** command will update all the existing attributes and any new attributes added.
- On the **Ribbon**, go to the **Insert** tab. Using the **Attributes** panel, click the **Synchronize** button:

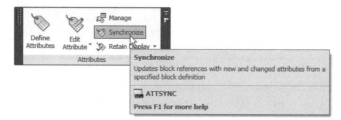

- The following prompt will appear:

```
Enter an option [?/Name/Select] <Select>:
```

- If you have memorized the spelling of the block name, type **n** and press [Enter]. The following prompt will appear:

```
Enter name of block to sync or [?]:
```

- Type the name of the block and the block will be synchronized instantly.
- If you do not recall the exact spelling of the block name, type **s**. The following prompt will appear:

```
Select a block:
```

- Select the desired block and you will see the following prompt:

```
ATTSYNC block Door? [Yes/No] <Yes>:
```

- To make sure you did not make a mistake, AutoCAD will show the name of the selected block (in our example, the name of the block is **Door**). You will be asked to confirm by selecting **Yes** or **No**. AutoCAD will respond accordingly.
- In the **Block Attribute Manager** dialog box, the **Sync** button in the upper right-hand corner will do exactly what the **Synchronize** command does.

- However, this button will not help if you are adding new attributes.

REDEFINING AND SYNCHRONIZING ATTRIBUTES

Exercise 14-4

1. Start AutoCAD 2011.
2. Open the file *Exercise 14-4.dwg*.
3. Make the **Door** layer current.
4. Insert the block **Door Type – 01** in an empty space and explode it.
5. Make the **Text** layer current.
6. All the attributes will appear.
7. Insert a new attribute below the last existing attribute. Specify the following:
   a. **Tag** = MANADD
   b. **Prompt** = Manufacturer Address
   c. **Mode** = Invisible, Multiple lines
8. Define the block again under the same name (while defining the block, do not forget to select objects first, then attributes in the correct sequence). Answer **Yes** if AutoCAD displays the message, "This block exists. Do you want to redefine it?"
9. Use the **Synchronize** command to reflect changes on the other **Door – Type 01** blocks. Notice the changes.
10. Double-click on any of these doors and make sure a new attribute has been added.
11. Use the **Block Attribute Manager** to make the following changes to **Door – Type 03**:
    a. Make the **Cost** attribute the second in the list.
    b. Make the **DOORH** attribute **Preset**, with **Default** value = 2.00.
12. In an empty space, insert **Door – Type 03** and check the attributes. Can you see the new changes you made?
13. Save and close the file.

14.9 EXTRACTING ATTRIBUTES

- After you are done with data entry for all of your blocks and all of your attributes for the current drawing or group of drawings, you can extract these values and arrange them using a table that can be inserted into the AutoCAD drawing, an Excel sheet, or a database engine.
- Use the **Data Extraction** command to extract attributes from drawing file(s).
- This command is a wizard that gives step-by-step instructions.

- On the **Ribbon**, go to the **Insert** tab. Using the **Linking & Extraction** panel, click the **Extract Data** button:

Step 1

- The following is the dialog box for the first step:

- You can select one of three options in this dialog box:
  - **Create a new data extraction**
  - **Use previous extraction as a template** (this will save time if there are similar extractions)
  - **Edit an existing data extraction**

- If you select to **Create a new data extraction** and click **Next**, the **Save Data Extraction As** dialog box will appear:

- As you can see, the file extension will be *.dxe*. Type the name and click **Save** and **Next**.

Step 2

- The following is the dialog box for the second step:

- You must now tell AutoCAD where it will extract the data from:
  - From objects in the current drawing file
  - From the entire current file
  - From a group of drawing files
- By default, you will extract all data from all blocks in the current file.
- If you want to extract from part of the current file, you must select the option **Select objects in the current drawing** and then click the small button at the right; the dialog box will disappear temporarily to give you the chance to select the desired blocks:

Add Drawings ...

- Click the **Add Drawings** button to select files from different drives and different folders:

Add Folder ...

- Click the **Add Folder** button to see the following dialog box:

- In this dialog box, you will specify a folder that contains all the drawings you want (you must be careful to include any unneeded drawing files in the desired folder).
- You must also control three options:
  - **Automatically include new drawings added in this folder to the data extraction**: This option allows you to include future drawing files in the extraction. This will keep the extraction process up-to-date.
  - **Include subfolders**: This option allows you to include any subfolders within the specified folder.
  - **Utilize wild-card characters to select drawings**: This option allows you to choose which files you want in the folder. You do so by typing a wild card. For example, if you type $c^*.dwg$, all drawing files (in this folder) starting with letter **c** will be included.
  - Click **OK** once you are done.

- Based on your choices, you will see a list of the files matching your selection. See the following dialog box for an example:

- Click **Next**.

Step 3

- The following is the dialog box for the third step:

- Because we are in the process of extracting attributes from blocks, make sure that the **Display options** are set as follows:
  - **Display all object types** is off
  - **Display blocks only** is on
  - **Display blocks with attributes only** is on
  - **Display objects currently in-use only** is off
- By default, all blocks are selected. If you do not want to include the attributes of certain blocks, you should specify this now.
- Click **Next**.

Step 4

- The following is the dialog box for the fourth step:

- This is where you will specify the needed information.
- As you can see from the right portion of this dialog box, there are six categories to choose from:
  - **3D Visualization**
  - **Attributes**
  - **Drawing**
  - **General**
  - **Geometry**
  - **Misc** (miscellaneous)

- For now, we are interested only in extracting the attributes. We will make sure that all other options are off.
- Now you can deselect any undesired attributes.
- Click **Next**.

Step 5

- The following is the dialog box for the fifth step:

- This is the place to refine the table that you will produce.
- Before we discuss the contents of this dialog box, you must understand the following:
  - You can change the width of the columns by dragging the line between any two columns.
  - You can change the position of any column by clicking and holding the title of the column, then dragging it to the new position.
  - You can sort the table according to any column by clicking the title of the column. The first click will make it **Ascending**; click again to make it **Descending**.

- If you right-click any of the column titles, you will see the following menu:

- Using this menu, you can:
  - Sort columns in either **Descending** or **Ascending** order.
  - **Rename, Hide**, or **Unhide** columns.
  - **Set Column Data Format**.
  - **Insert** a new **Formula Column**.
  - Choose to **Show** the **Count** and **Name** columns.
  - **Insert Totals Footer**.
  - Create a filter and choose **Filter Options**.
- Now specify the following options:
  - **Combine identical rows** allows you to combine rows that hold the same data.
  - Select whether to show the **Count Column**.
  - Select whether to show the **Name Column**.
- The **Link External Data** option allows you to establish a data link between the extracted data and an Excel spreadsheet.

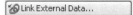

- **Sort Column Options** is a more sophisticated sorting feature that allows you to assign more than one column to sort according to order. See the following dialog box:

- In the preceding example, we assigned two sorting criteria. The first one is **COST**, in **Ascending** order; the second one is **Count**, in **Ascending** order.

- You can **Add** as many criteria as you wish.
- You can move them up and down in order of priority.
- Click the **Full Preview** button if you want to see how your table will look. You will see something resembling the following:

- Click **Next**.

Step 6

■ The following is the dialog box for the sixth step:

■ In this dialog box, select the type(s) of output you want.
■ You can select one or both of the following:
  • **Insert the data extraction table into the drawing**. (It is preferable to create a table style prior to the extraction process.)
  • **Output data to external file**. There are four types of file formats (*.xls* for an Excel spread sheet, *.csv*, *.mdb* for an Access® database, and *.txt*). If you select this option, specify where to save the file.
■ Click **Next**.

Step 7

■ The following is the dialog box for the seventh step:

Data Extraction - Table Style (Page 7 of 8)

Table style
Select the table style to use for the inserted table:

Door Schedule

Formatting and structure

○ Use table in table style for label rows
⦿ Manually setup table
   Enter a title for your table:

   Door Schedule

   Title cell style: Title
   Header cell style: Header
   Data cell style: Data

   ☑ Use property names as additional column headers

Title	
Header	*Header*
Data	Data
Data	Data
Data	Data
Data	Data
Data	Data
Data	Data

[< Back]   [Next >]   [Cancel]

■ Specify the **Table style** you would like to use. If you did not create the table style prior to this step (recommended), then click the small button and start setting up a table style now.
■ Leave the rest as default.
■ Click **Next**.

Step 8

■ The following is the dialog box for the eighth step:

Data Extraction - Finish (Page 8 of 8)

Click Finish to complete the extraction.

If you chose to insert a table, you will be prompted for an insertion point after you click Finish.

Any external files to create will be created when clicking Finish.

[< Back]   [Finish]   [Cancel]

■ Click **Finish** to conclude the extraction process.

EXTRACTING ATTRIBUTES

Exercise 14-5

1. Start AutoCAD 2011.
2. Open the file *Exercise 14-5.dwg*.
3. Make the **Text** layer current.
4. Start the extracting process, making the following changes:
    *   **Create a new data extraction** and save as **Door Schedule**.
    *   Click **Include current drawing** off.
    *   Click the **Add Folder** button and add your exercise folder.
    *   Click **Include subfolders** off.
    *   Click **Utilize wild card characters to select drawings** on, and input the following: **floor plan.dwg*. Click **OK**. Remove the two files that start with John Smith; only three files should be selected.
    *   Click **Display all object types** off. Make sure **Display blocks only** is on.
    *   Click **Display blocks with Attributes only** on.
    *   Click the block named **ISO A1 title block** off.
    *   Make sure to select only **Attribute** under **Category filter**. (You should be on Page 5 of 8 right now.)
    *   Move the **COST** column to the end of the columns.
    *   Hide the **DOORNO** column.
    *   Rename the **Count** column **Qty**, and move it to the left of the **COST** column.
    *   Rename **DOORH** as **Door Height**, and move it to the right of the **Name** column.
    *   Rename **DOORW** as **Door Width**, and move it to the right of the **Door Height** column.
    *   Rename **DOORMAN** as **Door Manufacturer**.
    *   Rename **DOORMAT** as **Door Material**.
    *   The **Data format** for the **COST** column should be **Currency**, with 0.00 precision.
    *   Right-click the **COST** column, and select **Insert Formula Column**.
    *   Name the new column **Total Cost**. The formula should be **COST · Qty** (you must double-click).
    *   Change the **Data format** to match the **COST** column.
    *   Sort the table according to **Name** in **descending** order.
    *   Select **Insert data extraction table into drawing**.
    *   The title of the table should read **Door Schedule**.

- Insert the table in the **Model Space**.
- If you click the table, you will notice it is **Locked** and **Linked** (we discussed this topic in Chapter 12).

5. Save and close the file.

14.10 XREF: AN INTRODUCTION

■ Imagine you are working in a firm and you are doing the layout of the beams and columns of the ground floor. You realize you need your colleague's drawing, which contains the footings of the same building, to use as a guide to create the correct structural layout. Until now, the only way we have learned to access such drawings is by using the **Insert** command, which will bring a drawing into another drawing.

■ Unfortunately, this method has three problems:
- You will import the whole file into your drawing; hence, your file size will increase significantly.
- The incoming file will bring along all of its components, including layers, blocks, text styles, dimension styles, etc., which will be very difficult to control.
- If the owner of the original file made some changes, you will not see them because there is no live connection between the two files.

■ **External Reference** (**XREF**) allows you to import a DWG, DWF, PDF, raster file, or DGN file to your current file, thereby solving the three problems as follows:
- Because **XREF** does not import the whole file to the current file, but merely a small part of it, the size added to the current file is greatly reduced.
- **XREF** separates all the incoming components from the existing layers, blocks, dimension styles, etc. A layer from an **XREF** file will look something like **First_Floor_Plan|Wall**. The first part is the name of the file, then a separator (|), then the name of the layer. Using this method, it is easy to distinguish the layers in your file from the layers in the **XREF** file. (The same applies to dimension styles, text styles, table styles, etc.)
- **XREF** keeps a live connection between the original file and its image in your file. Thus, if any modification occurs in the original file **XREF** will update the image in your current file.

14.11 XREF: INSERTING

- The first step is to open the file that will import the **XREF** file(s).
- To reach the **XREF** inserting command, do as follows: On the **Ribbon**, go to the **Insert** tab. Using the **References** panel, click the button in the lower right-hand corner of the panel:

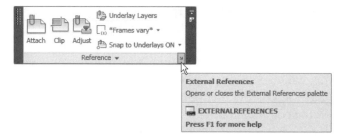

- You will see the **External References** palette, which offers many functions related to **XREF**:

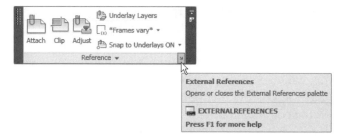

- Another way to access **XREF** is to issue the **Attach** command. This command
  will only help you attach an **XREF**. On the **Ribbon**, go to the **Insert** tab.
  Using the **References** panel, click the **Attach** button:

- You will see the following dialog box:

- Let's return to the **External References** palette. Click the small button in
  the top left-hand corner of the palette. You will see the following menu:

- You can see that this approach produces the same result as the **Attach** command.
- However, the palette offers many other functions that help you in attach the **XREF**. Thus, we prefer to use the palette.
- You can select one of the following file types to bring to your current drawing:
  - DWG (any AutoCAD drawing file)
  - Image (any raster file: *.jpg*, *.tif*, *.bmp*, etc.)
  - DWF (any Design Web Format file)
  - DGN (any Microstation® V8 file)
  - PDF (any Adobe® Portable Document File)

Attach DWG

- The **Attach DWG** command allows you to insert an existing AutoCAD drawing into your current AutoCAD drawing. Select the desired drive, folder, and file, then click **Open**. The following dialog box will appear:

- From this dialog box, you can see that AutoCAD saves the path of the file to track any changes that may take place.

- Specify the **Path type**. You will have three choices:

Path type

| Full path |
| Full path |
| Relative path |
| No path |

Rotation

- **Full path** means AutoCAD will save the exact path of the file. Each time an **XREF** is loaded using this option, AutoCAD will go to this specific folder.
- **Relative path** means AutoCAD will save only the name of the folder that contains the file. Even if you move the folder to another drive, AutoCAD will be able to locate it.
- **No path** means AutoCAD will not save any path for this **XREF**. Instead, each time an **XREF** is needed, AutoCAD will search the current folder and then the **Search** paths specified in **Tools/Options** on the **Files** tab (**Project paths** and **Support paths**).

- Specify the **Attachment Type**. Before we proceed, let's look at the following illustration:

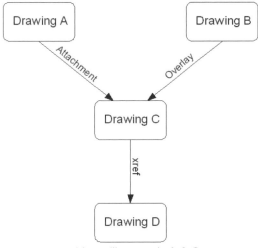

You will see only A & C

- Based on this illustration, while you are in Drawing C, you import two drawings: Drawing A and Drawing B. You close Drawing C, open Drawing D, and import Drawing C into it. What will you see?
- The answer: You will see Drawing C and Drawing A. You will *not* see Drawing B. Why?

- This is because of the **Attachment Type** chosen. Drawing A is an **XREF** as an **Attachment**. Drawing B is an **XREF** as an **Overlay**.
- Drawing B will be shown in Drawing C but not in any other drawing if Drawing C happens to be imported via **XREF** in another drawing.
- The rest of the dialog box is identical to the **Insert** dialog box.

Attach Image

- The **Attach Image** command allows you to insert a raster file into the current AutoCAD drawing.
- After you select the desired file, click **Open**. The following dialog box will appear:

- Each part of this dialog box was covered in our discussion on attaching DWG files.

Attach DWF

- The **Attach DWF** command allows you to insert a Design Web File (DWF) within the current AutoCAD drawing.
- After you select the file, click **Open**. You will see the following dialog box:

- The interesting thing in this dialog box is the part labeled **Select one or more sheets from the DWF file**. This option allows you to cover all the possibilities, as there are both single-sheet and multi-sheet DWFs. If you have the second type, select one of the sheets to attach to your current file.
- The other options in the dialog box have already been discussed.

Attach DGN

- The **Attach DGN** command allows you to insert a Microstation file (DGN) into the current AutoCAD drawing.
- After you select the file, click **Open**. You will see the following dialog box:

- A Microstation file always has two units: **Master** and **Sub**. Indicate which of the units should be converted to AutoCAD units.
- For example, an AutoCAD unit is either a millimeter or inch. Suppose you have a DGN file with **Master units** = foot and **Sub units** = inch. In this instance, you would select **Sub units**.
- The other options in the dialog box have already been discussed.

Attach PDF

- The **Attach PDF** command allows you to insert a PDF file into the current AutoCAD drawing.
- After you select the file, click **Open**. You will see the following dialog box:

- AutoCAD will assume that the PDF may be multiple pages and will ask you to select one or more of these pages.
- The example in the illustration is for a single-page PDF file.
- The other options in the dialog box have already been discussed.
- NOTE ▸ You can only attach a single copy of the same DWG file to your current file.
- You can attach multiple copies of the same image, DWF, DGN, and PDF file to your current file.
- The current layer will accommodate the whole **XREF**, so be sure you know which layer was current when you attach the **XREF**.

14.12 THE CONTENTS OF THE XREF PALETTE

- There are several parts of the **External References** palette that you should know.
- Each part holds different information.

- ◼ See the following views:
  - • In the upper part of the palette, there are two small buttons at the right side. See the following illustration:

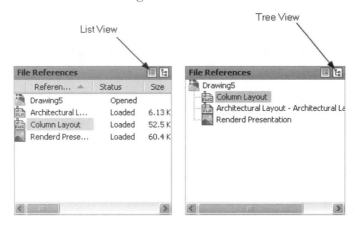

  - • In the lower part of the palette, there are two small buttons at the right side. See the following illustration:

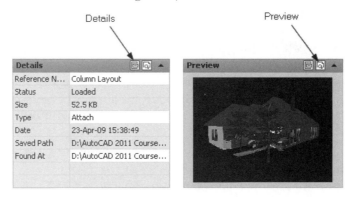

- NOTE ◼ Between the two parts, there is a small arrow at the right. If you click it, you will hide the lower part and allow more space for the upper part.

14.13 XREF LAYERS

- After you attach an **XREF** file, visit the **Layer Properties Manager**. You will see a dialog box resembling the following:

- You will see the layers that belong to your file, such as **Columns, Frame**, etc.
- You will also see **XREF** layers, such as **Footing Layout|Footing**, which are easily segregated from the layers in your drawing. You can further segregate **XREF** layers from one another.
- At the left part of the dialog box, you can see a filter called **Xref**, which is created by AutoCAD automatically.
- Note the following facts about layers and **XREF**:
  - You cannot make any of the **XREF** layers current; hence, you cannot draw on these layers.
  - You can change the color and linetype of an **XREF** layer. You can also turn it off, freeze it, and lock it. By default, all of these changes will be saved. If you do not want the changes to be saved, use the system variable **VISRETAIN**. By default, **VISRETAIN** = 1, so set the value to 0 (zero). Another method is through the **Options** dialog box. Use the **Open and Save** tab and turn off the option **Retain changes to Xref layers**. See the following illustration:

14.14 XREF FADING

- By default, the **XREF** files will look faded.
- You can control the fading percentage (by default, it is 70%).
- On the **Ribbon**, go to the **Insert** tab. Extend the **Reference** panel and adjust the **Xref Fading** slider:

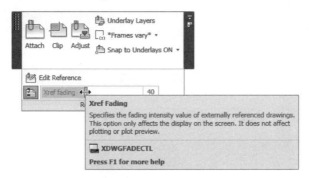

- The maximum value of fading is 90%.
- You can also turn off fading using the same panel. To do so, click the button beside the percentage slider:

ATTACHING XREF FILES

Exercise 14-6
1. Start AutoCAD 2011.
2. Open the file *Exercise 14-6.dwg*.

3. Using the **External References** palette, attach the following:
    - Attach *Footing Layout.dwg*, using 0,0, **Relative Path**, and **Scale** = 1.0.
    - Attach *Architectural Layout.dwf*, using 0,0, **Relative Path**, and **Scale** = 1.0.
    - In the **Architectural** layout, attach the image *Rendered Presentation.jpg* in the square at the upper right-hand corner of the layout, using **Specify on-screen** for both the **Insertion Point** and **Scale**, and making **Path** = **Relative Path**.
4. Decrease the **Xref Fading** to 30%.
5. Go to the **Layer Properties** palette and see the layers.
    - Can you differentiate between the layers in the drawing and the layers from the **XREF** file?
    - Did the DWF file or the image file import any layers?
    - Change the color of the layer **Footing Layout|Footing** from red to magenta (if needed, use the **REGEN** command).
    - Go to **Options** and make sure **Retain changes to XREF layer** is turned off.
    - Save and close the file.
    - Reopen the file. What is the color of **Footing Layout|Footing**? Why?
6. Make layer **Columns** current, then freeze layer 0. What happens? Why?
7. Thaw layer 0.
8. Save and close the file.

14.15 EDITING IN PLACE VERSUS OPENING

- Assume you attached a DWG file and then found that your colleague made a mistake in his or her file.
- AutoCAD allows you to change the attached file without leaving your file (i.e., **Edit In-Place**). Or you can open the file and edit it (i.e., **Open** the file).

Edit In-Place

■ To reach this command, do as follows: On the **Ribbon**, go to the **Insert** tab. Using the **References** panel, click the **Edit Reference** button:

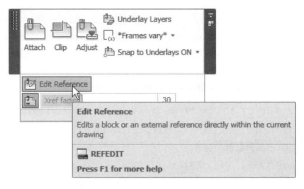

■ The following prompt will appear:

```
Select reference:
```

■ Select the **XREF** file. The following dialog box will appear:

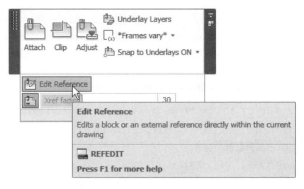

■ Click **OK**. Once you do so, all of the drawing except the **XREF** objects will be dimmed (you cannot edit the dimmed objects).
■ A new panel will appear called **Edit Reference**. It has four buttons. A description of each button follows:

- Click the **Add to Working Set** button. The following prompt will appear:

```
Select objects:
```

- Select the objects to be added.
- Click the **Remove from Working Set** button.

- The following prompt will appear:

```
Select objects:
```

- Select the objects to be removed.
- When you are done with your editing, you can either discard the changes as if nothing happened, or you can save the changes to the original block. Use either the **Discard** or **Save** commands, as described next.
- Click the **Discard Changes** button.

- The following dialog box will appear:

- If you are sure you want to discard all the changes you made to the block, simply click **OK**; otherwise, click **Cancel**.

- Click the **Save Changes** button.

Save
Changes

- The following dialog box will appear:

- If you are sure of the changes you made, click **OK**; otherwise, click **Cancel**.

NOTE
- Because it is dangerous to edit files that belong to your colleagues, they have the power to prevent you or any other user from editing them.
- To prevent others from editing your file, go to the **Options** dialog box and select the **Open and Save** tab. Under **External References (Xrefs)**, turn off the option **Allow other users to Refedit current drawing**, as shown:

External References (Xrefs)
Demand load Xrefs:

Enabled with copy

☐ Retain changes to Xref layers

☐ Allow other users to Refedit current drawing

Opening XREF File

- Another way to edit an attached file is to open the **XREF** file, edit it, and save and close it.
- Select the desired file in the **External References** palette and right-click it. From the menu, select **Open**. See the following illustration:

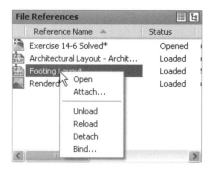

- You will see the open **XREF** file, and you can edit it as you wish. Once you are done, save and close the file.
- An alert will tell you that some changes took place in one of the files you are importing via **XREF** and that you may need to reload it (we will discuss this topic shortly).

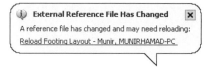

14.16 UNLOAD, RELOAD, DETACH, AND BIND XREF FILES

- While you are in the **External References** palette, you can select any **XREF** file, right-click, and do one or all of the following:
  - **Unload**
  - **Reload**
  - **Detach**
  - **Bind**

Unload

- The **Unload** command allows you to unload the **XREF** file while keeping the link.
- Using the **External References** palette, select the desired **XREF** file, right-click, and then select **Unload**:

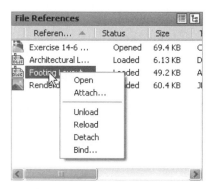

- You will see something like the following:

Reload

- The **Reload** command offers multiple functions, including:
  - Reload an unloaded **XREF** file.
  - Reload a file that you opened, edited, and saved.
- Select the desired **XREF** file, right-click, and select **Reload**.

Detach

- The **Detach** command is just like the **Unload** command, except that the link is lost in the process.
- When using this command, you must reattach the **XREF** Files, like the **Unload** command, where you can reload.

Bind

- The **Bind** command allows you to put the physical objects, layers, styles, and blocks in the current file; accordingly, it will cut any link to the original file.
- There are two binding types:
  - **Bind**
  - **Insert**
- They both function in the same way except for in the naming of the layers, styles, and blocks.
- Assume we have a layer named **Basement Plan|Deck**. The name will be changed as follows:
  - If you use **Bind**, the name will become **Basement Plan0Deck**.
  - If you use **Insert**, the name will become **Deck**.

- To use this command, select the desired **XREF** file from the **External References** palette, right-click, and select **Bind**. You will see the following dialog box:

- Select the desired type and click **OK**.

EDITING XREF FILES

Exercise 14-7

1. Start AutoCAD 2011.
2. Open the file *Exercise 14-7.dwg.*
3. Make the **COL-LAYOUT** layer current.
4. Attach the file *Column Layout.dwg* using the point 0,0 and **Relative Path**.
5. As you can see, all the columns fit in the right place except the one at the lower right part, which has drifted to the left.
6. Click one of the columns. When the **External Reference** tab appears, click **Edit Reference In-Place**. When the dialog box appears, click **OK**.
7. Zoom to the column you need to move. Using the **Move** command, move it to the right distance = 0.15, then zoom out.
8. Click the **Save Changes** button on the **Edit Reference** panel. In the dialog box, click **OK**.
9. Save the file.
10. Using the **External References** palette, select Column Layout **XREF**, right-click, and select **Unload**. What happens?
11. Select it again, right-click, and select **Reload**. What happens?
12. Select it once more, right-click, and select **Bind**. In the dialog box, select the **Bind** option. You should have two layers similar to each other; enter their names.
13. Save and close the file.

14.17 CLIPPING XREF FILES

- When you import an **XREF** file, the entire file will be shown.
- You can select to show only part of the file by clipping it.
- There is only one **Clip** command for all types of **XREF** files. Once you select the file, AutoCAD will show the appropriate options. On the **Ribbon**, go to the **Insert** tab. Using the **Reference** panel, click the **Clip** button:

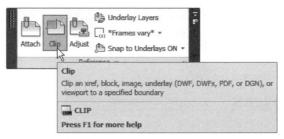

- Another way to reach the same command is to select the desired **XREF** and then right-click. The proper command will be shown for each type.
- We will discuss the clipping of a DWG as an example. This method applies to all file types.
- Once the command is issued, you will see the following prompt:

```
[ON/OFF/Clipdepth/Delete/generate Polyline/New boundary]
<New>:
```

- By default, the option selected is **New boundary**, which will create a new clipping boundary for the selected **XREF** file. Press [Enter] to accept the default option. The following prompt will appear:

```
[Select polyline/Polygonal/Rectangular/Invert clip]
<Rectangular>:
```

- Choose one of the following methods for the clipping boundary:
  - The default option **Rectangular** allows you to draw a rectangle around the desired area to be shown. The rest of the file will disappear.
  - The **Select polyline** option allows you to select a polyline if you have already drawn one.
  - The **Polygon** option allows you to draw an irregular polygon around the desired area to be shown. The rest of the file will disappear.
- After specifying the boundary, the command will end automatically, showing only the area you specified.
- The other options are **Off, On, Clipdepth, Delete, Generate, Polyline**, and **Invert Clip**.

Off

- The **Off** option allows you to turn off the clipping boundary and show the entire **XREF** file.

On

- The **On** option allows you to cancel the **Off** function.

Clipdepth

- The **Off** option allows you to control the front and back clipping planes in the Z-direction. Because we are dealing with 2D only (i.e., XY drawing), this option is not applicable.

Delete

- The **Off** option allows you to delete the clipping boundary. (Using the **Erase** command will not remove the clipping boundary.)

Generate Polyline

- The **Off** option allows you to draw a polyline identifying the clipping boundary if the **XREF** frame is turned off.

Invert Clip

- The **Invert Clip** option is the opposite of the clipping boundary. Instead of showing only the specified area and hiding the rest, in this command, the area you specify will be hiding and the rest will be shown.

Note 1

- While clipping is used to show some of the **XREF** file and hide some of it, it will not affect the performance of the AutoCAD file by reducing the **XREF** file size in your current file. You must turn on the **Demand Loading** option to benefit from clipping.
- From the **Application** menu, select the **Options** button, then select the **Open and Save** tab. Under **External References (Xrefs)**, change the settings of **Demand load Xrefs**. See the following illustration:

- You have three choices:
    - **Disabled**, which turns off this feature.
    - **Enabled**, which enables this feature but does not allow users to edit the file.
    - **Enabled with copy**, which enables this feature and allows users to edit the file.

Note 2

- In the **Reference** panel, you can show or hide the clipping frame by using the **Frames** button:

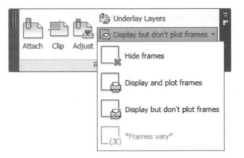

- You can select **Hide frames, Display and plot frames**, or **Display but don't plot frames**.

Note 3

- If the frame is turned on, then you can flip between what is hidden and what is shown using an arrow. See the following illustrations.
    - Suppose your frame appears as shown:

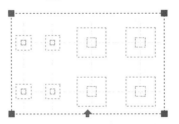

- After clicking the arrow at the bottom, it will appear as follows:

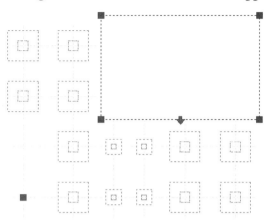

14.18 XREF PANELS

- If you click on an **XREF** (regardless of its type), AutoCAD will show a new tab with panels to edit and control this **XREF**.
- For each **XREF** type, there will be a different tab and panels.
- We will go through each of the five types in the following discussion.

DWG XREF

- If you click on a DWG **XREF**, you will see the following tab and panels:

- The available buttons are:
  - **Edit Reference In-Place**
  - **Open Reference**
  - **Create Clipping Boundary**
  - **Remove Clipping**
  - **External References** (to show the **External References** palette)
- We have discussed these commands previously.

Image XREF

- If you click an image **XREF**, you will see the following tab and panels:

- The **Adjust** panel includes three buttons—**Brightness, Contrast**, and **Fade**—which control the image sharpness and clarity.
- The **Clipping** panel has already been discussed.
- The **Options** panel includes:
  - **Show Image**, to show or hide the image.
  - **Background Transparency**, to change the background (if it exists) from black to transparent.
  - **External Reference**, to show the **External References** palette.

DWF XREF

- If you click a DWF **XREF**, you will see the following tab and panels:

- The **Adjust** panel includes two buttons—**Contrast** and **Fade**—which control the image sharpness and clarity. You can also choose between displaying the DWF in color or monochrome.
- The **Clipping** panel has already been discussed.
- The **Options** panel includes:
  - **Show Underlay**, to show or hide the DWF.
  - **Enable Snap**, to enable or disable the **Object Snap** to the DWF objects.
  - **External References**, to show the **External References** palette.

- The **DWF Layers** panel includes the **Edit Layers** button (the creator of the DWF should include layers with the file). If you click it, you will see the following dialog box:

DGN XREF

- If you click a DGN **XREF**, you will see the following tab and panels:

- These options are identical to those related to a DWF **XREF**.

PDF XREF

- If you click a PDF **XREF**, you will see the following tab and panels:

- These options are identical to those related to a DWF **XREF**.

- In the **Reference** panel, there are two buttons:

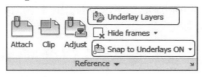

- The first button, **Underlay Layers**, will show the layer dialog box of the underlay regardless of its type.
- The second button, **Snap to Underlays (ON/OFF)**, will allow you to use **OSNAP** to snap to the objects of DWF, PDF, and DGN files.
- Both buttons were discussed previously.

CLIPPING XREF FILES

Exercise 14-8

1. Start AutoCAD 2011.
2. Open the file *Exercise 14-8.dwg*.
3. On the **Ribbon**, go to the **Insert** tab. Using the **Reference** panel, click the **Clip** button. Select one of the footings and create a new rectangular boundary for the four footings at the top right.
4. Select one of the four footings and a new panel will appear. Select **Remove Clipping**, then press [Esc].
5. Select one of the green lines (these are DWF objects), and a new panel will appear. Click the **Enable Snap** button (if it was not on already). Measure the length of the inner vertical line at the right. What is the distance? *(Answer: 14.6973)*
6. Go to the **Architectural** layout.
7. Zoom to the upper right-hand corner of the layout.
8. Select the image (if for some reason you cannot, press [Ctrl] + A, then deselect the frame).
9. Set **Brightness** = 75, **Contrast** = 27, and **Fade** = 20.
10. Clip the image to remove some of the background available.
11. Save and close the file.

14.19 USING eTRANSMIT

- Sending AutoCAD files from one company to another is a routine practice all over the world.
- Because **XREF** allows these companies to work together, designer use it heavily in their daily work.

- If you want to send a file that has several **XREF**s attached to it (especially if each **XREF** file already has other files attached to it) can you imagine how much work would be involved in sending this file?
- You would need to search for all of these files and their nested files, manually, group them together, then use a utility to compress them (e.g., WinZip) to create a *.zip* file or an *.exe* file if the receiver of this file does not have WinZip or WinRAR to uncompress the files.
- What if you want to send 100 files within half an hour? How would you do that?
- AutoCAD comes with a convenient solution to these problems: **eTransmit**. eTransmit will do the following:
  - Automatically collect all the files attached to a desired file, regardless of where they reside.
  - Assemble the font, hatch, linetype, etc., files so the receiver will not need any external help to open your file.
  - Compress all of these files (*.zip* or *.exe*) and set them ready to send via any available communication tool.
- Using the **Application Menu**, select **Send/eTransmit**.
- You will see the following dialog box:

- You can see from the **Files Tree** tab that all the files attached to your current file have been gathered.

- In our example, the **Files Tree** contains a JPEG Image, a DWF Underlay (another name for a DWF XREF), and External References (which is a DWG file XREF).
- Another view is the **File Table** tab, as shown:

- If you want to include more files in the transmittal package, click the **Add File** button. A normal file dialog box will be opened to select the desired file(s).
- To specify how to create the transmittal package, click the **Transmittal Setups** button. The following dialog box will appear:

- Click the **New** button to name and create a new setup (which can be used next time):

- Click **Continue**. You will see the following dialog box:

- Select **Transmittal package type** from *.zip*, *.exe*, or a folder containing the file.
- The rest of the options are self-explanatory.
- Once you are done, click **OK** and a file will be created. You can send it to anyone without having to worry about missing data.

■   When you are done, it is recommended you look at the report that AutoCAD produces. This report sums up all the information needed for the transmittal package. It will resemble the following:

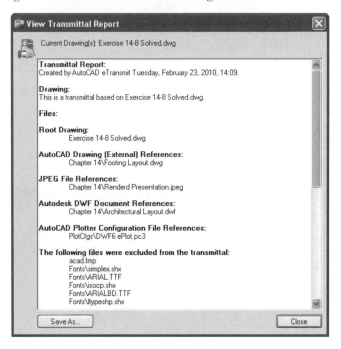

USING eTRANSMIT

Exercise 14-9

1. Start AutoCAD 2011.
2. Open the file *Exercise 14-9.dwg*.
3. Start the **eTransmit** command.
4. Make sure that all of the **XREF** files are there.
5. Check both the **Files Tree** and **Files Table**.
6. Create a new transmittal setup (call it **My First**) that includes:
   • **Transmittal package type** = Self-extracting executable (**.exe*)
   • **File format** = AutoCAD 2007
   • **Include fonts** = on
   • Select to save it in your Exercise folder
7. What is the difference between the transmittal package before and after creating the transmittal setup?

8. Create the transmittal package, and call it *Architectural files.exe*.

9. What is the size of the *.exe* file? (*Answer: almost 600 kB*)

10. Save and close the file.

CHAPTER REVIEW

1. In the **Attribute definition** dialog box, the **Default** value can be a
   _____.

2. Which one of these file types cannot be inserted into a drawing file using **XREF**?
   a. DWG
   b. PDF
   c. XLS
   d. DGN

3. You can extract attributes from your file and from other files as well.
   a. True
   b. False

4. You can control the DWF layers if they were imported into the file via **XREF**.
   a. True
   b. False

5. Which one of the following statements is false?
   a. You can edit attribute values locally and globally.
   b. In the case of adding a new attribute to a block, AutoCAD will add it to the inserted blocks automatically.
   c. You can delete an attribute from an existing block.
   d. **Preset** and **Constant** are two modes of attribute definition.

6. **Unload** and **Detach** are equal commands.
   a. True
   b. False

7. The best tool for sending a file that includes **XREF** files is _____.

CHAPTER REVIEW ANSWERS

1. field
2. c
3. a
4. a
5. b
6. b
7. eTransmit

Chapter **15**   **SHEET SETS**

In This Chapter

◊   An introduction to sheet sets
◊   The **Sheet Set Manager** palette
◊   Creation of sheet sets using an example
◊   Creation of sheet sets using an existing drawing
◊   The **eTransmit, Archive**, and **Publish** commands and sheet sets
◊   Label blocks and callout blocks

15.1 SHEET SETS: AN INTRODUCTION

- When an Architect Engineer Consultant (AEC) company designs a building, the most important output is the set of drawings, which includes Architectural, Structural, Mechanical, Electrical elements, etc.
- According to the U.S. National CAD Standard (NCS), there should be an order for the sheets, beginning with General and following with Hazardous Materials, Surveying/Mapping, Geotechnical, Civil Works, and so forth.
- Also, NCS requires Sheet Identification (also known as Sheet numbers). Complicated projects can use Sheet Identification with multiple parts, and small projects can use abbreviated Sheet Identification.
- Setting all of these requirements manually would prove tiresome.
- AutoCAD provides a tool that allows you to create a sheet set that adopts NCS (or any other system) requirements smoothly and without hassle.
- This tool is helpful for publishing (printing) and archiving projects.
- AutoCAD can help create sheet sets in two ways:
    - **Example sheet set**: Using a common organizational structure of sheets for different disciplines, AutoCAD will create sheet sets (but without sheets). You create the sheets and add stored views to them as **XREF**s. You then scale them to the desired scale factor.

- **Existing drawings**: You can use preexisting layouts in each drawing. The layouts include the company frame border and all of the other details, including viewports. This method considers each layout a sheet. It is easier and faster.

15.2 OPENING AND CLOSING EXISTING SHEET SETS

- There are two ways to open a sheet set:
  - While no file is open
  - While at least one file is open

No File Is Open

- If there is no file open, see the **Quick Access** toolbar. In the upper left-hand corner of the screen, you will see the following:

Sheet Set Manager

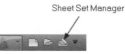

One File Is Open

- On the **Ribbon**, go to the **View** tab. Using the **Palettes** panel, click the **Sheet Set Manager** button:

- With either method, you will see the **Sheet Set Manager** palette:

- From the upper pop-up menu, select **Open**. A normal dialog box will be displayed. Browse to the desired location in your computer (or network) and select the file to be opened. The file extension for a sheet set is *.DST*.
- You will see something like the following:

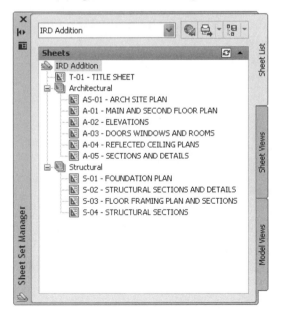

- ■ To close the sheet set, simply select its name and right-click, then select the
  Close Sheet Set option.

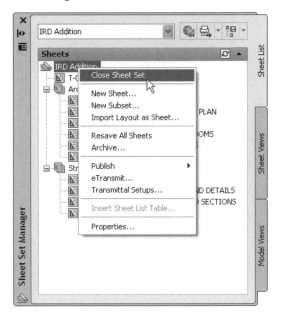

15.3 UNDERSTANDING THE SHEET SET MANAGER PALETTE

- ■ There are three tabs in the **Sheet Set Manager** palette:
  - **Sheet List**
  - **Sheet Views**
  - **Model View**s

Sheet List

- You will see the following:

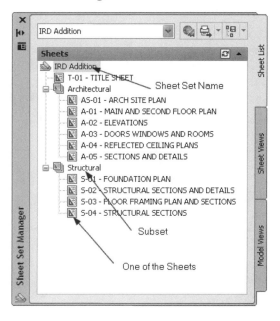

- In the **Sheet List** tab, you will see the sheets in the desired print order.
- The hierarchy consists of:
  - Sheet set name
  - Subsets
  - Sheets (may be linked to the sheet set directly or listed under a subset)
- Subsets are a way to arrange your sheets in groups. This arrangement is optional, but highly recommended.
- Each sheet has a number and a name, such as AS-01 ARCH SITE PLAN.

Sheet Views

- You will see something like the following:

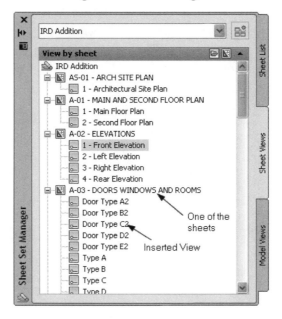

- In the **Sheet Views** tab, you will see the list of views inserted (by the creator of this sheet set) in each sheet.

Model Views

- You will see something like the following:

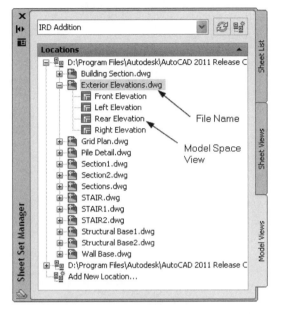

- In the **Model Views** tab, you will see the hard drive and the folder(s) that contain all of your drawings. You can also see the drawings and any stored **Model Space** views.
- In this tab, you can drag and drop views to an empty sheet (we will discuss this later).

■ While the **Sheet Set Manager** palette is open, you can do the following things:

• While in the **Sheet List** tab, if you point to one of the sheets, you will see the following:

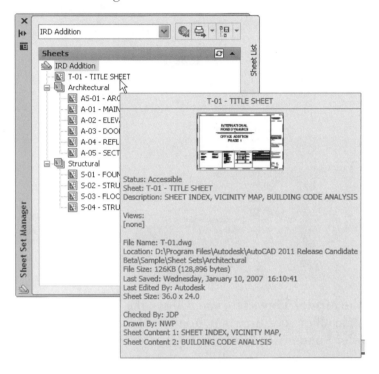

• This box displays a preview of the sheet and complete information about the sheet, including its **Status**, name and number, **Description, File Name**, etc.

• If you double-click any sheet, you will open it, and you change it as you wish.

- While in the **Sheet Views** tab, if you point to one of the views, you will see the following:

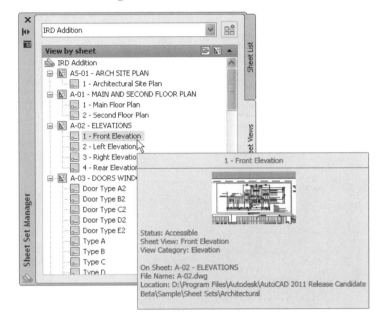

- This box displays the view and complete information about it.
- If you double-click the name of the view, it will open the sheet containing this view. When you move your cursor outside the palette, it will zoom to it.

- While in the **Model Views** tab, if you point to one of the listed files, you will see the following:

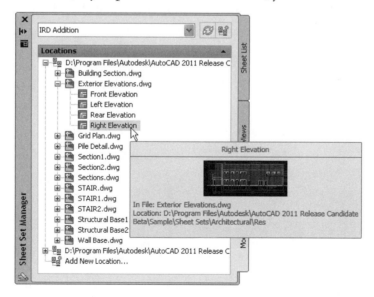

- This box displays a preview of the file and all the file details.
- However, if you point to one of the views, you will see the following:

- This box displays the view and all the needed information about it.
- If you double-click it, the file will open and zoom to the view.

15.4 SHEET SETS AND FILES

■ A very important note should be made here: The DST file contains only the associations and information that define the sheet set.

■ When you create a new sheet set, AutoCAD will automatically create a folder in the My Documents folder in your computer. It is highly recommended that you change the folder containing the sheet set file.

■ Let's return to our earlier example:

■ As you can see, there are 11 sheets. One is linked directly to the sheet set, six are linked to the Architectural subset, and four are linked to the Structural subset.

■ AutoCAD created a file for each sheet. You can name the files whatever you want. In our example, the names of the files are the same as the number of the sheets.

■ Each file contains one layout. The name of the layout is the name of the sheet (e.g., ARCH SITE PLAN is the name of the layout in the file named AS-01).

- If you go to the My Documents folder in your computer and browse until you reach the exact folder in which you stored your sheet set, you will see something like the following:

- You will find 11 files here, which is the exact number of sheets in the **Sheet Set Manager**.

USING THE SHEET SET MANAGER

Exercise 15-1

1. Start AutoCAD 2011.
2. Close all files.
3. Start the **Sheet Set Manager**. From the pop-up list, select **Open**.
4. Go to the following folder: \AutoCAD 2011\Sample\Sheet Sets\ Manufacturing.
5. Select the file *manufacturing sheet set.dst*.
6. Double-click on the first sheet: **01 – Cover Sheet**.
7. Zoom to the lower right-hand corner of the layout. You can see the name of the sheet and the sheet number as fields.
8. Close the file without saving it.
9. Point to the second sheet. You will see a preview and more information about the file.
10. Go to the **Sheet Views** tab.
11. Double-click the view **D-D**, noticing how the file opens and zooms to the view.
12. Close the file without saving it.

13. Go to the **Model Views** tab and click the plus sign at the left of the only folder available.

14. You will see the list of the files containing the views that will be imported as **XREF**s in the sheets.

15. Using the file *VW252-02-0300.dwg*, double-click the view **Detail A**. AutoCAD will open the file and zoom to the view.

16. Close the file without saving it.

17. Close the sheet set.

15.5 CREATING A NEW SHEET SET USING AN EXAMPLE

- As mentioned earlier, there are two ways to create a sheet set:
    - Using an example sheet set
    - Using existing drawings
- Before we continue, note the following:
    - We will assume from now on that the **Sheet Set Manager** palette is open.
    - You cannot create a new sheet set unless you have a minimum of one file open.
- To create a new sheet set, use the pop-up menu in the upper left-hand part of the **Sheet Set Manager**. Select the **New Sheet Set** option.
- The following dialog box will appear:

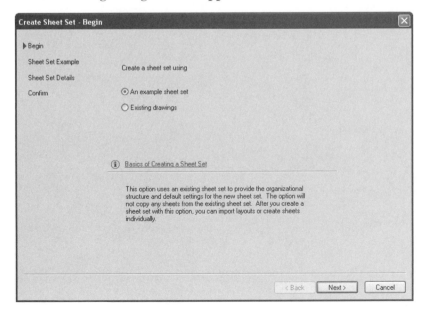

- Make sure that **An example sheet set** is already selected. Click **Next**.
- The following dialog box will appear:

- Select one of the examples provided (a brief description will appear at the bottom of the dialog box).

■ Remember, AutoCAD will only provide you with the subsets. No sheets will be added, as this is your responsibility. Click **Next** and the following dialog box will appear:

■ Type in the name of the sheet set.
■ Type in any description (if needed).
■ Select the location to store the DST file (by default, it will go in your My Documents folder).
■ Select whether you want to **Create a folder hierarchy based on subsets**.

- Click the **Sheet Set Properties** button. The following dialog box will appear:

- You must specify several things here. We will cover the most important:
  - **Sheet storage location** does not refer to the DST file, but to the sheets. It is highly recommended that you keep them in the same place as the DST file.
  - **Sheet creation template** is where you specify the path for the DWT file that all sheets will be based on.
  - **Project Control** and **Sheet Set Custom Properties** data are optional, but filling them in is useful.
- Click **OK**, then **Next**.

- The following dialog box will appear:

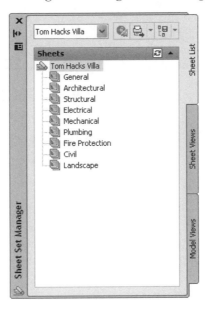

- Look at the preview. If you want to change anything, click **Back**. If not, click **Finish**.
- You will see something resembling the following:

Right-Click Subset

- As you saw in the preceding illustration, only subsets are visible.
- To create a new blank sheet inside a subset, do the following:
    - Select the desired subset.
    - Right-click and the following menu will appear:

Expand
New Sheet...
New Subset...
Import Layout as Sheet...
Rename Subset...
Remove Subset
Publish ▶
eTransmit...
Insert Sheet List Table...
Properties...

- Select the **New Sheet** option. The following dialog box will appear:

New Sheet

Number:	Sheet title:
A-01	Architectural Site Plan
File name:	A-01 Architectural Site Plan
Folder path:	C:\Documents and Settings\Munir\My Documents\AutoCAD Sheet Sets
Sheet template:	;e candidate beta\R18.1\enu\Template\SheetSets\Architectural Metric.dwt)

☐ Open in drawing editor

[OK]   [Cancel]   [Help]

- Fill in the number, the **Sheet title**, and the **File name**. Click **OK**.
- You will see something resembling the following:

Sheets

- Tom Hacks Villa
    - General
    - Architectural
        - A-01 - Architectural Site Plan
        - A-02 - Ground Floor Plan
    - Structural
    - Electrical
    - Mechanical
    - Plumbing
    - Fire Protection
    - Civil
    - Landscape

- If you double-click on any sheet, it will open and you will see items that came from the template file. The data you enter in the **Sheet Set Properties** will be entered accordingly in the sheet.

- Using the same menu, you can also create a **New Subset**, **Rename Subset**, and **Remove Subset**.

Right-click Sheet

■ Right-click the desired sheet. The following menu will appear:

Open
Open read-only

New Sheet...
Import Layout as Sheet...

Rename & Renumber...
Remove Sheet

Publish ▶
eTransmit...

Insert Sheet List Table...

Properties...

■ You can do the following:
  - **Open** the sheet (double-clicking the name will also open it).
  - Create a **New Sheet** inside the same subset.
  - **Rename & Renumber** the sheet.
  - **Remove** the sheet.
■ The other options will be discussed later.

CREATING A SHEET SET USING AN EXAMPLE

Exercise 15-2
1. Start AutoCAD 2011.
2. Make sure that there is one file open.
3. Start the **Sheet Set Manager** and create a new sheet set using an example sheet set.
4. Use the **Architectural Imperial** example.
5. The name of the new sheet set is **John Smith House**.
6. Store the sheet set in the following folder: Exercises\Sheet Set\John Smith House.
7. Click **Finish** to complete the creation of the sheet set.
8. Go to the **Model Views** tab, click **Add New Location**, and find the John Smith House Drawings folder.

9. Go back to the **Sheet List** tab and remove the **General** subset.

10. Under **Architectural**, create four new sheets and name them as follows:

    a. **A-01 Ground Floor – Overall**

    b. **A-02 Ground Floor – Architectural Details**

    c. **A-03 First Floor – Overall**

    d. **A-04 First Floor – Architectural Details**

11. Under **Structural**, create a sheet named **S-01 titled Column Layout**.

12. Leave this sheet set open; you will need it in the next exercise.

15.6 ADDING VIEWS INTO SHEETS

- Up until now, there has been no link between the drawings of your project (which you have already finished) and the sheet set.
- To make this link, you should add model views that have already been created in your drawings into your blank sheets.
- These will be imported as an **XREF** to the original files.
- You must scale each view before inserting them.
- Perform the following steps:
  - Make sure you are at the **Model Views** tab.
  - Double-click **Add New Location**.
  - A dialog box will appear to select the folder your files reside in.
  - You will see something like the following:

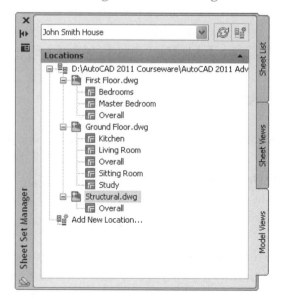

- If there is a plus sign at the left of the file, then there are named views in this file. Expand the file to see a listing of these views.
- Select the desired view, then drag and drop the desired sheet inside.
- You must specify the insertion point, but before you do, right-click to choose from a list of the available scale factors, as shown:

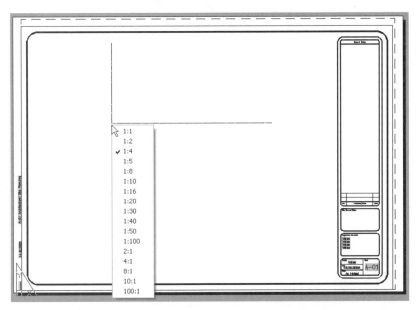

- Select the desired scale factor and specify the insertion point.
- You will get something like the following:

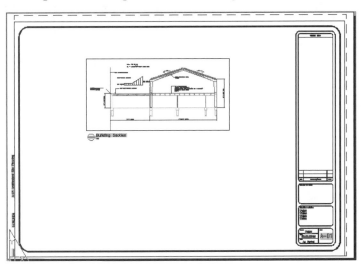

- Once you are done, look at the **Sheet Views** tab. You will see something like the following:

- You can see all the sheets and the layout views in each one.
- If you start the **View** command, you will see the following:

ADDING VIEWS INTO SHEETS

Exercise 15-3
1. Start AutoCAD 2011.
2. Open the sheet set we created in Exercise 15-2.
3. Double-click the **A-01** sheet to open the file.
4. Go to the **Model Views** tab and click the plus sign beside *Ground Floor. dwg*.
5. Click and drag the **Overall** view. Before you insert anything, right-click and select scale 1' = 1'.
6. Save and close.
7. Open the **A-02** sheet and apply the following settings from *Ground Floor. dwg*:
   a. At the left of the **Kitchen** view, set scale 2' = 1'.
   b. At the right of the **Kitchen** view, insert the **Living Room, Sitting Room**, and **Study** views using scale 1' = 1'.
8. Save and close.
9. Insert the **Overall** view from *First Floor.dwg* into the **A-03** sheet using scale 1' = 1'. Save and close.
10. Open the **A-04** sheet and insert the **Bedrooms** view at the top, using scale 2' = 1'. Beneath it, insert the **Master Bedroom** view, using scale 1' =1'. Save and close.
11. Open the **S-01** sheet and insert the **Column Layout** view from *Structural. dwg* using scale 1' =1'. Save and close.
12. Close the **John Smith House** sheet set.

15.7 CREATING A NEW SHEET SET USING EXISTING DRAWINGS

- ■ If you want to create a new sheet set using an existing drawing, you should read the following guidelines:
  - • Arrange your files by creating a hierarchy of folders. See the following example:

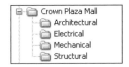

- Save all of your drawings within the respective folder.
- Make sure that each file contains only one layout. It is permissible to have multiple layouts to be converted to sheets in the same file, but if you plan to create your sheet set within a network that involves other users, Autodesk recommends keeping a single layout per file to avoid errors.
- The sheet set will convert each folder to be a subset, and each layout in each file will be converted to a sheet.

■ Select the **New Sheet Set** option. The following dialog box will appear:

- Select the **Existing drawings** option and click **Next**. The following dialog box will appear:

```
Create Sheet Set - Sheet Set Details                                      [X]

  Begin                  Name of new sheet set:
▶ Sheet Set Details      Crown Plaza Mall
  Choose Layouts
  Confirm                Description (optional):




                         Store sheet set data file (.dst) here:
                         C:\Documents and Settings\Munir\My Documents\AutoCAD Sheet Sets  [...]

                         Note: The sheet set data file should be stored in a location that can be
                         accessed by all contributors to the sheet set.


                              Sheet Set Properties


                                           < Back    Next >    Cancel
```

- Type in the name of the sheet set.
- Type in any description (if needed).
- Select the place to store the DST file (by default, it will go to the My Documents folder).
- Click the **Sheet Set Properties** button. The following dialog box will appear:

```
Sheet Set Properties - Crown Plaza Florida                                [X]

  Sheet Set                                                               ▲
    Name                          Crown Plaza Florida
    Sheet set data file           C:\Documents and Settings\Munir\My Docume...
    Description
    Model view
    Label block for views
    Callout blocks
    Page setup overrides file     C:\Documents and Settings\Munir\local settin...
  Project Control                                                         ▲
    Project number
    Project name
    Project phase
    Project milestone
  Sheet Creation                                                          ▲
    Sheet storage location        C:\Documents and Settings\Munir\My Docume...
    Sheet creation template       Arch D(C:\Documents and Settings\Munir\loca...
    Prompt for template           No




    Edit Custom Properties...        OK        Cancel        Help
```

- You must specify several data here. We will cover the most important:
  - **Sheet storage location**: It is highly recommended to keep the sheets in the same place as the DST file. (Note, this refers to the sheets, not the DST file.)
  - **Sheet creation template**: You should specify the path for the DWT file that the new sheets will be based on.
  - **Project Control**: These selections are optional, but filling them in is beneficial.
- Click **OK**, then **Next**. The following dialog box will appear:

- Before you browse to the desired folder, check the **Import Options** button. You will see the following dialog box:

- For the **Import Options**, you can do the following:
  - **Prefix sheet titles with file name**
  - **Create subsets based on folder structure**
  - **Ignore top level folder**

- After you finish the **Import** options, click the **Browse** button and select the folder(s) that contains the desired files. You will see something like the following:

- By default, all files and all layouts are selected. You can deselect any of these. When done, click **Next**. You will see the following dialog box. Click **Finish** or **Back**.

- The following will be shown in the **Sheet Set Manager**:

- You can do the following:
  - Rearrange the subsets and sheets by the drag-and-drop method.
  - Rename subsets, and renumber and rename sheets.
  - Create new subsets.
  - Create new sheets.

- If you right-click any subset, you will see the **Import Layout as Sheets** option. It allows you to import a single layout from other drawings to the selected subset as a sheet. See the following dialog box:

- Click the **Browse for Drawings** button to search for the desired drawing(s).
- Select the drawings, then click **Import Checked**.

CREATING A SHEET SET USING EXISTING DRAWINGS

Exercise 15-4

1. Start AutoCAD 2011.
2. Make sure that there is one file open.
3. Start **Sheet Set Manager** and create a new sheet set using existing drawings. Name it **Florida Villa** and save the DST file in the following folder: Exercise folder\Sheet Set\Florida Villa.
4. Click the **Import Options** button and make sure of the following:
   a. **Prefix sheet titles with file name** is turned off.
   b. **Create subsets based on folder structure** is turned on.
   c. **Ignore top level folder** is turned on.
5. Click the **Browse** button and select the drawings in the following folder: Exercise folder\Sheet Set\Florida Villa Drawings.

6. Click the plus sign near **Structural** and turn off the only sheet.

7. Click **Finish** to end the command.

8. Click the first sheet in the list and rename it **A-01 Ground Floor – Overall**.

9. Perform the following steps:

    a. Rename the *third* sheet **A-01 Ground Floor – Overall**

    b. Rename the *fourth* sheet **A-02 Ground Floor – Architectural Details**

    c. Rename the *first* sheet **A-03 First Floor – Overall**

    d. Rename the *second* sheet **A-04 First Floor – Architectural Details**

10. Rearrange them to be sorted by the numbers of the sheets.

11. Create a new subset and call it **Structural**.

12. Right-click the new subset, and select the **Import Layout as Sheets** option.

13. Select **Browse for Drawings** and select those in the following folder: Exercise folder\Sheet Set\Florida Villa Drawings\Structural. Then select *Structural.dwg*. A single layout is there. Click **Import Checked**.

14. Rename the sheet **S-01 Column layout**.

15. Save and close the **Florida Villa** sheet set.

15.8 eTRANSMIT, ARCHIVE, AND PUBLISH SHEET SETS

- We discussed and highlighted the advantages of the **eTransmit** command in Chapter 14.
- You can use eTransmit with sheet sets as well.
- According to the AutoCAD manual, eTransmit is for Internet transmittal. For internal work, the manual recommends using the **Archive** command.
- We believe that one command is enough and that eTransmit will do the job for both Internet and internal work.

eTransmit

- Using the **Sheet Set Manager**, select the name of the sheet set, right-click, and select the **eTransmit** option. The following dialog box will appear:

- A new tab, called **Sheets**, will show how the subsets and sheets are related to each other.
- The rest is the same as the **eTransmit** command discussed previously.
- NOTE ▶ AutoCAD will save the DST file with the transmittal package.

Archive

- Using the **Sheet Set Manager**, select the name of the sheet set, right-click, and select the **Archive** option. You will see the following dialog box:

- It is identical to the **eTransmit** dialog box, except that with this command, you cannot save the **Archive** setup. You can, however, change it if you want.

Publish

- If you select the **Publish** option, you will see the following menu:

```
Publish to DWF
Publish to DWFx
Publish to PDF
Publish to Plotter
Publish using Page Setup Override          ▶
─────────────────────────────────────────────
Edit Subset and Sheet Publish Settings...
Publish in Reverse Order
Include Plot Stamp
Plot Stamp Settings...
─────────────────────────────────────────────
Manage Page Setups...
Sheet Set Publish Options ...
Publish Dialog Box ...
```

- You will have the following options:
  - **Publish to DWF**: This option allows you to create a multisheet DWF file for all of the sheet sets. You will need Autodesk Design Review to open the file.

- **Publish to DWFx**: If you are using Windows Vista or Windows 7, you do not need Autodesk Design Review to open this file.
- **Publish to PDF**: This option allows you to create a PDF file for all of the sheet sets.
- **Publish to Plotter**: This option will send each sheet to the plotter configured inside the page setup.
- **Publish using Page Setup Override**: By default, each sheet contains the page setup that will be used once the **Publish** command is issued. Alternatively, you can create other page setups to override the default page setups. These should be configured inside the **Properties** dialog box, as shown:

- You will see something like the following:

- **Publish in Reverse Order**: This option is either turned on or off. By default, the publishing process will start with the first sheet. However, if you select this option, it will start with the last sheet.
- **Include Plot Stamp**: This option is either turned on or off. By default. the **Plot Stamp** is not included.
- **Plot Stamp Settings**: This option will present a dialog box that will help you select your requirements for the desired stamp to appear on all printed sheets. You will see something like the following:

- **Manage Page Setups**: This option will show you the **Page Setup Manager**, which was discussed in earlier chapters.

- **Sheet Set Publish Options**: This option is identical to the **Publish** options of the **Publish** command. You will see the following dialog box:

- Be sure to include all the necessary information inside the DWF file, including the **Layer, Sheet set, Sheet information**, and **Block information**.

- **Publish Dialog Box**: This option will show you the **Publish** dialog box, as shown:

eTRANSMIT, ARCHIVE, AND PUBLISH SHEET SETS

Exercise 15-5

1. Start AutoCAD 2011.
2. Make sure that there is one file open.
3. Open the **Sheet Set Manager**.
4. Open the **John Smith House** sheet set, which you created earlier.
5. Right-click the name of the sheet set and select the **eTransmit** option.
6. Review the sheets and files to make sure that AutoCAD included all of the necessary files.
7. Create an **eTransmit** package.
8. Right-click the name of the sheet set and select **Publish/Publish Dialog Box**.
9. Click the **Sheet Set Publish Options**, and make sure that **Sheet Set Information** and **Sheet Information** are both set to **Include**.

10. Make sure that **Publish to** = DWF.
11. Click **Publish** and save the DWF file in the same place as the DST file.
12. Close the **John Smith House** sheet set.

15.9 LABEL BLOCKS AND CALLOUT BLOCKS

- When you are creating a sheet set using an example and you add views to your blank sheets, a label block will be added automatically with data relevant to the current sheet. You will see something resembling the following:

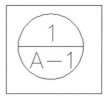

- The block contains the following data:
  - **View name**
  - **View number** (in this sheet)
  - **Scale**
- All of the these data are fields that will be input and updated by AutoCAD, not by the user.
- The callout block will look like the following:

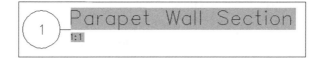

- The data included in this block are:
  - **View number** in this sheet
  - **Sheet number** containing the reference drawing
- All of the data are fields.
- You can specify the two types of blocks in the **Properties** dialog box of the sheet set. You have to specify whether the DWT or DWG contains both blocks:

Sheet Set	▲
Name	John Smith House
Sheet set data file	D:\AutoCAD 2011 Courseware\AutoCAD 201...
Description	Use the Architectural Imperial Sheet Set to cr...
Model view	D:\AutoCAD 2011 Courseware\AutoCAD 201...
Label block for views	Drawing Block Title(C:\Documents and Setting...
Callout blocks	Callout(C:\Documents and Settings\Munir\Loc...
Page setup overrides file	C:\Documents and Settings\Munir\Local Settin...

- Depending on the example sheet set you select, AutoCAD will assign the file you will get the two blocks from by default.
- AutoCAD comes with a folder called Templates. This folder contains some standard templates and two more folders. One of these folders, called **SheetSets**, contains three types of templates: **Architectural**, **Civil**, and **Manufacturing**. For each type, there are two templates, one for **Metric** and the other for **Imperial**.
- If you choose **Architectural Metric**, for example, the following will be assumed:
  - **Sheet creation template** = Architectural Metric
  - **Label block for views** = Architectural Metric
  - **Callout blocks** = Architectural Metric
- If you want to use your own template for the blocks, click the small button with the three dots. You will see the following dialog box:

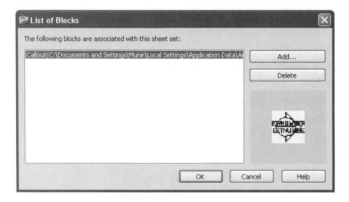

- Click the **Add** button. You will see the following dialog box:

- Click the small button with the dots inside it to select the desired file (it can be a DWG or DWT file).
- You can create your own blocks if you want and add all the desired fields that you want to show.

CHAPTER REVIEW

1. When you are creating a new sheet set using an example sheet set, you must:
   a. Create sheets.
   b. Create views in the files.
   c. Drag views as **XREF**s.
   d. All of the above.
2. While you are bringing in a view from a file, you must set the _____ of the view.
3. There are two methods used to create sheet sets in AutoCAD.
   a. True
   b. False
4. After you create a sheet set, you can:
   a. Archive it.
   b. Publish it using different file formats.
   c. Export it as a DXF file.
   d. A and B.
5. The label block for views and the callout block are preset, and you cannot create your own.
   a. True
   b. False
6. If you would like to import another sheet from a layout in a file after you create your sheet set, you must right-click the desired subset and select the _____ option.

CHAPTER REVIEW ANSWERS

1. d
2. scale
3. a
4. d
5. b
6. **Import Layout as Sheets**

Chapter 16

CAD STANDARDS AND ADVANCED LAYERS

In This Chapter
◊ Understanding CAD standards
◊ Creating CAD standard files
◊ Configuring and checking standards
◊ The **Layer Translator** command
◊ Using **Advanced Layer** functions
◊ Using the **Layer States Manager**

16.1 UNDERSTANDING CAD STANDARDS

- CAD (and AutoCAD in particular) is becoming increasingly complex, as every year a new version is introduced with new commands and techniques.
- Companies using AutoCAD are employing more and more CAD operators.
- Design itself is growing increasingly complicated.
- International bodies continue to issue new standards that address the changes in design and how they should be delivered.
- Companies of all sizes use CAD Managers. Without CAD Managers, the company would lack CAD standards, proper training, budgeting, etc.
- Part of the CAD Manager's duties is to establish CAD standards in his or her company by doing the following:
  - Adopting the right CAD standard for the industry his or her company is in.
  - Translating the standard inside AutoCAD into something tangible, such as layers, dimension styles, text styles, table styles, layouts, etc.
  - Ensuring that all the CAD operators within the company are using these standards consistently.

- Training all staff members to use these standards efficiently by outlining the importance of these standards for the workflow and for the success of the project and the company.
- Checking all drawings that are finished or partially developed to be sure that no standard violation took place.
- The AutoCAD **CAD Standard tool** enables CAD Managers to accomplish their duties swiftly.
- The large list of **Advanced Layer** functions allow users to control any drawing regardless of the number of layers inside it.

16.2 CREATING CAD STANDARD FILES

- Normally, each company has its own template files that include all of the following:
  - Layers (including the naming convention, color, linetype, lineweight)
  - Dimension styles
  - Multileader styles
  - Text styles
  - Table styles
  - Layouts (including the page setup, border block, and viewports)
- The best way to create a standard file is to open a template file and transform it into a standard file (from a DWT file to a DWS file) using the **Save As** command.
- Standard files can check for the following only:
  - Layers (anything related to layers)
  - Dimension styles
  - Text styles
  - Linetypes

Procedure

- Create a new file using the desired template file. Using the **Applications Menu**, click **Save As** and pick **AutoCAD Drawing Standards**, as shown:

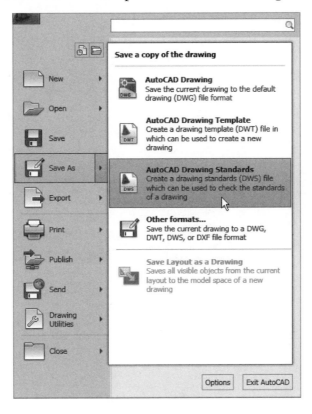

- The following dialog box will appear:

Save Drawing As

Save in: Munir's Stuff   Views ▼ Tools ▼

Name ▲   Size   Preview

History

My Documents

Favorites

Desktop

FTP

Buzzsaw

☐ Update sheet and view thumbnails now

File name: My Company   **Save**

Files of type: AutoCAD Drawing Standards (*.dws)   Cancel

- Type the name of the new standard file (*.*dws*) and click the **Save** button.

CREATING A CAD STANDARD FILE

Exercise 16-1
1. Start AutoCAD 2011.
2. Open the file *Architectural Standards.dwg*.
3. As you can see, it is an empty file that contains standards.
4. Go to the **Applications Menu** and select **Save As/AutoCADDrawing Standards**.
5. Save the file in your Exercise folder, naming it *Architectural Standards.dws*.
6. Close the file.

16.3 CONFIGURING AND CHECKING STANDARDS

- You will create a standard file once.
- There are still two steps to perform to complete this process:
  - **Configuring** the standard file (linking your current DWG to an existing DWS file).
  - **Checking** the compliance of your DWG by comparing it to the DWS file.

Configuring

- Open the desired DWG file to check its compliance.
- On the **Ribbon**, go to the **Manage** tab. Using the **CAD Standards** panel, click the **Configure** button:

- The following dialog box will appear:

- Click the button with the plus sign. A dialog box will appear allowing you to select your DWS file. Select your desired file and click **OK**.

- Click the **Plug-ins** tab. You will see the following:

Configure Standards

Standards | Plug-ins

Plug-ins used when checking standards:

☑ ⚠ Dimension Styles
☑ ≋ Layers
☑ ⟩ Linetypes
☑ A⟩ Text Styles

Description:

Purpose
Checks that names and properties of dimension styles in a drawing match those in an associated standards file.

Version
2.0

Publisher
Autodesk, Inc.
http://www.autodesk.com

[Check Standards...] [Settings...]   [OK] [Cancel] [Help]

- Clear the unnecessary plug-ins that you do not want AutoCAD to check for.
- Click the **Settings** button. You will see the following dialog box:

CAD Standards Settings

Notification settings

○ Disable standards notifications
○ Display alert upon standards violation
⦿ Display standards status bar icon

Check Standards settings

☐ Automatically fix non-standard properties
☑ Show ignored problems
Preferred standards file to use for replacements:
[None   ▼]

[OK] [Cancel] [Help]

- Choose which **Notification** method is suitable for you:
  - **Disable standards notifications**
  - **Display alert upon standards violation** (enabled while you are still working with the DWG file)
  - **Display standards status bar icon** (see the following illustration):

- Under **Check Standards settings**, you have the following options:
  - You can make the fixing process either automatic or manual.
  - You can either show or hide ignored problems (this refers to violations that you opt to ignore).
  - You can choose which standards file to use for replacements.

Checking

- Open the file you want to check for compliance.
- On the **Ribbon**, go to the **Manage** tab. Using the **CAD Standards** panel, click the **Check** button:

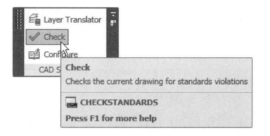

- The following dialog box will appear:

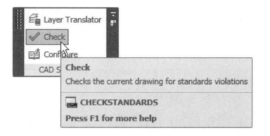

- There are three sections to be addressed:
  - **Problem**
  - **Replace with**
  - **Preview of changes**

Problem

- If any problems are found, they will be listed in this section:

```
Problem:
Dimstyle 'Standard'
Properties are non-standard
```

- In this example, the **Standard** dimension style has nonstandard properties.

Replace With

- AutoCAD will search the standard file and suggest a replacement for the existing style:

Replace with:	
Dimstyle	Standards File
Annotative	Architectural Standards
✓ Standard	Architectural Standards

- In this example, AutoCAD suggests replacing the standard file with either the **Annotative** dim style or the **Standard** dim style.
- Let's assume we choose **Standard**.

Preview of Changes

- AutoCAD will automatically show you what will happen if you choose this style:

Preview of changes:		
Property	Current Value	Standard Value
Arrow (DIMBLK)	Architectural tick	Closed filled
Center mark size (DI...	Type: [None] Size:[...	Type: [Mark] Size:[...

- If you choose this action, the following changes will be made to your current **Standard** dim style:
  - The arrow will change from **Architectural tick** to **Closed filled**.
  - The center mark will change from **None** to **Mark**.

Mark This Problem as Ignored

- In the bottom left-hand corner of the dialog box, you will see the following checkbox:

☐ Mark this problem as ignored

- Select this option if you want to accept this problem as is.
- You have two buttons to choose from: **Fix** and **Next**.
  - **Fix** allows you to fix the problem as the **Standards check** proposes.
  - **Next** allows you to ignore it this time, and the **Standards check** will show it as a problem again next time.
- When done, you will see the following message:

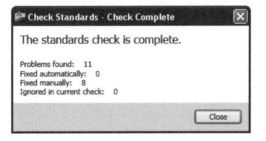

NOTE
- You can configure (link) the standard file to your file at any time.
- While you are working, if any of your changes violate the standard file, AutoCAD will display the following message:

> **ⓘ Standards Violation**   ☒
>
> A standards violation has occurred. Run Check Standards to view all standards violations in the current drawing.
>
> Run Check Standards

NOTE
- If the **Standards check** finds a layer that does not exist in the standard file, but you choose to include it inside an existing layer in the standard file, what will happen to the old layer? AutoCAD will move all objects from the old layer to the new layer and delete the old layer from this file.

CONFIGURING AND CHECKING STANDARDS

Exercise 16-2

1. Start AutoCAD 2011.
2. Open the file *Exercise 16-2.dwg*.
3. Go to the **Layer Properties Manager** and check the following:
   a. What is the layer **Door** color?
   b. Is there a layer called **Frame**?
   c. Is there a layer called **Partition**?
   d. Is there a layer called **Viewport**?
4. Start the **Configure** command and link the file *Architectural Standards.dws* to it.
5. Go to **Plug-ins** and make sure that all the options are selected.
6. At the right of the **Status bar**, make sure you can see the icon referring to the **Standard file**.
7. Start the **Check** command and change the following:

Problem	Action
Dim Style: Standard	Replace it with **Standard**.
Layer: Door	Replace it with **Door**.
Layer: Partition	Replace it with **Wall**.
Layer: Frame	Replace it with **Title Block**.
Layer: Centerline	Replace it with **Centerline**.
Layer: Column Layout	Select **Next**.
Layer: Viewport	Replace it with **Viewports**.
Layer: Hatch	Select **Next**.
Linetype: DASHDOT	Replace it with **DASHDOT2**.
Text Style: ISO Proportional	Replace it with **ISO Proportional**.
Text Style: Arial_09	Replace it with **Standard**.

8. Go to the **Layer Manager** tool palette and notice that layers such as **Partition, Frame**, and **Viewport** disappeared. Notice that the layer **Door** has a different color.
9. Save and close the file.

16.4 THE LAYER TRANSLATOR COMMAND

- When you are a CAD Manager, you have full control and authority over the company's staff, but you do not have the same power over those outside the company.
- Assume you are with an AEC firm and you are receiving some DWG files from a contracting company. After checking them, your staff wants to make some amendments. They are not happy with the company's naming convention and color choices.
- As a CAD Manager, you can translate the layers used in these files to something your staff feels comfortable with—your standard. But note, you can only do this for layers.
- On the **Ribbon**, go to the **Manage** tab. Using the **CAD Standards** panel, click the **Layer Translator** button:

- The following dialog box will appear:

- Click the **Load** button to load the file that contains your list of layers. You can load DWG, DWT, and DWS files.

■ After you load the file, you will see the following dialog box:

■ Click the **Map same** button. AutoCAD will find any similar naming of layers to exclude these layers from being mapped. You will see the following:

■ Now, select a layer from the **Translate From** list and a layer from the **Translate To** list. Click the **Map** button. The layer will move from the left list to the lower list.

■ Repeat until you are done.

- You can save the list you have mapped for future mappings with similar files (i.e., for the same company).
- At any time, you can click the **Settings** button to show the following dialog box:

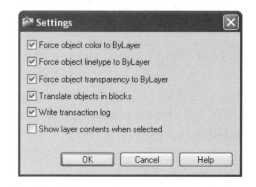

- When mapping, you can set any of the following:
  - **Force object color to ByLayer**
  - **Force object linetype to ByLayer**
  - **Force object transparency to ByLayer**
  - **Translate objects in blocks**
  - **Write transaction log** (to create a log file of the translation process)
  - **Show layer contents when selected**
- When you are done, click **OK**, then **Translate**.

THE LAYER TRANSLATOR COMMAND

Exercise 16-3
1. Start AutoCAD 2011.
2. Open the file *Ground Floor.dwg*.
3. Start the **Layer Translator** command.
4. Load *Architectural Standards.dws* to be the file to translate to.
5. Map the layers with the same name. You will have five layers left. Set the following:
   a. **Frame** to be mapped to **Title Block**
   b. **Partition** to be mapped to **Wall**
   c. **Viewport** to be mapped to **Viewports**
6. Do not translate the remaining layers.
7. Save the translation as *ABC Translation.dws* in your Exercise folder.

8. Click the **Translate** button.

9. Save and close the file.

10. Open file *First Floor.dwg*.

11. Start the **Layer Translator** command.

12. Load *ABC Translation.dws* (you must change the file type from DWG to DWS).

13. Notice that the layers were mapped automatically.

14. Click the **Translate** command.

15. In the folder, you will find two *.txt* files that are named after the two files. Open them and review their contents.

16. Save and close the file.

16.5 ADVANCED LAYERS: THE GENERAL APPEARANCE

- If you have a drawing with a large number of layers, use the **Property Filter**, accessed from the **Layer Properties Manager**, to create a filter based on a common property, such as **Name, Color, Freeze/Thaw, On/Off**, etc.

- Also, you can create a group of layers with no common thread by using the **Group Filter**.

- You can create a **Layer State**, which can save the state of the current layers and restore them for future use.

- On the **Ribbon**, go to the **Home** tab. Using the **Layers** panel, click the **Layer Properties** button:

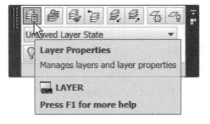

- The following palette will appear:

- Note the following:
  - In the lower left-hand corner of the palette, you will see the total number of layers:

  - At the left of the dialog box, you will see the **Filter** pane. By default, you will see something like the following:

  - There are two filters: **All** (which includes all used and unused layers) and **All Used Layers** (which includes only used [non-empty] layers).

- The **Invert filter** checkbox allows you to select the opposite of the current filter.
- In the upper left-hand corner, you will see three buttons:

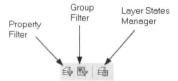

- In the preceding dialog box, you can also do the following:
  - Change the place of a column using the drag-and-drop method:

On	Freeze	Lock	Color	Linetype	Linev
♀	☼	🔓	■ white	Continuous	—
♀	☼				—
♀	☼	Freeze:			
♀	☼	Freezes or Thaws layer for entire drawing			—
♀	☼		□ yellow	Continuous	
♀	❄	🔓	■ red	Continuous	—
♀	❄	🔓	■ green	Continuous	

  - Sort the layers according to the column you choose (**Ascending** or **Descending**). In the following example, layers were sorted in descending order according to color:

S..	Name	On	Freeze	Lock	Color ▼	Linetype	Lineweight	Trans...	Plo
▱	Staircase	♀	☼	🔓	■ 27	Continuous	— Defa...	0	Col
▱	S-Grid	♀	❄	🔓	□ 9	DASHDOT2	— Defa...	0	Col
▱	Title Block	♀	☼	🔓	■ white	Continuous	— Defa...	0	Col
▱	S-Grid-Id...	♀	❄	🔓	■ white	Continuous	— Defa...	0	Col
▱	E-Legn	♀	☼	🔓	■ white	DASHDOT2	— Defa...	0	Col
▱	Defpoints	♀	☼	🔓	■ white	Continuous	— Defa...	0	Col
✓	0	♀	☼	🔓	■ white	Continuous	— Defa...	0	Col
▱	Frame	♀	☼	🔓	■ mage...	Continuous	— Defa...	0	Col
▱	A-Window	♀	☼	🔓	■ mage...	Continuous	— Defa...	0	Col
▱	Viewport	♀	☼	🔓	■ blue	Continuous	— Defa...	0	Col
▱	Text	♀	❄	🔓	■ blue	Continuous	— Defa...	0	Col
▱	C-Pron	♀	❄	🔓	■ blue	DASHDOT2	— Defa...	0	Col

- If you select any layer name and right-click, you will see the following menu (these options are self-explanatory):

- If you right-click the headings of one of the columns, you will see the following:

- You can show or hide any column and choose from several available tools.

16.6 ADVANCED LAYERS: THE PROPERTY FILTER

- Complex drawings contain a large number of layers.
- If you have many layers in the **Layer Properties Manager**, reaching the desired layer to freeze or lock will be difficult.
- AutoCAD provides a useful tool that allows you to see only certain layers based on a common property.
- Click the **Property Filter** button. You will see the following dialog box:

- First, fill in a name for the filter.
- If you use any of the fields available, you will see the result right away.
- In the preceding example, the **Name** field has been filled in with **S***. This means that any layer starting with "S." is considered a wild card; hence, it can take the place of anything. You can use it before a letter, after a letter, or both. For example, ***plum*** would produce any layer containing the word **plum**, whether at the beginning, the middle, or the end of the name.
- You can filter using **On/Off, Freeze/Thaw, Color, Linetype**, etc.

- When you are done, click **OK**. You will see the following:

- In the lower left-hand corner of the palette, you will see the name of the filter and the number of the layers that fit the criteria.
- Next, go to the **Home** tab and look at the **Layers** panel to see the following:

- As you can see, only the layers of the example filter—plus layer 0, which is the current layer in this case—are shown.

16.7 ADVANCED LAYERS: THE GROUP FILTER

- We have just discussed how the **Property Filter** works, but what if you want to create a group of layers that have nothing in common? You must create a group filter.
- Click the **Group Filter** button in the **Filters** pane. You can then type in the name of the new group filter.
- You can drag and drop layers from the layer list into the filter you just created. See the following illustration:

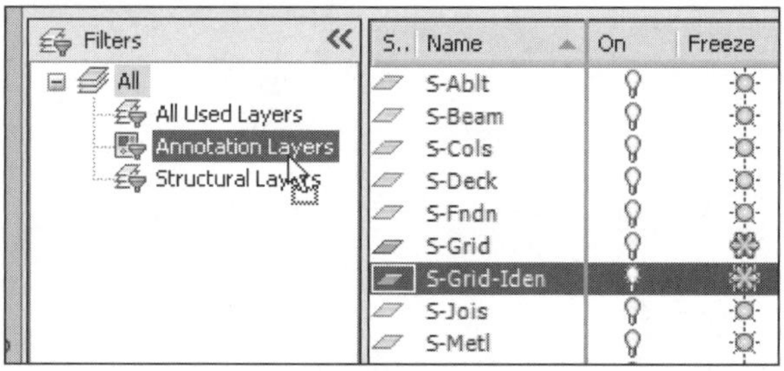

16.8 ADVANCED LAYERS: RIGHT-CLICKING A FILTER

- What happens if you right-click a property filter or a group filter?
- How do filters help speed up your production?

Right-Clicking a Property Filter

- Because these layers are connected, we can perform collective actions that will affect all of them at once.
- If you right-click a property filter, you will see the following menu:

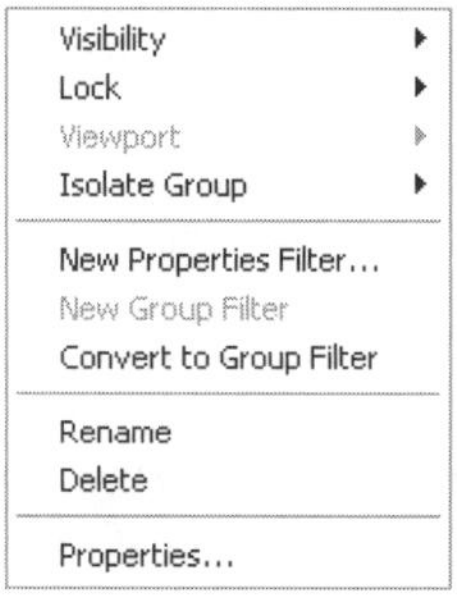

- **Visibility** presents you with the following submenu:

- You can turn all layers **On/Off**, or you can **Thaw/Freeze** all layers.
- **Lock** presents you with the following submenu:

- You can **Lock/Unlock** all layers.
- **Viewport** presents you with the following submenu (you must be in **Layout** for this option to be active):

- You can **Freeze/Thaw** all of these layers in the current viewport.
- **Isolate Group** will be discussed later in this chapter.
- **New Properties Filter** allows you to create a new property filter.
- **Convert to Group Filter** will not add a new layer to the list even if it fits the criteria of this filter.

- **Rename** and **Delete** allow you to rename or delete a filter, respectively (another method is to double-click the filter name).
- **Properties** allows you to modify the filter (another method is to double-click the filter name).

Right-Clicking a Group Filter

- If you right-click a group filter, the following menu will appear:

- This menu is identical to the **Property Filter** menu, except that the last choice is **Select Layers**.
- The **Select Layers** option is useful when you wish to include new layers inside the filter without naming them. Instead you can select objects that reside in the filter.
- The following prompt will appear:

```
Add layers of selected objects to filter...:
```

- Select an object in the desired filter to be added into the group filter.

ADVANCED LAYERS: THE PROPERTY AND GROUP FILTERS

Exercise 16-4
1. Start AutoCAD 2011.
2. Open the file *Exercise 16-4.dwg*.
3. Start the **Layer Properties Manager**.
4. How many layers are in this drawing? (*Answer: 74*)
5. How many used layers are in this drawing? (*Answer: 14*)

6. Using the drag-and-drop method, make the **Freeze** column the second column from the left.

7. Hide the **Description** column.

8. Sort layers in descending order according to their color. What is the name of the first layer now? (*Answer:* ***A-Area***)

9. Create a new property filter and name it **Structural Layers**. This layer will include all layers that start with "S."

10. How many structural layers are there? (*Answer: 11*)

11. Create a new group filter and name it **Annotation Layers**. Include the following layers:

    a. **A-Dim**

    b. **Text**

12. Right-click the **Annotation Layers** filter and choose **Select Layers/Add**. Select one of the grid lines and one of the circles.

13. Go to the **Annotation Layers** filter. You will find that two more layers were added. What are their names?

14. Right-click the **Annotation Layers** filter and select **Visibility/Frozen**.

15. Close the **Layer Properties Manager**, and review the effect of your changes.

16. Save and close the file.

16.9 ADVANCED LAYERS: THE LAYER STATES MANAGER

- While you are working in a drawing, you will specify many layer properties—**Freeze/Thaw, On/Off**, colors, and so on.

- At a certain stage of the development process, you can save the current state of the layers as is and retrieve it later.

- From the **Layer Properties Manager**, click the **Layer States Manager** button. You will see the following dialog box:

- Click the **New** button to create a new layer state. The following dialog box will appear:

- Type in the name of the new layer state and click **OK**. AutoCAD will save the current state of the layers.

- The question is, will AutoCAD save all of the elements related to the layers, or will it only save some of them?
- To answer this question, go to the lower right-hand corner of the dialog box and click on the small round button with an arrow pointing to the right. You will see the following:

- Under **Layer properties to restore**, select the desired properties.
- At any time, you can select options such as the following:
  - **Save** allows you to save the selected layer state.

- **Edit** allows you to edit the selected layer state. You will see the following dialog box and can change the properties as you wish:

- **Rename** and **Delete** allow you to rename or delete the selected layer state, respectively.
- **Import** and **Export** allow you to import layer states from other files or to export to other files, respectively.
- Once you are done, click the **Restore** button to restore the selected layer states, or click the **Close** button to close the dialog box without making any changes.
- NOTE ▶ You can issue the same command from outside the **Layer Properties Manager** as follows: On the **Ribbon**, go to the **Home** tab. Using the **Layers** panel, click the pop-up list above the layers list, then select **Manage Layer States**:

- You can also see the current layer state from the same panel:

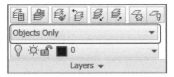

THE LAYER STATES MANAGER

Exercise 16-5

1. Start AutoCAD 2011.
2. Open the file *Exercise 16-5.dwg*.
3. Start the **Layer Properties Manager**.
4. Start the **Layer States Manager** and create a new state called **Original**. Enter the following description: "Original states without any change from my side."
5. Click **Close** to close the **Layer States Manager** dialog box.
6. Freeze the following layers: **A-Dim, S-Grid, S-Grid-Iden**, and **Text**.
7. Change the color of the **A-Wall** and **A-Wall-Prht** layers from yellow to blue.
8. Change the color of the **A-Window** layer from magenta to red.
9. Start the **Layer States Manager** and create a new state called **Objects Only**. Enter the following description: "Showing objects without annotation with some color changes."
10. Make sure all options are selected.
11. Click **Close** to close the **Layer States Manager** dialog box, then close the **Layer Properties Manager** palette.
12. Using the pop-up list in the **Layers** panel, restore the **Original** and then **Objects only** states.
13. Start the **Layer Properties Manager**.
14. Click the **Layer States Manager**, select **Objects Only**, and click **Edit**.
15. Change the color of the **A-Furn** layer to magenta.
16. Test the change.
17. Make sure that the current layer state is **Original**.
18. Start the **Layer Properties Manager**.

19. Select all layers, then deselect the **A-Wall** and **A-Wall-Prht** layers. Freeze all selected layers.

20. Start the **Layer States Manager** and create a new state called **Walls Only**. Enter the following description: "To show only the walls with the original colors."

21. Click **Close** to close the **Layer States Manager** dialog box, then close the **Layer Properties Manager** palette.

22. Try the three states you just made.

23. Save and close the file.

16.10 ADVANCED LAYERS: LAYER TRANSPARENCY

- You can control the visibility of a layer.
- By default, the transparency value for all layers is 0%, but it can be set as high as 90%.
- If you are making a test plot for a drawing with lots of solid hatching, you can set the visibility low to save ink.
- You can use the same color for several layers and control the visibility of the layers by giving each a different tone of the color.
- When you start the **Layer Properties Manager**, you will see a column called **Transparency**. If you are at a layout, you will see another column called **VP Transparency**:

- You can control the visibility of the new objects as follows: On the **Ribbon**, go to the **Home** tab. Using the **Properties** panel, you can set the visibility of the new objects by adjusting the slider, or you can use the **Transparency** button:

- If you select the **Transparency** button, choose either **ByLayer, ByBlock**, or **Transparency Value** (which will set the transparency to 0%).
- You can also set the transparency value for object(s) using the **Properties** palette, as shown:

- You can save the layer transparency as part of your layer states, as shown:

- Finally, using the **Status Bar**, you can choose whether to show or hide the transparency value:

ADVANCED LAYERS: LAYER TRANSPARENCY

Exercise 16-6

1. Start AutoCAD 2011.
2. Open the file *Exercise 16-6.dwg*.
3. As you can see, the solid hatching is very dark.
4. Using **Layer Properties Manager**, select the **Solid Hatch** layer and set **Transparency** = 50%.
5. For the **Wall Solid Hatch** layer, set **Transparency** = 60%.
6. Select the solid part of the corridor area, start the **Properties** palette, and set **Transparency** = 80%.
7. Using the **Status Bar**, click on **Show/Hide Transparency**.
8. Save and close the file.

16.11 ADVANCED LAYERS: THE SETTINGS DIALOG BOX

■ In the **Layer Properties Manager** palette, click the **Settings** button. You will see the following dialog box:

■ This dialog box consists of three parts:
   • **New Layer Notification**
   • **Isolate Layer Settings**
   • **Dialog Settings**

New Layer Notification

- In accordance with the CAD standards discussed at the beginning of this chapter, the user should not add any new layers to his or her drawing, whether intentionally or unintentionally.
- AutoCAD will notify the user if layers are added. See the following:

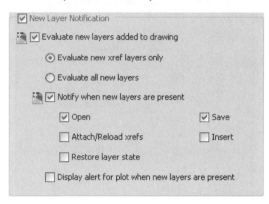

- First, select whether you would like to be notified.
- If yes, select whether to **Evaluate new layers added to drawing**.
- If yes, select which type of layers (**XREF** layers or all layers).
- Now select when you would like to be notified (e.g., when opening the file, when saving the file).
- Lastly, you can choose to be alerted if any new layers have been added when you use the **Plot** command.

Isolate Layer Settings

- The **Isolate** command will be discussed shortly. You must decide how you want the other layers that are not isolated to appear. You can **Lock and fade** them (you can select the fading percentage), or you can turn them **Off**. The following shows the user selecting the **Lock and fade** option:

- The following shows the user selecting the **Off** option:

  > Isolate Layer Settings
  >
  > Setting for layers not isolated
  >
  > ○ Lock and fade
  >
  >   🔒   Locked Layer Fading   50%
  >
  > ◉ Off
  >
  >   In paper space viewport use
  >
  >   ◉ Off
  >
  >   ○ VP Freeze

Dialog Settings

- These three settings apply to the **Layer Properties** palette. See the following:

  > Dialog Settings
  >
  > ☑ Apply layer filter to layer toolbar
  >
  > ☑ Indicate layers in use
  >
  > Viewport override background color:
  >
  > ☐ 203,236,255

- Select whether to **Apply layer filter to layer toolbar**.
- Select whether to **Indicate layers in use**. See the following:

  > | S.. | Name | |
  > |---|---|---|
  > | ✔ | 0 | |
  > | ▱ | A-Area | |
  > | ▱ | A-Clng | |
  > | ▱ | A-Detl | |
  > | ▱ | A-Dim | |
  > | ▱ | A-Door | |
  > | ▱ | A-Elev | |

- Layers in use are the layers that contain a single object. Can you tell from the preceding illustration which layers are in use?
- In Chapter 10, we discussed the layer override in viewports. To distinguish them from the others, what is the suitable background color?

Unreconciled Layers

- If a new layer is added, AutoCAD will inform you according to the method you chose in the preceding dialog box.

- The information will be displayed in the **Status Bar**, as follows:

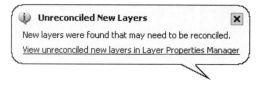

- When you click **View unreconciled new layers** in the **Layer Properties Manager**, you will see something like the following:

- As you can see, AutoCAD created a new filter called **Unreconciled New Layers**. You can see these layers at the right.
- To reconcile any of these layers, simply right-click the name of the layer and select the **Reconcile Layer** option.

16.12 ADVANCED LAYERS: ADVANCED LAYER FUNCTIONS

- We will now cover a group of functions that will make your life much easier!
- Advanced layer functions enable you to carry out a variety of tasks with a single click.

- To access these commands, do as follows: On the **Ribbon**, go to the **Home** tab. Using the **Layers** panel, select from the options shown in the following illustration:

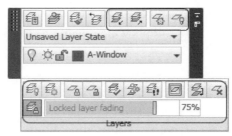

- You will see the **Isolate** and **Unisolate** buttons.

- **Isolate** a layer allows you to turn off (or lock) every layer except the desired layer. The following prompt will appear:

```
Current setting: Hide layers, Viewports=Off
Select objects on the layer(s) to be isolated or [Settings]:
(Select the desired object.)
Layer A-Doors has been isolated.
```

- **Unisolate** allows you to turn on (or unlock) the other layers. There are no prompts for this function.
- You will see the **Freeze** and **Off** buttons.

- **Freeze** and **Off** allow you to turn off a layer by selecting an object that resides in the layer. The following prompts will appear:

```
Current settings: Viewports=Vpfreeze, Block nesting
level=Block
Select an object on the layer to be frozen or [Settings/
Undo]: (Select the desired object.)
Layer "A-Doors" has been frozen.
Select an object on the layer to be frozen or [Settings/
Undo]: (Select another object, and so on.)
```

- You will see the **Turn All Layers On** and **Thaw All Layers** buttons.

- These commands allow you to reverse the effects of the **Freeze** and **Off** commands.
- There are no prompts for these two commands.

- You will see the **Lock** and **Unlock** buttons.

- **Lock** allows you to lock layer(s) by selecting an object that resides in the layer. The following prompts will appear:

```
Select an object on the layer to be locked:
(Select the desired object.)
Layer "A-Plumbing" has been locked.
```

- You can lock one layer at a time.
- **Unlock** will reverse this command. There are no prompts for this function.
- You will see the **Change to Current Layer** button.
- This command allows you to move selected objects from their layers to the current layer. The following prompts will appear:

```
Select objects to be changed to the current layer:
(Select an object.)
Select objects to be changed to the current layer:
(Continue selecting. When you are done, press [Enter].)
3 objects changed to layer "A-Doors" (the current layer).
```

- You will see the **Copy Objects to New Layer** button.
- This command allows you to create a copy of selected objects and transfer them from one layer to another. The following prompts will appear:

```
Select objects to copy: (Select desired objects.)
Select objects to copy: (When you are done, press [Enter].)
Select object on destination layer or [Name] <Name>:
(Either type a name of the layer, or select an object in the
desired layer.)
3 object(s) copied and placed on layer "Partition".
Specify base point or [Displacement/eXit] <eXit>: Specify
second point of displacement or <use first point as
displacement>:
```

- As you can see, the last three prompts are identical to the **Copy** command.
- You will see the **Layer Walk** button.
- If you click this button, you will see a dialog box. By default, all layers are selected. If you click any layer name, the objects that reside in this specific layer will be shown and the others will disappear.

- You can select multiple layers by holding [Ctrl] and selecting. See the following example:

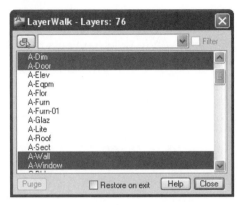

- You will see the **Isolate to Current Viewport** button.
- In Chapter 10, we discussed how to freeze a layer in one viewport and thaw it in another.
- Using this command, you can freeze a layer in all viewports except the current viewport. The following prompts will appear:

```
Current settings: Layouts=Current Layout, Block nesting
level=Block
Select an object on the layer to be isolated in viewport or
[Settings/Undo]: (Select the desired object.)
Layer Text has been frozen in all viewports but the
current one.
Select an object on the layer to be isolated in viewport or
[Settings/Undo]: (Continue selecting objects until you are
done, then press [Enter].)
```

- You will see the **Merge** button.
- This command allows you to merge one or more layers into another layer by selecting objects that reside in these layers. The last layer selected will stay, and the others will be deleted. The following prompts will appear:

```
Select object on layer to merge or [Name]:
Selected layers: A-Doors.
Select object on layer to merge or [Name/Undo]:
Selected layers: A-Doors, A-Windows.
Select object on layer to merge or [Name/Undo]:
Select object on target layer or [Name]:
******** WARNING ********
You are about to merge 2 layers into layer "Partition".
Do you wish to continue? [Yes/No] <No>: Y
```

```
Deleting layer "A-Doors".
Deleting layer "A-Windows".
2 layers deleted.
```

- You will see the **Delete** button.
- This command allows you to delete objects in the selected layer and purge them. The following prompts will appear:

```
Select object on layer to delete or [Name]:
Selected layers: Partition.
Select object on layer to delete or [Name/Undo]:
******** WARNING ********
You are about to delete layer "Partition" from this drawing.
Do you wish to continue? [Yes/No] <No>: Y
Deleting layer "Partition".
1 layer deleted.
```

THE SETTINGS DIALOG BOX AND ADVANCED FUNCTIONS

Exercise 16-7
1. Start AutoCAD 2011.
2. Open the file *Exercise 16-7.dwg*.
3. Start the **Layer Properties Manager** and click the **Settings** button.
4. Turn **New Layer Notification** on and make the following changes:
   a. **Evaluate new layers added to drawing** = on
   b. **Evaluate all new layers** = on
   c. **Notify when new layers are present** = on
   d. **Open** = on
   e. **Save** = on
5. Under **Isolate Layer Settings**, make the following changes:
   a. **Lock and fade** = on
   b. **Fade %** = 75%
6. Under **Dialog Settings**, make the following change:
   a. **Indicate layers in use** = off
7. Close the dialog box and the **Layer Properties Manager**.
8. Start the **Isolate** command and select one object in the **A-Wall** layer. Press [Enter] to finish the command.
9. If you approach any other object, you will notice that the lock symbol appears, indicating this object is locked. You will also notice the fading percentage.

10. Use the **Unisolate** command to return to the original settings.

11. Start the **Layer Walk** command and click inside the dialog box to remove any selection. Select the **A-Wall, A-Wall-Prht, A-Door**, and **A-Window** layers.

12. Turn off **Restore on exit** and click **Close**. At the alert, click **Continue**.

13. Start the **Layer Properties Manager** and notice how the other layers are turned off.

14. Close the **Layer Properties Manager**.

15. Click the **Turn All Layers On** button.

16. Start the **Merge** command and click any object in layer **A-Wall-Prht** (the inner partition objects), then press [Enter]. Select any object in **A-Wall**. When the question "Do you wish to continue?" appears, click **Yes**. Check the layers. What happens to layer **A-Wall-Prht**?

17. Add a new layer called **A-Furn-01** and save the file. Does AutoCAD give you any warning concerning unreconciled layers? Click the bubble to check the unreconciled layers. Select the name of the layer, right-click, and select the **Reconcile** option. What happens to the filter?

18. Save and close the file.

CHAPTER REVIEW

1. The **Layer Translator** command is a good alternative to CAD standards.
   a. True
   b. False

2. If the layers you want to put together have nothing in common, use the _____ **filter**.

3. You can control whether the isolated layers are turned off or locked.
   a. True
   b. False

4. Which of the following statements is *not* correct?
   a. You must create a DWS file to be eligible to check CAD standards.
   b. A DWS file is a file you create using the **Save As** command.
   c. A DWS file is a file you create using the **CAD Standards** panel and the **DWS Create** button.
   d. You must link your DWG file to DWS to check CAD standards.

5. Which one of these statements is *not* true about the **Isolate** command?

    a. There is a **Unisolate** command.

    b. You can **Isolate** more than one layer using the same command.

    c. Other layers will be frozen.

    d. You can control the fading percentage from the **Settings** dialog box and the **Layers** panel.

6. If you want to delete a layer and put all of its objects in another layer, you must use the _____ command.

CHAPTER REVIEW ANSWERS

1. b

2. **Group**

3. a

4. c

5. c

6. **Merge**

Chapter 17

AUTODESK DESIGN REVIEW AND THE MARKUP SET MANAGER

In This Chapter
◊ The **Publish** command
◊ **Autodesk Design Review**
◊ DWF files and markups
◊ **Markup set manager**
◊ Comparing DWF files

17.1 INTRODUCTION

- We have already discussed how important the DWF file is to the AutoCAD user and how it can solve multiple problems.
- To view a DWF file, you must have Autodesk Design Review.
- Autodesk Design Review comes with many markup tools that help design teams conduct their reviewing process electronically.
- The following is a hypothetical scenario illustrating how engineering firms did their work prior to electronic reviews:
  - When an engineer (or draftsman) finished a drawing, he or she printed it and took it to the supervisor for review and commenting.
  - Assuming the drawing was not lost among stacks of paper, the supervisor would review it, adding revision clouds, remarks, comments, and so on.
  - The supervisor would call the engineer and sit down with him or her to discuss all the remarks and notes added to the drawing.
  - The engineer would return to his or her desk, load the AutoCAD drawing, and make the requested alterations.
  - The engineer would print the revised drawing and send it again, possibly forgetting to attach the old drawing with the remarks to the new printout.
  - The boss would review the new drawing and request more adjustments.
  - Most likely, no one was keeping track of all of these changes, resulting in an inaccurate final design.

- In this process, we can easily highlight the following costs:
  - The supplies required to produce repeated drawings, including ink, paper, and electricity.
  - The time for the employee to leave his or her desk to send the drawing, pick it up, resend it, and so on (bearing in mind that he or she may need to leave the building if the boss is located elsewhere).
  - The inability to precisely track the changes to the drawing.
- These factors could all lead to errors in the final drawing and, therefore, a bad output or product.
- If we truly learn to use the process of AutoCAD and Autodesk Design Review, and if we master the tools available, our reviewing process will be faster, more efficient, and more accurate.

17.2 THE PUBLISH COMMAND

- You can publish DWF files in AutoCAD using three different commands:
  - The **Plot** command uses a *DWF6 ePlot.pc3* printer that will produce a single-sheet DWF.
  - The **Publish** command will produce a multisheet DWF file and include information such as layers, block information, views, etc.
  - The **EXPORTDWF** command will also produce a multisheet DWF file and include information such as layers, block information, views, etc.
- We will concentrate on the **Publish** command.
- On the **Ribbon**, go to the **Output** tab. Using the **Plot** panel, click the **Batch Plot** button:

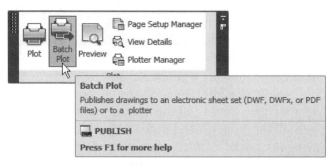

■ The following dialog box will appear:

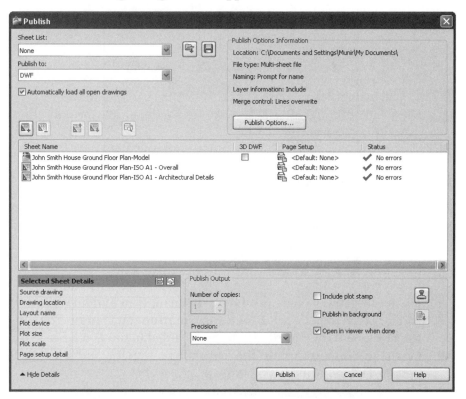

■ This dialog box was covered in earlier chapters, but we will now look at some features that have not been discussed.

Publish Options

■ The **Publish Options** dialog box dictates what the DWF does and does not contain.

- You will see the following:

- Do not forget to include the **Layer Information** in the DWF file.
- Also, you can include the **Block Information** (attributes). You must select the blocks and their attributes to be included in the DWF file.
- Go to the **Block template file**, click the pop-up list, and select the **Create** option. The following dialog box will appear:

- Click the **Scan for Blocks** button. A list of blocks and their properties will be shown.
- Beneath the block list, you will find an option to **Exclude blocks without attributes**. Check this box if you want the DWF file to include only block information related to blocks with attributes.
- Beneath the properties list, you will find an option to **Exclude general block properties**. Check this box if you want the DWF file to include only attributes.
- The dialog box will resemble the following:

- Once you are done, click **Save**. AutoCAD will show the **Save As** dialog box, and you will save it as a DXE file. The next time you want to publish a DWF file and you want to include the same information, you can call this file instead of going through the whole process again.

THE PUBLISH COMMAND

Exercise 17-1
1. Start AutoCAD 2011.
2. Open the file *Exercise 17-1.dwg*.

3. Start the **Publish** command.

4. Remove the **Model** sheet from the sheet list.

5. Make sure that **Publish to** = DWF.

6. Click the **Publish Options** button and make sure of the following:

   a. **Type** = Multisheet file

   b. **Layer Information** = Include

   c. Change **Precision** = For Architecture

7. Save the DWF file in your Exercise folder and name it *Ground Floor.dwf*.

8. Save the DWG file and close it.

17.3 AUTODESK DESIGN REVIEW

- Autodesk Design Review comes on the same DVD as AutoCAD 2011. You can also download it from the Autodesk website at no charge.

Autodesk
Design Review

- Double-click the Autodesk Design Review icon on your computer's desktop to start the software (you can also double-click any DWF file to start the software).

- You will see the following:

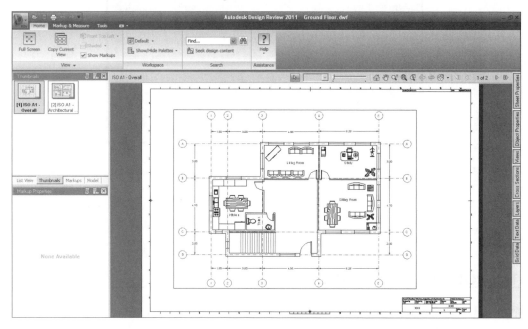

- The interface is similar to the AutoCAD interface (**Ribbons, Application Menu, Quick Access Toolbar**, etc.).
- You will notice a few other elements on your screen:
    - There are several palettes on the left-hand side.
    - The **Canvas** and **Canvas toolbar** cover most of the screen.
    - On the right-hand side, there are tabs showing various details about the DWF file.
- By default, when you open a DWF file, the **Thumbnails, Sheet Properties, Object Properties**, and **Layers** palettes will display information.

Thumbnails

- The **Thumbnails** palette will resemble the following:

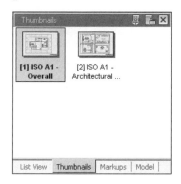

- Another view is the **List View**:

- Using either view, you can see the sheets by clicking either the thumbnail or a name in the list.

NOTE ▶ ■ If you use the **Canvas toolbar** at the top right-hand portion of the **Canvas**, you will see something like the following:

◁॥ ◁ 2 of 2 ▷ ॥▷

■ You can browse through the sheets forward and backward. You can also go to the beginning and end of the list of the sheets.
■ At the right, there is a group of tabs that will show information about the DWF file or its components.

Sheet Properties

■ If you hover over the **Sheet Properties** tab, you will see something like the following:

Sheet Properties	
Name	Value
⊟	
Author	Munir
Creation Time	28-Feb-10 16:29:43
Modification Time	28-Feb-10 16:29:43
Sheet Name	ISO A1 - Overall
Sheet Size	841.0 x 594.0 mm
⊟ **AutoCAD Drawing**	
Author	
Comments	
Copyright	
Creation Time	19-Oct-08 12:14:22
Creator	AutoCAD 2011 Relea
Description	
File Name	Exercise 17-1 Solved
Keywords	
Layout Name	ISO A1 - Overall
Modification Time	28-Feb-10 16:19:39
Subject	
Title	ISO A1 - Overall

Object Properties

■ If you hover over the **Object Properties** tab, you will see the properties you chose to carry with you from the DWG file.
■ To select the desired block, you must be in the **Select** mode, which you will find in the **Canvas toolbar**:

■ You will see something like the following:

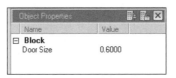

Object Properties	
Name	Value
⊟ **Block**	
Door Size	0.6000

Layers

- If you hover over the **Layers** tab, you will see something like the following:

On	Name
♀	A-Doors
♀	A-Walls
♀	A-Windows
♀	Centerlines
♀	Centerlines-TAGS
♀	Dimensions
♀	Furniture
♀	Staircase
♀	Text
♀	Title Block
♀	Viewport

- You can turn on or off any layer you wish.
- NOTE ▶ You cannot open more than one file per Autodesk Design Review session.
- However, you can open more than one session of Autodesk Design Review software at a time.

17.4 PANNING AND ZOOMING

- You can pan and zoom a DWF file inside Autodesk Design Review using the mouse's wheel just as you would do with a DWG in AutoCAD.
- In addition, there are some extra functions available in the toolbars and menus that will help you pan and zoom.
- You will see the following:

Panning and Zooming

- You can use:
  - **Zoom Rectangle** (**Zoom Window**)
  - **Fit to Window**
  - **Zoom In/Out** (**Zoom Realtime** in AutoCAD)
  - **Pan**
  - **Home**
  - **Select**

Steering Wheel

- The **Steering Wheel** is mainly a 3D tool. You can use it in 2D drawings as
  well, but it is not as effective. Start the **Steering Wheel** command from the
  toolbar. You will see the following:

- You can pan if you are in the outer circle. Simply click and hold.
- You can zoom if you are in the inner circle. Again, simply click and hold.

17.5 THE FORMATTING PANEL

- The **Formatting** panel, which is accessed from the **Markup & Measure**
  tab, allows you to format your markup if you need to add text or a shape
  (e.g., line, box, circle, callouts).

Text Formatting

- Start the **Text** command (it will be discussed shortly).
- The panel appear as follows:

- You can do the following:
  - Change the size of text.
  - Change the color of text.
  - Make text bold or regular.

Line Formatting

- Start the **Object Creation** command to format lines, polylines, rectangles, etc.
- The panel will appear as follows:

- You can do the following:
  - Set the lineweight.
  - Set the line color.
  - Set the linetype.
  - Set the fill color.
  - Set the fill transparency.
  - Select whether to use borders.
  - Set the line endpoint style for the start and end.

17.6 THE CALLOUTS PANEL

- The **Callouts** panel allows you to insert callouts with different shapes.
- The panel appears as follows:

- There are nine different callout shapes, some with revision clouds and some without.
  - If you do not have a revision cloud, you will specify two points—the first one at the start of the line segment and the second one at the location of the callout. You will see something like the following:

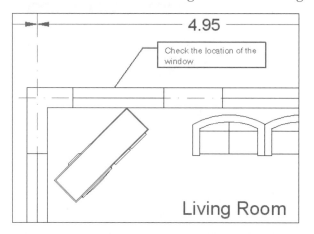

  - If you have a revision cloud, you will first specify the revision cloud by specifying two opposite corners (as you did for a rectangle); second, specify the location of the callout. You will see something like the following:

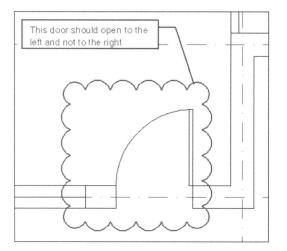

17.7 THE DRAW PANEL

- The **Draw** panel allows you to draw any shape you want in your DWF.
- The panel appears as follows:

- You can do the following:
  - Draw lines (one segment at a time).
  - Draw polylines (multisegment).
  - Draw freehand shapes.
  - Draw rectangles.
  - Draw ellipses (or circles).
  - Write text.
  - Use the freehand highlighter.
  - Use the rectangle highlighter.
  - Insert rectangular clouds.
  - Insert polyclouds.

17.8 THE MEASURE PANEL

- Before you use this tool, make sure that **Snap to Geometry** is active (to do so, go to the **Home** tab and select it from the **View** panel):

- The **Measure** panel appears as follows:

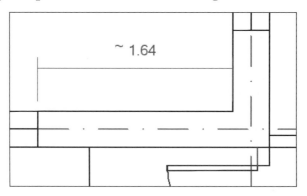

- Only three options are available for 2D DWF files: **Length**, **Area**, and **Polyline**.

Length

- You can measure a length between any two points and any angle.
- Specify two points. You will see something like the following:

~ 1.64

Area

- You can measure the area of any shape with straight lines.
- Specify the points. You will see something like the following:

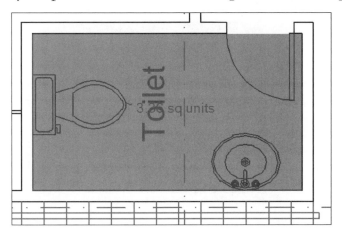

Polylines

- You can add up the length of line segments.
- This method allows you to measure the perimeter of an object that consists of straight lines.
- Specify the points. You will see something like the following:

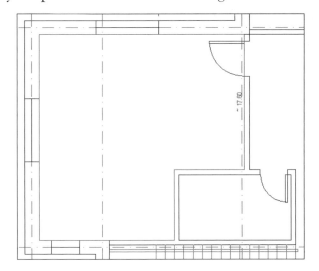

17.9 THE STAMPS AND SYMBOLS PANEL

- You can add stamps to the DWF declaring the current status of the file.
- You will see the following panel:

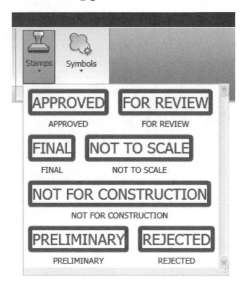

- To apply a stamp, simply click on a suitable place in the file.

17.10 EDITING MARKUP OBJECTS

- Once you add **Markup** objects to your DWF file, you will be able to edit these objects.
- To edit, you must do the following:
    - Make sure you are in the **Select** mode before you start editing.
    - Click the desired object (you can select multiple **Markup** objects by holding [Shift] and clicking objects).
- As an example, let's consider the process of inserting a callout. This same process is used for inserting all **Markup** objects.

Callouts

■ Click the callout and you will see something like the following:

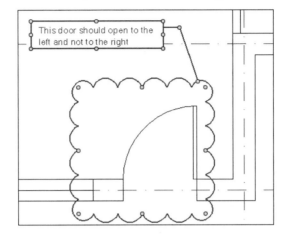

■ You can do the following:
  • Resize the revision cloud.
  • Resize the box containing text.
  • Double-click the text for editing and formatting (you can use the **Formatting** panel to format the text).
  • Delete the callout by pressing [Delete].

17.11 SAVING MARKUPS

■ After adding all of your markups, you can view the **Markups** palette, which will resemble the following:

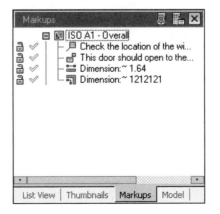

- All the markups are sorted by time of insertion.
- You can click any one of these to zoom to it and select it.
- The **Markup Properties** palette will show a full description of the selected markup, as shown:

- When you are satisfied with your markup process, save all of these markups to your DWF file.
- From the **Application menu**, select **Save**.
- You can also use **Save As** if you want to save it under another name. However, saving it under the same name is better for revision follow-up and history tracking.

MARKUP OF A DWF FILE

Exercise 17-2

1. Start AutoCAD 2011.
2. Double-click the file you created in the previous exercise, *Ground Floor. dwf.*
3. Browse to see the two sheets. Zoom in and zoom out, and use pan.
4. Using the **Overall** sheet, measure the inner width and height of the **Living room**. What are they?

5. Calculate the area of the **Study room**. What is it (in m²)?

6. Input a rectangular cloud with a rectangular callout around the small toilet beside the kitchen. In the callout, type the following statement: "I want to see you to discuss the location of the toilet."

7. Turn off the layer **A-Door** and check how many doors turn off.

8. Turn off the layer **Dimensions** and check if the other doors disappear.

9. Turn on layer **A-Door** and **Dimensions**.

10. Zoom to the door of the small toilet and make a rectangle callout showing the following statement: "This is the only door in the **A-Door** layer. The rest are in the **Dimensions** layer."

11. Create a text box near the same door and type, "Flip the door opening."

12. Put a **For Review** stamp in the **Overall** sheet.

13. Check the **Markups** palette. To review the different markups, you can click on each one to make sure you input the right words and remarks.

14. Save the DWF file under the same name, and close the file.

17.12 THE MARKUP SET MANAGER

- After your supervisor finishes reviewing your DWF, you will need to make the requested corrections.

- To see the markup in AutoCAD, you must load the **Markup Set Manager**. On the **Ribbon**, go to the **View** tab. Using the **Palettes** panel, click **Markup Set Manager**:

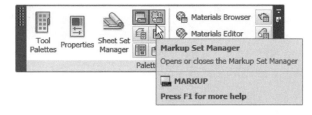

- You will see the following palette:

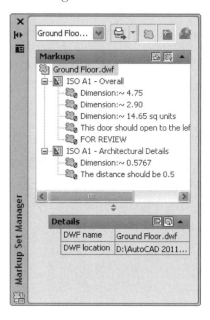

- From the drop-down menu, select **Open**. An **Open file** dialog box will appear, allowing you to select a DWF with markups.
- You will see the following:

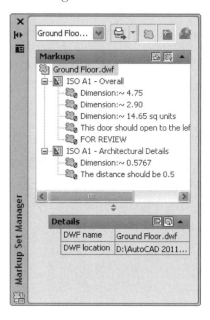

- You can see the markup as a tree.
- If you click the sheet node of the tree using the **Details** button, you will see the following:

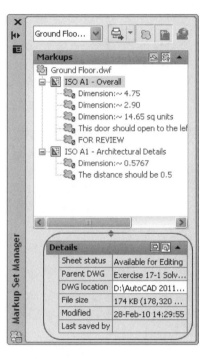

- The two most important pieces of information are **Parent DWG** and **DWG location**. As you can see, the only editable field is the location, which means if your file has moved for some reason, you can use the **Markup Set Manager** to find the file again.
- You can see the markup as a tree. If you click (not double-click) one of the markups, you can see **Details** and **Preview**.

Details

- In the **Details** portion, you will see the following:

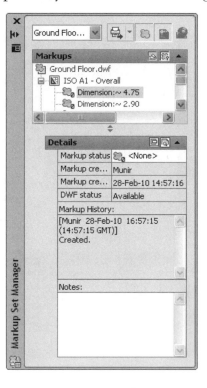

- There are six settings you can control:
  - **Markup status** allows you to set the status of your current markup. You can choose from **None, Question, For Review**, and **Done**:

  - You can post the status according to your case. For example, if you did what your supervisor specified, then change the status to **Done**.
  - **Markup creator** and **Markup created** allow you to add the name of the person who made the markups and the time these markups were made.

- **DWF status** indicates whether this DWF is available for editing.
- **Markup History** keeps track of the markups (who made them and when).
- **Notes** allows you to post special notes.

Preview

■ In the **Preview** portion, you will see the following:

■ If you double-click any markup, the original DWG will be opened along with the DWF file with the markups. AutoCAD will zoom to the markup selected. At the top right-hand side of the palette, you will see the following:

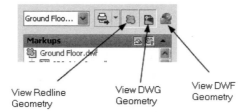

■ The two buttons at the right—**View DWG Geometry** and **View DWF Geometry**—cancel each other out; therefore, by default, the first is turned on and the second is turned off.
■ When you make your changes, turn off the DWF geometry.

- The third button allows you to turn off the redlining that took place in the Autodesk Design Review software.
- Once you make your changes, you can republish the DWF file with the adjustments. Click the **Republish Markup DWF** button. You will see the following:

- Choose between **Republish All Sheets** and **Republish Markup Sheets** only.
- It is highly recommended you rename the file in a manner that indicates the revision number, such as *name_rev_01.dwf*. This way, you can compare versions of the file.

THE MARKUP SET MANAGER

Exercise 17-3

1. Start AutoCAD 2011.
2. Create a new file.
3. Using the **View** tab and the **Palettes** panel, click the **Markup Set Manager**.
4. Click **Open** and locate the DWF you changed in Exercise 17-2.
5. Double-click **ISO A1 – Overall**. The file will open with markups.
6. Double-click **Dimension: ~ 4.75 m and 2.90 m** and change the markup status to **Done**.
7. Double-click **Dimension: ~ 14.63 m²** and change the markup status to **Done**.
8. Double-click "I want to see you to discuss the toilet location," and change the markup status to **Question**. In the **Notes** part, type, "Kindly specify time and location."
9. Change the layer of the doors to layer **A-Doors** (you can do so in the **Model space**). Also, flip the door of the small toilet to open to the left, not the right.
10. Double-click "This is the only door…" and change the markup status to **Done**.
11. Change the status of "Flip the door opening" to **Done**.

12. Double-click **For Review** and change the markup status to **Done**.

13. Select **Republish Markup Sheets**, rename the file *Ground Floor Rev 01.dwf*, and save it in the Exercise folder.

14. Close the **Markup** DWF.

15. Save and close the DWG file.

17.13 MAKING COMPARISONS

- Up until now, we have performed the following steps:

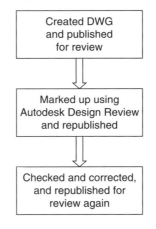

- The next step is for the supervisor to review the DWF again, comparing the first file to the new file to confirm that the appropriate edits were made.

- When you open the modified file, check the **Markups** palette. You will see something like the following:

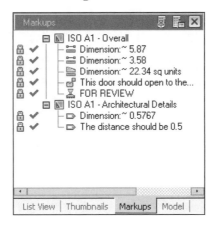

- This palette will tell you about the markups and their current status.
- In our example, the user marked the status as **Done** for all the markups.
- To make sure, compare the two files.
- To compare sheets, do as follows: On the **Ribbon**, go to the **Tools** tab. Using the **Canvas** panel, click **Compare Sheets**:

- The following dialog box will appear:

- Click the **Browse** button and select your old file. You will see something like the following:

- Click the **Options** button. You will see the following dialog box:

- Any addition will be shown in green, and any deletion will be shown in red.

- Click **OK**, then **OK**.
- You will see something like the following:

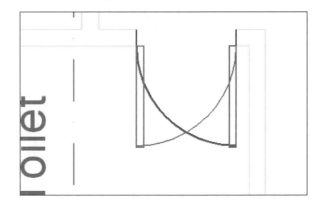

- You can see the markup, the old opening of the door, and the new opening of the door.

COMPARING TWO DWF FILES

Exercise 17-4
1. Start Autodesk Design Review.
2. Open the *Ground Floor Rev 01.dwf* file you created in Exercise 17-3.
3. Click the only markup with a question mark (**?**). Go to the **Markup Properties** palette.
4. You can see the label and its current status. Check the **History** field and you will see the note that you posted in AutoCAD.
5. Click **Compare Sheets**, load the old file (*Ground Floor.dwf*), and select **ISO A1 – Overall**.
6. You can see the previous status of the door and the new status of the new door.
7. Save the DWF file and close it.

CHAPTER REVIEW

1. You can include layer information in the DWF file.
   a. True
   a. False
2. The name of the software that comes with AutoCAD to read and mark up a DWF is _____.
3. Which of the following are you unable to do in a DWF while viewing it?
   a. Measure a distance.
   b. Calculate an area.
   c. Change the layer of an object.
   d. Insert a cloud with a callout.
4. Which of these statements is *not* true about marking up?
   a. You can republish a DWF with modifications in AutoCAD.
   b. AutoCAD cannot load DWF files.
   c. You can change the status of the markup inside AutoCAD.
   d. The **Markup Set Manager** is the tool used to load DWF files.
5. You can input a markup with a hexagon-shaped callout.
   a. True
   b. False

CHAPTER REVIEW ANSWERS

1. a
2. Autodesk Design Review
3. c
4. b
5. b

Appendix A

CREATING A TEMPLATE FILE

In This Appendix
◇ What is a template file?
◇ Which elements are included in a template file?
◇ How is a template file created?

A.1 INTRODUCTION

- Companies using AutoCAD are always seek:
  - Ways to unify their work to a certain standard (homemade or international).
  - Ways to speed up the process of producing a drawing.
- Template files are the answer
- Template files reassure the decisionmakers in any company that premade settings for the drawings are already included in the templates, thus cutting production time by at least 30%.
- Templates also guarantee that everyone will be using the same source.
- Template files have the extension *.dwt*.

A.2 WHICH ELEMENTS ARE INCLUDED IN A TEMPLATE FILE?

The following elements are included in a template file:
- **Drawing units**
- **Drawing limits**
- **Grid** and **Snap** settings
- **Layers**

- **Linetypes**
- **Text Styles**
- **Dimension Styles**
- **Table Styles**
- **Layouts** (including **Border blocks** and **Viewports**)
- **Page Setups**
- **Plot Style tables**

NOTE ➤
- There is no need to include blocks in the template file; instead, store them in files and put each category in a separate file (e.g., Architectural, Civil, Mechanical, etc.).
- You cannot save **Tool Palettes** inside a template file. Tool Palettes are unique to each computer.

A.3 HOW IS A TEMPLATE FILE CREATED?

- Start AutoCAD.
- Do the paperwork to prepare the necessary settings. This step may require consultation with other people who operate AutoCAD within the same company.
- Create a new file using the simplest template file *acad.dwt*.
- The new file will contain the minimum drawing requirements.
- Build all the necessary elements inside this file (as described in the previous section).

- Once you are done, select **Save As** and **AutoCAD Drawing Template** from the application menu:

- The following dialog box will appear:

- Type in the template file name.
- By default, you can save your file in the same template folder that comes with the AutoCAD software. Or you can create your own folder to accommodate all of your template files.
- It is highly recommended that you store your files in a different folder away from the AutoCAD folders.
- You can create as many templates as you wish.

■   If you want to edit an existing template, simply do the following:
    •   Select **Open**, then **Drawing** from the application menu:

- At **Files of type**, select **Drawing Template (*.dwt)**:

- Open the desired template and make the desired changes.
- Save it under the same name or use a new name.

Appendix **B** **I**NQUIRY **C**OMMANDS

In This Appendix
◊ Introduction to inquiry commands
◊ The **Distance** command
◊ The **Radius** command
◊ The **Angle** command
◊ The **Area** command

B.1 INTRODUCTION

- Inquiry commands are used to:
  - Measure a distance between two points.
  - Measure the radius of a circle or arc.
  - Measure an angle.
  - Calculate the area between points or of an object.
- AutoCAD provides a single command—the **MEASUREGEOM** command—that includes all of these functions.
- You can also reach these functions from the **Ribbon** by using the **Home** tab and selecting the **Utilities** panel.

B.2 THE DISTANCE COMMAND

- Use the **Distance** command to measure the distance between two points.
- On the **Ribbon**, go to the **Home** tab. Using the **Utilities** panel, click the **Distance** button:

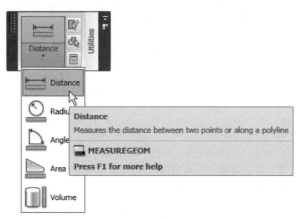

- AutoCAD will display the following prompt:

```
Specify first point: (Specify first point.)
Specify second point: (Specify second point.)
```

- After clicking on the two desired points, AutoCAD will display something like:

```
Distance = 10.0000,  Angle in XY Plane = 0,  Angle from XY
Plane = 0
Delta X = 10.0000,  Delta Y = 0.0000,   Delta Z = 0.0000
```

B.3 THE RADIUS COMMAND

- Use the **Radius** command to measure the radius of a circle or arc.
- On the **Ribbon**, go to the **Home** tab. Using the **Utilities** panel, click the **Radius** button:

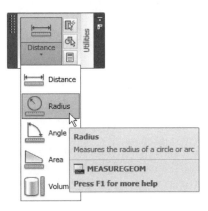

- AutoCAD will display the following prompt:

Select arc or circle: *(Select the desired arc or circle.)*

- After selecting the desired arc or circle, AutoCAD will display something like:

Radius = 6.6294
Diameter = 13.2588

B.4 THE ANGLE COMMAND

- Use the **Angle** command to measure the angle between two lines included in an arc, between a circle's center and two points, or between a selected vertex and two points.

- On the **Ribbon**, go to the **Home** tab. Using the **Utilities** panel, click the **Angle** button:

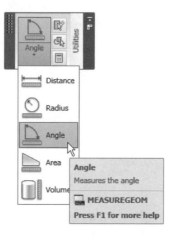

- AutoCAD will display the following prompt:

```
Select arc, circle, line, or <Specify vertex>:
```

- These are identical to the requirements of the **Angular dimension**.
- After selecting the desired arc or circle, AutoCAD will display something like:

```
Angle = 120°
```

B.5 THE AREA COMMAND

- Use the **Area** command to calculate the area between points or the area of an object.
- On the **Ribbon**, go to the **Home** tab. Using the **Utilities** panel, click the **Area** button:

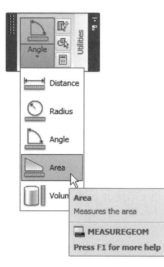

- You can calculate the area for:
    - Points, assuming there are lines connecting them.
    - Objects such as circles or polylines (closed or open).
- You can calculate two types of areas:
    - *Simple* areas (single area).
    - *Complex* areas (areas inside areas for which you want the net area).
- If you start the **Area** command and specify the points or select the object, AutoCAD will calculate the simple area.
- To calculate the complex area, you must start with either **Add** or **Subtract**.
- Click the **Area** button.
- AutoCAD will display the following prompt:

```
Specify first corner point or [Object/Add area/Subtract area/
eXit] <Object>:
```

Specify the First Corner

- A simple area consists of points connected by lines or arcs. Specify the first point and AutoCAD will prompt:

```
Specify next point or [Arc/Length/Undo]:
Specify next point or [Arc/Length/Undo]:
Specify next point or [Arc/Length/Undo/Total] <Total>:
(After the third point, you can ask for the total value of
the area measured.)
Specify next point or [Arc/Length/Undo/Total] <Total>:
```

- Continue specifying points until you press [Enter] to get the total value of the measured area. The following message will appear:

```
Area = 33.3750, Perimeter = 23.6264
```

Object

- To calculate the area by selecting an object such as a circle or a polyline, press [Enter], as the **Object** option is the default option. You can also type **O** or right-click and select **Object**. AutoCAD will prompt:

```
Select objects:
```

- Once you select the desired object, AutoCAD will report the following (in this example, the object is a circle):

```
Area = 28.2743, Circumference = 18.8496
```

Add Area/Subtract Area

- You need the **Add Area** mode and the **Subtract Area** mode to calculate a complex area—which is an area inside another area—in order to get the net area.
- Start with either one of these two modes, and AutoCAD will assume that you are starting with **Area** = 0.00. Hence, you will add the outer area, then subtract the inner areas; or you can subtract the inner areas, then add the outer area.
- Assume you started with the **Add area** mode. AutoCAD will prompt you:

```
Specify first corner point or [Object/Subtract area/eXit]:
```

- You can specify the area(s) using either points or an object. When you are done, switch to the **Subtract area** mode, and so on.
- While you are adding and subtracting, AutoCAD will give you the current value of the area until the last area is added/subtracted.
- Once you are done, press [Enter] twice and AutoCAD will report to you the final value of the area.

Add Area/Subtract Area

- The following are possible prompts for **Add area/Subtract area**:

```
Specify first corner point or [Object/Add area/Subtract area/
eXit] <Object>: A
Specify first corner point or [Object/Subtract area/eXit]: O
(ADD mode) Select objects:

Area = 44.0000, Perimeter = 30.0000
Total area = 44.0000
(ADD mode) Select objects:
Area = 44.0000, Perimeter = 30.0000
Total area = 44.0000

Specify first corner point or [Object/Subtract area/eXit]: S
Specify first corner point or [Object/Add area/eXit]: O
(SUBTRACT mode) Select objects:
Area = 3.1416, Circumference = 6.2832
Total area = 40.8584
(SUBTRACT mode) Select objects:

Specify first corner point or [Object/Add area/eXit]:

Total area = 40.8584
```

- You will see something resembling the following illustration:

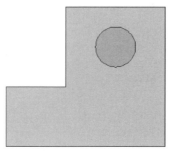

Appendix C   WORKSPACE

In This Appendix
◊ What are workspaces in AutoCAD?
◊ What do workspaces consist of?
◊ How are workspaces created and modified?

C.1 INTRODUCTION

- We all like to change the interface of any software to suit our personal preferences.
- In most software packages, we call this "interface customization."
- AutoCAD has two tools for interface customization:
  - Workspace
  - Profile
- Starting with AutoCAD 2009, AutoCAD adopted a new interface using **Ribbons**, which looks and feels like Microsoft Office 2007.
- **Ribbons** consist of two parts:
  - Tabs
  - Panels
- **Ribbons** offer users more screen space than toolbars.
- However, if you like the old AutoCAD interface, you can still use it by restoring other workspaces that come with AutoCAD.

C.2 INTRODUCTION TO WORKSPACE

- Showing or hiding any of the following will determine your workspace:
  - **Menus**
  - **Toolbars**
  - **Palettes**
  - **Ribbons** (**Tabs** and **Panels**)
- The workspace will memorize the location of each choice and whether it is should be floating or docked.
- In very simple terms, you can decide what to show and what to hide, and where the different items will be located. You save these preferences as your workspace.
- As a result, you can restore your settings at any time.

C.3 WORKSPACE COMMANDS

- AutoCAD comes with four predefined workspaces:
  - **2D Drafting & Annotation** is the default workspace.
  - **3D Basics** is used for 3D commands.
  - **3D Modeling** is used for 3D commands.
  - **AutoCAD Classic** restores the old look (before AutoCAD 2009).
- To reach these four predefined workspaces and other commands, use the button on the **Quick Access Toolbar**:

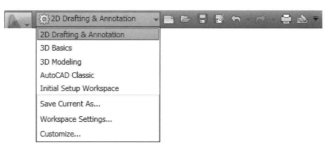

- Click the name to restore any of the four workspaces.

Save Current As

- If you made any changes to your current workspace, you can save the workspace under a new name.

Workspace Settings

- If you start the **Workplace Settings** command, you will see the following dialog box:

- You can make the following changes:
  - Change the order of the saved workspaces by moving them up or down, which will affect their listing in the menu on the **Quick Access Toolbar**.
  - Add a separator (simple line) between the workspace names in the menu.
  - By default, AutoCAD will not save any changes you make to your workspace unless you save the workspace under another name. However, you can tell AutoCAD to save the changes automatically.
- The following illustration shows changes made to the menu using the commands we just discussed. We changed the order and added a separator:

C.4 USING THE RIBBON

- Because the **Ribbon** is an essential component of the new interface, we will take some time to consider how to use it effectively.
- If you right-click any tab, you will see the following menu:

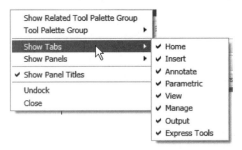

Show Tabs

- If you click **Show Tabs**, you will see the following menu:

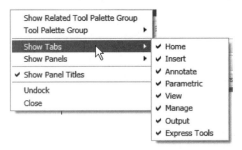

- You can select which of the existing tabs you want to show or hide.

Show Panels

- If you click **Show Panels**, you will see the following menu:

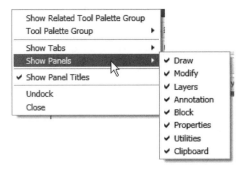

- Select which of the panels you want to show or hide in the current tab.

Show Panel Titles

- Select whether to show the panel titles. See the following illustrations:

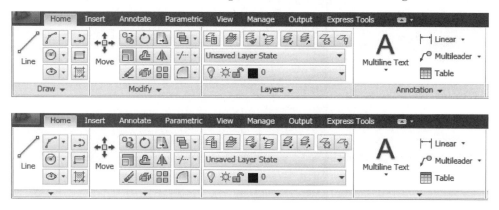

Undock

- By default, the **Ribbon** is docked at the top of the screen.
- You can undock it to make it floating, then move it to the right, left, or bottom of the screen.
- The following is an example of docking the **Ribbon** at the left of the screen:

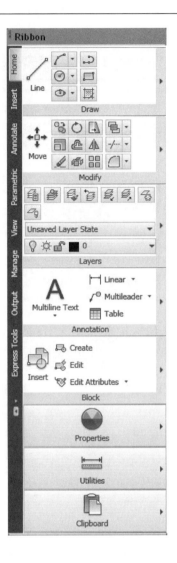

Close

- Closing the **Ribbon** is not recommended.

INDEX